The Sovereign State and Its Competitors

PRINCETON STUDIES IN

INTERNATIONAL HISTORY AND POLITICS

Series Editors
John Lewis Gaddis
Jack L. Snyder
Richard H. Ullman

History and Strategy by Marc Trachtenberg (1991)

George F. Kennan and the Making of American Foreign Policy, 1947–1950 by Wilson D. Miscamble, c.s.c. (1992)

Economic Discrimination and Political Exchange: World Political Economy in the 1930s and 1980s by Kenneth A. Oye (1992)

Whirlpool: U.S. Foreign Policy Toward Latin America and the Caribbean by Robert A. Pastor (1992)

Germany Divided: From the Wall to Reunification by A. James McAdams (1993)

A Certain Idea of France: French Security Policy and the Gaullist Legacy by Philip H. Gordon (1993)

The Limits of Safety: Organizations, Accidents, and Nuclear Weapons by Scott D. Sagan (1993)

We All Lost the Cold War by Richard Ned Lebow and Janice Gross Stein (1994)

Mercenaries, Pirates, and Sovereigns: State-Building and Extraterritorial Violence in Early Modern Europe by Janice E. Thomson (1994)

Who Adjusts? Domestic Sources of Foreign Economic Policy during the Interwar Years by Beth A. Simmons (1994)

The Sovereign State and Its Competitors: An Analysis of Systems Change by Hendrik Spruyt (1994)

The Korean War: An International History by William W. Stueck (1995)

Cooperation among Democracies: The European Influence on U.S. Foreign Policy by Thomas Risse-Kappen (1995)

Cultural Realism: Strategic Culture and Grand Strategy in Chinese History by Alastair Ian Johnston (1995)

Does Conquest Pay? The Exploitation of Occupied Industrial Societies by Peter Liberman (1996)

Satellites and Commisars: Strategy and Conflict in Politics of Soviet-Bloc Trade by Randall W. Stone

The Sovereign State and Its Competitors

AN ANALYSIS OF SYSTEMS CHANGE

HENDRIK SPRUYT

PRINCETON UNIVERSITY PRESS

PRINCETON, NEW JERSEY

Library of Congress Cataloging-in-Publication Data

Spruyt, Hendrik, 1956–
The sovereign state and its competitors / Hendrik Spruyt.
p.   cm. — (Princeton studies in international history and politics)
Includes bibliographical references and index.
ISBN 0-691-03356-0
ISBN 0-691-02910-5 (pbk.)
Title. II. Series.
JC327.S65 1994 320.1' 5—dc20 94-10759 CIP

This book has been composed in Bitstream Caledonia

Princeton University Press books are printed
on acid-free paper and meet the guidelines
for permanence and durability of the Committee
on Production Guidelines for Book Longevity
of the Council on Library Resources

Second printing, and first paperback printing, 1996

Printed in the United States of America
by Princeton Academic Press

2 3 4 5 6 7 8 9 10

FOR LUCY LYONS
AND MY PARENTS,
DOLORES AND HENDRIK SR.

CONTENTS

LIST OF MAPS AND TABLES

THE FIRST "research" for this project started roughly twenty-five years ago when I participated in the 750th anniversary of the founding of my hometown. I was puzzled by the fact that virtually every town and village in the region seemed to be celebrating the same thing, because they all seemed about equally old. I ascribed it to either chance or a desire among the townspeople to engage in continual festivities.

I did not know then that similar activities were taking place in much of Europe, particularly in the northwest. These events, commemorating the foundation and independence of cities, were in fact evidence of a great political and economic transformation that occurred some seven centuries ago. It was that transformation, due especially to a surge in trade, that allowed political entrepreneurs and social groups to create new institutions to displace the older feudal and ecclesiastical arrangements. Not all of these institutions are with us today. Indeed, only one—the sovereign, territorial state—really survives, although shadows of other forms of organization are ubiquitous and discernible to the observing traveler throughout Europe.

The idea that the anarchical nature of the international system imposes a rational choice problem on the actors in the system is essentially a description of a historically contingent situation. The international system has not historically been, and consequently in the future need not be, of its present nature. This book tries to explain how the current state system arose, why it has existed for so long, and how the process of its demise might come to pass.

This work is not a novel historical analysis. Although I use historical materials, those in search of a dramatic interpretation of heretofore unknown archives will be disappointed. Instead I attempt to draw attention to the oft-neglected case that only in hindsight looks anomalous and quaint. Thus, although I look at France, the Hanseatic League, and Italian city-states, this work is only in a secondary sense the history of any one of these. Instead, these serve as exemplars of the general question of why sovereign territoriality displaced nonsovereign and nonterritorial logics of organization, and how this affects international affairs.

I have incurred many debts. Peter Cowhey and Tracy Strong read more versions of the manuscript than they probably care to remember. They did so, however, with great care and intelligence and offered continual support. The same holds true for John Ruggie, whose inspirational work set me on the course of this project even before I knew him. I hope that I have taken advantage of these colleagues' insights.

Special thanks also go to Stephen Krasner who read the entire manuscript with minute care and who provided trenchant critiques and suggestions which helped me state my argument with greater precision. John Hall likewise read and commented on the manuscript with insightful suggestions. Victor

Magagna's comparative historical knowledge was indispensable to carrying out this project.

It has never been explained to me why spouses are usually mentioned in the last part of acknowledgments. Oblique references to spousal support under the rubric of "last but not least" simply do not do justice to the support of my wife. I thank Lucy Lyons for all her help.

I also particularly thank Deborah Avant with whom I shared many drafts, critiques, and ideas and a fair number of large cappuccinos. David Bartlett, Ellen Commisso, Eric Fredell, Scott Gates, Martha Howell, Walter Prevenier, Robert Ritchie, and Donald Wayne read all, or parts, of this work and provided many useful suggestions and comments. Dan Deudney, Miles Kahler, John Mundy, Phil Roeder, and Wim Smit provided help along the way both in substantive terms and in suggesting relevant literature. I also greatly benefited from the assistance of the faculty and staff of the Institute of War and Peace Studies at Columbia University.

Economic forces held not only the future of Europe in sway. At the University of California, San Diego, and at Columbia University, I benefited from the financial support of the Institute on Global Conflict and Cooperation, the Josephine de Karman Fund, and the Columbia Council for Research in the Social Sciences.

The maps in this book have been reproduced by the kind permission of the following presses: Map 5.1 has been reproduced from Reinhard Bendix, *Kings or People: Power and the Mandate to Rule*. Copyright (c) 1978 The Regents of the University of California. Map 5.2 has been reproduced from Elizabeth Hallam, *Capetian France, 987–1328*. Copyright (c) 1980 of Longman Group UK Ltd. Map 6.1 has been reproduced from Donald Matthew, *Atlas of Medieval Europe*, by permission of Andromeda Oxford Ltd., Abingdon, UK (c) 1983. And Map 7.1 is from *Power and Imagination* by Lauro Martines, maps by Rafael Palacios. Copyright (c) 1978 by Lauro Martines. Reprinted by permission of Alfred A. Knopf, Inc.

At Princeton University Press, I am indebted to Malcolm DeBevoise for his advice and confidence in this project. Liz Pierson scrutinized the manuscript with great intelligence and care. I also thank Tim Bartlett, Jane Low, and Alessandra Bocco for guiding the manuscript to its final form.

The Sovereign State and Its Competitors

Remnants of the past that don't make sense in present terms—
the useless, the odd, the peculiar, the incongruous—are the signs of history.
They supply proof that the world was not made in its present form.
When history perfects, it covers its own tracks.[1]

HISTORY has covered its tracks well. We often take the present system of sovereign states for granted and believe that its development was inevitable. But it was not. The sovereign, territorial state had its own peculiar rivals that very well might have held the day. Now that dramatic changes within and between states are taking place, it is appropriate to rethink our explanations of the origins of the state system, analyze the forces that shaped it, and reflect on the possibility of its demise.

Where we are today is the result of a long historical process. At the end of the Middle Ages, the international system went through a dramatic transformation in which the crosscutting jurisdictions of feudal lords, emperors, kings, and popes started to give way to territorially defined authorities. The feudal order was gradually replaced by a system of sovereign states.

The new element introduced by the late medieval state was the notion of sovereignty. This was the critical turn in the political organization of the Late Middle Ages, not the particular level of monarchical administration or royal revenue, nor the physical size of the state.[2] Instead it was the concept of sovereignty that altered the structure of the international system by basing political authority on the principle of territorial exclusivity.[3] The modern state is based on these two key elements, internal hierarchy and external autonomy, which emerged for the first time in the Late Middle Ages.[4] When scholars focus on the emergence of the state, they often really mean the growth of formal government. The critical question in my analysis is instead why some governments took the form of sovereign, territorial rule whereas others did not. This book, therefore, does not look at the growth of government vis-à-vis society but analyzes the development of hierarchy within polities and the effects of sovereignty on the relations between states.[5] It further seeks to explain why, over time, sovereign states have become the sole constitutive elements of the international system at the exclusion of others.

Some argue that another epic change is currently taking place. Factors such as economic interdependence, ecological disasters, and globalization of financial markets have led to a search for new ways to organize domestic and international politics.[6] Consequently, social scientists have started to re-examine the origins of the state system and have begun to discuss the possibility of its transformation.[7]

The contemporary era requires us to confront the question of how new forms of organization might emerge and whether different types of political organization might fundamentally change the character of international conduct. The problem is that we not only lack answers to such questions, we do not even have appropriate means to think about these questions theoretically. My major aim in this book is to address that issue and to explain how the elements that constitute the international system change over time. I further seek to demonstrate how international relations are influenced by the character of the system's constitutive elements.

Much of the literature that tries to explain systems change suffers from a common conceptual problem.[8] It sees institutional evolution as unilinear. Consequently, these theories explain the demise of feudalism and the triumph of the sovereign state as a unilinear evolutionary process. They account for the rise of the state by comparing it to the previous feudal order.

As I will argue in Part I, this is theoretically and empirically incorrect. Theoretically, unilinear theories of change affirm the consequent. Because these theories only focus on one observed outcome—the rise of the sovereign state— a variety of explanations appear plausible. Such theories might, for example, argue that increased economic interaction, new military technology, or shifts in medieval mentality led to the decline of the old feudal order. However plausible these may be, in fact such views are descriptive accounts. In order to see which variables were relevant in bringing about change, a theory of change should account for variation in the observed outcome.[9]

Moreover, such accounts do not do justice to history. Empirically, the transformation did not occur unilinearly. In fact, the decline of the feudal order produced a flurry of institutional innovation. Urban leagues, independent communes, and city-states, as well as sovereign monarchies, emerged to challenge the existing institutional order of empire, church, and feudal lordships. A satisfactory account should acknowledge this variety of political forms. Any explanation of change must thus first account for institutional variation. Part II of this book focuses on the question, what sparked the emergence of this multiplicity of new institutional types?

However, it is also clear that the alternatives to the state have died out. The powerful city-leagues that organized northern commerce and united considerable urban resources are no more. Similarly, the city-states, which consisted of the rule of one predominant city over others, have ceased to exist. Any explanation must, therefore, also explain how the state consolidated itself. Part III of this book thus turns to the question, why did many of the new institutional arrangements become extinct?

Unilinear views only examine how the state proved to be superior to feudal organization. For this reason the question of the origins of the state is commonly assigned to comparative politics. Such views focus, for example, on the extractive capabilities of the state vis-à-vis society. Growth of the "modern" state is explained by comparing it with the weaker capacity of the feudal state. By contrast, this work examines how states superseded their synchronic alter-

natives and compares their territorial and hierarchical authority with alternative forms. That is, why did sovereign states survive while city-leagues and
city-states proved to be institutional dead ends?[10] Both of those organizational
forms were also more efficient than feudal types, and hence we cannot suffice
with the explanation that states became the dominant type of organization
simply because they were more efficient than the previous feudal order. The
question of the origins of the state needs both a domestic and international
explanation.[11]

The causes of the emergence of the sovereign state are not, therefore, the
same as the causes that explain selection among synchronic institutional alternatives. Unilinear evolutionary theories, however, contract the causes of the
demise of feudalism with the causes of the rise of the state system. Explanations
of the former, however, need not explain the latter. Explanations of the latter
need not explain the former.

By abandoning the idea of unilinear progress and by acknowledging the variety of political institutions, one can better identify the causal sequences of institutional development. Moreover, by recognizing the wide range of empirical
possibilities, one does not conflate the reasons for the decline of the feudal
order with the reasons for the success of the sovereign state.

This book, therefore, revolves around three elements, which together form a
theory of change. First, it focuses on the variety of institutional forms that
emerged in the later Middle Ages. I examine three empirical cases: the sovereign state of France, the Hanseatic League, and the Italian city-states. All three
were successors to feudal organization, and all were responses to the changing
environment. Second, I seek to explain why sovereign states, rather than the
alternatives they displaced, became the constitutive elements of the international system.[12] And third, I examine how an understanding of this previous
transformation can help us explain change in the international system in
general.

AN OUTLINE OF THE ARGUMENT

This study argues that unit type influences international relations. Although I
take the transhistorical nature of anarchy as a given—that is, there never has
been a world government—units do not operate in a structureless vacuum.
Chapters 1 and 2 discuss some critiques of neorealism and argue that neorealism is ill suited to account for system transformation. I then clarify my method
of analysis and suggest a causal model for understanding unit change. I also
elaborate on the argument that structure is partially determined by the prevalent type of units. A change in the constitutive elements of the system means a
change in the structure of the system.

Chapter 3 discusses the logic of older forms of organization—feudalism,
church, and empire—which characterized the early Middle Ages. The discussion of the Hanseatic League, the Italian city-states, and the French state will

illustrate how these forms, instead of feudal, imperial, or theocratic structures, emerged to dominance. Following the period of growth and economic expansion in western Europe during the eleventh and thirteenth centuries, which I discuss in Chapter 4, the relative position of social groups changed. The ascendent mercantile groups and urban centers had different material interests than the warrior nobility or the clergy. They also differed in their ideological perspectives. The burghers, therefore, sought political allies to change the existing feudal order.

I contend that the impact of the exogenous variable, trade, led to a variety of social coalitions in Italy, Germany, and France.[13] The different coalitions and bargains between kings, aristocracy, and towns accounts for institutional variation across Europe. As I explain in Chapters 5 through 7, these coalitions created different institutions which better met the coalitions' material interests and ideological perspectives. Depending on the nature of these coalitions, sovereign states, city-leagues, and city-states emerged from feudalism. This variety of institutional forms, which arguably were all superior to the feudal mode of organization in terms of resources and economic potential, dispels the notion that evolution is a unilinear process.

In France the social bargain between king and burghers allowed for recentralization of monarchy, by asserting royal sovereignty over the church and nobles. In Germany the reverse took place. The German king allied with the feudal nobles against the towns. His policy failed, and feudal decentralization resulted. The German towns formed independent leagues to protect and further their interests against the lords. In Italy the failed imperial policy of the German king, who was simultaneously the Holy Roman Emperor, led to independent communes which gradually developed into city-states. Unlike the German aristocracy, the Italian nobles engaged in urban, mercantile pursuits, and hence the feudal-urban dichotomy that characterized Germany failed to appear. Italian towns did not ally with the king, nor did they band together to form city-leagues.

The resulting realignments in Europe led to a variety of new political institutions: the sovereign, territorial state, the city-league, and the city-state. These new institutions differed from the institutions that dominated the earlier part of the Middle Ages: the empire, the feudal lordships, and the theocratic church.

Part III clarifies that not all of these new units were equally efficient and effective. The dynamic of competitive advantage selected out those units that were less effective and less efficient than others. Sovereign authority proved to be more adept at preventing freeriding, standardizing weights and coinage, and establishing uniform adjudication. Equally important were the abilities of sovereign actors to coordinate their interactions with one another. Sovereign states proved to have significant advantages over city-leagues in this matter because the latter had no distinct locus of authority. Furthermore, territorial sovereignty proved incompatible with nonterritorial logics of organization, such as that of the Hansa. States thus increasingly only recognized similar units as legitimate actors in international relations.[14]

The interaction between internal and external spheres is a two-staged process. At first, changes in the external milieu lead to domestic shifts in relative power between social and political actors. Those actors then realign to form new types of institutions. The new institutions then become part of the external environment which consists of the whole array of institutional possibilities at that historical juncture. Some of the institutional arrangements will be eliminated because they are not as competitively efficient as the leader. Moreover, because actors need to devise some means of structuring their interactions with others, some forms of organization will prove to be less attractive than others. So in the second stage of social evolution, the internal changes of units alter the external environment in which other actors operate.

At the end of this work, I recapitulate my general views on the nature of unit change and reflect on the possibility of institutional change in the contemporary era.[15] A change in the units of the present system—that is, a decline of the state—will have to be studied by examining whether a serious change has occurred in the overall international environment, whether the preferences of social and political actors have changed, and whether there has been a significant shift in the relative power of particular social groups. Given the variety of political bargains during such transformatory phases, we should expect a multiplicity of alternatives to arise. Institutional change will occur through a twofold process: a stage of institutional emergence and a subsequent stage of systemic selection.

The account of social evolution presented here provides some justification for the claim that institutional change is an infrequent phenomenon.[16] Change in institutions imposes costs, and hence social groups and political actors will be unwilling to experiment with new institutions unless a serious exogenous shock alters internal political alignments. Units will otherwise continue in the form they have taken at a particular historical juncture. Change will take the form of a punctuated equilibrium—a dramatic shift along several dimensions simultaneously in response to a powerful environmental change. Usually the status quo prevails and institutional change is marginal rather than fundamental. The task before us is to ponder whether or not a change in the current system of sovereign states is likely, and whether we may be witnesses to profound alterations in the conduct of international affairs. This work examines the past to provide clarity in our meditations on the future.

Contingency, Choice, and Constraint

CHAPTER 1

Structural Change in International Relations

In a Europe without states and without boundaries the concept of "foreign affairs" had no meaning.[1]

The rise and decline of various types of entities and state systems must of necessity be a fundamental concern of a comprehensive theory of international change.[2]

DESPITE Robert Gilpin's exhortation, international relations theory has paid little attention to change in the types of units that constitute the international system. Gilpin himself, after having classified unit change as the most fundamental type of transformation, turns his attention to the distribution of capabilities—the standard research program for neorealists.

However, if Gilpin is correct that the change from city-state to empire, from empire to feudalism, and so on, is important for understanding international politics, then we need to seriously engage the questions of how units change and how such change affects the international system. These questions have been raised most explicitly by critics of neorealism. These critics have specifically focused on the feudal-state transformation as an example of systems change.[3] How did the sovereign state emerge? How has its rise affected international relations? This chapter begins with a discussion of these questions and proceeds to argue that the constitutive type of unit in the international system is a critical facet of structure.

With the feudal-state transformation as a starting point, this chapter also explores various accounts of unit change. Most of these accounts explain institutional evolution as a unilinear process. Such a perspective is both theoretically and empirically flawed.

Because a unilinear view sees the development of units, specifically the feudal-state transformation, as a process of sequential stages, it affirms the consequent. Methodologically, the absence of any real variation on the dependent variable—one only seeks to explain the emergence of the state—makes it impossible to select among rival independent variables. Empirically, unilinear accounts fail because they neglect the multiplicity of institutional alternatives that were available during this historical change. As a consequence, the competition between different institutional arrangements is neglected, and analysis is performed solely on the internal dynamics of particular polities. International relations thus gives way to comparative politics.[4]

NEOREALISM AND ITS CRITICS: THE ORIGINS OF THE STATE
AS AN ISSUE IN INTERNATIONAL RELATIONS

In Kenneth Waltz's interpretation of Durkheim's theory, the international system is structured according to organizing principle, functional differentiation, and distribution of capabilities.[5] Because of the lack of organizing authority, that is, because of anarchy, the second element of the structure drops out. Under anarchy, actors will pursue self-sufficiency rather than division of labor and subsequent reliance on others. For Waltz, the international system is similar to Durkheim's premodern society based on mechanical solidarity.[6] Because of the absence of central authority, little or no functional differentiation is possible.[7] Consequently, under anarchy only the distribution of capabilities matters for the structure of the system. The character of the unit and unit change are thus unimportant for understanding structure.[8] This view, by the way, is also upheld in the literature spawned by this neorealist perspective.[9]

John Ruggie has launched a sustained critique of this view. He argues that Waltz's view of Durkheim is mistaken. In contrast to Waltz, Ruggie suggests that functional differentiation does occur. Waltz neglects the dynamic element in Durkheim's theory. The cause of evolutionary progress in society lies in the increase in dynamic density—the total volume of transactions and communications.[10]

Ruggie adduces Medieval Europe as an empirical case to demonstrate that a strict application of neorealist theory fails to capture the logic of international relations as conducted at that time. As with all forms of political organization, feudal authorities occupied a geographical space. But such authority over territorial areas was neither exclusive nor discrete. Complex networks of rival jurisdictions overlaid territorial space.[11] Church, lords, kings, emperor, and towns often exercised simultaneous claims to jurisdiction. Occupants of a particular territorial space were subject to a multiplicity of higher authorities.

Given such a logic or organization, it is impossible to distinguish the actors conducting "international" relations, operating under anarchy, from those conducting "domestic" politics, operating under some hierarchy. Bishops, kings, lords, and towns all signed treaties and waged war.[12] There was no one actor with a monopoly over the means of coercive force.[13] The distinction between public and private actors was yet to be articulated.[14]

To understand such interactions as international relations under anarchy is an anachronism. Were lords subject to the king? Was the king subject to the church? Was the church subject to the emperor? The answers to those questions were inevitably contextual and intersubjective. Warring lords might subject themselves to royal jurisdiction for mediation, yet at other times rebellious lords might wage war on the king himself. Richard of England and Philip Augustus of France, at war in the later twelfth century, submitted to papal demands to end their dispute and join forces for a crusade. Yet in many instances they also acted as independent kings without recognizing higher authority. Indeed the very word *international* is a posterior and an anachronistic conceptualization of that era. It suggests that there was a distinct realm of national (internal) affairs which was conceptually distinguishable from a realm of international (external) affairs. In other words, we can only speak of international affairs as synomous with actions under anarchy because the feudal-state transformation defined the realms of domestic and interunit behavior. The condition of anarchy, as we apply it today, implies the existence of a particular type of unit. The neorealist view of anarchy presumes that there are discrete units with mutually exclusive spheres of jurisdiction.[15] The medieval system, however, was quite different than that of the contemporary state system. Jurisdiction was neither discrete—jurisdictions overlapped—nor exclusive—different authorities might claim final jurisdiction on the same matter. The medieval case thus demonstrates how the character of the units has dramatic implications for the structure of the system. Certainly there was anarchy in the sense of a lack of world hierarchical authority. But when that condition applied, or to whom it applied, were in fact indeterminate.[16]

Ruggie's analysis is partially based on structuration and poststructuralist theory. Structuration theory criticizes neorealism for not accounting for the formation of structure.[17] Because of its empiricist orientation, neorealism objectifies structure as a given entity rather than as the result of interaction by agents. Anarchy is perceived as an observable, objective entity rather than as a social construct. Alternatively, structuration theory seeks to establish how interaction between agents creates a specific structure and how, in turn, structure constrains agents. Agents and structure, that is, units and system, are mutually constitutive.

Although the freedom of the individual is constrained by a given structure, this constaint is not such that the agent is determined by that structure. By redefining the nature of their interactions, individuals create a new structure which imposes constraints on others. In many ways, the agent-structure debate resembles the classic micro-macro problem.[18]

Poststructural theory is even more radical than structuration theory in its critique of neorealism, for the epistemological orientation of poststructural theory lies closer to that of critical theory and Foucault.[19] Poststructural theory views neorealism's particular depiction of international relations as a manifestation of a dominant conceptual framework. Neorealists understand the anarchical condition of exclusive entities as a natural and inevitable phenomenon because they have unreflectively accepted a particular way of thinking about the world. They do not recognize the state system as a social construction that has a specific historical origin. Poststructural theory, in contrast, advocates an archaeology of the state.

In short, both structuration theory and poststucturalism suggest that neorealism takes the ontological nature of the system as constant and as consisting of discrete units. As Ruggie shows, this was not always historically true. Neorealism does not acknowledge this because of its objectivist perspective which defines anarchy as a given, ahistorical condition. By contrast, Ruggie suggests that we need to account for the emergence of territorial discreteness—the exclusivity of authority over fixed space, which is typical of the modern state.

Structuration theory and poststructuralism thus wish to make the emergence of the sovereign state a fundamental issue in the study of international relations. They indicate, furthermore, that the emergence of an anarchical state system was not merely due to a reordering of the social and political map in a material sense but was equally due to the reconceptualization and rearticulation of social and political order. The sovereign state had to be invented.[20] Any account of state formation will have to take this notion of conceptual change into consideration.

Both structuration theory and poststructuralism, however, are not without problems of their own. Arguably, poststructuralism has, as of yet, offered little in the way of substantive theory.[21] It is, by its own account, largely a metatheory. Structuration theory, at least in some versions in the realm of international relations theorizing, professes to use a Lakatosian research methodology. Hence, it claims additional empirical explanatory power to realism but accepts the general epistemological position of realist research.[22] Consequently, one should expect its empirical focus to be more explicit than that of poststructuralism.

However, it is not entirely clear how to operationalize this program. More specifically, if one takes structure and agency as mutually constitutive in all instances, then structure must be understood in a constructivist sense as the poststructuralists do. That is to say, structure would be primarily, if not completely, a creation of individual agents. Consequently it would be difficult to specify what the constraining characteristics of a particular structure are given its amenability to continual reconstruction and reinterpretation.[23]

The second problem with operationalizing a structurationist program is that agent-structure problems permeate all levels of politics. It depends on what one takes to be the agent and what the structure. The individual can be embedded in the structure of a bureaucratic organization. That organization, taken as an agent with a particular corporate identity, is in turn embedded in a larger political structure, and so on.

The research method that I propose circumvents both problems. It takes the agent-structure problem to bear on two sets of issues. First, it focuses on the interaction of individuals and the state. It takes a methodological individualist approach to explain how the state came into being but embeds these choices in the constraints of the existing political structure and relative distribution of power. On a second level, it takes the state as agent and sees it as embedded in the structure of a system that imposes constraints on it—the state system. In so doing, one stays closest to a deductive understanding of the system, in the neorealist sense, while at the same time problematizing the emergence of that system.[24] I argue, therefore, contra Waltz, that systems theorizing that takes the dominant type of unit into account is not reductionist.

VARIATION IN UNITS AS VARIATION IN SYSTEMS STRUCTURE

In his seminal work on neorealism, Waltz compares the international system to a market.[25] The distribution of capabilities between units is analogous to market share distribution. The polarity of the system is the conceptual equivalent of oligopolistic or monopolistic markets. The distribution of market share leads to expectations about individual firm behavior. One can a priori expect that firms will behave in a particular way if a given distribution of market shares occurs. The major powers in international politics are the logical analogue of price setters in the market.

Against Waltz, I argue that the market is not uniquely determined by the distribution of market share. The constraints imposed by the market are not simply determined by the number of firms but also by the *type* of firms that dominate that market. The relative efficiency of units, that is, of rival companies, puts constraints on companies to organize similarly. This is not simply a question of size. For example, American firms may face pressure from more efficient Japanese or European firms in terms of organizational makeup. Fordist production might be obsolete in the face of craftlike production.[26] This, too, can be understood as imposing a structure to which the firm has to conform. However, these constraints do not follow from the interactions between actors; these are not inductive "rules of the game."[27] Given a particular economic milieu—the technology to alter production quickly, the flexibility of demand, etc.—a particular type of organization, once created, compels others to follow suit. Competitive efficiency dictates unit, that is, firm behavior. Although the distribution of market share is important, it is not the only structural trait of the environment faced by actors.[28]

A similar logic operates in unit transformation in the international system. Here, too, the units are faced with the necessity of competitive efficiency and effectiveness. Once new unit types have been generated, they operate in competition with others. The unit that is best able to capitalize on environmental changes, which caused the search for new forms of organization in the first place, exerts a competitive, marketlike pressure on the others. This is the first sense in which new units create a different structure.

But the international system, unlike the market, also selects units by mutual empowerment of actors.[29] In this sense the structurationist critique that neorealism objectifies the system is correct. Here the analogy between the state system and the market does not hold. The selection of firms in a market environment does not work by the mutual empowerment of like firms. The market does not reflect mutual agreements by firms to allow only similar firms.[30] The metaphor of the market differs in that respect from the international system.

Historically, the establishment of a state system led to a recategorization of who was entitled to exercise the means of violence. In the feudal system, the exercise of violence followed crosscutting obligations. Feudal lords had multiple superiors to whom they owed allegiance. The medieval system further lacked any conception of private versus public authority. Kinship structures, for example, claimed the legitimate use of violence and retaliation.[31]

The state system, by contrast, has led to a specific categorization of what is to count as internal or external violence and who may exercise such violence. The state claims a domestic and external monopoly of force. As a consequence, nonstate actors are stripped of coercive means—mercenaries and privateers thus have disappeared.[32]

The state system, or rather the state actors who made up that system, thus recognized or denied certain forms of organization as legitimate international actors.[33] The Hansa, for example, was not allowed to be an equal participant at the Peace of Westphalia. Individual free cities, however, were permitted to participate at conferences and sign treaties. This was not just a matter of material power; it was also a question of whether such actors were compatible with a statist form of organizing international transactions.[34] Likewise, the modern system empowers third world actors as states, even though they internally diverge from the standard European pattern.[35]

Similarly, universal empires are difficult to accommodate in a state system. Traditional universalist empires, such as the Ottoman, were based on a different logic of organization. Such empires sought to exercise political control over their sphere of economic production and trade, and herein they diverge from the statist logic of organization where political rule and sphere of interaction are separated. China and the Parthian Empire, for example, could exist in their respective spheres of influence without having to formally agree upon borders. "Similarly, the Roman Empire conceived the limes not as a boundary, but as a temporary stopping place where the potentially unlimited expansion of the Pax Romana had come to a halt."[36] The limits of political control were measured by that which was maximally feasible and economically desirable. Such empires existed with indifference to the pursuits of the other—short, of course, of military incursions on their respective spheres of influence. The contemporary state system, by contrast, is explicitly based on the premise that the sphere of interaction is much larger than the sphere of political control.[37]

The empowerment of particular actors, however, should not be understood as social norms or rules in the Grotian perspective. Hedley Bull, for example, argues that diplomatic procedures led to a particular structuring of international behavior.[38] Actors needed to conform to these rules and norms in order to participate in the international system. In this account the Ottomans could play no role in the European state system because they lacked the shared understanding of international "rules of the game" of the European states.

This book is sensitive to the notion of shared conceptual frameworks, but unlike Grotians, it seeks to account for why they exist. Grotian theory provides no such accounting and thus cannot help us explain why the nature of international politics changed so dramatically in Europe.

I submit that these rules are consequences of different logics of organization. The argument that the Ottoman Empire was excluded because it was not part of European society and culture does not hold. The alleged shared civilization of Europe, for example, did not prevent Francis I from seeking Ottoman support against Spain in the sixteenth century. I agree that the Ottoman Empire was fundamentally at odds with a state system and could only play an ad hoc role in the European diplomatic process. However, the real reason why the Ottoman Empire was excluded from the European theater had less to do with its understanding of diplomatic rules of the game than with its universalist logic of authority. As Bernard Lewis suggests:

> In the Muslim world view the basic division of mankind is into the House of Islam (Dar al-Islam) and the House of War (Dar al-Harb). The one consists of all those countries where the law of Islam prevails, that is to say, broadly the Muslim Empire; the latter is the rest of the world. Just as there is only one God in heaven, so there can be only one sovereign and one law on earth.[39]

Universalist imperial systems do not confine their authority by mutually agreed upon spatial parameters, that is, borders.[40] It is thus antithetical to the external equality of states which sovereign territoriality presupposes.

Dislike units are thus based on different conceptions of internal and external politics. The development of sovereignty meant a formal demarcation of political authority on territorial grounds. Unlike universalist empires or the translocal organization of the Hansa, states thus have very precise limitations to their claims to rule. States, unlike empires or the Hansa, do not extend political control over the entire sphere of principal economic interaction.

Consequently Gilpin is right in suggesting that conflicts during periods of systems change are likely to be multidimensional. Changes in unit type are simultaneously changes in domestic and external politics. Such changes are thus tied up with changes in social coalitions regarding material interests and conceptual perspectives.[41] The emergence of sovereign states meant, therefore, a dramatic break with older institutional forms, such as empire and papacy, which claimed to rule over the entire Christian community.

In essence, the agents that make up the state system thus create a particular structure of interunit behavior. The very fact that some institutions are empowered as states, whereas others are denied that status, demonstrates how constraints have been placed on the subsequent choices of social actors.

The ordering of translocal interaction by spatial borders and internal hierarchy also allowed for a mechanical conceptualization of politics.[42] By restricting violence to sovereign entities, by recognizing formal borders, and by agreeing on specific channels of communication, such as embassies, some management of competition became possible. Mattingly rightly sees the Peace of Lodi (1454) between the city-states of Italy as the first true balance-of-power system.[43]

I thus argue that unit change imposes a particular structure on international relations. The structure of the system is also determined by the particular type of unit that dominates the system in a given historical period. Such structure is not derivative of the interactions between units, nor is it an aggregation of unit-level attributes. Hence the view that I advocate is not a reductionist understanding of the system.[44]

UNILINEAR EXPLANATIONS OF CHANGE

If unit change, such as the shift from feudal organization to sovereign, territorial state, changes the structure of the international system, what accounts for
such change? What explains, particularly, the emergence of the sovereign, territorial state? There are of course a great variety of accounts that deal with the
emergence of the state. Much of this literature, however, suffers from a similar
conceptual error; it argues that evolution is a unilinear process.[45] Such accounts
suppose a progression of subsequent stages with a new type of unit superseding
the old.

The decline of the feudal system, however, did not straightforwardly lead to
a system of states but gave rise to multiple institutional arrangements, any one
of which—at that time—appeared to be viable. The institutional evolution of
the international system was therefore not unilinear.

Many unilinear accounts of state emergence are, at least implicitly, driven by
the classical accounts of Marx, Durkheim, and Weber.[46] Even accounts that
pay more attention to the predatorial nature of international politics sometimes
commit the same error. These latter types of accounts are correct in their attempts to explain change by looking at the relative ability of different forms of
economic or military organization.[47] Some institutional arrangements are better
at performing certain tasks in a new economic or military environment. Where
they go wrong is in affirming the consequent, that is, by focusing solely on the
winners. Hence, existing institutions are presumed to be efficient.

Evolution, however, is driven by fits and starts. At critical junctures a multiplicity of new forms emerge.[48] Gradually some of these alternatives are weeded
out. We must therefore first explain not merely why states superseded feudal
organization but why a variety of alternatives emerged following feudalism. We
need, secondly, to account for the superiority of the state vis-à-vis these alternatives. Standard accounts do not do this.

Unilinear theory in its purest form assumes necessity in evolution. One type
of organization logically and inevitably follows the other. Unilinear theory also
assumes continuity in history. The new is explained by the reasons for demise
of the old. For example, the capitalist state is believed to be a solution to the
problems that emerged from the objective limits of feudalism. Socialist states
become inevitable because of the logical contradictions of capitalism. As I will
try to demonstrate, I disagree with the claims of necessity and predictability.

In the world systems variant of neo-Marxism, the emergence of the state can
be explained by the emergence of the world capitalist system.[49] For Wallerstein, the evolution of the world economy determines the nature of the unit.
"The states are thus, we are arguing, created institutions reflecting the needs of
class forces operating in the world economy."[50] The emergence of the state is
due to unilinear historical progress.[51]

There is, however, nothing inevitable about the emergence of the sovereign,
territorial state. It arose because of a particular conjuncture of social and politi-

cal interests in Europe. Functionalist and teleological accounts cannot explain the variation in types of institutional arrangements other than the sovereign state. As a consequence, world systems theory misdates the emergence of states. States preceded the development of a capitalist world economy, rather than the reverse. Indeed, the differentiation of Europe into different states might be the very reason why capitalism developed in Europe and not elsewhere.[52]

Wallerstein is thus susceptible to the structurationist critique that he cannot account for the particular nature of the system. Since the system is wholly determinate of the unit, he cannot really account for change in the system. He presents an agentless history and thus "is forced into an explanation of that transition [feudal to capitalist] in terms of exogenous shocks and the teleological imperatives of an immanent capitalist mode of production."[53]

Even Perry Anderson, who is more sensitive to variation in European political organization, explains the decline of the feudal system by the fact that it had reached its "objective limits."[54] The absolutist state emerges as "a redeployed and recharged apparatus of feudal domination, designed to clamp the peasant masses back into their traditional social position."[55] As with Wallerstein, Anderson's account remains decidedly within a teleological framework. It is an account wherein economics determines politics. Only the specific nature of feudalism determines the next phase of development. The emergence of states can thus be reduced to explaining change in the mode of production.

For Durkheim, the internal social environment is the ultimate cause of social evolution.[56] Durkheim attributes societal evolution to the gradual increase in population, rising levels of moral and legal interaction, and increasing dynamic density which require a new division of labor. Durkheim, therefore, also suggests a unilinear evolutionary account.[57]

Max Weber is far less susceptible to the critique that he has a unilinear view. Indeed, some see his work primarily as a taxonomy of how particular elements of economy, authority, and culture interrelate without a theory of development.[58] From another perspective, however, Weber does advance an evolutionary theory that depicts the unilinear development of instrumental rationality in society. Society is ever more based on formal and hierarchical modes of authority and rests on instrumental rational calculations.[59]

Some accounts that focus on relative ability take a unilinear view when they argue that given a particular technology of war, or a particular economic milieu, a given type of unit will emerge that is optimally suited for that environment.[60] Depending on the theorist, the state is believed to have displaced feudal organization either because it was better at waging a new type of war or because it was better suited for a new economic climate. Whether military or economic dynamics are the trigger for change, such theories share common ground in arguing that new functional necessities required a shift in the economies of scale of political units.[61] Bean, for example, argues that change in the character of warfare necessitated a certain change of scale. His argument suggests that the size of the feudal manor was inadequate to provide the resources for larger armies. Bean creates the impresssion that feudal units must have given way to states because increased army size was the most efficient way of fighting war. Because of its larger scale, the state could raise larger armies and extract more revenue. The state was thus simply due to an increase in size.

Explanations that focus on the comparative superiority of one form of organization over the other do not, of course, have to be unilinear. In fact, my own account relies heavily on the logic of competitive selection. The problem is that many of these explanations often compare institutions diachronically rather than synchronically. As a result, they end up with a linear sequence of successive and progressive types.

THE FALLACY OF THE UNILINEAR EVOLUTIONARY IMAGE

The neo-Marxist, neo-Durkheimian, neo-Weberian, and some forms of competitive efficiency explanations commit the same conceptual fallacy. They try to explain how states displaced feudal units, but they do so with a bias toward unilinear evolution. For neo-Marxists, states are an answer to economic contradictions in feudalism. For neo-Durkheimians, the state evolves because of increasing dynamic density. Some neo-Weberians see an evolutionary drift toward instrumentally rational, formal organizations—as evinced by the modern state. Competitive efficiency arguments submit that states were militarily and economically more competitive than feudal units, particularly in terms of scale. All of these thus suggest that evolution is unilinear wherein through a straightforward process the more efficient form displaces the older form. Such an interpretation of change, however, is wrong.

The unilinear evolutionary view is incorrect on several counts. First, because it neglects the variation in different types of units, such an explanation in effect perceives no variation in the dependent variable. Consequently this literature cannot accurately specify which independent variables were critical in explaining change. It focuses solely on one case—the feudal-state transition—and uses *post hoc ergo propter hoc* arguments.

Second, the unilinear evolutionary view fails to distinguish between the causes that led to the emergence of various institutional types and the causes of subsequent selection. The reasons that explain the emergence of the state need not explain why states won in the selective process vis-à-vis their institutional alternatives, for example, city-leagues and city-states. By not recognizing this, one fails to acknowledge the advantages of state sovereignty vis-à-vis other types of organization that existed simultaneously. The process of subsequent evolutionary selection is different from the process that generates a particular form—just as is the case in biological evolution.[62]

Third, one cannot say the state displaced feudal organization because it was more efficient. City-leagues and city-states were also more efficient than feudal organization in mustering resources and fostering trade. A good account of social evolution will therefore have to explain how different alternatives arose and how sovereign states displaced their synchronic alternatives.

Fourth, some of this literature imputes preferences from outcomes. At critical junctures, however, individuals cue in to many new institutional opportunities rather than to one specific type. This literature uses "as if" arguments to link individual preferences to the functions that an institution performs, but there is little examination of the real choice process.[63]

Moreover, I take for granted that changes in military and economic milieu affect which type of organization might be more efficient and effective. But the type of institution that emerges is the result of individual bargains in response to those changes. For example, territorial states developed that were superior to feudal lordships in war because some political entrepreneurs, specifically kings, had incentives to adopt new technology. In short, shifts in military milieu alone cannot explain the development of particular institutional arrangements. Rather, the reverse is true: sovereign, territorial states made adoption of new technology imperative. As Eugene Rice notes, there were other places, notably China, that had access to gunpowder technology before Europe but never developed its military uses in full.

> This difference suggests the existence in Renaissance Europe of a very powerful pressure to exploit the new invention for military purposes. This pressure, becoming acute about 1450, came from the larger territorial princes and derived its force from a fundamental political reality of the age: the consolidation in Europe of . . . the sovereign territorial state.[64]

The fundamental reality that existed in Europe before the military revolution was thus the failure of empire. It was exactly because discrete territorial units existed in constant competition that political entrepreneurs desired technological innovation.[65]

Finally, the institutions that individuals create need not be optimal. Survivability is not derived from the conditions imposed by the deeper environmental milieu, whether it be economic or military. Institutions might be caught in low-level equilibrium traps.[66] Instead, survivability of an institution derives from its competitive ability vis-à-vis its synchronic competitors which have been created by other coalitions.

The next chapter clarifies my proposed alternative methodology. I propose that a microlevel account can explain the variation in types of units during their generation without contracting generative cause and subsequent selection.[67] This account is partial to recent discussions in both economic history and historical sociology.[68] I submit that different material interests and belief systems of social groups and political actors lead to variations in political alliances. The impetus to form new coalitions came from changes in the overall milieu. The variation of these coalitions explains the emergence of a plurality of institutional types at the end of the feudal era.

Organizational Variation and Selection in the International System

> Most available explanations fail because they ignore the fact that many different
> kinds of states were viable at different stages of European history, because they
> locate explanations of state-to-state variation in individual characteristics of
> states rather than in relations among them.[1]

THIS CHAPTER presents my model of change. It begins with a discussion of two theories of change which have informed my nonlinear view of institutional evolution. I argue that a change in the constitutive units of the system is only likely to occur after a broad exogenous change, or an environmental shock, if you will. Such an exogenous change will lead to political and social realignments.[2] The divergent composition of these political alliances accounts for the variation in new institutional types. In the long run, however, some institutions will disappear given the competitive nature of the international system. In short, following a broad, contingent change in milieu, actors choose to create institutions that meet their material interests and ideological perspectives. But the subsequent viability of institutions is constrained by their relative competitiveness.

A NONLINEAR VIEW OF EVOLUTIONARY CHANGE

This book is influenced particularly by the images of change proposed by two theorists, Fernand Braudel and Stephen Jay Gould. Both classify change by periodization and pace. Fernand Braudel, the French historian, suggested that the pace of change operates at three levels.[3] This parallels the different types of systems change in international relations. Gould's view of Darwinian selection, specifically the punctuated equilibrium model, serves as a useful metaphor in classifying institutional change.

Braudel argued that the pace of history can be captured by a threefold classification. It is fastest at the level of everyday occurrences, a heterogeneous tapestry textured by individuals' decisions and events in life. This is *l'histoire evenementielle*, the history describing continually changing microlevel actions. The tempo of such change is rapid and is paced by *individual time*. At the intermediate level, history is less transitory. Economic changes and political shifts are more structural in nature. This is social history that aggregates individuals and human structures. Change, particularly in economic affairs, fluctu-

ates in cycles of ten, twenty, or perhaps even fifty years. Using not only the
metaphor of economic cycles but even its terminology, Braudel called this the
history of *conjunctures*. Finally, there is the level of history that seems to move
at a virtually imperceptible pace. Looking at his own rural roots, Braudel saw
little change in village life between the Middle Ages and the early twentieth
century because the objective conditions of life had not altered all that much.
Demography, geographic conditions, and the technology of communication all
conspired to make life appear unchanged to the individual. Such forces, however, were critically important in explaining the long-term fortunes of geographic areas such as the Mediterranean basin, or in demonstrating the relative
similarity in conditions facing the French farmer of the Middle Ages and of the
nineteenth century. The objective conditions that created such structural stasis
made for the history of the *longue durée*.

In the Braudelian scheme, the tempo of change thus varies between the
instant, the cyclical, and the longue durée. The task of the historian is to demonstrate the interplay between these three. Seen from another perspective,
l'histoire evenementielle and longue durée occupy opposite ends of the spectrum of agency and structure. Through microlevel choices, individual agents
create a history of events. Conversely, factors such as weather and mortality
rates often structurally determine the course of history over a long time frame.

Braudel's taxonomy of pace resonates across disciplines.[4] Scholars of international relations have been similarly confronted with the problem of how to
categorize change.[5] One way of doing so strongly resembles Braudel's categorization of tempo. Change in international relations might be categorized as interaction change, rank order change, or change in the constitutive units.[6] Interaction change, the change of diplomatic practices, is the most susceptible to
individual decision making. Such practices are influenced by the presence of
particular decision makers and by specific strategic choices. By contrast, shifts
in the distribution of capabilities occur less frequently.[7] Changes in relative
power, and the subsequent challenges to the existing rank order by ascending
powers, occur, by some accounts, every century or century and a half. Such
changes might correspond with periodic cycles in the economy. Finally, unit
change, for example, the change from city-states to empires, or from empires to
feudal organization, occurs the least often. When a particular type of unit
comes to dominate the international system, it transforms the deep structure of
the system. The more frequent changes in interactions and rank order occur
without affecting the particular character of this deep structure. For example,
diplomatic practices and the rank order of states have changed in the past decades, but all this has happened without affecting the existence of a system of
sovereign, territorial states. These historical periods in which particular types
of units tend to dominate constitute the longue durée of international politics.

But using a Braudelian scheme does not explain why such transformations
occur infrequently or how such changes might look when they do occur. Here
the punctuated equilibrium model can be of some use.[8] This second image of
change comes—somewhat ironically—from biology.[9] Stephen Jay Gould

rearticulates the Darwinian perspective and challenges common interpretations of Darwin's view of evolution as a linear and progressive process.[10] Both the "ladder" and the "cone" views of evolution are, according to Gould, mistaken. In the ladder interpretation, evolution is defined as progression along steps of a linear process. Each step follows from and is superior to the preceding step. In the cone view, evolution is perceived as a process of continual change wherein life becomes progressively more diversified and more complex, and hence more advanced. Both of these views are wrong. "Evolution, to professionals, is adaptation to changing environments, not progress."[11] One explains evolution not by suggesting that the existing life form is superior to the previous—Gould beautifully illustrates that early life forms were highly complex—but by demonstrating how it is well suited to exist in the new environment.

Gould differs from Darwin, however, on the pace of evolution. In Gould's view, change can be dramatic and very quick. It takes the form of "punctuated equilibrium." Stages of relative tranquility are interrupted by sudden and dramatic changes. Such broad exogenous change—punctuation—will lead to a flurry of radically new forms.[12] In the long run, some of these forms may die out and a period of relative tranquility will ensue—a period of relative equilibrium. Whatever forms survive are not explained by reference to the types preceding the exogenous shock but by reference to the new environment and the now simultaneously existing forms which emerged after the shock.[13] Gould's discussion of this two-staged nature of evolution is worth emphasizing in detail.

> Darwinism, on the other hand, is a two-step process, with different forces responsible for variation and direction. Darwinians speak of genetic variation, the first step, as "random." This is an unfortunate term because we do not mean in the mathematical sense of equally likely in all directions. We simply mean that variation occurs with no preferred orientation in adaptive direction.... Selection, the second step, works upon *unoriented* variation and changes a population by conferring greater reproductive success upon advantageous variants.[14]

Gould's view of evolution serves as an alternative to the unilinear imagery that I criticized in Chapter 1. But is it appropriate for social science, and international relations in particular? Social and biological evolution are different, and the critical difference between them is intentionality in the first, variation, phase of evolution. Although biological organisms mutate at random, social groups may intentionally form political coalitions to deal with particular environmental constraints. Nonetheless, even here Gould's theory proves to be a useful metaphor.[15] First, the institutional outcomes of such bargains need not be efficient responses to external challenges. Furthermore, these outcomes are not a priori predictable because they involve elements of political strategy (more on this below). Moreover, the actors, when forming these coalitions, are incognizant of the long-term ability of their preferred institutions to compete with rivals. Created institutions are thus unoriented toward their long-run survivability, and the causes behind their emergence are different from the causes of their demise.

Second, empirically we can distinguish periods in which particular units (feudal, imperial, or territorial states) have become dominant following a dramatic change in military organization, economy, or culture. That is, changes in political organization seem to be preceded by broad shifts in constraints and opportunities imposed on social actors by the external milieu. Punctuations such as defeat in war, revolution, or emergent capitalism lead to a flurry of institutional innovations. Such phenomena are the sociopolitical equivalent of speciation events in biology.

Third, there are good reasons why actors do not redesign institutions unless conditions force them to do so. Transaction costs, set belief systems, and standard operating procedures mitigate against frequent overhaul. Moreover, given the fact that institutions reflect a particular distribution of power, such changes are unlikely to occur without fundamental shifts in that distribution.[16] Once one form has established itself as dominant, relative stability in institutional types should follow.[17] There is a certain path dependency in institutional design.

In short, the uneven nature of political change is well captured by the punctuated equilibrium model. Given that existing institutions cater to particular interests and reflect specific distributions of power, institutions will be "sticky." Only when dominant coalitions change, or interests and perceptions shift, will there be an opportunity for institutional transformation.

Most importantly, this metaphor warns us that history does not work by optimal design. The species or institution that proves to be successful over time is only successful vis-à-vis its synchronic alternatives. Following a punctuation event, type A might prove to be better than type B or C. But type A need not be an optimal response. Indeed, if type A did not emerge as a type in the variation stage, type B might become dominant in the subsequent selective process with C. For example, changes in the economic and military milieu of China did not lead to territorial states there. Yet it is clear that the Tang and Sung empires were well ahead of European development. But neither expanding trade nor gunpowder caused territorial states to emerge.[18] As in the first step of Darwinian evolution, the emergence of new types is not predictable by the change in milieu alone. However, once some new types have established themselves, the second step of the Darwinian process—selection—will reward only some or even only one of these.

A PROPOSED CAUSAL MODEL FOR EXPLAINING INSTITUTIONAL VARIATION AND SELECTION

I essentially argue that broad-based external change has a variety of internal repercussions. In response to such an external change, new political coalitions will form, based on material interests and shared conceptual frameworks. The expansion of trade was the critical external change that set this process in motion during the High Middle Ages. The variety of novel institutional arrangements—city-leagues, city-states, and sovereign, territorial states—can be explained by the particular nature of new political coalitions in response to the changing environment. The three cases I examine—the Hanseatic League, the Italian city-states, and the French territorial state—are all explained in this fashion. The growth of trade and corresponding increase in urban centers gave birth to new sets of arrangements between kings, aristocracy, burghers, and church.

Many theorists have argued that the internal developments of a country cannot be understood without taking into account that country's position within its external environment. This view lies at the heart of Hintze's explanation of how a state's external vulnerability, because of geographic location, might lead to authoritarianism.[19] The argument that changes in the economic market led to political realignment lies at the basis of Barrington Moore's explanation of authoritarianism and democracy.[20] Theda Skocpol's explanation of revolutions and Peter Gourevitch's account of foreign economic policies also follow this logic.[21]

Similarly, social realignments explain the emergence of new types of political organization, for example, during the High Middle Ages.[22] Actors have particular interests and perspectives and corresponding preferred forms of organization. An external change, a change in the overall milieu in which that society is placed, will lead to a shift in the relative power of social and political actors. Individuals will seek to capitalize on their improved relative position and change the existing political institutions. I thus take a methodological individualist perspective. Individuals have reasoned preferences to support one institution over another. The emergence of new institutions must thus be traced back to the ability of actors to pursue those preferences.

The outcome of such realignments, however, is not a foregone conclusion.[23] Realignments are essentially permutations and combinations of bargains based on material interests and shared belief systems.[24] Some actors choose in a satisficing way. They might lack information or might be ignorant about the probability of achieving their most preferred outcome. Moreover, because powerful actors may have widely divergent preferences, second-best solutions and compromises abound. Furthermore, actors work with divergent discount rates. The long-term future of the city-state clearly was not in anybody's mind in the period leading up to the Italian Renaissance. Political entrepreneurs and burghers were more concerned with immediate success in war or profit. To make matters worse, outcomes might even be serendipitous or accidental to what actors set out to achieve. Finally, institutions might be caught in low-level equilibrium traps.[25]

In short, we cannot simply deduce institutional outcomes from preferences or impute preferences from observed outcomes. The pure rational choice variant of methodological individualism, in assuming outcomes from efficient calculations, runs the risk of committing the *post hoc ergo propter hoc* fallacy. Institutions are interpreted "as having arisen because of the functions they must have served, when they in fact appeared for purely adventitious reasons."[26] As Keohane notes, a sound functional analysis should show a causal connection between the functions of an institution and its existence. Similarly, James Caporaso criticizes rational choice for not examining the actual choice process.[27]

For these reasons, my research tries to inductively ascertain what preferences individuals actually had and what choices they made. I further examine how preferences were aggregated and played out in political bargaining. In doing so, the role of beliefs and norms must be taken into account, in conjunction with the material interests of the individuals in question. Beliefs and norms inform one's preferences. Hence, in order to ascertain the actual preferences of an actor, that individual's belief system must be examined. To label particular types of behavior, for example, a noble's pursuit of honor, as irrational by holding it to a strict cost-benefit logic misses the point. The choice of that individual should be understood by the conceptual context through which that individual's preferences are formed.[28] Weber's notion of elective affinity is one way of reconciling material interests and belief systems, without claiming the priority of the first and reducing the latter to epiphenomenal status. By using his insight, I try to demonstrate the preferences I ascribe to individuals.[29]

The focus on individuals' ideas is important, moreover, because it addresses a problem that is neglected in some accounts of rational bargaining but that should be clearly central to it. Such accounts, although they correlate interests to outcomes, fail to clarify how second-order collective action problems are overcome. Even when new institutions might benefit the members of a potential political coalition, that coalition might not form because of freeriding. The existence of shared beliefs will thus make the link between material preferences and institutional outcomes more plausible.

I will analyze three cases: the rise of the sovereign, territorial state in France, the emergence of the Hanseatic city-league, and the rise of the Italian city-states.[30] My analysis of the three cases starts at roughly the end of the tenth century. In France, the Capetian Dynasty ascended to the throne. In three centuries it would extend its control from a small royal domain around Paris to an area roughly similar to contemporary France. In those same three centuries, German imperial pretensions came to naught. Both Germany and Italy fragmented into a variety of urban leagues and city-states. It is in this period, then, that feudal lordships, universalist claims by the church, and German imperial designs started to give ground. Instead, sovereign statehood, urban leagues, and city-states made their appearances.

My discussion ends at about the time of the Peace of Westphalia (1648), which formally acknowledged a system of sovereign states.[31] This is not to say that the process of eliminating alternatives to states had been completed by then. But it did indicate that the variety in the types of units that existed in the Late Middle Ages was gradually being reduced, until later only a system of states remained.

I chose these cases for several reasons. First, I argue that all three were affected by the rise of trade, my independent variable. During the eleventh, twelfth, and thirteenth centuries, Europe went through a remarkable period of economic growth. This exogenous variable set a process of realignments in motion. Second, the variation in types of units allows me to demonstrate that the success of the state was not a foregone conclusion, as many theories on the rise of the state suggest. Third, the differences in capacities—not necessarily in favor of the state—clarify that the rise of the state was not simply a matter of efficiency of scale, that is, of size. As shown in this study, all these cases were viable contenders with states. Fourth, this variation dispels some alternative explanatory accounts. Emergent capitalism (neo-Marxist theory), dynamic density (neo-Durkheimian arguments), military technology (competitive ability perspectives), and conceptual shifts (neo-Weberian theory) do not suffice as ultimate explanatory variables. Each of the three cases were susceptible to emergent capitalism and increased transactions. All of these also had access to the new military technologies and sets of ideas. Yet they demonstrate different institutional solutions.

In short, by acknowledging this variation in contending alternatives, I can more accurately identify the causes of unit change. Furthermore, this variation allows me to suggest reasons why the other forms were inferior, without simply affirming the consequent.[32]

Critical to my analysis is the separation of the generative causes of such new institutional arrangements from the causes that led to the demise of some. It is clear from the contemporary state system that states have displaced other forms of organization. The second part of the explanation of unit transformation therefore requires an account of the selective process that favored states over these other types. The full account of this selective process is presented in Part III of this book.

I will argue that selection occurs both by systemic pressure on the less competitive types and by societal choices of actors who switch their allegiances. Systemically, from a top-down perspective, there are three main reasons why states survived and displaced other forms of organization. First, the internal logic of organization of the sovereign state had less deficiencies than its rivals. Sovereign, territorial states were better at rationalizing their economies and mobilizing the resources of their societies.[33] Second, state sovereignty proved to be an effective and efficient means of organizing external, interunit behavior. Sovereign states could more easily make credible commitments than their non-sovereign counterparts. Third, sovereign states selected out and delegitimized actors who did not fit a system of territorially demarcated and internally hierarchical authorities. The organizational principles of territorial states and city-leagues were mutually incompatible, exactly because the latter had no specific borders.

Selection, however, also occurs by social choice, from the bottom up. Since sovereignty is an institutional mechanism which creates a focal point for coordinating behavior, members of sovereign societies can achieve gains from long-run, iterative cooperation. If the benefits of long-term cooperation outweigh the benefits of short-run defection, social actors have an incentive to defect from institutions that do not provide for these benefits.[34]

Institutional mimicry constitutes a second form of social choice.[35] For example, once the benefits of sovereign statehood became apparent, the German feudal lords started to behave like territorial rulers. They started to call themselves princes and to perform regalian tasks such as regulating weights and measures, standardizing coinage, and rationalizing justice. Although technically still part of the empire (which would last in name until 1806), these principalities gained all the trappings of sovereign statehood. The Peace of Westphalia formally acknowledged their status and granted them all the rights of state actors, such as signing treaties, exchanging diplomats, and waging war (albeit not against the empire itself).

My key point, therefore, is that institutional structures have particular domestic and international consequences. This is not a comprehensive theory of late medieval and early modern Europe. Readers searching for a detailed account of the Hundred Years War, the defeat of Burgundy, or a clarification of the implications of the new Atlantic trade routes will search in vain. Instead my focus is on the advantages of fixed territorial borders and the benefits and costs of weakly established hierarchy. I do not deny the specific importance of individual traits of kings, weather patterns, or fortunes of war to clarify the rise and fall of specific states. But this is not an argument about specific states. In a sense, this is not even the history of France, Germany, or Italy. Instead it is an argument about the relative merits of particular logics of organization. The historical cases should be seen as examples of a larger set of diverse organizations—France was not the only territorial state, the Hansa was not the only city-league. My account suggests why some actors preferred one form of organization over others and why in the long run only sovereign territoriality survived as a logic of organization.

A NONLINEAR ACCOUNT OF STATE FORMATION THROUGH WAR

Charles Tilly suggests, as I do, that any account of change in the type of units must deal with the nature of institutional variation that existed in medieval Europe and the subsequent consolidation of the state. He explicitly recognizes the omission of this in some of his earlier work.[36] He also gives one of the few accounts of change that takes internal and external variables into account.

Tilly's recent model of explanation is extremely powerful.[37] The explanation he presents explicitly acknowledges the variety of institutional types that differed from the national state. Indeed, in its broad outline, Tilly's formula parallels my own. Shifts in the milieu lead to internal crises. Domestic factors produce a certain outcome. Then international systemic factors eventually lead to the dominance of one of the organizational forms. It is precisely the similarity in general perspectives that makes Tilly's model a valuable benchmark for evaluating my analysis. It will also clarify how my argument differs from a commonly held view that the rise of the sovereign state must be primarily attributed to warfare.

Tilly argues that the creation of new types of units in Europe basically proceeded along two dimensions. The first dimension was coercive intensive and the second was capital intensive. "In the coercion intensive mode, rulers squeezed the means of war from their own populations and others they conquered, building massive structures of extraction in the process."[38] This method of resource mobilization occurred in regions that lacked strongly developed towns, such as Brandenburg and Russia. Areas that had well-developed towns, such as Italy and the Netherlands, had to make bargains with capitalists—the capital-intensive mode of resource mobilization.

National states such as England and France combined both coercive- and capital-intensive modes. "In the intermediate capitalized-coercion mode, rulers did some of each, but spent more of their effort than did their capital-intensive neighbors on incorporating capitalists and sources of capital directly into the structures of their states."[39]

Gradually, competitive pressure selected out those organizations that used only one of the two methods of resource mobilization. The national state, which utilized both of these methods, proved to be better at waging war.[40] The series of wars that permeated Europe from 1500 on thus selected out the city-states and city-leagues. These unit types proved unable to muster the resources that national states could bring to bear.

My account differs from Tilly's on several issues. First, Tilly explains the variation between types of organization by differential responses to the functional demand of waging war. My account is based on the impact of economic change and subsequent politics of coalitional bargaining. I see the economic transformation of medieval Europe as the primary independent variable which made new political coalitions possible. These coalitions embarked on different institutional paths prior to the military revolution. Second, Tilly explains selection among rival modes of organization by their ability to wage war. From my perspective, the ability to wage war is itself determined by the efficacy of particular institutional arrangements. For example, the ability of a particular mode of organization to raise revenue and prevent freeriding will affect its war-making capacity. That is, the ability to wage war is an intervening variable, itself determined by institutional makeup. Third, Tilly's focus is different from mine. Tilly is primarily concerned with the state's ability to raise revenue from its society for war. Given this focus, there is no doubt that the military revolution led to an exponential increase in state demands on society following the Middle Ages. By contrast, I am interested in the question of how sovereign territoriality became one of the logics of organization that emerged in the Middle Ages. Thus, although I am also concerned with the capacity of government to extract resources, I focus more specifically on the emergence of sovereign territoriality in contrast to nonterritorial and nonsovereign types of organization.

Given Tilly's focus and presuppositions, it is logical that he sees the variety of coercive-intensive or capital-intensive paths emerge particularly after 1400. This corresponds with major breakthroughs in military technology—artillery, modern fortifications, massed infantry—after 1400 or even later by some accounts. This environmental change forced governments to seek more revenue from their populations in order to guarantee the security of their respective polities.

However, some historians, such as Joseph Strayer, place the origins of the state at an earlier date. Tilly suggests that if Strayer is right, then his own argument is flawed.[41] It is not merely a question of the exact dating of the origins of the state. As I discuss in Chapter 5—and this is the critical point if Strayer's chronology is correct—centralization cannot be explained by war making alone. First, weak kings were not the logical providers of protection. Second, given that there was no increase in competitive pressure, since the military revolution had not yet occurred, central governments must have provided other inducements to powerful groups.

The French Capetian kings started from a very weak material basis. Powerful lords, such as the duke of Normandy, wielded more military might. If war making were the primary explanatory factor, then such lords should have been more successful than the king. That is, if state making were simply a bargain for protection, there is no reason to assume that the king would be the logical provider of protection, or that a centralized kingdom should be the result. The question thus becomes, how could weak kings bargain their way to greater strength?

This suggests that a focus on social alliances will be more fruitful. To argue that national states centralized and accumulated coercive force by combining elements of the coercive- and capital-intensive path still leaves unanswered how this occurred. A focus on social alliances will, for example, clarify why rulers started to protect property rights[42] and will thus suggest why centralized rule was more attractive than feudal rule.[43] This is of course Douglass North's point. Although Tilly views North's theory as a direct counterargument to his own,[44] I believe that a closer analysis of microlevel incentives and political bargains, such as North's or my own, actually fills some gaps in Tilly's argument.

I agree that the relative strength of towns is the first step in explaining the variation between states (city-states, national states, etc.). However, the relative power of the towns alone cannot explain everything. One needs an account of how towns bargained or allied with rulers. For example, one could not predict that many German towns would become independent solely by taking their relative power into account. The course of German urban independence was equally determined by Frederick II's choice to ally with the lords against the towns. The specific strategy pursued by political coalitions remains, therefore, important.

Furthermore, if towns are critical, as Tilly suggests—and I agree with him— then their presence needs to be explained. I argue that the emergence of many of the new towns in northern Europe, and the growth of the Italian towns, can be precisely attributed to the economic dynamics of the Late Middle Ages.

Hence, this reinforces my point that the important change in milieu is the change in the economic system, which preceded changing methods of warfare.

In short, Tilly explains the variation in unit type by different responses to the functional necessity of waging war. These different responses can in turn be explained by regional variation in the strength of towns. I argue, by contrast, that variation can be explained by different responses to a changing economic environment. The particular different responses can in turn be explained by the nature of internal political coalitions.

The second difference with Tilly's model is his account of international selection. For Tilly, selection is rooted in the unit's security performance. From my perspective, the critical variable is institutional structure. This in turn explains the ability to wage war. Whether or not a particular type of organization will survive depends on its ability to prevent freeriding, its credibility to commit in international treaties, compatibility with other types of organization, and the benefits that it provides to its subjects (in order to prevent defection).

Sometimes Tilly's account appears to explain the success of national states simply by the amount of resources under control, not by the particular mix of coercive-intensive or capital-intensive means. The national state centralized and accumulated more coercive means than its rivals.[45] The physical size of the state makes the difference. Tilly suggests, for example, that "large states" replaced other types.[46] The Italian city-states fell to the French and the Netherlands to England, not because they were capital intensive but because they were not large enough to muster sufficient resources.

I locate competitive ability in the nature of the unit's organizational structure.[47] One cannot argue that capital-intensive states lost out to national states because the latter could use coercion and capital-intensive means to mobilize resources. One could very well argue that the more capital-intensive units were more suited to purchase resources for war. In fact, states that rely more on coercive means to extract resources might be at a disadvantage.[48]

My alternative explanation of variation and selection has several benefits over Tilly's perspective and similar accounts that focus predominantly on warfare. If, as Tilly proposes, war making is the crucial selecting mechanism, then it is difficult to explain why so many small states survived. Why, for example, were the minuscule German states recognized as treaty signees equal to France or England, even in the middle of the nineteenth century? As Tilly himself notes, he regards some small entities such as Monaco or San Marino today as states, because other states treat them as such.[49] In other words, it is the empowerment by other states of such entities that allows them to continue to operate in world affairs rather than their ability to wield force. Furthermore, if the size of the national state is actually the explanation, how can smaller states replace a larger? Why did the Netherlands replace Spain? In my account this can be explained by looking at possible institutionally superior arrangements.[50]

In summary, I basically disagree with Tilly on two dimensions. First, I explain institutional variation by the specific nature of social coalitions following economic change rather than by different responses to the functional prerequisite of war making. Second, I argue that whereas war is an important factor, the ability to wage war itself needs to be explained by institutional analysis. I would argue that on these dimensions, however, my theory complements Tilly's analysis by specifying the particular bargains underlying the state-making process.

Modes of Nonterritorial Organization: Feudalism, the Church, and the Holy Roman Empire

> The conflict between this Duplicity and the requisite Unity becomes the starting-point for speculative discussions of the relation between Church and State. The Medieval Spirit steadily refuses to accept the Dualism as final. In some higher Unity reconciliation must be found. This was indubitable; but over the nature of the reconciling process the great parties of the Middle Age fell a fighting.[1]

> The king, therefore, did not rule the entire territory of his realm in the same way as the modern state governs within its boundaries. In this sense the modern state is a "territorial state," whereas the medieval state was not. In this sense one may speak of a state based on personal ties as well as of lordship over land and people.[2]

IF POLITICS is about rule, the modern state is verily unique, for it claims sovereignty and territoriality. It is sovereign in that it claims final authority and recognizes no higher source of jurisdiction. It is territorial in that rule is defined as exclusive authority over a fixed territorial space. The criterion for determining where claims to sovereign jurisdiction begin or end is thus a purely geographic one. Mutually recognized borders delimit spheres of jurisdiction.

As John Ruggie has pointed out, rule need not have, and historically often has not had, these two characteristics.[3] Clans, tribes, and kinship groups, for example, are not bound by territorial rule. Clan leaders and tribal elders exercise authority over individuals as members of that collectivity. The area occupied or controlled by such a group is thus derivative of the prior classification of individual membership of the clan. Some forms of territorial rule, moreover, need not be fixed. One's claims to authority over a particular space might vary with the seasons or trade routes. For example, in the case of nomadic tribes, one might claim a right over particular grazing areas that fluctuate with the seasons. Finally, rule need not be exclusive. A variety of authorities might claim the right to govern and exercise jurisdiction over the same space. Ruggie notes how medieval Europe was of that nature.

Thus the modern state defines the human collectivity in a completely novel way. It defines individuals by spatial markers, regardless of kin, tribal affiliation, or religious beliefs. Individuals are in a sense amorphous and undifferentiated entities who are given an identity simply by their location in a particular area. Thus one must *make* Acquitanians, Normans, and Bretons into French people.[4]

We should also note that the contemporary state is not only territorial but is internally sovereign. That is, it is externally demarcated from others. It makes no claim to rule outside its borders and, conversely, recognizes no authority above it within them. Internally it claims final authority. In Weber's terms, it claims the monopoly of violence or, put in more general political terms, it is the final locus of jurisdiction.

Systems of rule in the early Middle Ages had vastly different characteristics. They were nonterritorial, and sovereignty was, at best, disputed. Yet it would be wrong to think that these systems of rule did not control a particular geographical space. As Robert Dodgshon argues, all forms of organization—hunter-gatherer tribes, nomadic kinship structures, empires, and states—occupy a certain space.[5] The question is whether the system of rule is predicated on and defined by fixed territorial parameters. The medieval period lacked not only exclusivity but also territoriality. Even in the feudal system of rule, where lords might have jurisdiction over manors and lands granted to them, territoriality was not the defining trait of that logic of organization.

I will argue in this chapter that feudalism, the church, and the Holy Roman Empire lacked territorial fixity and exclusivity. Rule was not premised on territorial delimitation. Feudal organization was essentially a system of rule based on mutual ties of dependence without clearly defined hierarchy. So although one might say that feudal rule occupied a given space, inclusion in the feudal structure was not defined by physical location. That is, territory was not determinative of identity and loyalty. One's specific obligations or rights depended on one's place in the matrix of personal ties, not on one's location in a particular area.

The church, with its clear perception of hierarchy, saw itself as a community of believers with no geographic limits to its authority. Inclusion in the membership of the church meant being part of a religious community. There were believers and infidels. Logically, there were no territorial limits to the inclusion of such faithful.[6] But as the name indicates, the Holy Roman Empire claimed that very same constituency and legitimated its power by a semireligious status of its own. The emperor claimed superiority over all other rulers. Frederick II thus claimed to rule as *dominus mundi*, "lord of the world."

In short, in none of these was authority contingent on, or defined by, control over a specific territory with fixed boundaries. Although there were of course pragmatic limits to the factual exercise of power, their claims to rule were not defined by territory. Church and empire were universalist forms of organization. By their very nature they could not admit any rival authority as legitimately equivalent. There could only be one church, since it was sanctioned by God. There could only be one empire, since it was the secular arm of the church.

To reiterate, the sovereign state, by contrast, is an organization that is territorially defined. Authority is administrative control over a fixed territorial space. It is delimited in an external sense, vis-à-vis other actors, by its formal borders. Unlike the church or empire, it advances no superiority over other rulers.[7]

In none of the three modes of organization under study can we define or distinguish domestic from international politics. Feudal lords, church, and empire operated in systems of crosscutting jurisdictions. Juridical competence depended on the specific issue at hand. Indeed, the system of rule looked remarkably like the patterns of authority we ascribe to premodern rule in non-European parts of the world. "In different contexts, different subdivisions of the whole take collective action for the purposes for which they are autonomous; so that if such action is the criterion of a political community, there are series of overlapping political communities."[8]

At the end of the first millennium it was hardly predictable that the decentralized nature of feudalism and the systems of rule of church and empire would be challenged and in many ways superseded by new logics of organization. Nevertheless, by 1300 all three had started to give way to city-states, city-leagues, and sovereign, territorial states.[9]

The critical aim of this chapter is to clarify the specific logics of organization of church, empire, and feudalism. This will set the tone for upcoming discussions of the interests of territorial rulers and emergent towns which ran contrary to the systems of rule of the early medieval period.

FEUDALISM: RULE BY PERSONAL BONDS

There are few concepts in historical analysis as ambiguous and contested as the concept of feudalism. It is ambiguous, not in the least because the very term was unknown to its medieval practitioners. The term was first coined in the seventeenth century. It is contested in that debates about feudalism are inherently declarations of theoretical and political dispositions. They involve polemics on the nature of constitutionalism, the origins of capitalism, and the sequence of political evolution. Some historians have even gone so far as to suggest that the term should be scrapped altogether.[10] Given that these debates are essentially irresolvable, and given that one's position on these matters is largely a consequence of one's chosen analytic and ideological focus, I will not discuss the intricacies of these disagreements.

I argue that feudalism is a highly decentralized system of political organization which is based on personal ties.[11] I therefore essentially follow Strayer in defining feudalism as a mode of political organization. "To sum up, the basic characteristics of feudalism in Western Europe are a fragmentation of political authority, public power in private hands, and a military system in which an essential part of the armed forces is secured through private contracts."[12] Most important for our purposes is the contrast between the feudal logic of political organization and the sovereign, territorial state. In order to understand this feudal system of rule, we must start by retracing its historical origins.

The Roots of Feudalism

Feudalism finds its roots in the decline of the Carolingian Empire in the early ninth century. The breakup of central authority coincided with increasing raids by Maygars, Saracens, and Vikings.[13] One common explanation sees the rise of feudalism as a response to these ubiquitous and sudden threats which necessitated the presence of local defense.[14] Standing armies, far away, were of no avail. Individuals sought and found protection from local strongmen. These local strongmen were the knights who had constituted the heavy cavalry of Charles Martel, Pepin, and Charlemagne in their conquests. Now the knights provided local protection by the presence of their strongholds. Feudalism emerged out of an already existing warrior elite.[15]

A second explanation of the emergence of feudalism focuses on the nature of military technology. It emphasizes the development of heavy shock cavalry by the Franks.[16] This was an expensive mode of warfare. Since only the wealthy could afford horse and armor, this inevitably led to concentration of power by a small military elite.[17] It was this stratum of great men that became rivals of central authority.

Others see a strong Germanic influence. Like the old Germanic chieftains who fought the Roman imperial legions, Frankish kings were seen as leaders in war. These leaders had a reciprocal relation with their followers. "As described by Tacitus, at any rate, the comes was a free warrior who voluntarily, by a solemn obligation (sacramentum), agreed to become the devoted follower of a military chief (princeps), sharing his fortunes even to the death in return for sustenance, equipment, and a share of the booty gained in war."[18] The retinue of the king thus expected spoils for military service. The quid pro quo that we find in the lord-vassal relation thus has its origin in an ancient custom.[19]

Whatever explanation we wish to accept, it should be clear that Frankish kingship evolved around mounted knights who expected some form of return for their services. Indeed, if the chieftain could not deliver his end of the bargain, the vassal could renounce his obligation to the superior, provided this was done explicitly and before witnesses. Superimposed on this military basis developed the later theory of feudalism proper,[20] complete with a particular mode of economic production and sources of legitimation.

Feudalism, therefore, placed military force directly in the hands of the vassal. The decentralizing tendency of localized military force, however, was initially mitigated by a variety of policies. The Carolingians managed to control fragmentation of political rule until the end of Charlemagne's reign. While the empire was still in existence, and trade and coinage were still available, service was rewarded by monetary payment.[21] Monetary payment from the center curtailed the decentralizing tendencies of feudalism.[22] Moreover, these warlords were forced to rotate their residences. They would only reside at particular areas for several years at a time. The king also traveled throughout his domain exercising on-site control. Although there were established administrative centers, such as Aachen, the king would tour his domains while residing at the castles and churches of his inferiors. In other words, the king tried to maintain direct supervision over his vassals. Where he could not be himself, he sent vassi dominici, paid administrators who acted in his name.[23]

The theoretical point is that as long as the economic infrastructure was still strong, there was no inherent reason why local military strongholds had to be decentralizing. A focus on only the military logistics of the time is too narrow. Remuneration from the center, effective administration, and other means of controlling agents can counteract the logistics of local force.[24]

However, with the decline of the empire and the incursions of Viking, Saracen, and Maygar raiders, trade and the availability of coinage declined. Reciprocal military obligations now had to be repaid in-kind—by land. It was this repayment in-kind that had such a decentralizing effect and that led to feudalism proper.[25] Vassalage was now not merely a form of military organization; it became the nexus around which economic production was organized.

The resulting system of rule consisted of two sets of obligations, well described by Bloch.[26] Feudalism is first the set of reciprocal military obligations where the weaker seeks the protection of the stronger, in return for military service when required by the superior. Sometimes the guarantee of protection would suffice, but usually military service was rewarded by the superior in the form of a benefice, a gift, which later usually became a land grant, a fief.[27] When the vassal became a holder of lands under his own jurisdiction, this gave rise to the second set of obligations. These relations were hierarchical, nonreciprocal, and did not involve military relationships. These were the manorial relations.[28] At first the tilling of the soil was primarily done by free men, but gradually serfdom became more prevalent. The peasants would till the soil and transfer portion of the crops to the manorial holder.

In short, one can say that feudalism "has analogies with barter economics, its duties, protections and services being exchanged rather than bought or sold."[29] It was an explicit bilateral relation with specific duties and obligations. Because of the emergence of in-kind rewards, this logic of organization led to fragmentation of political rule.

Differences between Feudal Organization and Sovereign Statehood

There are three main differences between the logic of feudal organization and organization based on sovereign territoriality. First, feudal rule lacked hierarchy. Second, territorial rule was not exclusive. Third, feudal rule of territory was imperfect. Manorial relations in some ways resembled territorial rule the closest. One would be subject to the jurisdiction of a lord by one's residence in a given area. However, seen as a system of larger political rule, the territorial holdings of the lords were dependent on the specific personal relations in which they were embedded. Feudal relations superseded the manorial.

The logic of feudal organization lacked a sovereign, a final source of authority and jurisdiction. Service was owed to those with whom one had entered into vassalage. It was not uncommon to have lands from several lords, all of whom were entitled to service from that vassal for the lands held from them. Thus one could simultaneously be the vassal of the German emperor, the French king, and various counts and bishops, none of whom necessarily had precedence over the other. For example, the Count of Luxemburg was a prince of the empire and hence nominally subject to the emperor, but he also held a money fief (a pension) from the French king and was thus also subject to him.[30] A vassal might recognize different superiors under different circumstances. Consequently a vassal might be caught in crosscutting obligations which are very difficult to comprehend within our understanding of "international" relations. A mind-boggling example is provided by John Toul who tried to balance rival obligations to four lords—Lord John of Arcis, Lord Enguerran of Coucy, the Count of Champagne, and the Count of Grandpré—with the latter two having equivalent status but precedence over the first two.

> If it should happen that the count of Grandpré should be at war with the countess and count of Champagne for his own personal grievances, I will personally go to the assistance of the count of Grandpré and will send to the countess and count of Champagne, if they summon me, the knights I owe for the fief which I hold of them. But if the count of Grandpré shall make war on the countess and count of Champagne on behalf of his friends and not for his own personal grievances, I shall serve in person with the countess and count of Champagne and I will send one knight to the count of Grandpré to give the service owed from the fief which I hold of him. But I will not myself invade the territory of the count of Grandpré.[31]

Whether John Toul actually had to oppose his own knights we do not know. But we do know from the biography of William Marshal, the trusted aide of several kings, that he in fact was engaged in a similar balancing act. First, Marshal was indebted to the English King Richard, but he also held lands from John, Richard's brother who was in rebellion against the king. Marshal tried to fulfill his obligations to both. Later, when Normandy fell to the French king, Marshal was indebted to Philip Augustus for his lands there. William Marshal worked out a formula where he would be King John's man in England and King Philip's man in France.[32] And indeed both monarchs maintained him as lord of his lands.[33]

Not only was hierarchy diffuse, but one could question whether there was indeed any hierarchy at all. For example, the king of France was enfeoffed to several bishops for land he held from them. It is only later with the principle of ligesse, the superiority of some types of homage over others, that hierarchy started to be established.[34]

Such relationships did not necessarily reflect factual material power of the superior lord. For example, Henry II was king of England, duke of Acquitaine, Count of Anjou, and duke of Normandy. But although he was king of England, he only held Normandy in the title of duke and was thus, according to feudal theory, obliged to pay homage to the French king. Henry II did indeed pay Louis VII such homage, although in pure material terms the French king was much weaker.

Not only was the feudal logic of organization in many ways nonhierarchical, but rule over territory was also not exclusive. Jurisdiction over a particular territorial area was seldom absolute. Ecclesiastics, for example, were to be tried by religious courts and canon law rather than by territorial lords. Likewise the king was entitled to proceeds of bishoprics that fell outside his royal domain or that of his vassals.

Consequently, one can question whether the feudal logic of organization is even properly conceived as a system of territorial rule. Instead it is better conceptualized as organization based on personal bonds. "The performance of political functions depends on personal agreements," and "political authority is treated as private possession."[35] Feudalism is thus rule over people rather than land. One speaks, therefore, of the king of the English (Rex Anglorum) in the twelfth century, rather than the king of England (Rex Anglie).[36] Similarly, one spoke of the king of the French (Rex Francorum) because the idea of what the kingdom exactly encompassed (the Regnum Francie) only came into existence after the king had established himself over and above the lords. There is considerable debate in German medieval historiography over whether the German duchies of the tenth century should be perceived as administrative areas or rather as tribal aggregations, the so-called stem duchies.[37] The difficulty of applying contemporary notions of territorial rule to the feudal situation also shows itself in the indeterminacy of the boundaries of the royal domain of the early Capetians. As Elizabeth Hallam argues, in the early Capetian period, when the kings were little more than princes among equals, the royal domain was best conceived as a package of rights rather than as rule over a specific territory. The king was thus entitled to income from sources, such as bishoprics, outside his domain over which he also might have jurisdiction.[38] The acquisition of authority over territory was thus subsidiary to the personal bonds which gave one such authority over a given geographic space.

Because feudal organization was so heavily based on personal ties, markers were developed to distinguish those privileged to engage in reciprocal obligations and rights from those who were not so privileged.[39] Hence, rule was reinforced by the special legal status of nobility and by the particular legitimation of their authority. The feudal aristocracy constituted a caste. The bearing of arms differentiated who were servile and who were free. Those who paid homage and bore arms were considered free, regardless of the number of overlords they had. Rituals and symbolism reinforced this differentiation. The act of homage, the kneeling in submission to the superior, was unique to the military relations of feudalism. Fealty, the swearing of an oath, was reserved for members of the clergy and the nobility.[40] Nobles married within the aristocracy and were buried with their fellow nobles. Nobility connoted pure "blue" blood.[41] "On every occasion, documentary and narrative sources attribute to the nobility a spirit and attitudes of a class, even of caste."[42]

Nobility thus constituted a new type of kin group to replace older tribal kin-group affiliation.[43] Nobility distinguished itself from others by superior lineage. This did not imply equality among these knights. As in every military organization, there were superiors and inferiors. However, the nobility acknowledged that they were related as a group, which was quite distinct from others. "Despite differences in power and property, as nobles all are of equal birth; as a later term has it, all are dynasts."[44]

From the tenth century onward, the nobles' distinctive character and the legitimacy of their privileged position were further developed by the theory of the three orders. I discuss this in greater detail in Chapter 4. Suffice it to say for now that the theory of the three orders divided society into the clergy, the warriors, and the workers. This division was perceived to be homologous to that of heaven. Hence, the warrior could justify his position as the defender of those who prayed.

This personalistic system of rule had corresponding legal arrangements. First of all the nobility formed a special legal category. It was entitled to free, allodial holdings. On these holdings it had rights of command and justice (banal lordships). Nobles were entitled to sit on courts with their peers (the mallus). And they were entitled to have an armed retinue.[45] If a noble was murdered, the money required for compensation of the kin, the wergild, was higher than for nonnobles.[46] The scale of compensatory damages to kin clearly reveals the inequality before the law.

Laws were a mixture of prefeudal elements, remnants of Roman law mixed with Germanic customs, and edicts of the Germanic kings who came after the decline of the empire. Most law, however, was customary.[47] Contracts would be sealed by gestures or specific formulas. To remember obligations or important events, mnemonic devices were used.[48] In such an environment one could hardly expect well-defined property rights. Feudal law only recognized seisin, or Gewere, which was possession over time. Disputes were settled by querying neighbors.[49] Written law would only emerge after 1100 because of the demands of merchants and the drafting of urban statutes.

The legal context thus reveals the larger social and conceptual order of the time. Saltman is right when he argues that legal relations go beyond their immediate pragmatic use. "[T]he initial legal principles are grounded in sets of social relationships and attain intelligibility in this particular social order. Thus these principles are ontological rather than mere abstractions."[50]

Given that military and economic organization consisted primarily of the network of personal ties, well-defined property rights would hardly be necessary even if they were conceivable. Exchanges occurred largely by in-kind transfer with little ramifications for third parties who were not immediately part of the deal.[51] In a highly abstract and monetarized economy, the nature of property rights of course becomes critical to the working of the market. Indeed, it establishes the very principle of a "market."

In summary, the feudal logic of rule differed from sovereign territoriality in that it lacked territorial delimitation[52] and lacked a final locus of jurisdiction. It was a system based on personal ties conferring rights and obligations across territories. These ties were reaffirmed by the construction of nobility as a caste, a special legal class which demarcated itself by cultural markers such as dress, manners, and rituals and which claimed superiority simply as a birthright.[53]

UNIVERSALIST CLAIMS OF THE CHURCH

It has been said that the state is inconceivable without the church.[54] The clash between the universalist modes of organization of church and empire preceded, and laid the basis for, the emergence of sovereign, territorial states. Had these two modes of organization reconciled their differences, or had one conceded to the other, then the pattern of European state formation might have looked quite different. Although both empire and church increasingly developed a theory of sovereignty, a view of final authority, they were decidedly translocal. Neither recognized territorial boundaries to its authority. It was the very tension between the idea of a Christian Commonwealth and the legacy of the old Roman Empire that was responsible for the later conflict. I begin, therefore, with a brief description of the historical origins and structure of the church. From the very beginning, the fates of church and empire were intertwined.

The Historical Development of the Universalist Church

From the beginning, Christianity had a paradoxical relation with the Roman Empire. On the one hand, it managed to spread throughout the empire with considerable speed. Michael Mann suggests that this occurred because the Christian doctrine appealed to traders and merchants, who, in their mobile occupations, could spread the faith.[55] Should Christianity have taken root, then it might have united the various segmented and heterogeneous groups of the late Roman Empire.[56]

For a long period, however, Rome persecuted the Christians. It did so because Christians could not accept the claims of divine emperorship. Furthermore, the Roman Empire had acquired its territory without ideological conversion. It did not engage in religious dissemination, despite the cultural extension of citizenship and law. Christianity by its very nature saw conversion as a primary mission. Hence, the tolerance of pluralism under the Pax Romana was contradictory to the aims of Christian conversion.

Moreover, because Christianity had a particular appeal for middle-class artisans and traders, this caused particular concern among Roman rulers. Christians tended to organize in local, usually urban congregations. These congregations were linked by communications and exchanges with fellow believers elsewhere. In so doing, the Christian community established an interstitial organization, outside the Roman imperial structure. Rome persecuted the Christians because it saw in them a contrasting form of potential, translocal mobilization to rival that of imperial rule.

Finally, Christianity seemed to distance itself from secular rule. The kingdom of God was after all not of this world. Powerholders, therefore, could not easily use it as a source of legitimation, despite the fact that Christianity would extend the power basis of the empire. A more inclusive ideology based on universality and cosmopolitism might have mobilized the empire when it was faced with the barbarian invasions.[57]

Consequently, Christianity came to flourish only after the decline of the empire. When imperial authority declined, Christianity as a church, as a formal organization, stepped in. It took over many of the functions that had been previously performed by Roman administration. And like imperial administration, the organization of the church centered around cities. Ecclesiastical territory was divided along the same lines as the empire. Indeed, the boundaries of the bishoprics were based on the perimeters of the old Roman territorial units of dioecesis and civitas, which became the diocese and the city—the latter being the location of the bishop's church.[58] Thus, when secular authority crumbled, the church remained a translocal form of organization, uniting tribes, different ethnic groups, and local administrations.

Moreover, the church performed many functions and acted in many ways like the empire before it. For example, many of the invading barbarians were absorbed in the faith, as previously Germanic tribes had been absorbed in the empire. Furthermore, monasteries became local nexi of economic production. The church also became the repository of translocal knowledge, law, Latin, and of course cosmological interpretation.[59] In so doing it performed the capstone functions that were previously fulfilled by Roman administration.

Whereas Christianity was originally confronted by an already existent empire, the situation was reversed by the time of Frankish ascendence.[60] From the eighth century on, attempts to reconstitute the empire would have to recognize the considerable powers of the church. The Franks recognized astutely that the church could enhance their material power and could provide for legitimation of their rule.

But the church was only willing to do so if rulers met the interests of the church. The spiritual power of the church needed secular armies to defend it against its enemies, specifically the Muslims and Lombards. Secular power was to be, in the spiritual perception, the sword of God on earth. For that purpose Charlemagne was crowned emperor in Rome on Christmas Day of the year 800. He was acclaimed by the words: "To Charles Augustus, crowned by God, great and peace giving emperor of the Romans, life and victory."[61]

The symbolism is illustrative. Charlemagne's father had been anointed with holy oil, a practice performed on priests and prophets. He received staff and ring, symbols of bishops.[62] And now Charlemagne himself had become emperor by God's grace in the capital of the Christian Commonwealth on one of its holiest days.

The Frankish Empire itself was justified by intricate religious interpretations. According to the prophesy of Daniel, there were to be four empires before the end of time. Three had passed, the Babylonian, the Persian, and the Macedonian. The Roman Empire, the fourth, had not really ceased to exist but continued in the Frankish Empire.[63] Thus, empire was not simply a form of political domination but a marker of the end of time.

It is important to realize that by this doctrine, and by the anointing of kings as bishops, a king gained theocratic powers, which were enhanced by his role as defender of the faith. The emperor became Vicar of Christ, responsible for all souls on Judgment Day. The pope was merely the Vicar of St. Peter.[64] The emperor could therefore rightly claim that he was the ruler of the Christian Commonwealth whereas the pope was merely a bishop of a very important see, but a bishop nonetheless. This sowed the seeds for the later struggles between emperor and pope.

By legitimating Frankish kingship in this vein, the church accomplished two goals. First, it made the empire the secular extension of translocal authority; the ecumene of Christianity became a political reality. Second, by extending its support to secular authority in purely religious terms, it sought to make such authority if not subject to, then at least partially dependent on the church. If part of the king's status derived from his theocratic position, then surely he had to be subject to Rome.

In short, historically the church emerged as a translocal authority. Consequently the church supported those rulers who sought a return of empire, provided this was to be an empire under God, that is, subject to the dictates of the pope. The struggles with the German emperor would not originate from the German imperial claims but from imperial unwillingness to accept papal rule above him.

In this sense the logic of a universalist doctrine and translocal organization differed from sovereign, territorial rule. The church ruled the community of believers. By its very nature it could doctrinally not admit to territorial limits. "Therefore in all centuries of the Middle Age Christendom, which in destiny is identical with Mankind, is set before us as a single, universal Community . . . Therefore that it may attain its one purpose, it needs One Law and One Government."[65]

Consequently, territorial rulers, such as the French king, were bound to later come into conflict with the dictates of the church. Sovereign authority can brook no outside interference, even from someone who speaks in the name of all believers of the true faith.

The Translocal Resources of the Church

The church commanded considerable material power to back up claims of dominion over the Christian community. It was the largest landholder in Europe and could obtain revenues from those lands, as well as from taxes on clergy and laity. This material basis made it a viable political organization and not merely a preferred but unobtainable social order. As Randall Collins states, the church was a cultural, economic, and political actor.[66] The papacy, and the secular and the regular clergy, all had means of levying taxes.

The papacy could get revenue from a variety of sources.[67] First, the pope himself, in his capacity of bishop of Rome, commanded considerable property in Italy. According to the Donation of Constantine, the emperor had rescinded control over these lands to the pope.[68] Second, the monasteries made direct payments to the papacy in exchange for the pope's support against members of the secular clergy. The secular clergy were sometimes at odds with the monastic orders, that is, the regular clergy, because of their different religious function and because the monasteries tended to usurp clerical revenue. Third, the pope could obtain direct payment from secular rulers. For example, the Peter's Pence was a payment by the English king to the pope, allegedly equivalent to one pence for every household in the kingdom.[69] Furthermore, the pope could give certain benefices (land grants) to bishops or other members of the clergy, just as any feudal overlord could. The pope would receive servitia (services) or annates, such as one third of the first year's revenue of the new benefice. As another source of revenue, the pope could ask for subsidies from the clergy for particular events such as a crusade. Finally, the pope could impose direct taxes on laity and clergy for a specified number of years.

The secular clergy had its own revenue sources. This group, which provided service to the laity directly, received their primary revenue from the tithe. This was a tax levied on all Christians.[70] It was a tax of one-tenth of gross income. Agricultural producers had to surrender a tenth of their crops. Those who engaged in animal husbandry had to surrender a similar portion of their animal products. Other activities also required payment of one-tenth of the yearly income. In short, few people managed to escape it. Aside from the tithe, members of the secular clergy could draw revenue as feudal lords in service of secular rulers. Churches and bishoprics, prior to the reforms following the Investiture Conflict, had become transferable holdings. In many ways they were no different from the regular feudal holdings. Bishops thus obtained revenue from these lands, maintained armed retainers, and provided administrative services for the secular overlord.

The regular clergy differed from the secular clergy in that they lived according to certain rules (regula). They lived communally and followed the dictates of their abbot, in communities that sought to become as independent as possible from any authority.[71] Their revenues derived primarily from the yields of their holdings.[72] The Clunaics, a later development within the Benedictine order, were particularly successful. Later orders such as the Augustinians and the Cistercians also did very well.[73]

I have highlighted these various sources of revenue to demonstrate that the church was more than a religious organization as we understand it. Its translocal economic operations covered Christian Europe and affected every level of society.[74] Thus, the economic power of the church, in addition to its ability to legitimate secular authority, made it into a desirable ally, or a formidable foe, for any territorial magnate. Given the small tax basis for the period, it is evident that the revenues of the church made it an attractive ally for aspiring secular rulers. From the opposite view, however, clerical taxes eroded the opportunity for rulers to raise large amounts of revenue themselves.

The Hierocratic Organization of the Church

Before the Gregorian reforms of the late eleventh century, religious administration was subject to considerable secular control. When the church tried to diminish such influence, and tried to extend its translocal control in earnest through strict hierarchical control from Rome, conflict with secular rulers became unavoidable.

The church started its existence as a loose affiliation of urban communities of believers.[75] As said, the church adopted the Roman imperial pattern. Bishops were appointed to cities to supervise the Roman community, the civitas. The area of their administration was the diocese, which formerly had been a subunit of the Roman province. Archbishoprics were aggregations of bishoprics and coincided with the Roman province, the provincium. The heart of the organization revolved around the bishopric. Hierarchical control from Rome was weak at best.

Secular support had always been important to the papacy. Indeed, the privileged position of the Bishop of Rome had to be established with imperial support. There was no pragmatic reason why the bishop of Rome should have a privileged position, certainly in view of important Christian communities in Antioch (Syria) and Alexandria. To support Rome's claims, however, some theological scholars referred to a passage in the New Testament (Matthew 16:18–19) wherein Christ said that Peter was the rock upon which he would build his church. This was interpreted to mean that Peter was the superior of the other apostles. Peter, as bishop of Rome, had passed this capacity on to his successors. The bishop of Rome thus claimed to be the hierarchical center of the ecclesia. This view, the Petrine doctrine, was enforced by imperial dictate.[76]

Such secular support was only the beginning. Bishops were to be chosen by the clergy and the people they would serve. "No one is to be consecrated as a bishop unless the clergy and people of the diocese have been called together and have given their consent."[77] The clause "by the clergy and the people" was of course highly ambiguous. Which members of the clergy were the electors? Who would speak for the people?

The clergy were initially represented by the priests in the diocese where the bishop served. Gradually representation was taken over by members of the church, the cathedral canon, where the bishop actually resided. The cathedral canon differed from the secular clergy in that the members of the canon did not perform religious service and lived according to rules similar to a monastic order. They performed administrative and juridical functions for the bishop.

Consent by the people initially meant nothing more than popular acclamation. This was factually replaced by consent of the secular rulers. Thus kings and emperors had a direct say in who was to become bishop. Gradually, as central authority broke down, even feudal dukes and counts appropriated the capacity to appoint clergy. To what extent lesser secular rulers appointed higher clergy is a matter of debate, although the appointment of bishops apparently was performed mainly by kings, whereas the lesser nobility controlled parish churches and monastic houses.[78]

The election of the bishop of Rome, the pope, differed slightly because of the special capacity of this bishop. The bishop of Rome was elected by several bishops around Rome and priests who served in the diocese of Rome and around the city. The latter were called cardinals and could serve in churches other than their own.[79]

Secular consent for the election of the bishop in Rome meant de facto that the election was controlled by the local powerholders in Rome. Consequently even the papacy was directly subject to secular domination by two aristocratic factions, the Crescentii and the Tuscalani.[80] In the tenth century, the papacy had virtually become inheritable.

The papacy could only manage a semblance of independence of these Roman magnates if it could draw on the support of the emperor against the local Italian factions. Thus Emperor Henry III deposed several rival popes, supported by the Tuscalani and the Crescentii, to finally install his own preferred candidate in 1046. Of the seven German popes in history, five reigned between 1046 and 1058.[81] Ironically, therefore, early attempts to forge a stronger papacy were supported by the emperor. A strong pope, dependent on imperial support against local factions, was a useful ally for legitimation of the imperial title.

In addition to the election procedure, secular control was made possible by the ambiguity of the Gelasian doctrine. At several points in the Bible there was mention of two swords: the sacerdotal and the secular. But it was highly unclear which one was superior. Christian doctrine was ambiguous about how church and secular power were to interact. As early as the ninth century some prelates had put forward the claim that the church was superior to secular rulers. The archbishop of Rheims, Hincmar (845–882), argued that "the episcopal dignity is greater than the royal, for bishops consecrate kings, but kings do not consecrate bishops."[82] But given the weak and fragmented nature of the church at that time, the claim had little validity.

If one further takes into account that kings had considerable theocratic status of their own—recall that they were anointed with holy insignia—it is clear that kings were reluctant to see the clergy as their superiors. Indeed, kings and emperors could claim that it was the duty of the clergy to help the ruler carry out his holy task. Certainly in view of the secular machinations in all bishopric elections, their claim cannot be seen as implausible. Bishops and popes were in many ways feudal lords by another name.

One cannot, therefore, simply depict the later conflict between church and empire as one between secular and spiritual rule. The two were indistinguishable before the Investiture Conflict (1075). Rule was per definition spiritual.

Victory in war, just as trial by ordeal, was an indication of divine approval. Ecclesiastical offices fulfilled many of the tasks that we today would see as governmental. Moreover, many ecclesiastics were relatives and appointees of feudal lords and kings.

The Investiture Conflict

It was quite common, until the Investiture Conflict between pope and German emperor which started in 1075, for secular rulers to endow the clergy, particularly abbots and bishops, as vassals to kings and emperors. The clergy were valuable assets for such rulers. They could serve as literate and educated administrators, they could provide for efficient agricultural production, and (theoretically) their lands resorted back to the lord after they died because they had no heirs.[83]

Moreover, the German kings had come to rely on their ecclesiastical lords to a greater extent than their French and English counterparts. This was partially due to the strength of the stem duchies. Ever since the revolt of the dukes in the middle of the tenth century, the kings had sought to ally themselves with the German church.[84]

Consequently, despite the fact that its members controlled properties and revenue, the church lacked hierarchical organization prior to the Gregorian Reform of the eleventh century.[85] As we have already seen, the position of the pope, as bishop of Rome, was ill defined and pragmatically under the control of local factions. Aside from this lack of a well-defined center, the local clergy had their own particularized affinities and interests. They were indebted to the ecclesiastical or secular overlords from which they had fiefs and tithes.[86] The local clergy, therefore, often had quite different interests than the bishop of Rome who sought to establish hierarchical control over the church. In order for any centralization of the church to be successful, the papacy, therefore, inevitably had to tackle the issue of lay investiture of spiritual offices. As long as secular rulers could appoint bishops and priests, any control from Rome would be illusory.

The papacy started to assert this control from the middle of the eleventh century on. First, the church started to interpret the Gelasian doctrine in its favor. As stated, the doctrine originally suggested the existence of two swords: the sacerdotal and the secular. According to theological doctrine, Pope Gelasius (492–496) had written to the emperor Anastasius: "Two there are, august emperor, by which this world is chiefly ruled, the sacred authority (auctoritas) of the priesthood and the royal power (potestas)."[87]

However, it was highly unclear from Gelasius's letter and his other writings which of the two, or if either of the two, he meant to be superior. Now the papacy started to advance the claim that the sacerdotal was the superior, and the secular subject to it. At this point the pope was only claiming spiritual, not absolute temporal, authority. That is, the pope claimed that he, not the emperor, was the Vicar of Christ, the leader of the Christian community and responsible for souls on Judgment Day. But the denial to the emperor of spiritual legitimation had important consequences for the emperor's political rule.[88]

The Investiture Conflict revolved around the imperial investiture of bishops in Germany. Given that the pope denied spiritual powers to the emperor, he could not permit the emperor to install men of his choice in a spiritual office. The move to reorganize and centralize the papacy which had started in the middle of the eleventh century now had come full circle. In 1046 the emperor had deposed two rival popes and had elected a third against local factions. The ensuing decades saw a rise in reorganization efforts by the papacy against secular influences on the church. Now the pope asserted his autonomy even from the emperor himself. The result was embodied in a set of theses drawn up by Gregory VII. Among his twenty-seven theses, in the Dictatus Papae (1075), he claimed the following rights:

> 2. That the Roman Pontiff alone is rightly to be called universal.
>
> 3. That he alone can depose or reinstate bishops.
>
> 12. That he may depose Emperors.
>
> 22. That the Roman Church has never erred, nor ever, by the witness of Scripture, shall err to all eternity.
>
> 27. That the Pope may absolve subjects of unjust men from their fealty.[89]

Naturally the claims were inacceptable to the emperor. First, they denied his supremacy over the church and his role as a spiritual leader of Christianity. But the political implications also created a zero-sum game. The denial of investiture to the emperor meant that the control over ecclesiastical holdings, and revenue, would pass directly to the pope. What the emperor lost, the pope gained. Henry IV's response was commensurate. Gregory VII was labeled a usurper of the papacy.

> Henry, King not by usurpation, but by the pious ordination of God, to Hildebrand, now not Pope, but false monk: . . . Our Lord, Jesus Christ, has called us to kingship, but has not called you to priesthood . . . I, Henry, King by the grace of God, together with all our bishops, say to you, Descend! Descend, to be damned through the ages![90]

Gregory VII then excommunicated Henry IV, and many lords supported the pope therein. "The turbulent princes of medieval Germany were never willing to submit to a powerful, centralized monarchy. . . . The announcement of the king's excommunication and deposition was therefore very welcome to many of the nobles."[91] The emperor thereupon embarked on the famous journey to Canossa to do penance and ask for the pope's forgiveness, which he obtained.

But the struggle was far from over and was to rage for decades beyond this. Intermittently, emperors would recognize antipopes and ally with groups that opposed the incumbent pope. Conversely, popes would ally with German lords to support antikings. In Italy, the pope would seek support from the Normans who controlled southern Italy and from the communes of the north which feared a dominating empire as well.

The overall outcome of the conflict was, however, more a compromise than an outright victory for either side. In effect the issue was never fully resolved. The emperor would no longer appoint bishops with clerical insignia—the staff and the ring—but imperial approval of bishops was still required.

The revolutionary impact of the Investiture Conflict was therefore twofold.[92] First, in separating the two realms, it necessitated secular rule to justify itself by other than spiritual means. Second, in distinguishing and separating these two realms, which both had claims to universality, the two became rivals. Which one was to be subject to the other? As a result, both camps had to seek political allies, search for new sources of legitimation, and rationalize their administrative and legal machineries. The Investiture Conflict in a sense necessitated rulers to invent "secular" rule.

In the long run both positions were eroded by the struggle. Both sides could appeal to local groups who opposed either emperor or theocratic papacy. The papacy consistently sought material allies, first in the Normans, then in territorial rulers such as the French kings, to fight the empire. In the thirteenth century the papacy even went so far as to suggest a political deal with the Byzantine emperor. If the Greek church would consent to papal rule from Rome, the papacy would recognize the Byzantine emperor, not the German, as the legitimate ruler of Christendom.[93]

During the struggle the papacy continued to improve hierarchical control and administration within the church. One of the instruments for doing so was the development of canon law.[94] Canon law was unique in that it referred back to classical Roman sources and used a dialectical method of contrasting different solutions to a given problem. Arguments for and against particular positions were the preferred style of argument, rather than reasoning by authority.

The success of the papacy's administrative reforms shows, for example, in the vastly increased amount of correspondence that went out from Rome.[95] The papal administration became specialized in four different branches: the Penitentiary, the Chancery, the Camera, and the Rota. The Penitentiary dealt with matters of faith; the Chancery was in charge of correspondence; the Camera handled finances; and the Rota performed judicial tasks. In short, there was functional specialization. As a consequence the papacy increased in size. It is estimated that even the papacy in exile in Avignon had an administration of roughly 450 to 650 people.[96]

Furthermore, in an attempt to minimize secular influences on the papal election, the Lateran Council of 1059 was convened. The election procedure was now formally established in the body of cardinals. This still did not eliminate secular influence since kings and lords continued to sway their preferred cardinals. But it did foreshadow the separation of secular and spiritual authorities.

The medieval church thus did not delimit its authority in any territorial sense but advanced the universalist claim to rule over the Christian community of believers. Economically and administratively the church was organized translocally. It increasingly favored hierarchical control by Rome, despite misgivings of the local clergy. In terms of economic revenue, both local clergy and Rome affected every activity in life. No area of Christian Europe escaped the extractive capability of the church.

In the long run, conflict with territorial rulers would erupt on cultural, economic, and administrative dimensions. Universalist claims to authority could not be conceptually reconciled with the principle of sovereignty. In the economic sphere, the king objected to the transfer of resources to Rome. Furthermore, the holdings of the church were attractive assets in their own right. Administratively, bureaucratic hierarchy from Rome undercut control of secular rulers over their local clergy, who operated as lords and administrators. The logic of universal ecclesiastical rule and the logic of sovereign territoriality were fundamentally at odds.

THE HOLY ROMAN EMPIRE

Traditional empires have usually had a universalist system of rule. They have basically aspired to exercise political control over their relevant sphere of economic interaction. The spatial extension of political control ideally corresponds with the market. In Roberto Unger's words, empires aspired to be autarkic. "Its most tangible feature is the overall coincidence of economic and political boundaries."[97] Moreover, such empires legitimated their existence by spiritual claims. Universal empires tended to claim some form of cosmological justification.[98] Whereas there were of course factual limits to the exercise of their power, theoretically they denied other actors an equivalent status. "Empires in other words have had a universalizing quality within their own territories."[99]

The empire that the German kings tried to establish from the tenth century onward was no different. The empire did not define itself by control over a given territory. It had "border regions—we cannot speak of borders yet— around the mid eleventh century."[100] By its very nature it could not have fixed boundaries. "The empire was not a geographical entity, but a military and spiritual authority."[101]

Like the church, the Holy Roman Empire made universal claims. Indeed, the empire was premised on the control of several kingdoms, supposedly of ancient stature—the Italian kingdom, Burgundy, and the Germanic kingdom. Its universalist claims find their origin in the legacy of the Carolingian Empire. Given that the ideal form of rule was analogous to that of heaven, there could be only one world ruler. Symbolically this was represented by the imperial orb which supposedly contained soil from all four corners of the world. The legitimate rule of empire first transferred from Rome to Constantinople and then to the Carolingian Empire was now transferred to the German.[102]

German imperial claims, however, confronted two problems which eventually negated the imperial possibility.[103] First, the German emperor was increasingly faced by rival universalist claims of the pope. Second, the heterogeneous nature of German principalities made any pursuit of an imperial strategy abroad always a hazardous undertaking. In order to deal with these issues, the German king—the Holy Roman Emperor—chose a feudal strategy against the towns.[104]

The Historical Legacy of Empire

The later centuries of the Roman Empire witnessed the influx of peoples who previously had lived beyond the frontier of the empire. The Franks were one of the Germanic tribes caught in the great pattern of migration in the fourth and fifth centuries. They finally settled down in what is today northern France and Belgium. Like all barbarian invading and migrating tribes, the Franks were heavily influenced by the Roman legacy. They tailored Roman law to their particular needs and converted to Christianity.

Gradually the Merovingian and later the Carolingian line expanded the Frankish realm. With the capability of their cavalry, they conquered the other kingdoms that had established themselves in France. They defeated the Burgundians and pushed the Visigoths into Spain. They halted the Muslim advance and set up a border province across the Pyrenees.[105]

The secular expansion of the Franks was matched by their success in creating an alliance with the church. When the pope needed secular allies to defend Italy against the Lombard invaders in the north, and the Byzantine emperor was increasingly unable to provide secular support, the Franks seemed like a logical choice.[106] Simultaneously, the chancellor of the household, the major domus Pepin, wished to replace his Merovingian overlords. The Merovingian kings had increasingly become figureheads, and the chancellors had in fact become the main political administrators. In order to legitimate such usurpation, Pepin sought and got the approval of the pope. Pepin was anointed king by the archbishop, the pope's legate. The pope hereby gained an ally against his secular enemies. The Carolingian king in turn gained the approbation of the church and, after the Carolingian defeat of the Lombards in Italy, the Franks also obtained territorial holdings south of the Alps. They returned to the pope a large amount of these holdings, which then became the heart of the independent papal lands.

Charlemagne, Pepin's successor, went on to expand Carolingian territory to the east. Carolingian rule encompassed areas from the North Sea to Italy and was bordered to the east by the Hungarian plains. To seal the consolidation of political power and sacerdotal status, Charlemagne was crowned emperor by the pope on Christmas Day of the year 800.[107] As previously stated, the religious symbolism was meant to convey the theocratic standing of the empire.

The Frankish unification of western Europe was short lived. One of the main factors contributing to the decline of the Carolingian Empire was the absence of primogeniture—inheritance by the eldest son alone. Instead, the Carolingians divided inheritance among all male heirs. Consequently the empire was divided into four kingdoms in 817, and its divisions were periodically altered. In 843, by the Treaty of Verdun, the kingdoms were redrawn and the empire was partitioned into western, middle, and eastern kingdoms. The treaties of Meersen and Ribemont redrew boundaries again in 870 and 880. The result of continual fratricidal wars was the establishment of a West-Frankish kingdom, an East-Frankish kingdom, Upper and Lower Burgundy (the latter also called Arles after its capital), and the kingdom of Italy. The papal lands (the patrimonium petri) remained independent and were uninfluenced by the alterations in the Frankish Empire.

The weakening of central authority gave rise to five powerful duchies in the East-Frankish kingdom: Franconia, Saxony, Thüringen, Bavaria, and Swabia.[108] When the Carolingian lineage died out at the beginning of the tenth century, the Saxons proclaimed Henry I king. He went on to subject the dukes, and his son Otto the Great was crowned king, whereas the dukes became part of the royal entourage. During his second Italian campaign, the pope crowned Otto as emperor in 962. This marked the foundation of the empire, and indeed Otto saw himself as a direct successor to Charlemagne. His son, Otto II (973–987), argued for restoration of the old Roman Empire consisting of Germania, Roma, and Gallia. Otto III (983–1002), his successor, accepted the title "servant of the apostles" to signify the unification of empire and church. The empire was not, therefore, simply a secular political authority that controlled a certain area. It claimed jurisdiction over the Christian community as the secular arm of God. In this sense it was universalist.[109]

Although the Holy Roman Empire lasted in name until 1806, the empire was from the very beginning subject to internal tensions. As we will see, the political bargains that the king had to make in order to deal with these tensions ended by directing Germany on a course that was the reverse of that pursued by the French king.

The Internal Weaknesses of the Empire: Universalist
Claims Superimposed on Heteronomous Lordships

The problems that faced the German emperor arose from two sources. The first lay in the strength of the dukes. In the East-Frankish part of the Carolingian Empire, feudalism had not initially progressed as far as it had in France. Fragmentation was initially less severe. Although it had broken into several duchies, it did not proceed beyond that.[110]

It is debatable to what extent these duchies were tribal in character. The names of the duchies themselves suggest that they were to some extent indeed tribal. The Carolingians had tried to break up these duchies and rule through counts, but after Carolingian decline these powerful duchies returned.[111] These duchies acquired a semiregal character. The continued strength of these principalities would constitute the first roadblock to any attempts by the emperor to form a consolidated realm in Germany.

To counter these powerful lords, the German kings had to ally themselves with the German church. But there they encountered a second problem. This obstacle consisted of the rivalry between church and emperor which we have discussed in the context of the Investiture Conflict. The local clergy, bishops and abbots, were often incorporated as vassals in royal administration. The loyalty of such clergy, however, became increasingly doubtful, particularly after Rome established an effective bureaucracy and claimed papal jurisdiction over these members of the clergy.

Although the pope had crowned Otto the Great emperor in 962, papal and imperial objectives were basically antithetical to each other. The life-and-death struggle between papacy and empire resulted from the very fact that both sought to administer the same areas of political life. Both sought to reestablish the old notion of the Roman Empire, to control investiture of the clergy, and to unite the disparate domains, including Italy and Germany. The problem was that neither would submit to the other's final jurisdiction.[112]

In the end it proved impossible to reconcile an imperial policy focusing on Italy with a policy focusing on Germany. In Italy the emperor faced political opponents in the pope and the wealthy communes. Moreover, these might ally to other powers such as the Normans in Sicily. In order to combat these, the emperor would have to drain German resources which would tax his ducal support. Moreover, these lords would already have incentives to ally with outside powers, such as the pope, to mitigate any centralizing tendency of the king. A reverse policy, focusing on Germany, would jeopardize imperial claims to northern Italy and Burgundy, which were desirable sources of revenue. Moreover, that would not square with the universalist logic of the empire. The imperial response was a variety of often inconsistent strategies that ultimately crippled territorial development and divided Germany up to the late nineteenth century.[113]

The Failure of Imperial Strategy

Imperial strategy failed, first because it could only reach a compromise with the papacy at considerable expense. The compromise, concluded in the Concordat of Worms, conferred to the emperor the right of approval, but he could no longer appoint the bishop with sacerdotal insignia, the staff and ring.[114] This was more than mere symbolism and meant that the emperor did not have jurisdiction over bishops in the emperor's capacity as member of the clergy. This was particularly problematic for the German king because he relied to a far greater extent than his French and English counterparts on ecclesiastical lords.[115]

The Investiture Conflict is thus an important illustration of the ability of local powerholders, both clerical and temporal, to utilize the strife between emperor and pope as an avenue to further their own interests. It also meant that the pope or any rival to the throne in Germany could tap into this local dissent to keep the emperor at bay. On occasion, popes would recognize antikings supported by coalitions who opposed the incumbent emperor, and the emperor would do the converse. During the Investiture Conflict, Pope Gregory supported the nobility's election of Rudolf of Swabia as antiking against Henry.

The emperor appointed an antipope, Clement III. Likewise they appointed bishops and antibishops, so that bishoprics had two claimants.[116]

A second major conflict between pope and emperor was the control of lands in Italy outside the papal estates. Attempts by Frederick II (1212–1250) to bring Sicily and northern Italy into the German empire particularly threatened the independence of the papal state. Consequently the Italian cities in the north, which sought independence from the empire, allied with the pope. Despite some initial success in his imperial campaigns, Frederick II ultimately failed to subdue these towns, and all German claims to de facto overlordship in Italy evaporated. A century later (1356), the Italian territories were formally surrendered by Charles, who in exchange retained the imperial title.[117]

Geoffrey Barraclough argues that Frederick II's Italian policy sealed the fate of the Holy Roman Empire. Frederick II deliberately opted to focus his attention on Italy rather than Germany. The main reason might have been that Italy provided him with large amounts of revenue, but he also had ideological reasons of his own. He apparently had megalomaniacal tendencies and embellished claims of his messianic status. "[H]e presented himself as the Emperor of the End of Time, the savior who was to lead the world into the golden age."[118] After his death, myths continued to circulate about the second coming of this emperor who would unite Christendom.

Imperial strategy was always built on a shaky foundation. The German lords were reluctant to concede their independence, and any king on campaign across the Alps always had to fear rebellion at home. Frederick II, possibly the last emperor who might have succeeded in maintaining the empire, tried to avert losses in Germany by conceding the princes' semiregalian rights. In two bulls, particularly in the bull of 1232 (Statutum in favorem principum), he granted extensive claims to the princes. He also recognized the princes' right to election of the emperor which had previously been practiced but not officially recognized. The princes denounced hereditary monarchy and would from then on consciously put weak candidates on the throne. Papal acclamation became an addition, not a prerequisite to imperial status.

Both the feudal strategy in Germany and the imperial strategy in Italy failed. Germany thereupon evolved into a heterogeneous system of independent lordships and city-leagues. The end of Frederick II's reign was a turning point in German history and, pragmatically speaking, the end of the empire.

CONCLUSION

I have suggested in this chapter that the church, the Holy Roman Empire, and feudalism were nonterritorial logics of organization. Feudal organization was a network of personal ties. Church and empire claimed authority over the community of believers and invoked the legacy of the Roman Empire. Moreover, all three systems of rule coexisted. Individuals could be subject to multiple authorities because government was not defined by mutually exclusive criteria.

Even though the emperor and pope claimed final jurisdiction vis-à-vis the other, this still was not sovereignty in a territorial sense. For example, the emperor had to concede Roman control over ecclesiastical holdings in the empire, and lords maintained many powers which made them virtually independent.

The modern state, by contrast, is premised on the notion of sovereignty. Sovereignty per definition consists of internal hierarchy and territorial demarcation. The scope of authority thus requires the existence of formal borders.

In feudalism, by contrast, since authority was defined by personal ties—the obligations and rights between individuals—hierarchy was diffuse. Personal obligations were ad hoc and case specific. As a result, the status of the individual, the "quality" of the person, became an important ingredient in maintaining social order. Feudalism, as a system of personal obligations, hinged on distinctions of birth, ability to bear arms, and other markers that demonstrated the individual's place in society.

Nor did the church define its authority in spatial terms. Its authority was based on its role in guiding the community of believers. The scope of authority extended over the Christian ecumene. It was thus one's status as a believer that made one subject to this mode of authority.

Within the church, the pope gradually asserted his supremacy over the other bishops and attempted to make secular and regular clergy subject to his dictates from Rome. Externally the pope claimed universalist supremacy; all other powers were subject to him. Emperors and kings only held their power by papal approval.

Consequently the church was economically and administratively set up as a translocal organization. It operated as far as the community of believers stretched. The pope could extract revenue from all corners of Christian Europe. Yet at the same time, the dictates of Rome could permeate to the most local level of society. The scope of the church's authority was wide, and its effects on society ran deep.

The Holy Roman Empire was a strange mixture of conflicting elements of organization. First, it claimed a legacy to the old Roman Empire. Based on that view, some argued that the empire should encompass Gallia, Italia, Germania, and parts of eastern Europe. Second, the new empire had also adopted the religious logic of a community of believers. The empire was thus to consist of Christian Europe, thereby basing its authority on a nonterritorial criterion. Even though the German kings de facto could not follow through on their claims of supremacy over the French and English king, in principle the latter were considered inferiors. The principle of imperial rule was thus in a theoretical sense universal. Its aim was to unite all individuals in a Christian empire.

This duality of secular and religious legitimation led to the absence of clear hierarchical authority. From one perspective, the emperor had universal authority over all other rulers including the pope. The church, however, claimed the same scope of authority. There were two swords, but the secular was to serve the spiritual.

The confusion regarding scope and hierarchy of imperial authority was further exacerbated by the feudal influence on imperial strategy. In order to further imperial claims to Italy and Burgundy, the German emperor conceded considerable rights to princes—so much so that he could not claim exclusive jurisdiction within the area over which he was nominally the lord.

The struggles of this period can be described as "a three cornered conflict between a secularized episcopate (anxious to preserve its customary prerogatives against papal centralization), the imperial power (which saw papal centralization as a menace to its own monarchical authority) and the Papacy (which saw centralization as the only way to a reformed and purified Church)."[119] As John Morrall notes, at the same time this was a struggle between unifying forces and local, particularistic ones which opposed central authority. The result of these struggles and the way in which these struggles were fought influenced the development of sovereign states in several ways.

First, by denying the legitimacy of each other and by allying with local forces, emperor and pope weakened each other. Moreover, there was no secular force that could have played a similar role as the German empire in undershoring the papacy. "It may thus be said that the fall of the one universal power brought with it that of the other."[120]

Second, because the emperor and pope supported the particularistic forces that opposed their rival, Germany and Italy embarked on a course of fragmentation rather than centralization. Lombard communes could find support from Rome and the Normans to oppose the emperor. In Germany, high nobles and ecclesiastics could count on the pope as well. Conversely, Italian aristocratic families who opposed the pope could count on the emperor's support.

Third, the papacy turned to territorial rulers for support in its fight with the empire. Thus, as we will see in Chapter 5, the French kings could count on papal support and revenue when they set about to unify their kingdoms against the feudal lords.

Moreover, the necessity of domestic German support forced German kings to appease particular domestic groups. The German kings opted for a strategy that curtailed the liberties of towns and surrendered Germany largely to the lords. This strategy differed markedly from that of the English and French territorial rulers.

Finally, the struggle between papacy and emperor led to new modes of organizing and justifying rule. Whereas the papacy turned to canon law, secular rulers would find justification for their sovereignty in Roman law. Henry IV had already recognized this mode of justification in the Investiture Conflict, but it still had some way to go in its development. A century later, however, Frederick Barbarossa made his argument very explicit on the basis of Roman law and encouraged the development of universities.[121] That development would also play an important role in the organization of sovereign states and the structuring of property rights.

The Emergence of New Modes

of Organization

The Economic Renaissance of the Late Middle Ages

This age marked Europe's true Renaissance . . . two or three hundred years
before the traditional Renaissance of the fifteenth century.[1]

Sovereignty is not a fact. It is a concept which men in certain circumstances
have applied—a quality they have attributed or a claim they have counter-
posed—to the political power which they or other men were exercising.[2]

THE CATALYST: THE EXPANSION OF TRADE AND THE GROWTH OF TOWNS

In the later stages of the eleventh century the European economy started to
expand dramatically. Agricultural production rose, forests and wastelands were
cleared, and migration to previously uncultivated areas increased. As a result,
trade grew, new towns emerged, and older towns expanded. For Marc Bloch,
the French medieval historian, this period was unique and distinct from the
early medieval period—it was a second feudal age.[3]

There were many causes of this economic expansion, and they are still de-
bated. What is clear, however, is that a variety of events occurred to stimulate
trade. Agricultural production accelerated with the development of the heavy
plough and the three-field system. The climate seems to have become milder.
The invasions by Vikings, Maygars, and Saracens halted. Finally, there was a
dramatic growth in population. All of these factors led to an upswing in consumer demand and production.

The causes of this economic upswing need not concern us here.[4] The important point is that the increase in economic production foreshadowed the return
of local and long-distance trade. In contrast to the old, largely local, and often
in-kind nature of exchange, the newly expanding monetary economy encouraged the division of labor and the growth of towns.

Monetarization of the economy had a profound impact on the existing political structure. It inevitably affected the system of in-kind transfers, the linchpin
of feudal organization. Lords started to commute their military service into
monetary payments, scutage. Likewise, rather than receive agricultural products, they preferred land rents from their peasants. Most important, however,
was the rise of the towns.

Henri Pirenne was one of the first to assert that the growth in size and the
increase in the number of towns were critical to European development.

Towns and long-distance trade were inexorably linked. "It was therefore trade on a big scale or, if you prefer a more precise term, trade over long distances, that was characteristic of the economic revival of the Middle Ages . . . in step with the progress of trade, towns multiplied."[5] The increasing level of urbanization, particularly in northwest Europe, was thus directly linked to the expansion of trade. More recently, Fernand Braudel likewise argued for the importance of urban centers in the early European economy.[6] Although a variety of critiques have been leveled against Pirenne's work (particularly against his argument that the Muslim takeover of the eastern Mediterranean led to a decline of trade following the seventh century), his thesis regarding the connection between urbanization and trade has stood the test of time.[7]

Pirenne's thesis states that the growth of trade, from the eleventh century on, led to the emergence of merchants with distinct interests. In order to evade feudal and ecclesiastical rule, the merchants moved outside the existing towns and created walled areas of their own, the suburbia, which were distinct from the older feudal strongholds.[8] They called these *newbourghs* or *newburgs* to differentiate them from the old feudal fortification, the burg. In Dutch and English they were called *portus* (hence *port*), meaning a point of transfer, not necessarily on the sea, for merchandise. Their inhabitants were thus called *burghers* and *poorters*. In addition, merchants founded new towns altogether. Fritz Rörig, also a proponent of the importance of long-distance trade, argues that in Germany "the most important towns of the twelfth and also of the early thirteenth centuries were created in the main by enterprising burghers of the Old German towns.[9]

Many European towns that exist today can be traced to this period. The towns that do not find their origins in this era of expansion date from the Roman period. As we will see in the following discussions of France and Germany, new urbanization was particularly prominent in frontier areas, which had been relatively underdeveloped.[10] Both high lords and kings, eager to capitalize on new economic opportunities, and associations of merchants from old towns founded these new urban centers. The expansion of trade created incentives to found many new villages and towns in previously underdeveloped areas and allowed existing towns to increase in size, expand their revenue, and foster specialization of labor.

This trade expansion set a great economic transformation in motion. This does not mean, however, that agriculture disappeared. Most people continued to live outside the towns, and the economy remained agricultural. My argument is not that the medieval renaissance led to a predominantly mercantile and industrial economy. Instead I argue that the towns improved their relative position and had an influence on the old economic and political order far beyond their objective share of the overall economy.[11]

The result of this economic dynamism was that a social group, the town dwellers, came into existence with new sources of revenue and power, which did not fit the old feudal order. This new social group, the burghers, had various incentives to search for political allies who were willing to change the existing order. Neither the burghers' material preferences nor their belief systems fit

TABLE 4.1
A General Explanation of Unit Change

Generative Phase	
Independent variable:	Economic growth and expansion of trade (1000–1350).
Intervening variable:	New coalitions become possible because of shifts in relative power caused by economic expansion. Towns emerge that do not fit the old feudal order. They seek to create new institutions by allying with political entrepreneurs.
Outcome:	A variety of new institutions—sovereign, territorial state; city-state; and city-league.
Selective Phase	
Causes of selection:	Competition
	Mutual empowerment
	Mimicry and exit
Outcome:	Sovereign, territorial state.

the existing institutional and conceptual frameworks. "The new trading and commercial classes of the towns could not settle into the straightjacket of the feudal order, and the towns became a chief agent in its final disruption."[12] The causal argument to come is captured schematically in Table 4.1.

Some General Expectations on the Preferences of Towns

Towns, that is to say the burghers, had two competing preferences. On the one hand, they had a preference for the greatest amount of independence possible. Given that political authority tended to exploit the towns for revenue or military service, the bourgeois had reasons to resist political domination by outside forces. On the other hand, a stronger central authority would benefit translocal trade. Protection from robbers, pirates, and demanding feudal barons, as well as reduction in the prolific amount of feudal exactions and tolls, would benefit long-distance trade. Poggi succinctly states the reasons for towns to support central authority:

> Generally speaking, the towns' interests were favored the wider and more uniform the context of rule within which they operated [*sic*]—at any rate insofar as it fell upon that context to police the traffic, to provide a reliable coinage, to enforce market transactions, etc. This is why, between the two forces whose relations defined the feudal system of rule—the territorial ruler and the feudal powers—the towns tended to favor the former.[13]

Preferences depended on the level of urbanization made possible by the extension of trade and on the specific nature of trade. Where trade was significant, wealth and population accumulated, and consequently an advanced division of labor emerged.[14] The significance of trade might be measured in terms of volume and value. Given the wide diversity of towns, it is very difficult to make generalizations about the profit margins and volume of French trade. There were hundreds of small local markets where trade dealt primarily in agricultural bulk goods. Yet there were also a few towns such as Bordeaux where traders could make substantial profits by shipping more expensive goods such as wine. Moreover, it is extremely difficult to get exact data for these small-scale transactions because records simply were not kept.[15]

Nevertheless, it is fair to say that in France the impact of trade was relatively low.[16] French medieval towns did not generally participate in the long-distance trade of the Middle Ages. Instead, most of them catered to regional markets. France remained a highly rural and agricultural society. "France was a peasant nation, rather cut off from large scale commerce."[17] Trade was primarily of relatively low volume and of low added value. It may be true that profit margins for maritime trade could be as high as 30 to 40 percent. It seems more likely, however, that the profit margins of this bulk trade were closer to the profit margins of the Hansa which were between 5 and 25 percent. Profits on local trade and investments in land, which as I said were far more usual in the French case, were between 5 and 10 percent.[18] As a consequence, urban development was relatively modest except for the areas in the north, particularly Flanders.[19] Most towns, except Paris, were thus relatively small and accumulated only modest amounts of capital.

Trade in Germany was more significant. In particular, the towns along the North Sea coast and the Baltic as well as the towns along major rivers such as the Rhine engaged in long-distance trade. This trade was primarily of high volume but of low added value. "So in their heyday the Germans of the north monopolized a commerce predominately in bulk goods of relatively low value, unlike those trades in luxuries or bullion which elsewhere developed under Italian and Iberian control."[20] That is, the towns of the Hanseatic League traded primarily in bulk goods such as timber, grain, and herring. As said, profit margins ranged from 5 to 25 percent.

Italian towns engaged in long-distance commerce more than any others. Towns such as Florence, Venice, and Genoa traded many goods, including bulk items such as grain, but the trade in luxury goods of small quantity especially created the wealth and size of the Italian towns. The trade in high-quality textiles and spices led to profit margins ranging from 20 to 150 percent.[21] This type of trade encouraged a highly advanced division of labor. As a consequence, the Italian towns were large and abundant.

By measuring the volume and value of trade, we can conjecture what the towns preferred political organization might have been (see Table 4.2). Both the German and French towns faced roughly similar environments. These towns were relatively small in size and wealth and thus required some form of organization that could pool their resources together as an effective force against their political adversaries. Given that towns had to contend with political opponents who wished to subject cities for their own benefit, for example,

TABLE 4.2
Expected Preferences of Towns Based on Character of Trade (generative phase)

	Character and level of trade	*Expected preferences*
French towns:	low volume low added value	Corresponding level of urbanization relatively low, with the exception of Flanders and northern France. Towns prefer central organization to provide protection and improve economic climate (standardization, reduction of transaction costs, etc.).
German towns:	high volume low added value	Moderate level of urbanization. Towns need a central actor or league to pool their resources for defense and to improve economic environment (standardization, reduction of transaction costs, etc.).
Italian towns:	moderate volume high added value	High level of urbanization. Large towns with considerable resources do not need central actor for protection. Predatorial market suggests competition rather than collusion. Competition for market shares with high payoffs.

to gain revenue, towns would have to band together or seek territorial lords who were less predatorial than others. Hence, towns required either city-leagues to pool their resources or high territorial lords who were willing to mitigate their exactions from rival lords.

Furthermore, because these towns faced a competitive market environment where there were many suppliers and buyers and where profit margins were quite slim, they would benefit from a central authority which could override the drawbacks of the feudal system. Because of political fragmentation in the feudal environment, merchants had to engage in multiple overlord-peddler deals.[22] In addition, the multiple jurisdictions with their tolls and different weights, measures, and coinage were highly inefficient. In economic terms, these towns would benefit from central organization which could lower transaction costs.

Additionally, it would have been difficult for any one town to capture a large share of the market on its own. Although city-leagues as a whole would try to bar entry to outside competitors—indeed the very name *Hanse*, or *Hansa*, is derivative of guildlike organizations of merchants—no one town could obtain a monopoly position by itself. Although some towns were far more important than others—Cologne and Lübeck, for example, were leaders of the Hansa—there were still dozens of others that could compete with them.

The Italian towns faced quite a different situation. Because of their size and wealth, they could yield considerable force of their own. Genoese revenues at the end of the thirteenth century outstripped those of France, and Genoa could mobilize almost 40,000 troops by 1295.[23] Towns were large and strong enough to oppose political foes alone. They did not need to band together or seek protection from any territorial lord.

Furthermore, within their market, individual towns could try to capture a trade-route monopoly. Because trade was of relatively small volume but very high in added value, towns were predatorial rather than cooperative, and attempts were made to capture particular trade routes in order to secure monopolies.[24] There was a lot to be gained by knocking out the competition.[25]

Although these might have been the towns' preferred political outcomes, political outcomes clearly cannot be predicted by the towns' preferences alone. Powerful political opponents, most notably the secular and ecclesiastical lords, had to be overcome. To accomplish that, towns needed political allies. But those political allies had agendas of their own. Highly diverse organizational outcomes were shaped by how these internal realignments were settled in the different regions. In short, although expanding trade was the impetus for change, it can only provide a partial explanation, for it alone cannot explain actual outcomes.

The variation in outcomes across the three cases of this study—France, the Hansa, and the Italian city-states—must be explained by variant combinations of social and political actors. These political coalitions form my intermediate explanatory category.

First, as I just suggested, the composition of the social coalition will depend on the level of impact of the external change.[26] France, for example, benefited from the growth in trade, but it did not have great trading cities strong enough to oppose political foes alone. French towns could prove to be a valuable ally to the king,[27] but they were not strong enough to further their own interests without a sovereign.[28] The relative power of towns is thus a first predictor of the political alliance.

Second, the coalition will be determined by the specific material interests of the various groups. In France, for example, the towns wanted to be relieved from the onerous feudal burdens and sought royal protection. In Italy towns sought primarily to curtail exactions by the emperor and to gain a monopoly over trade. Material interests thus depend on the type of trade that cities engage in, but they are also influenced by the composition of the ruling coalition. In France feudal lordship had developed much further than in northern Italy. In Italy much of the aristocracy had early on turned toward mercantile pursuits. Indeed, the whole nature of Italian towns was different. These towns were largely of Roman origin, whereas the German and French towns were products of the second feudal era. The dichotomy of bourgeoisie and aristocracy was thus less pronounced in Italy than in France and Germany, and this influenced the burghers' preferences.

Finally, the composition of the alliances is determined by the specific preferences of the actors involved. We shall see, for example, that although German towns might have wanted a centralizing authority, the German king opted in-

TABLE 4.3
Historical Paths of Institutional Development (generative phase)

	Expected preferences of towns	*Actual political coalitions*	*Outcome*
France:	central actor	Weak kings ally with towns. Bargain based on shared material interests regarding tax structure and royal administration as well as shared perspectives on preferred social order. Aristocracy and clergy paid off by pension schemes and tax exemptions.	sovereign, territorial state
Germany:	central actor	German king (Holy Roman Emperor) pursues imperial strategy in Italy and surrenders control over the German towns to the feudal lords. After failure in Italy, the king becomes a figurehead. Towns form leagues against the lords.	city-leagues and independent lordships
Italy:	urban independence	Urbanized aristocracy. Unlike Germany or France, no clash between towns and lords. Bourgeois and nobles resist central control by German emperor or pope.	city-states

stead for an Italian strategy. To pursue that, he surrendered Germany to the lords (see Table 4.3).

I argue that the fundamental transformations of the late medieval period were set in motion by the dramatic changes in the economic environment. The expansion of trade is thus the independent variable in my account.[29] Trade created new incentives and shifted the distribution of relative power in society. Political entrepreneurs and social groups created new coalitions to alter the existing set of institutions. However, these coalitions did more than reshuffle the benefits and gains produced by existing institutions. They redefined the realms of the possible and invented altogether new rules of authority. These coalitions were made possible by the shift in material power, but substantively the content of their political bargains was a conceptual revolution as well.

IMAGINING THE SOVEREIGN STATE

In the systems of rule that we have discussed so far, authority is exercised on the grounds of some readily identifiable shared affinity. The identity of the political community derives from shared kinship, similar religious beliefs, or highly personalistic ties of mutual aid and submission. But as Michael Walzer has pointed out, the sovereign state needs to be imagined and personified before it can exist.[30] Or, as German medieval scholars phrased it, the transition from feudal lordship to territorial state required reification and objectification of authority.[31] Feudal relations in many ways resembled a form of artificial kinship, quite often fortified by real kinship ties through marriage alliances. In feudalism, one entered into explicit bonds of mutual service and dependence. In a theocracy, shared faith is the marker of those who form part of the community—shared rituals, gatherings, and feast days reinforce the presence of the community of believers. But what does it mean to be part of a territorial collectivity?

The emergence of sovereign, territorial rule was, therefore, not merely a fight between the forces favoring fragmentation versus centralization; it was a contest about the very nature of authority and kingship. Early kingship was perceived to derive from the person. The kingdom was the king's personal possession. He could do with it as he pleased. When the king died, the king's peace ceased. Sudden deaths of monarchs required an immediate investiture of the next in line. There was no differentiation between the office and the person, no difference between the kingdom and the possessions of the king. Yet when Louis XIV supposedly equated himself with the state, he contravened the realities of political discourse of the seventeenth century. Realm and royal possession had been separated centuries earlier in the Late Middle Ages. Thus when the French king wished to sell a part of the realm during the Hundred Years War, he was admonished that the public realm was inalienable. The king had become protector of the common weal.[32]

Moreover, as Holzgrefe, Kratochwil, and Ruggie indicate, sovereignty introduced a radically different way of ordering international transactions as well.[33] Political authority recognizes mutually agreed upon spatial demarcation of its authority and conversely grants the other political actors the same right. The sovereign state system is based on the principle of juridical equivalence. In this sense the emergence of the sovereign state and a state system represent a cognitive shift. A pure materialist explanation does not suffice. Despite similar patterns of economic growth and expansion outside Europe, sovereign territoriality never gained acceptance there.[34] We must therefore account for the confluence of material changes and conceptual transformations which together propelled the European development of a system of territorially defined and juridically equivalent authorities.

The idea of the state required a reorientation in the existing set of beliefs. How did this new idea of spatial and hierarchical organization win?[35] How did the idea that exclusive territoriality should become the dominant principle of order gain support?

I will argue that shared perspectives led to royal-burgher affinity and the subsequent empowerment of new ideas. New belief systems emerged to justify alternative patterns of rule and simultaneously provide meaningful interpretations of new activities. But although this shift in beliefs and values was important, it alone cannot explain the decline of the medieval order. Much of Europe was exposed to similar new ideas and values, yet political outcomes differed. For example, although the emergence of a monetarized economy and pursuit of profit brought with it a revaluation of manual labor and economic gain, this was true throughout much of western Europe. Moreover, Germany, France, and Italy all had access to Roman law, and consequently all their social and political elites were familiar with the idea of sovereignty. Yet institutional outcomes differed quite radically in all three. Changes in belief systems alone cannot explain the institutional variation.[36]

Following Max Weber, I take the position that there is an elective affinity between ideas and certain material practices. Individuals who engage in particular activities such as warfare or the pursuit of monetary gain will be predisposed to ideologies that explain and justify the activity to the agent.[37] Elective affinity is a predisposition to certain ideas, not the instrumental construction of values or ideas solely to serve one's material interests. Weber does not deny the independent status of ideas. There are always charismatic individuals who can determine the limits of the possible and redefine the contours of the permissible. But whether such ideas become routinized will depend on their material support. The carriers of such ideas will often depend on economic power or coercive means to spread and develop these ideas. Social groups will look for political allies who can advance their preferred order. Conversely, political elites have an incentive to propagate and foster new ideas to gain support from social groups. They manipulate cultural symbols for their own instrumental reasons.[38] It is thus the correspondence of interests and ideas that brings actors together in a coalition and thereby empowers new sets of ideas in political practice.[39]

For these reasons this explanation ultimately places primacy in changed material conditions. Without the broad changes in overall milieu and the upswing in trade, those political and social actors who favored new ideas about legitimate authority and who had alternative views of validation of labor and profit would not have succeeded. That is, whereas the creation of new belief systems is not epiphenomenal to these material changes, new beliefs do depend on material conditions for their routinization. The shift of beliefs in the late medieval period is thus an intermediate explanatory variable.[40]

The Medieval Belief System[41]

All logics of organization contain some assumptions about time and space.[42] George Dumezil believed the phenomenon is cross-cultural, that the ruler "must try to appropriate time for the same reason that he appropriates space."[43] Medieval ideas about space and time were largely determined by the church. Christian religion determined space by the boundaries of the community of the faithful. The church occupied space but did not define its claims of authority by it. Its rule did not derive from exclusive control over fixed territorial areas. Moreover, as a consequence of religious practice and material conditions, the medieval view of geographical space was at once local and particularized but, paradoxically, also translocal and distant.

Jacques Le Goff speaks of an itinerant society. Some were pilgrims, others were crusaders in search of adventure and economic gain, and others were simply people uprooted by war and pestilence. At the same time, life was localized. The nucleus of economic organization remained the manor. Real political control was in the hands of local feudal lords, even keepers of particular castles. Written law was sparse. Custom dominated. Claims to ownership were established by the principle of seisin; simple occupation over time established one as a just claimant. Currency, language, law, all these varied widely across small areas of geographic space. In sum, what was in name a Christian ecumene was in another sense an incredibly localized world.

Likewise time existed on two levels. First, there was time in terms of life and afterlife. In an ephemeral sense, in the doctrine expounded by St. Augustine, all believers were but pilgrims in search of eternal salvation. All moments on earth were but a prelude to eternal time ahead. The reckoning of time was thus reckoning by the Holy Book. History was therein revealed. Unknown to the believers, but indicated to them by prophecy, there would be a time when God would end this earthly existence. The end of the millennium was a natural marker for many Christians.[44]

On the level of everyday activity there was a general indifference to time.[45] Only the members of the church kept time. The church marked the passage of the year by Christmas, All Saints Day, and other holy days. The passage of the day was reckoned by the time before and after services.[46] The church thus had a monopoly on time. It alone kept the day and times of year, it told people which days were holy and which not, it determined when to work and when not to; that ability itself tells us something about the dominant position of the church in the social order.

Overall, the measurement of time varied widely. The year began on different dates in different countries depending on the dominant religious tradition. Thus the year began on Easter in France. January 1, a later demarcation, was apparently based on the dating of the circumcision of Christ. Likewise, the day began at different points—sunset, midnight, or noon—depending on locality.

The clergy also advanced a theory of social stasis, the theory of the three orders. In its simplest form it asserted the supremacy of the clergy over the nobility and of the nobility over the peasantry. The distinguishing mark was the activity in which the individual was engaged: the life of contemplation, the life of combat, or the life of toil.[47] This was not simply a preferred social order but an order that reflected divine regulation. It was homologous with heaven.[48] It was thus a way of understanding one's place in the world. Stratification and hierarchy were reflections of cosmological design. Other activities, such as commerce, had no meaning if they were not directed to a religious purpose.

The church used a variety of ways to implement this proposed stratification. For example, only nobility and clergy could take oaths. Oath taking was thus a marker of perfection, the ability to comprehend the word of God. The church for that reason supported the nobles' suppression of peace societies. These societies, which were voluntary associations of manual laborers, were based on oaths of mutual support. But oaths could only be taken by those within the assigned strata. Hence, to take an oath was to defy hierarchical authority. It introduced dangerous notions of equality in association and the idea that compacts before God could be valid without the approval of the church hierarchy.

The effect of this restriction on taking oaths was to make legal practice the exclusive province of members of the elite.

Clerical texts also constructed lists of licit and illicit trades.[49] These lists were quite lengthy and encompassed many trades. Spiritual activity was superior to material activity. The church condemned any activity specifically geared to making profit. Usury and education for pay were condemned as well. The taboo on money played an important role in the struggle between societies living within the framework of a natural economy and the invasion of a monetary economy. "This panic flight before the precious metal coin incited medieval theologians like Saint Bernard to pronounce curses on money and aroused hostility against merchants—who were attacked, in particular, as usurers and exchange agents—and, more generally, against all handlers of money, as well as wage earners."[50] Scholarly activity for remuneration was also considered an illicit activity. Knowledge, like time, was possessed by God. Since all true knowledge belonged to God, it was a sin to be paid for providing knowledge, that is, to instruct for payment. The church thus justified its monopoly on knowledge.[51]

The medieval legal order reflected these views and reinforced the social stratification advocated by church and nobility. After the decline of the Roman Empire, the influx of Germanic tribes had transformed, if not driven out, the written Roman law. In northern France particularly, the invading Goths and Franks had diluted Roman law. In general there had developed two sets of coexisting legal systems: laws that pertained to the non-Romans, such as the Lex Burgundium and Lex Visigothorum; and laws for the Romans. Law thus had become personalized. Distinct races had their own system of law. By contrast, those areas that were still populated by a large number of Roman people maintained a relatively strong sense of Roman law, as was the case in southern France and Italy. These differences gradually evolved into the difference between droit coutumier, the unwritten customary law of the north, and droit écrit, the written law of the south.[52]

The feudal era depersonalized law in the sense of dissociating legal standing from race. Jurisdiction was exercised by specific lord-vassal and lord-peasant relations. However, because of the decentralization of power, this meant a high degree of particularism. The local lords would adjust their legal systems to fit local customs and conditions. Because of this localized system of adjudication and regulation, there could be no comprehensive notion of private property. As said, seisin, continued use of a piece of land for a length of time, established legitimate title. If there was any dispute, seisin would be ascertained by querying the neighbors of the landholder in question. "For nearly all land and a great many human beings were burdened at this time with a multiplicity of obligations differing in their nature, but all apparently of equal importance. None implied that fixed proprietary exclusiveness which belonged to ownership in Roman law."[53]

Evidentiary proceedings were unknown. Trial by ordeal and combat were preferred means of discovering the truth. Innocence or guilt, for example, were proven by immersing the accused in water. If the accused sank to the bottom, he or she was innocent. Another procedure consisted of having the accused carry hot iron over a specified distance. Truth was ascertained by the nature of the wound after a set amount of days.[54]

Finally, the medieval belief system placed a high premium on religious and military frames of mind. Nobility attempted to demarcate itself from supposedly inferior groups. As we saw in Chapter 3, the feudal warrior elite distinguished itself as a caste. Rank was delineated, as it was later in Tokugawa Japan, by the ability to bear arms. The higher one's rank, the more obvious the display of weaponry. The feudal elite clearly recognized the bourgeoisie as its archenemy. Despite a lack of clear economic differences, particularly at the lower end of the nobility scale, the inability to bear arms was always considered a mark of inferiority.[55]

Moreover, nobility was seen as a genealogically acquired superiority. The nobles' special status was legitimated by the argument of superiority by birth.[56] This took bizarre proportions. Respected ecclesiastical scholars constructed genealogies demonstrating that the kings of France were related to the Trojans. The lineage of the Count of Flanders could apparently be traced back to Priamus.[57] The wealth of merchants did not matter. Their inability to bear arms and their birth marked them inevitably as inferior. "The assumption was that nobility had merit and merit again was innate in blood."[58] Nobles were not to associate with these inferiors in marriage or even in death—hence the practice of separate burial areas for the nobility.

Consequently the importance of personal ties always weighed heavily. As Bloch points out, violent conflict in the Middle Ages was to a considerable extent the conflict of rival kin groups. Going back to ancient Germanic custom, wrong to one's kin group needed to be addressed according to the rules of the feud. Nobility in a sense constructed a new type of kinship, not based on tribal affiliation but on genealogical superiority and caste differentiation. Knights recognized members of this caste across the boundaries of duchies and counties— hence the practice of acquisition by marriage.

The Serendipitous Effects of Church Renewal

The role of the church during the Late Middle Ages is fraught with paradox. It opposed kinship structures yet reaffirmed the personal ties of feudal bondage. While it lamented the pursuit of monetary gain, the papacy sought to streamline its revenue intake. The attempt of the church and the papacy to create order in an anarchic, fragmented political environment, and their desire to create a hierarchical organization of their own, therefore led to a departure of some of the features of the earlier medieval system of rule and affected the older belief systems. The instruments that the church used to rationalize its proceedings were later appropriated by aspiring territorial rulers and modernizing elements in late medieval society.

First, the church had led the way in diminishing the role of kinship structures. It particularly had propagated the idea of primogeniture, because consolidated holdings would increase ecclesiastical revenue through wills.[59] It thus broke up older tribal and kin relations and made it impossible later to organize market exchange along those lines.[60]

Second, the church had tried to diminish the level of ubiquitous violence by outlawing war on particular days and regulating certain modes of combat. In proclaiming the Peace and Truce of God, the church thus appropriated the role of a public actor.[61] One function of this authority was to maintain the general peace. In so doing the church created the idea that one of the roles of government was to provide for the collective good.

Third, in arguing for a hierarchy of feudal rule rather than a grab bag of cross-cutting and multiple obligations, the church moved against fragmentation of political order. That is, it argued for a feudal pyramid. In Strayer's words, feudal rule in the twelfth century became a real system.[62] Indeed, the principle of a strict feudal hierarchy, where obligations to some lords, particularly to the king, outranked the others, was largely established in the twelfth century when the actual power of the nobility was already declining vis-à-vis central authority.

Moreover, because of its contest with the empire and its desire to create a rational administrative machinery, the church engaged in the codification of systematic written law. Canonical law was established to deal with affairs pertaining to the church and affairs that fell under its jurisdiction.[63] In response, secular rulers turned to systematic and written law to justify their own positions. Roman law, which contained the concepts of sovereignty and exclusive jurisdiction, seemed particularly favorable for the purpose.[64] As Kantorowicz put it, Christ centered kingship became law centered kingship.[65]

Finally, as we saw in Chapter 3, the contest between church and empire eroded the basis of both sources of authority. It delegitimized both papacy and empire. Popes had to contend with antipopes, the emperor faced rivals supported by lords and pope, and some bishoprics had two bishops. Pope and emperor branded each other as false monks, usurpers, and heretics. In addition to delegitimizing each other, the contest also made secular rulers aware that ecclesiastical support was a dangerous basis for political rule. Ultimately, ecclesiastical lords would have to answer to Rome. In a sense the denial of sacral status to political rule necessitated that secular rulers find alternative justifications.

By pursuing these policies, the church had, somewhat unintentionally, created the space for institutional innovation and reinterpretation of individuals' activities. Political entrepreneurs and social groups would use some of the church's arsenal against it. Moreover, by seeking to establish a hierocratic and sovereign church, the papacy set in motion forces that opposed that very idea.

The Commercial Revolution and Conceptual Transformation

Some of the new ideas and sources for legitimation were soon appropriated by various individuals, political entrepreneurs, and social groups who did not fit the old medieval set of values. The upswing in economic activity had given rise to practices that were irreconcilable with the medieval social and institutional framework. The growth of trade and corresponding increase in wealth had improved the material position of merchants. But material gain and the pursuit of profit were anathema to the medieval belief system and the values propagated by church and nobility. The affinity of burghers for the older set of ideas and beliefs was therefore slight.[66] The belief system propagated by the church, and its corresponding social order, were unacceptable to the merchants and townspeople.[67] If society was indeed ordered homologously to heaven, then there was no salvation for them. The burghers had to justify their activities in some other way.

The bourgeois, furthermore, perceived time and space differently. Time was no longer the ephemeral time of the afterlife. Nor was the time of the year and day marked by the activity of the church. Business activity required formalized calculation of time. Time and space had been undifferentiated concepts, beyond the control of humans. Those with knowledge of ultimate ends, the clergy, claimed to have the ability to interpret the world, but they did not claim to make it. Proponents of the new beliefs did exactly that. They appropriated time and space by making them products of mortal calculation.

For example, if money was lent, interest rates had to be calculated with mathematical precision. After all, the lending of money entailed an opportunity cost. The church, however, dissuaded usury because it was considered to be the sale of God's possession. That is, usury was seen as a charge on time, not as the cost of money. Since only God possessed time, the charging of usury was an irreligious act. If one is indifferent to time, if one does not have a sense of chronological progression of time, the value of a good (money) should not increase. Contrary to the medieval belief that time was winding down (*mundus senescit*, "the world grows old," was the medieval adage), the bourgeois acquired a sense that time itself had value.

Business activity thus required timekeeping. Mechanical clocks rather than church bells became the markers of time. The twenty-four-hour day came into being. Throughout western Europe towns constructed clock towers which were strategically placed opposite belfries of the churches. The bell tower of Bruges was thus placed on the market, larger and taller than the church just down the road; it symbolized the new powers in this mercantile town. Likewise, business activity required exact delineation of space. Businesspeople sought certitude in their business environment. In an unstructured world of crosscutting jurisdictions and boundaries, businesspeople were constantly faced with new and unpredictable obstacles. Fixed boundaries and uniform jurisdiction were therefore preferable to the crosscutting environment of medieval feudalism. Space had to be ordered.[68]

In other words, the demarcation and conceptualization of time and space are essentially contested concepts. "Against the merchant's time, the church set up its own time."[69] The traditional medieval conceptualization of spatial and chronological order did not correspond to the new beliefs of society.[70] The burghers had very different views about time and space. Time and space did not exist in forms homologous to heaven; they did not exist transcendentally but were constructed and designed by mortals. Such new images made the later articulation of authority in and over geographical space possible.

Furthermore, business activity could not be organized according to the theory of the three orders or the knightly system of personal bonds. The businessperson depersonalizes ties. Contracts between entrepreneurs are not the same as the contract of lord and liege. The latter is personal.[71] Business contracts are upheld merely for the exchange of commodities, not because they signify some deeper bond. If service is required, it is depersonalized, circumscribed for a particular time and amount. One is buyer or seller, role players in the circulation of goods.

Marvin Becker argues that there was a critically important shift from literal bonds to abstract ties. This shift made abstract economic exchange and credit possible. The early medieval era was based on narrow allegiances and kinship ties. Given the nature of the insecure material environment, exchanges had to be face-to-face and transacted immediately. "The notion that writing in itself could be a cause of obligation was tenuous at best. This, then, was a world of narrow tribal loyalties, demanding kinship ties and exacting primary allegiances. The individual was encadred in a literal world where the materiality of bonds was immediate and certain."[72]

Such personal ties and lack of confidence in the material environment made economic exchange difficult to conduct. Consequently, gift giving was highly important. Such exchanges were ceremonial and tribal in character, conferring mutual entitlements and obligations. But these should not be regarded as trade.[73] Becker, surveying the area of Lucca and Florence, notes that before 1000, 80 to 85 percent of transactions, primarily land deals, were in the form of gift exchange and donations. By 1150, however, monetary sales had become far more important, accounting for about 75 percent of all transactions.[74]

The necessity to have circumscribed areas of clear jurisdiction, and the desire to substantiate private property combined with the necessity of more formalized interaction which could exist independent of the specific actors, renewed interest in Roman law. "There was the attraction—especially felt by merchants—of more convenient and more rational procedures."[75] Reliance on seisin and custom were insufficient guarantees of property. Contracts could not depend on oaths of the initiating actors. Sometimes these contracts might have to carry through beyond the death of the original contractors. "They needed access to rapid legal processes to enforce contracts without excessive delays and to machinery which would assist them to recover debts from those with whom they had dealings."[76] The written law, Roman law, mitigated some of these problems. It had well-developed theories of private property. The adoption of Roman law had other benefits as well. It had well-developed means of trial. Because of the nobles claim to trial by combat, burghers could not very well take men who were skilled in armed combat to court.[77] Overall burghers desired more evidentiary court proceedings. An attempt was made to adduce the truth by witnesses and written documents rather than rely on the understanding that individuals had of the prevalent customs. Jurisprudence once again had to become the domain for professionals.[78] In short, the outlook of the burghers differed dramatically from that of the nobility and clergy.[79] Mystical and cosmological views increasingly started to give way to instrumentally rational beliefs on how to structure time, space, property rights, and juridical procedures. Inevitably that meant a shift in preferences for a new political order.

CONCLUSION

About the middle of the eleventh century a dramatic expansion of the European economy occurred. This expansion went hand-in-hand with an increase in long-distance trade. The growth in trade made further division of labor possible. Towns increased in size and number. These settlements had widely different material interests from the old feudal and ecclesiastical order. Consequently the burghers were motivated to change existing institutions. To accomplish this, they either formed political alliances with other actors, such as an aspiring territorial ruler, or they pursued the largest amount of independence possible. Whether these towns pursued autonomy on their own, formed leagues, or allied with some centralizing authority depended first of all on the size and strength of the individual towns. Few towns, save the Italian, were strong enough to go it alone. The second factor influencing the urban set of preferences was the nature of trade. The relatively low-volume, high-profit trade of the Mediterranean, the trade in luxury goods, suggested that individual towns might try to capture a monopoly position on their own. By contrast, the low-profit, high-volume trade of the north made that policy impossible. No one actor could individually monopolize the bulk trade of the Baltic and the North Sea. Moreover, the low profit margins made actors sensitive to competition and high transaction costs. Towns not only had divergent material interests, but they had different perceptions than church and nobility regarding legal procedure, licitness of trade, and the nature of profit making. Consequently the burghers would seek to ally with actors who had an affinity with their interests and beliefs. The next three chapters explore how the towns fared in pursuit of these goals.

CHAPTER 5

The Rise of the Sovereign, Territorial State
in Capetian France

> A second precondition for coming to think of the State as the main subject-
> matter of political philosophy is that the independence of each regnum or civitas
> from any external and superior power should be vindicated and assured. . . .
> A further precondition for arriving at the modern concept of the State is that the
> supreme authority within each independent regnum should be recognized as
> having no rivals within his own territories as a law-making
> power and an object of allegiance.[1]

THE ECONOMIC transformation between 1000 and 1300 was paralleled by political innovation. The sovereign, territorial state was one of the new logics of
organization which emerged against the background of the late medieval renaissance. Contrary to the crosscutting and nonhierarchical personal ties of
feudalism, the Capetian Dynasty (987–1328) claimed final authority over all
inhabitants of the realm. And unlike empire and church, it did not infuse its
political rule with claims over a translocal community as did the Christian
Commonwealth. Instead it defined its authority territorially. Within fixed
boundaries the Capetians claimed to have final power, but they made no claims
to rule beyond those borders.

The success of the Capetians was hardly foreseeable when they first assumed
the throne. Gaining the kingship by consent of the barons after a long period of
civil war, they were—at best—only first among equals. The puzzle before us
then is to explain how these weak kings managed to assert their control over the
heavily fragmented area that was to become France. In addition, they also managed to impose the principle of territorial exclusivity upon universal actors,
particularly against the wishes of the pope. Within the borders of the kingdom,
even members of the clergy had to recognize that ultimate jurisdiction lay in
Paris, not Rome.

Contrary to the common explanation that states emerged as the result of
changes in warfare, I argue that the sovereign state emerged as the result of a
social coalition based on the affinity of interests and perspectives between in-
cipient monarchy and burghers. Changes in the nature of warfare might explain
the growth of government, particularly following the fifteenth century, but they
do not explain why some governments were structured on the principles of
sovereignty and territoriality, whereas other governments were not.

THE BEGINNING OF THE FRENCH STATE: THE CONSOLIDATION
OF THE CAPETIAN DYNASTY (987–1328)

On Christmas Day in the year 800, Pope Leo III crowned Charlemagne emperor of the Christian world. He was deemed to be successor to the Caesars and
protector of the Roman church. When Charlemagne died, he left to his heirs an
area stretching from northern Spain to Poland and from northern Italy to the
lowlands.

This great Carolingian Empire was not to last. Shortly after Charlemagne's
death, the empire disintegrated into western, middle and eastern kingdoms.
The latter two became the basis for the later German Empire. But the fragmentation did not end there. The lack of established primogeniture, the invasions
by Vikings, Saracens, and Maygars, and the decline of the monetary economy
eroded any semblance of central authority. In the West-Frankish kingdom,
royal authority existed only in a nominal sense.

By the end of the tenth century, feudalism was fully entrenched.[2] It legitimated itself by justifying the supremacy of warrior and priest, and it subjugated
others to menial existence as inferior laborers. Political control had even
slipped away from the fifty-five dukes and counts to the level of individual
castle-holders.[3] The localization of market exchange and legal procedures
meant that any identification with a larger political authority evaporated.
"France" came to refer only to the area between the Loire and the border of
Lotharingen, or sometimes only to the area immediately surrounding Paris.[4]
Even after royal control had extended considerably by 1300, officials in Toulouse would sometimes still speak of "sending messengers to France," that is,
Paris.[5]

It was under these circumstances that Hugh Capet was elected to replace
the disputed Carolingian lineage in 987. With him started the dynasty of Capetians which would rule until 1328. After decades of civil war, however, the
actual area under their control was not more than a dot on the map of the
former West-Frankish kingdom. The royal domain consisted only of the surrounding area of the Île-de-France, some territories around Orléans, and a
smattering of even smaller areas. In total it comprised about 2,600 square
miles.[6] Moreover, Hugh Capet had only gained the throne by the support of
particular nobles who opposed the Carolingian branch. In 887 the Carolingian
line was without a direct heir. In West Francia the nobles then elected Eudes,
the Count of Paris, as king.[7] This was the beginning of the Robertian, later
called the Capetian, line. When the fortunes of war turned against Eudes, some
nobles favored a return to members of the Carolingian line, even though the
succession of Charles the Simple was disputed. The consequence was a century
of civil war with nobles frequently switching sides and favoring one house then
the other. All in all, royal power meant little to such powerful lords as the dukes
of Normandy, Acquitaine, or Burgundy. The king, after all, had only recently

been one of their rank. The dukes and counts believed they had established an elective monarchy.[8]

Yet after three centuries of Capetian rule, we find the basis of a sovereign state, so much so that Joseph Strayer, focusing mainly on France, can argue that by 1300 the state had become the dominant form of political organization in Europe.[9] Although Strayer perhaps overstates the point, his argument is convincing that in France the basis of a sovereign, territorial state had been laid by the beginning of the fourteenth century. By then the Capetians had reduced the power of such rivals as the Counts of Champagne and the dukes of Normandy. They also diminished the vast holdings of the English king.[10] By the end of the thirteenth century, the English king held no more than the area of Gascogny in the southwest (see Maps 5.1 and 5.2).

The Capetians also installed a regular system of administration from the center. From there they supervised local administration by seneschals and baillis. They began to establish various forms of revenue production. The Capetians, particularly Philip the Fair, curtailed the church in their domain and were victorious in their confrontation with the pope.

It would be too much to suggest that we find modern France in the 1300s. There was still a protracted war with England to come, years of religious turmoil, and domestic opposition by cities, nobility, and clergy. Nevertheless, we do already find the essential traits of modern statehood. The first notions of sovereign authority developed in this period. The French king was regarded as emperor in his own kingdom. The beginnings of territorial demarcation by formal boundaries date from that dynasty. Where these boundaries exactly lay was of course a different matter, but there was a distinct territorial unit, a distinct "Regnum Francie."[11] From the Capetian reign also dates the beginning of royal justice and the use of written Roman law—both essential to the concept of public authority.

The Capetians thus curtailed their feudal rivals and constructed a mode of organization that was not based on personal ties nor laid claim to universal domination as did the church and Holy Roman Empire. How did this come about? How did the insignificant royal domain of Hugh Capet expand in the face of opposition by feudal lords, and how did the French king manage to defeat powerful enemies such as the pope where the German emperor had failed?

For some historians, there is no puzzle. Susan Reynolds, for example, suggests that there always existed an idea of the kingdom as a community.[12] Even Fawtier, who greatly extolled the state-making abilities of the later Capetians, argued that the kings differed from other nobles in their ideological position. They were not "petits signeurs" of the Île-de France but were powerful lords in their own right.[13]

No doubt such social ideas are important, but the existence of a social idea and its influence on political practice are two different things. As I have suggested in previous chapters, ideas can have considerable influence, but they

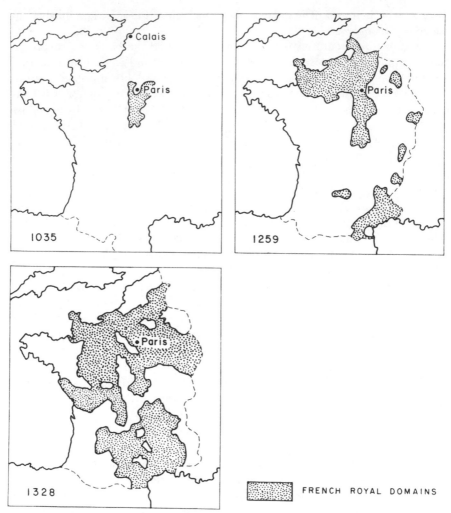

5.1 The Extent of the Capetian Royal Domain (Source: Reinhard Bendix, *Kings or People: Power and the Mandate to Rule*. Berkeley: University of California Press, 1978, p. 322.)

need material bases of support in order to be routinized. Ideas need to be empowered before they can become political practice. Feudal practice differed markedly from the ideal. Vassals often disobeyed the king. Indeed, during the eleventh century, the low-water mark for the Capetian Dynasty, many vassals did not bother to travel to Paris to do homage. Even within the royal domain, the land held directly by the king, he had to fight individual castle-holders. The more powerful lords, such as the Counts of Flanders, the dukes of Normandy, and the rulers of Brittany, would on occasion call themselves rulers over "regna," rulers of kingdoms in their own right.[14] Moreover, as we have seen, feudal vassalage was not hierarchical. The king himself was indebted to some

5.2 France in the Mid-eleventh Century (Source: Elizabeth Hallam, *Capetian France, 987–1328*. New York: Longman, 1980, p. 5.)

bishops from whom he held land. Finally, the early Capetian monarchy can hardly be compared with the later kings who claimed exclusive authority and based their rule on Roman law, in which the king was the supreme fountain-head of laws. That qualitative shift from personal rule to public authority was not contained in the earlier medieval notion that the kings had a privileged ideological position as first among equals.

The task before us is to explain how the principle of sovereign, territorial rule emerged and how that principle was empowered. Which material interests and belief systems came together in order for the idea of sovereign, territorial kingship to become the system of rule in France? Indubitably the king had an ideological position which differentiated him from other high lords. But de facto there were dozens, if not hundreds, of independent feudal lords who had little incentive to support royalist centralization. To combat such opposition, the king must have found allies to support him. Who were these political allies of the king?

WHY THE EMERGENCE OF THE FRENCH STATE DOES NOT FOLLOW FROM THE CHARACTER OF WARFARE

In one explanation, changes in the nature of warfare account for the rise of the state. The thesis that the rise of centralized monarchy in France can be explained by war plays an important role in the works of, for example, Charles Tilly, Michael Mann, Richard Bean, and Margaret Levi. Richard Bean explains the rise of states by the changes in the art of war and the ability of sovereigns to tax. Charles Tilly once suggested that "wars made states."[15] Similarly, Margaret Levi suggests that kings provided their subjects with military security in exchange for revenue.[16]

Interpretations of these theories are roughly of two varieties. The first variety sees states simply as larger units compared to feudal lordships. Efficiency of scale favored the king over dukes and counts. It is basically a macrostructural account which pays little attention to social bargaining. The operative dynamic consists of Darwinian selection. Smaller units fell by the wayside.

The second, and more persuasive, interpretation explains the emergence of the state by the exchange of revenue for the provision of security by the monarch. From that perspective the king can be seen as the provider of protection in exchange for the consent of individuals to be taxed. Since military security became increasingly expensive because of the ever-rising costs of warfare, taxes had to be raised accordingly.[17] Corresponding with the growth of taxation was the rise of centralized administration and a bureaucratic apparatus.

Can these theories explain the emergence of a sovereign, territorial state in France? Despite their valuable insights, I do not think they ultimately can.[18]

Warfare and Efficiencies of Scale

One interpretation of the theory that warfare determines the particular logic of organization argues that the scale of the unit changes in response to the dynamics of warfare. Some types of military technology favor the formation of large political units such as empires. Other types of technology lead to small political organizations such as in feudalism. Changes in military technology thus alter existing efficiencies of scale. The decline of the Roman Empire, for example, can be attributed to the increasing success of cavalry. The efficiency of scale of cavalry favored smaller political units. Hence the Roman borders contracted.[19]

In a similar vein, the transition from a feudal system to a system of states is often explained by the rising costs of warfare and the increasing size of armies in the later Middle Ages. The introduction of organized infantry and (cross)bowmen made the feudal mode of warfare obsolete. Heavy cavalry simply could not hold the field against archers and organized infantry.[20] The appearance of gunpowder weapons on the battlefield completed the process. The use of artillery required changes in the style of fortification.[21] All this meant a dramatic rise in the costs of warfare.[22] This mode of warfare therefore favored a large tax basis and centralized authority. Feudal units lacked the sheer size required for this warfare. Efficiencies of scale dictated centralization of states.

Although the mode of warfare did change in the later Middle Ages and particularly during the Renaissance, we cannot see the emergence of sovereign states simply in terms of efficiencies of scale. First of all, this explanation is too deterministic.[23] Because of its macrostructural bias, it implies a uniform outcome of technical shifts. Essentially it contends that Darwinian selection leads to a single response. In reality, however, the impacts of technological changes are always mediated through the dominant groups in power.[24] To reinforce this point, one need only realize that the impact of military technological changes led to widely diverse outcomes throughout Europe. Although the technologies of war were generally available—that is French, Italian, and German actors all had roughly similar access to such technologies—they did not have the same political effect. Many parts of Europe did not centralize. Witness Germany and Italy, which decentralized, and they survived well into the nineteenth century. The nature and size of units in these two areas had little to do with the nature and availability of military technology but were instead the result of different political strategies and alliances—as we will see in the chapters ahead.[25] The interaction between emperor, feudal lords, and towns, not the character of warfare at the time, explains the decentralization of Germany and Italy. And perhaps most significantly, these small units survived well beyond the military revolution of the fifteenth century.

Moreover, this "efficiency-of-scale" argument suggests a functional, teleological process. It posits states as the inevitable result of exogenous constraints and thus commits the fallacies of unilinear explanations which I have criticized in earlier chapters. Society does not necessarily generate the most efficient solution to an environmental change. Society consists of a variety of identifiable actors who pursue a complex set of objectives. Political entrepreneurs seek to expand their power, burghers seek economic security, peasants might desire less control by their feudal and ecclesiastical lords, and so on. Out of these competing interests come social alliances which create institutions. One cannot argue that a particular institution emerged as an efficient response to the environmental stimulus. That would be to deduce preferences from outcomes. Although selection clearly occurs, the selective process only explains the subsequent relative efficacy and efficiency of that institution vis-à-vis other institutional arrangements. It does not explain the reasons why individuals preferred one type of institution over another, or how that preference won out in the political process. One cannot simply say that states *emerged* because they waged war more effectively and more efficiently than feudal organization. One can perhaps say that states *survived* because they were better at waging war than synchronic and rival forms of political organization. We know with twenty-twenty hindsight that states survived while other forms of organization atrophied or died out. As in all evolution, death is the final arbiter. But one must distinguish the causes for the emergence of territorial states from the reasons why they survived in the long run. One cannot deduce which forces gave rise to the first states from the continued survival of states. One must first explain the variation in individual choices and political bargains before one can explain why sovereign, territorial states proved more successful than their synchronic institutional rivals.

Finally, one might also argue against the efficiency-of-scale theory that the issue of relative efficiency and effectiveness is actually one of efficiency of institutional makeup rather than size.[26] For example, the revenues of some Italian city-states were equivalent if not higher than those of rival states. The Netherlands and England managed to defeat far larger and more populated enemies by virtue of their ability to raise revenue, stemming from well-defined property rights, and their overall economic strength. Size is an imperfect predictor of success in military competition.

The French State as a Protection Bargain

A stronger version of state formation by war sees the rise of the state as the result of a political bargain. Given the change in the nature of warfare, individuals perceived the king to be the logical provider of protection, and in exchange for that protection they consented to taxation. Such accounts are more persuasive than simple efficiency-of-scale arguments because they are able to suggest reasons for the institutional variation across Europe, and they are less determinist in that the impact of technology is viewed as mediated by social groups and political entrepreneurs.[27] The question is whether the king was indeed the logical provider of protection and whether protection explains the rise of a centralized, sovereign monarchy.

Although this account is more powerful, it too is flawed. First, it tends to deduce preferences from outcomes.[28] Since history has moved in the direction of states, we deduce from the outcome that individuals "contracted" for that result. Such views suggest that changes in the character of war inexorably forced social actors to accept the dominance of a central authority. It is clear, however, that feudal aristocracy had very good material and ideological reasons to prevent centralization of the means of violence.[29] The question is, why did the feudal nobility not succeed in preventing the adoption of these new techniques of warfare and new systems of raising revenue?[30]

Second, the implications of changes in military technology were not straightforward. For example, it was not clear if the construction of stone castles made local resistance easier or whether it led, because of higher expenses, to more centralization.[31] Although we can say from our contemporary vantage point that feudal cavalry was gradually becoming obsolete, this was not immediately perceived by its practitioners. Mounted knights remained a critical element of armed force well into the fifteenth century. It is also clear that other areas with a high degree of insecurity did not centralize. Witness the German Empire; there feudal lords dominated the king. In short, one cannot unequivocally argue that the change in military technology necessitated political bargains for central protection by the king. The implications of such change were far from clear.

Third, the historical evidence suggests that the success of the Capetian kingdom preceded the expensive developments of large infantry armies, artillery, and redesigned fortifications. By 1300 the royal domain encompassed the area west of the Rhône, along the Saône and Meuse rivers to the east, the Scheldt River in the north, and the Pyrenees as the southern boundary.[32] In short, the small domain of the early Capetians around Île-de-France and Orléans had almost expanded to France's contemporary size between 1000 and 1300. The most significant developments in military technology and strategy came after this centralization and expansion.[33] Medieval armies remained relatively small.[34] Artillery was first invented in the early fourteenth century and did not make its appearance on the battlefield until after several decades. Hand firearms only appeared in the sixteenth century. Consequently both Tilly and Bean see the major military changes occurring after 1400. Geoffrey Parker locates the military revolution in the sixteenth century, as does Lawrence Stone. Stone tellingly suggests that central administration preceded and made possible modern warfare rather than the other way round. We should also recall that the centralized domain that the Capetians had built up was most threatened in the Hundred Years War when the kingship was contested. The strong principalities reasserted their political power with some success when the kingdom was challenged by England.[35] Warfare, in other words, threatened to fragment rather than centralize the kingdom.

Fourth, it was not obvious that the early Capetian kings were the logical providers of protection. I do not think that "monarchs needed more funds to win battles and were the obvious persons to organize war."[36] As I have already pointed out, the king was in title defender of the realm, but pragmatically the noble domains were larger, produced more revenue, and could bring more military resources to bear on any opponent. The royal domain was very small. Even vassals who had paid homage to the Capetian king, and castellans within the royal domain, would on occasion rebel. If there was a preference for larger units with greater military strength, then the larger duchies and counties should have been preferred. Considering the weak position of the Capetian Dynasty at the outset, it is unclear why they would be the preferred providers of protection.[37] For such explanations to be able to account for the growth of royal control, they need to explain how the weak Capetian kings could become the providers of protection in the first place.

Fifth, the explanation that individuals consented to royal rule for protection only applies to areas where such control had already been established. Why would individuals outside the domain seek protection from the king? If one was not under the factual control of the king, it is difficult to argue that the king would be a better provider of protection. The king of France, from a purely material perspective, did not possess the resources to be the most efficient provider of protection. This type of argument tends to beg the question. It suggests that the king can legitimate and expand his rule as the provider of protection and therefore can raise taxes. It does not explain how the king achieved such a capability in the first place.

One might counter my argument by suggesting that analysis of state revenue indicates that most of royal revenue was devoted to war. I agree that this was the case until the rise of the welfare state and the increasing involvement of the state with modern economies. Fiscal historical analysis demonstrates this quite clearly. But this in itself does not explain the emergence of a sovereign, territorial state in France and other institutional arrangements elsewhere. Whereas the primary expenditures of the Capetian monarchy were devoted to war, this was also true for other logics of organization. City-leagues, city-states, and feudal lordships all undoubtedly devoted the major portion of their expenditures to war.[38] In short, the level of war expenditure in any one type does not explain individuals' institutional preferences to choose one type over the other. I do not deny that governments spent most of their resources on warfare, but that in itself does not explain why some governments were based on sovereign, territorial forms of organization whereas other governments exercised power on nonsovereign and nonterritorial principles.

We need, therefore, to explain the social processes by which a weak French king expanded his domain without having great material resources at his disposal. Like Strayer, I suggest that state formation was due to the acquiescence of privileged classes.[39] I argue that the emergence of the towns permitted new social bargains, which enabled the Capetian kings to centralize their authority. There were benefits for the bourgeois to side with the French king and support his policies against the nobility and church.

THE CONFLUENCE OF MATERIAL INTERESTS OF MONARCHY AND TOWNS

As discussed in Chapter 4, the impact of trade was relatively modest in France compared to Italy and some of the German areas. Although regional trade did lead to the formation of new towns, these towns were relatively small. France remained bereft of long-distance trading centers. Only in Flanders, whose count was technically a vassal of the king, did towns of considerable size emerge, because of their connection with the wool trade.[40] The type of trade in which most towns engaged was basically of low volume and low added value. Most of the goods in which merchants of the French towns dealt were agricultural, bulk commodities. The French did not tie in to the long-distance trade

TABLE 5.1
Estimated Population of Major French Towns[a]

Town	Population	Year
Beziers	14,000	early 14th century
Lyons	30,000	early 14th century
Montpellier	40,000	1300
Narbonne	25,000	1300
Orleans	25,000	1300
Paris	60,000	1250
Paris	80–120,000	early 14th century
Paris	80–210,000[b]	1400
Strasbourg	25,000	1300
Toulouse	25,000	early 14th century

Sources: Ennen, *The Medieval Town*, p. 186; Mundy and Riesenberg, *The Medieval Town*, pp. 30, 66; Hilton, *English and French Towns*, pp. 45, 51, 96–99.

[a] From the wide variation in Paris's population, the reader can surmise the difficulties in estimating town populations. Records were often inaccurate, quite often described only the amount of hearths (the basic tax unit), and sometimes involved deliberate misrepresentations, for example, when towns were asking for more churches. For a discussion of the difficulties of this enterprise, see Ennen, *The Medieval Town*, p. 186f; Hilton, *English and French Towns*, p. 51.

[b] I have omitted the estimate by Hohenberg and Lees who suggest that Paris's population in 1400 might have been as large as 275,000. *The Making of Urban Europe*, p. 11. This strikes me as too high given the other estimates. J. C. Russell argues that Paris had upward of a 100,000 people in 1348. "Population in Europe 500–1500," pp. 34–35. Ennen notes that most towns in the Middle Ages were relatively small, usually not above 10,000. Ennen, *The Medieval Town*, p. 185. By way of comparison, London probably had in the neighborhood of 40–50,000 inhabitants in the fourteenth century. For a comparison with Germany and Italy, see Chapters 6 and 7.

that the Italians developed in the Mediterranean and that the Hanseatic cities developed in the north.[41]

As suggested in Chapter 4, the particular impact of this trade had two consequences. First, the size of the towns and their moderate revenues prevented them from acting independently (see Tables 5.1 and 5.2). Unlike Venice or Florence, whose revenues and military power equaled that of any sovereign, territorial state, the French towns needed some form of organization to pool their economic and political resources to gain their objectives. Yet as Robert Fawtier suggests, they could not become independent or form leagues because they were too small.[42]

Second, the nature of the trade, with its low profit margins, was an inducement to search for forms of organization that could reduce costs and introduce more certitude in the business environment. The towns would prefer a system

TABLE 5.2
Estimated Population of Major Flemish Towns

Town	Population	Year
Antwerp	5,000	1347
Antwerp	20,000	1440
Bruges	50,000	1300
Bruges	125,000	1400
Brussels	30,000	1300
Ghent	60,000	1300
Ghent	70,000	1400
Louvain	45,000	1300

Sources: Ennen, *The Medieval Town,* p. 187; Hohenberg and Lees, *The Making of Urban Europe,* p. 11. Blockmans suggests that Ghent, Antwerp, Bruges, and Brussels were all larger than 32,000 in 1450 and that there were seven other towns that were between 16,000 and 32,000. "Princes Conquérants et Bourgeois Calculateurs," p. 175. J. C. Russell argues that Ghent was larger than 50,000 by 1348, whereas Bruges's population was between 20,000 and 50,000 that same year. "Population in Europe, 500–1500," pp. 34–35. Mundy and Riesenberg give a rough estimate suggesting that the larger Flemish towns were between 20,000 and 40,000 in size. *The Medieval Town,* p. 30.

with standardized taxes and more regulation of weights and measures. In economic terms, the towns would prefer a form of political organization that could reduce transaction and information costs.[43]

Although the expansion of trade provides for a first approximation of the institutional preferences of the French towns, it alone does not explain political outcomes. We can conjecture from the size and revenues of towns and the nature of their trade what the burghers preferred, but those preferences, of course, need not have translated into outcomes. Other social groups and political actors—aristocracy, church, and king—might have had alternative preferences. Moreover, although trade might have improved the relative position of the towns, it is by no means certain that the towns would be able to overcome political opposition to the institutional arrangements they desired. In short, we need a more detailed look at how political coalitions were constructed and what types of organization the participants of those coalitions preferred.[44]

The emerging towns thus had become important actors in the politics of late medieval France because as new partners they could alter the existing political coalitions; "towns now held the key position in the political order."[45] My argument in this section focuses on the affinity of interests between the French monarchy and the burghers on taxation and administration. The analysis of royal taxation reveals how both monarchy and mercantile groups preferred regularized taxation which also allowed for urban negotiation. The development of centralized administration enabled the king to construct a bureaucracy on a nonfeudal basis. Moreover, it offered the bourgeoisie and lesser nobility career opportunities and input into royal decision making. Although the church was initially a powerful ally of the French king, it inevitably became one of his opponents because of its universal claims to authority.

The increasing ability to raise revenue was thus fundamental to the formation of a stronger, more centralized monarchy. More specifically, it enabled the Capetians to construct an army and an administration that were based on monetary payment rather than in-kind transfers. This differed from the personalized structure of feudal obligations.[46] This also allowed the king to later encroach upon the influence of Rome. Alternative sources of royal revenue gave the papacy less leverage on the king. Finally, the gains in revenue allowed the king to pay off opponents whom he could not challenge directly.[47]

The nature of taxation also reveals the ability of the state to impose demands on society. Since taxation for any length of time requires at least a minimum of compliance, analysis of taxation also indicates something about social acquiescence to the objectives of the taxing authority.[48] The particular nature of the tax illuminates the political relations between actors. Who are the actors on which the heaviest demands are imposed? Who are exempted? The nature of taxation reveals how costs and benefits are distributed in a society and thus illuminates underlying social coalitions.

By the end of the fifteenth century the French kings, building on the early efforts of the Capetians, had established a system of regularized taxation, administered by a central bureaucracy. The taille, the direct royal tax, accounted for 85 percent of the entire revenue.[49] How did the kings establish this revenue basis given that early medieval taxation was haphazard and irregular?[50] The basis for royal taxation of the kingdom was laid by the Capetians and was later formalized and regularized by the successors of the Valois Dynasty.

The Correspondence of Urban and Royal Interests in
Standardized Taxation

In the eleventh and twelfth centuries the taille was far from popular. The taille was a direct, personal tax levied on commoners, and it denoted servility. It was levied by any lord and was thus called the seigneurial taille.[51] Neither clergy nor those with some form of military obligation were subject to it. Moreover, the taille was imposed on an irregular basis and varied in its incidence. The tax was "a levy effected by the lord on whatever his subjects had put by, as often as he felt need of it."[52] It was thus particularly unappealing for merchants. The abbot of Saint-Denis, an ecclesiastical lord, noted how the bourgeois complained about the taille. "For that custom seemed to the said bourgeois inordinately bad and hateful, in that it kept them in constant fear; and so, not daring to display their goods, they made little gain. Wherefore, not only were outsiders afraid to settle in the town, but even the natives were impelled to move elsewhere."[53] Stephenson goes on to note that the abbot conferred the arbitrary and unpredictable assessment to a fixed rent and left the raising and allocation of the tax to the citizens.

Furthermore, since the taille was a tax that was due any lord to whom that person was subject, and since infeudation could work on many levels, an individual might owe tax to a variety of authorities. Several lords might seek to extract revenue from the subject, and thus each would search for the very limit of what the taxed laborer could possibly sustain. The conflicting set of jurisdictions made taxation very ambiguous. If a commoner owed several lords taille, who was to be paid first? This form of taxation, the old form of the taillage, was thus neither for the commoner nor the lord efficient.

The economic upswing of the late medieval era sowed the seeds for change. The growth of the towns and their increased wealth made them attractive sources of revenue for the king, ecclesiastical lords, and aristocracy. One way to tap this new source of wealth was to charter new towns or to grant more liberties to those already in existence. Because the economic boom led to labor scarcity, chartering new towns and offering them liberties were strategic policies to attract more labor.[54] King and higher lords gained by attracting more subjects; "lords began to vie with one another in guaranteeing privileged status to residents within their jurisdiction."[55]

Commoners benefited from this process. Aside from having to pay the taille, rural laborers were also subject to other taxes and feudal exactions. The ability to evade such forms of taxation, by moving to a chartered town and by paying a fixed taille to the chartering king or lord, must have seemed attractive.[56] Towns made it standard practice to grant freedom to any individual who had resided in that town, uncontested, for a year and a day.[57] They thus provided a commoner the opportunity to escape the burden of serving a multitude of masters as a peasant.

The towns were eager to capitalize on this newfound opportunity for freedom. Because of their growing importance and because of the competition between rival lords, they could make considerable demands. They often formed communes, sworn associations of equals. One of the most important demands of the communes was the decrease in burdensome taxes and exactions. The privileges granted in the Charter of Lorris by King Louis VII in 1155 were imitated throughout northern France. Some of its provisions illustrate the nature of urban demands.

> 2. No inhabitant of the parish of Lorris shall be required to pay a toll or any other tax on his provisions.
>
> 9. No one, neither we or any other, shall exact from the burghers of Lorris any tallage, tax, or other subsidy.
>
> 15. No inhabitant of Lorris is to render us the obligation of corvée.[58]

During this process of chartering and granting liberties to towns, the taille went through a transformation. Although it was still a tax on commoners, it became more and more institutionalized. This benefited the bourgeois. The tax became a fixed incidence rather than an irregular levy.[59]

The tax was increasingly paid by the town as a whole. Indeed towns would negotiate for the right of self-assessment.[60] The distribution of the tax burden would lie with the town leadership.[61] By acting as a group, the town could negotiate with the taxing party on the incidence level. The regularity and predictability of the taille in its new form also made it easier to anticipate as an expenditure in the normal practice of business. "It made more sense to pay the king's predictable taxes than to continue to yield to the irregular exactions of the local nobility."[62]

Towns constantly sought to adjust the level of taxation. The king or his intermediaries, the seneschals and baillis, thereupon engaged in ad hoc negotiations. The assessment would then be fixed for the town as a whole, with the individual tax incidence determined by local town patricians. This enabled the town oligarch to engage in patronage and allocate the burden according to local power constellations.

To a considerable extent this ad hoc bargaining was due to nonpolitical conditions. The size of the country and the variety of customs, languages, and absence of efficient administration made localized bargaining unavoidable.[63] Furthermore, the gradual incorporation of various areas into the royal domain was accomplished by a process of mutual acquiescence, marriage alliances, and sometimes force. But in all cases such incorporation was based on particularistic deals. Unlike the forced centralization of Anglo-Saxon England after Hastings and the conquest of Wales, centralization of France was never a decisive process.[64] Local laws and customs remained constant obstacles to central administration. The seneschals and baillis, as upper administrators, could be mainly recruited from the center. The lower level administrators, however, were necessarily from the area in which they operated.[65] The king needed to be sensitive to local customs and established prerogatives.

This ad hoc procedure, however, also had political benefits for king and towns. From the monarch's perspective, it allowed the king to divide possible opposition. Indeed, the national assembly of the three estates seldom met to discuss taxation matters. If convened by the king, they were usually brought together to demonstrate their agreement with a particular policy. From the towns' perspective, local bargaining suited the patrician ability for patronage and left the opportunity to renegotiate bargains.[66] Political negotiations thus took place within the local representations or by informal procedures. "There were many interests which a town might have to discuss with the government; but was it necessary to discuss them in an assembly? Backstairs representations and bargaining with their ruler were a perpetual theme throughout the period in towns which varied in their status from that of Lyons to that of Millau."[67]

This also allowed the king to be selective with the benefits he wished to distribute. The liberties that some towns would gain need not be given to others. This strategy allowed the king to clamp down on the independence of towns once this power basis was secure.[68]

The chartering of towns thus particularly favored powerful lords such as the king and dukes and thus decreased the power of independent castle-holders and lesser lords. It worked against political fragmentation. This process, however, particularly favored the king for several reasons. First, according to feudal theory, the king formed the top of the feudal hierarchy and hence had the legal ability to create new feudal relations.[69] Towns were willing to put this social idea into political practice and thus favored a more centralized system. Consequently, towns did not overtly contravene feudal theory. Instead they understood their association, the commune, to be a physical body which could be incorporated into the feudal system just as any vassal. But because they sought to be independent, they attempted to be placed as high as possible in the feudal hierarchy. The best possible situation, therefore, was to be the direct vassal of the king and nominally not subject to any other lords. "It was an attempt of communities to rise by force of union in the feudal hierarchy and themselves to rank side by side with feudal seigneurs; sometimes as their vassals, but whenever possible, as suzerains themselves and tenants-in-chief of the Crown, privileged and independent of all but nominal allegiance."[70]

To acknowledge vassalage to a lesser lord would mean that the town acknowledged that it was also subject to the feudal superiors of that charterer of the town. Since towns strove for the maximum amount of independence and the least amount of burdens, they tended to favor royal protection over that from other lords.[71] It allowed them to get rid of crosscutting obligations and the exacting taxes of their lords. Ecclesiastical overlords were particularly disliked. Laon, for example, killed its ecclesiastical lord, the bishop, and sought royal tutelage. Rheims chased the archbishop out of town and claimed communal rights under protection of the king. Lyons, an important trading town, likewise sought protection from the king, Philip the Fair.[72]

Lesser lords lost out for additional reasons. The uncultivated areas in which new towns were settled often belonged to high lords since no manorial holders had yet established themselves. Moreover, lesser lords often lacked the revenue to set up fairs and establish towns. Poggi notes that towns preferred larger territorial organizations to facilitate trade.[73] In short, lesser lords had less to offer.

The second major factor favoring the king over other lords was the basically antiseigneurial disposition of the towns.[74] The towns did not merely want another feudal lord; they wanted a different basis of rule altogether—a rule that fit that of more rational, central administration. The villes libres and the communes, sworn associations of equals, were antithetical to the feudal, personal mode of obligation.

> The idea of personal bondage disappeared within the walls of the towns; the innumerable relationships of dependence in the countryside—in short, the feudal ordering of society—were broken and subdued. This was the burghers doing, and it laid the basis for their subsequent designation of the proper relationship of the individual to this state as "citizen of the state, not a subject."[75]

This does not mean that the inhabitants of the cities were equals in terms of power and wealth. The towns had their own division of patricians and poor. However, the difference with the feudal order was that the cities lacked fixed stations and personal bondage. There was relative social mobility and juridical equality.

Finally, the kings deliberately pursued the alliance with the towns as part of their overall strategy to centralize the kingdom. Hence they were willing to offer the towns better deals than some of their comital and ducal rivals. For example, the granting of favorable terms to Lorris by King Louis VII contrasted with the County of Champagne wherein serfdom remained more prevalent.[76] When the kings acquired new territories in Poitou, Normandy, and the Midi, they solidified urban loyalty by granting the burghers generous privileges and liberties.[77] Even where the king was not yet established, he would intervene in affairs beyond the royal domain by offering towns protection.[78]

Kings thus faired particularly well by pursuing urban tutelage, and kings were well aware of their advantages. John Baldwin describes how Philip Augustus chartered seventy-four towns during his reign. Chartering did not always entail forming new towns but also the granting of specific urban liberties and customs to existing ones. "Recognizing the importance of the growing urban communities produced by the upswing of commercial activity in the early twelfth century, these kings issued charters to towns throughout the northern half of France."[79] Elizabeth Hallam confirms Baldwin's observations: "Often such successes [of communes seeking independence from overlords] were gained initially by an appeal to the king for support. . . . The territorial princes and the king profited from the communal movement as far as they could."[80]

From the thirteenth century onward, revenue started to flow increasingly from new monetary sources rather than from traditional agrarian incomes.[81] Thus the taille that Philip Augustus collected was predominantly from the towns, not from peasants. Towns and commerce produced about 20 percent of total ordinary income, with most of this coming from the tailles. The agricultural domain still produced most of the income, about 50 percent of total ordinary income, through farm produce and tolls. Church and justice only contributed 5 percent and 7 percent respectively, with a host of other categories making up for the rest.[82]

When the political bargain broke down or did not yield sufficient results, the French kings would divert the burden to groups who were not crucial to his objectives. Properties and money of Jews were confiscated, or the Jews were taxed inexorably. Defaulting on loans from Italian bankers was another remedy. Philip the Fair accused, imprisoned, and executed the Templars who had acted as the Treasury after he had defaulted on loans from Italian bankers. Their goods became part of royal revenue. Such strategies were, however, onetime actions. Likewise the debasement of coinage was a practice that could only yield momentary benefits. Unlike confiscation of the properties of differentiated groups such as Jews or Templars, debasement of coinage proved to be

TABLE 5.3
Some Estimates of Annual French Royal Revenue[a]

Reign	Revenue	Year
Louis VII (1137–1180)	30–60,000 l.p.	no year
	60,000 l.p.	no year
	228,000 l.p.[b]	no year
Philip Augustus (1180–1223)	100–103,000 l.p.	1202
	228,000 l.p. approx.	1228
Louis IX (1226–1270)	200–250,000 l.p.	1250
	250,000 l.t.	no year
Philip the Fair (1285–1314)	450,000 l.p.	1290
	550,000 l.t.	no year
	650,000 l.p.	1290s

Sources: Hallam, Capetian France, pp. 167, 292; Dunbabin, France in the Making, p. 298; Baldwin, The Government of Philip Augustus, p. 152f.; Jordan, Louis IX, p. 79; Given, State and Society, p. 135; Strayer, The Reign of Philip the Fair, p. 258, particularly note 59.

[a] These figures should be treated with great caution. Extraordinary revenues, such as feudal reliefs and revenue from tithes for Crusades, might have greatly altered these estimates in certain years. Where no year is given, the revenue is a suggested average for that reign. Four livres parisis (l.p.) equal 5 livres tournois (l.t.). Strayer, The Reign of Philip the Fair, p. xvii.

[b] This very high estimate is from Fawtier, Capetian Kings of France, p. 100.

highly unpopular and encountered social opposition. Philip the Fair had to cease the practice.[83] Thus, periodic revenue-raising methods were dramatic, but at the heart of the basic revenue process lay a social coalition of commoners and kingship with more regularized means of taxation. Although there was no direct royal tax over the kingdom by the end of the Capetian reign, the Capetian kings had, through changes in the nature of taxation and exactions, laid the basis for its introduction shortly thereafter. Strayer believes that Philip the Fair was the first king to impose general taxes.[84] Overall, the monarchy gradually expanded its general revenue intake. A very rough set of estimates is suggestive of an upward trend (see Table 5.3).

Tax Exemption and Pensions for the Nobility

Being a vassal meant that one had to aid his lord in military service. Each vassal had to bring a certain amount of men to the field. Usually the fixed period for such service was about forty days. Special regulations pertained to the Crusades which, of course, necessitated more time.

Increasingly from the twelfth century onward, the king or great lords to whom service was due would accept monetary compensation in lieu of service, the payment of scutage.[85] This could be paid at any level of the military order. The higher the feudal rank, the higher the payment due since one not only had to substitute service for oneself but also for one's subordinate vassals and their knights. This was a deviation of feudalism proper since it replaced service in-kind with a monetary payment by vassals. As a consequence, by enabling the king and high lords to obtain mercenaries, the warrior aristocracy eroded the very basis of its existence.

A second deviation from feudalism was, in turn, monetary payment by the king for specific services. In the traditional feudal system, vassals put their military skills at the disposal of their overlord. In return, the overlord granted them land, titles, and shares in the spoils of war. Once rewarded, the king effectively lost control over these vassals. However, as the king built up a centralized administration, he paid his men in money. As Strayer points out, Philip the Fair established fixed sums of payment and pensions after service. The royal administration thus became an attractive source of employment for the middle- and lower-range aristocrats. They performed administrative, judicial, military, and financial tasks. But they did this on the basis of payment rather than exchange military service for land.

With troops at his disposal to whom he need not forfeit land, the king had increasingly less reason to require powerful lords such as the Counts of Foix or Champagne to serve militarily and bring troops to the field. Moreover, it was questionable whether the king had the capability to enforce obligations on powerful dukes and counts. Rather than rely on those who by feudal theory were his vassals, but in fact were his rivals, the king preferred to acquire military service by payment.[86] This was another reason why towns were important for royal objectives. The towns provided troops through the military levy and provided revenue for mercenaries.[87]

Rather than confront the high lords, the king sought to appease them by sharing the proceeds of centralization. In some cases kings would grant considerable pensions and rents to nobles to accede to royal demands or dissuade them from forming alliances against him. For example, nobles who resided in areas that became part of the royal domain would receive pensions of several hundred pounds and were thus pulled into the royal orbit.[88] Philip the Fair paid the duke of Brabant a pension of 2500 l.t. (livres tournois) to remain neutral and not aid the Count of Flanders who was in rebellion. He offered the Count of Hainaut 6000 l.t. annual rent.[89] To put it bluntly, money bought allies. Nobles also routinely received a percentage of tax receipts for their area. When the royal taille became increasingly regularized from the 1380s onward, the clergy and nobility were exempted. This was to be the French system for the next few centuries. "The direct tax system of seventeenth century France was largely in place by 1379."[90] This is one of the reasons why representation never became as important as in England. The French nobility took little interest in the meetings of the estates.[91] They were appeased by their tax exemption and pension schemes.

In short, the French king was too weak to tax the nobles. Instead he obtained revenues from other sources and bought noble acquiescence by tax exemption or outright payments.

The End of a Beautiful Friendship: Paris Confronts Rome

The church had acquired considerable holdings throughout the Middle Ages. Indeed, in some sense we might regard the monasteries of Europe as the innovators in agricultural production.[92] The church's wealth was also due to its control of wills and marriages. Such acts required oaths taken before God and were thus under the exclusive jurisdiction of the church. To secure salvation, people would often include the church in their wills. Because they could guarantee the validity of oaths, and signed documents in general, the clergy were natural notaries. They were, for example, witnesses for royal edicts. It is obvious, then, that the church must have appeared as a lucrative revenue source for aggrandizing kings and lords.

The kings of France were able to extract considerable revenue from the church. Initially this was possible because the papacy and the Capetian kings were allies. Indeed, the church recognized the right of the king to nominate certain bishops and derive revenue from those bishoprics.[93] Eventually, however, the principle of royal sovereignty and the transterritorial jurisdiction of the church clashed. When that confrontation finally came, after the Capetian kings had already made significant inroads into consolidating the realm, the king of France emerged victorious.

There were historical and theoretical justifications for secular taxation of the clergy. Taxes raised for the "defense of the faith" accorded with church policy. Such taxes were upheld by the theory of the just war.[94] In its starkest form, a just war might consist of a crusade against enemies of the faith—Muslims or heretics. The most common type of taxation was payment of the tenth. That is, a payment of ten percent of the value of moveables in possession of the church. The pope could motivate secular rulers to embark on crusades to the Holy Land by making such sources of revenue available. It should be clear, without denying the religious motives of kings and high nobility, that one way to obtain considerable amounts of revenue was to take up the cross.[95]

The granting of ecclesiastical taxes allowed the pope to acquire allies against his spiritual and secular enemies alike. The papacy supported the buildup of centralized kingdoms in order to form a counterweight to the secular challenges by the German emperor and the Normans in southern Italy. Indeed, after the Germans had acceded to the Norman state through marriage alliances, it was the French, with papal support, who displaced the Germans in southern Italy in the middle of the thirteenth century. The French king was also a useful ally in combatting heretical movements such as those of the Cathars in southern France.

Conversely the king also needed the church for a variety of reasons. The church offered institutional resources besides revenue. It was a model of efficient hierarchical organization which collected revenue from faraway parishes. It also managed to dispense authority by an effective administrative machinery. And, most important perhaps, the clergy were men of knowledge who could be used within the royal bureaucracy. Thus, the chancellor was, from the end of the Carolingian Empire until Philip Augustus's reign, a member of the clergy. In return for such service, the king would often grant his clerks a small benefice and perhaps a pension. In accepting, they would become nominal vassals of the king. For clerical members, service to the king was also a stepping stone in the administration of the church. In an environment where church and secular authority sought each other's support, clerks who worked as liaisons made rapid promotion. Finally, the church was an attractive ally to the king because it could even provide military resources. In 1194, for example, twenty monasteries provided the king with 1,500 sergeants.[96]

The church was also important for the king for legitimacy. The church had the juridical ability to absolve oaths between vassals and an excommunicated member of the church. Excommunication was thus a powerful tool because it released lords from their formal duty to abide by the oath they took to serve the king. As long as the king sought legitimacy as the highest overlord in the feudal hierarchy, he needed the church's sanction.

In conclusion, the alliance of pope and king was beneficial to both actors in many ways. The pope gained a secular defender to carry out the task of Rome. The king gained a source of revenue, able administration, and basis for legitimation. And so it is not surprising to see Louis IX (1226–1270), crusader in Egypt, Montaillou, and Tunisia, become St. Louis, blessed by the church.

Despite all the benefits that cooperation between church and king yielded, however, their alliance was ultimately based on divergent interests. At the heart of the king's endeavor lay an attempt to obtain sole control over the resources within his domain and to expand the area of that domain. This clashed with the church's claim of jurisdiction over all clerical affairs and of ultimate superiority over rulers on secular matters as well. "The Church never accepted the royal right to tax as a matter of principle."[97] The breach between pope and king came only one generation after St. Louis. It was his own son, Philip IV, Philip the Fair, who brought matters to a head.

The conflict started with the war in Acquitaine. Ever since Eleanor of Acquitaine had married the English king in 1152, Acquitaine had been under English control. In 1294, Philip the Fair sought to raise an army and invade it. In order to do so, he imposed taxes on the church under his territorial control. The pope decided that this was not a war to defend the faith, nor a case of legitimate self-defense. Hence he decided that no clerical duties were due. This became the first conflict between Philip and Boniface VIII.

Boniface excommunicated Philip and ordered the important French prelates to come to the pope for counsel. Contrary to the pope's expectations, many of the French prelates did not come. They feared a loss of their benefices should they go to the pope. The fortunes of the French monasteries, bishoprics, and parishes depended more on good relations with the French secular authority, which was close at hand, than on the distant dictates of the pope.

The pope soon came to realize how badly he needed secular support. The king forbade any revenues from the ecclesiastical authorities in France to leave the country. This hurt the pope since the revenues from France were the most important source of finance for papal opposition to the German emperor. To make things worse, the pope's legitimacy was called into question by powerful opponents in Italy. The pope, therefore, had to yield. Philip's army then occupied Acquitaine.[98]

Six years later a similar conflict occurred. Once again Philip the Fair sought to expand his domain by force. This time it was Flanders that opposed the king. And again Philip imposed taxes in opposition to the church's wishes. Against all odds, the Flemish decimated the king's men near Courtrai.[99] Simultaneous with this defeat occurred a conflict over final jurisdiction. In 1300 a bishop in Languedoc, Bernard Saisset, had been arrested on grounds of treason, blasphemy, and insulting the king. Despite being a bishop and thus only subject to canon law, he was tried by royal officials and thrown into jail. This represented an important assertion that the king had supreme jurisdiction, even over members of the clergy. The pope rescinded his earlier compromise, "Etsi De Statu," made in 1297 after the conflict over Acquitaine, and months of mutual accusations followed. Finally the pope summoned the French prelates to come to Rome in the fall of 1302.

Claiming a national emergency because of Courtrai, Philip refused to let them go. Only half of the summoned prelates disobeyed Philip, which demonstrated the divided loyalties of the local clergy.[100] Pope Boniface, enraged by this defiance and perhaps encouraged by the king's setbacks in Flanders, thereupon issued the famous papal bull "Unam Sanctam": there was but one authority sanctioned by God. Secular authority was subject to the religious authority. The pope's solution to the Gelasian theory of the two swords was thus not a reconciliation of the two but a clear advancement of supremacy of the church over ecclesiastical and temporal matters. In short, sovereign authority and universalist claims clashed head-on.

In the final act of this drama, Nogaret, an advisor to the king, left for Italy with his troops. He colluded with the domestic opposition of the pope, the Colonni, and took the pope prisoner at his summer residence. The pope was soon released but apparently died of shock two weeks later. The subjection of the papacy to Paris was symbolized by the move of the papacy to Avignon, just outside the French realm but well within the Capetian's sphere of influence.[101]

Philip's argument was not with the church per se. Indeed, we have already noted that the clergy, like the nobility later, became officially exempt from the royal taille. The king's strategy was directed against the limitation of his sovereignty by an authority outside the kingdom, which had denied him access to revenue and which denied him supreme jurisdictionary power on all matters within the kingdom. "As for the two powers with claims to world domain, the empire and the papacy, each of them was pursuing an ideal which could not be in accordance with the particular ideas of the kings of France."[102] Philip argued that there were kings before popes, hence popes could not be superior. Unlike the German emperor, the French kings had the means to back up their claims.

The Benefits of Royal Administration

For the early Capetians, private household and public administration were virtually synonymous. The king's personal staff were at the same time his important advisors. The butler, master of the stables, and chamberlain were not merely his personal helpers but were influential in policy making; "the King's court, the centre of government was nothing but an enlarged household."[103] As the kingdom expanded, the inner cohort increased in size. Nevertheless, the inner sanctum of personal advisors, the Curia Regis (council of the king), did not differentiate itself by functions. It remained a nonspecialized council consisting of the king's entourage.

Scarcely three centuries after the ascent of the Capetian Dynasty, however, royal administration consisted of distinct departments. These were functionally specialized and oversaw provincial field agents on a regular basis. Taxation, judiciary, police, and military functions had to a considerable extent been centralized and affected the activities of society on a regular basis.

The growth and nature of centralized administration reveal the strategy of the king to extend his power. Royal administration provided the king with the ability to carry out an antifeudal policy through professional agents who were less inclined to pursuing their own interests than vassals who were remunerated in-kind.[104] The administration also provided the bourgeois with career opportunities, standardized rule, and adjudication, while simultaneously allowing for local bargaining and input from the third estate.

The extension of royal administration took place in roughly four phases.[105] The logic behind each particular type of administration reveals the constraints under which kings had to work, the reasons why they favored particular types of administration over others, and how each different structure reflected the social alignments of the period.

The Capetian kings did not operate in a historical vacuum. In many ways their bureaucracy reflected similar administrative processes of the fifth century. The Merovingian kings sent out general field agents (pagi), who were often rewarded with land grants since coinage had became scarce after the Roman retreat.[106] Charlemagne reversed this process. Because of centralization and stability, currency came back into use and the field agents could be paid rather than rewarded with land.[107] These were not permanent or hereditary positions. To ensure that his orders were obeyed, the emperor sent personal supervisors into the field (missi dominici). These supervisors spoke on his behalf. That is, they represented the emperor with full powers and traveled the provinces in his capacity. After Charlemagne, the system rapidly fell into disuse. As discussed earlier, feudalism proper formally established itself. Administratively this meant that the pagi, the emperor's representatives, consolidated themselves into larger counties or duchies which in turn were subinfeuded to viscounts. All of these offices became hereditary and factually independent entities.

From this weak basis the Capetians set out to establish an effective bureaucracy. In the early Capetian administration, the kings sent out provosts (prévôts), general field officers.[108] They were supposed to raise revenue, perform judicial functions, and keep the peace. Such provostships were farmed offices; entrepreneurs entered bids for the provost position of certain territories.[109]

The interests of provosts and king were in many ways compatible. Because the income of the provostship, which gradually became a hereditary post, depended on the proceeds he managed to raise, the provost was always eager to extend his control over more taxable subjects. Thus the provost encroached upon actors outside the domain who were nominally subject to the king but factually independent. Within the kingdom they opposed exemptions for social groups such as the church. In so doing they furthered the interests of the king who likewise wanted to expand the domain.

In the second phase, around the latter part of the twelfth century, the Capetian kings started to exert more influence over their field agents. They sent itinerant, generalist supervisors into the field. Partially influenced by the Norman efficiency of administration and the Carolingian notion of missi dominici, the kings established bailiffs (baillis). In the more recently acquired areas of the kingdom they were called seneschals.[110]

Again the logic of this administrative order is illustrative of the deeper purposes of the French kings. First, the bailiffs were appointed to control provost abuse of their position and to make sure enough of the revenues came through. Moreover, bailiffs were to control various provostships which were aggregated into bailiwicks. With this larger administrative unit, the bailiffs could claim jurisdiction in feudal disputes between lords whose areas laid within the bailiwick. For that reason, Fesler has called this a deliberate antifeudal strategy. Lastly, the bailiffs were generalists who duplicated the royal presence in the field.[111]

In the third phase of extension of royal administration, at the beginning of the thirteenth century, bailiffs were permanently stationed in particular areas. Because of the expansion of the domain, itinerant bailiffs proved to be less effective. Moreover, on-site permanence may have enhanced their ability to supervise the provosts. The thirteenth century thus saw the establishment of a real centralized bureaucracy. The number of bailiwicks doubled during that century to about two dozen, with each of them comprising three to sixteen provostships. (Estimates vary because different regions were organized differently.)

The bailiffs maintained their generalist character. They represented the king in the field and were thus the highest officials outside Paris. They raised revenue, or rather they were the hierarchical superiors of the provosts. They sat as judges and performed police and military functions. The bailiffs acted as the court of the king acted, and their salaries were compatible with the advisors to the king in Paris.

The recruitment pattern of the bailiffs further demonstrates the antifeudal strategy of the king. Initially the clergy played an important role as royal administrators. However, they could not function as bailiffs. Members of the clergy could not fulfill the military functions required of bailiffs, nor could they pass blood sentence, for example, the death penalty. In addition, bailiffs could not be recruited from higher nobility, for bailiffs were the king's instruments against his political rivals. They were therefore recruited from the bourgeoisie and lower nobility. "They were normally laymen, often of bourgeois or lesser knightly origin rather than noble families."[112] Jean Dunbabin stresses the importance of nonpersonal ties in such administration. The bourgeois were, furthermore, preferred administrators because they were literate and numerate.[113] Business knowledge was applicable to running a government.

Bailiffs were not indigenous to the areas they supervised. To prevent them from being captured by local interests, they were assigned from the outside. Thus the seneschals, the bailiffs in the south who controlled relatively new areas, were usually brought in from the north. They were rotated every three to four years, could not marry local inhabitants, and could not acquire property in the areas they administered.[114]

For individuals entering into such high office, this meant career service.[115] They were correspondingly rewarded by high pay. Bailiffs would receive from 365 to 700 l.t. a year.[116] Pensions were considerable.[117] Unlike administrators rewarded by feudal land grants, royal administrators were continually dependent on monetary rewards from Paris.

The bailiffs continued to oversee the lower officials. They acted as the link between center and the lesser ranks. These lesser ranks did, in contradistinction to their superiors, have local roots.[118] Often they were indigenous to the area of administration. This, too, was a felicitous way of organizing. Recall from our discussion on taxation that much bargaining took place on local levels. Regional estates were more important than the estates general. Furthermore, local officials who had resided in that area were more knowledgeable of its customs. Prior to the ascendence of Roman law, customary law was still important, particularly in the north where Roman influence had been less strong.

The activities of bailiffs and king mirrored each other. As the king sat in Paris and mediated and judged particular issues on many areas, so the bailiffs represented the king as generalists and exercised regalian authority with the help of the lesser ranks of administration. But just as the center, the Curia Regis, was gradually specialized between the middle of the twelfth century and the end of the thirteenth, so too were the bailiffs increasingly replaced by functionally specialized agents. The end of generalist agents came at approximately the beginning of the fourteenth century. This was the fourth phase in the development of French field administration.[119]

The reasons for specialization were several. For one, the Curia Regis was gradually differentiated into Parlement, Privy Council, Chamber of Accounts, and Chancery. Hence, the bailiff was from then on supervised by various organs. Furthermore, increasing specialization eroded the position of the bailiff. For example, required knowledge of Roman law led to his replacement by the juges-maires. The increasing desire for control by the center led to reintroduction of touring supervisors, the enquêteur-réformateurs, now ironically to supervise the bailiffs, who were once itinerant supervisors themselves.[120]

To conclude, royal administration was based on and provided opportunities to bourgeois and lesser nobility. "In short, the royal administration was a service which attracted Frenchmen of the middle classes because it offered them a path to wealth, position, and rank."[121] Elizabeth Hallam makes similar observations: "As the great officials declined in power, the kings drew more and more on men of low birth to carry out routine administrative tasks."[122] In this increasing process of rationalized, central administration, higher nobility and clergy were less important, if not outright targets of royal agents.

This administrative system was not simply the reflection of increasing division of labor in society at large. Instead, the internal structure of the administration, and the goals of that administration, reflect a compatibility of bourgeois interests and royal policy.

> Philip Augustus II was certainly a true friend of the French bourgeoisie. There were internal reasons for the connection. The royal system of government with its well-paid officials stood much closer to the bourgeois world than to the feudal one which it was to supersede. . . . He also called upon the bourgeoisie to carry out state duties on a grand scale, by giving it a share in the general governmental duties of the country.[123]

In turn, the king benefited by having a professional and remunerated bureaucracy. No doubt the improved financial position of the king depended directly on the ability to raise revenue (see the discussion above on taxation). This allowed the king to remunerate his officials rather than reward them with in-kind transfers, particularly land grants.[124] This ability to pay officials increased the loyalty of the king's officers, since these positions did not provide the same security as feudal land grants which quickly became hereditary. Consequently, remuneration halted the decentralizing tendencies caused by the granting of lands in return for feudal service.

SHARED PERSPECTIVES AND SOCIAL COALITIONS

John Ruggie has rightly pointed out that the transformation from feudal rule to that of the sovereign, territorial state involved an important epistemic shift.[125] The transformation did not merely entail a change in who exercised power; it redefined what was to count as power and as legitimate rule. The origins of late medieval ideas, such as public authority rather than personal rule, the position of the king as fountain of law, and the concept of exclusive authority over goods and land, are highly complex and difficult to trace. We can describe the content of such ideas and present a history of their development, but we have not thereby explained their inception.[126] Therefore, I do not engage in that enterprise. However, following up on the discussion in Chapter 4, I will suggest how some of these ideas, particularly the idea of sovereign authority, became empowered and routinized in late medieval France.

I argue that the social ideals of the bourgeois and the transformation of the institutional order that the towns envisioned corresponded with the views of the Capetians. They had similar views regarding authority and justice. They particularly had a mutual preference for written, Roman law. This was not merely an alternative institutional preference but a conceptual reorientation of what should count as proof and truth. Such reorientation was complex and included clashes on collective versus private property; personal rule and public authority; divine versus secular law; and the challenge of territorial rule to universalist actors.

Early rulers had legitimated themselves as discoverers of law. Greek leaders justified their authority as interpreters of the nomoi, existing norms which only had to be discovered. Similarly, Macedonian kings legitimated their rule by claiming divine status which gave them access to hidden perennial truths. Laws were timeless, divine revelations. They were revealed, rather than made, by those with special status.

The idea that the law originated from the emperor was uniquely Roman. The Romans, however, did not completely develop the modern concept of sovereignty. They developed a notion of internal sovereignty but not of external sovereignty. They did not confer juridical equivalence to other states so that sovereignty could become a principle of international conduct.[127] Furthermore, the Roman emperor was above the law, but his position did not have the status of an abstract public office. He was not a lawgiver in the modern sense, but it was his personal capacity as emperor that made him fountainhead of laws.

Late medieval kings and emperors returned to this body of law to enhance their position vis-à-vis their rivals. Particularly influential in the later Middle Ages was the Codex Justinianus, the codification of Roman law by the Byzantine emperor Justinian in the sixth century. In the twelfth century, the archbishop of Milan used that codex to argue for the benefit of the Holy Roman Emperor, Frederick Barbarossa: "What pleases the prince, has the power of law."[128]

French kings were quick to note that they too were princes. Hence they justified their rule as the sole legitimate authority of adjudication and law making. Scarcely a century later, around 1250, we therefore find the dictum "The King of France is prince in his realm, since he recognizes no superior in temporal affairs."[129] That is, the claim of the Holy Roman Emperor that he was supreme fountainhead of all laws was now claimed by the king in his realm. Contrary to the religious view and the view of Aquinas that human law was a manifestation of divine law, the king advanced the idea that law was created and made by mortals.[130] This changed ecclesiastical kingship into jurisprudential kingship. The king became the embodiment of law: *Lex est Rex*, "the king is the law."[131]

The church initially supported the claims of the French king. The pope, after all, needed royal support against the German emperor.[132] Moreover, at that time the king only seemed to claim sovereignty in temporal affairs. Because of this recognition, the French king was able to draw on the support of the church to a much larger extent than the dukes and counts surrounding his domain. Hence, the support of the church for the king was an important factor in the early formation of the concept of sovereignty.

Ultimately, however, this notion of sovereignty was at odds with the concept of universal authority—as we have already seen in the clashes of Philip the Fair and Boniface. Although a completely developed theory of sovereignty only emerged with Bodin in the sixteenth century, the idea had taken hold during the last Capetians. The idea of sovereignty as internal hierarchy and external demarcation had spread over the kingdom, not just the royal domain, by the thirteenth century.[133] After Boniface's defeat, the pope officially conceded the de facto independence of the king. "The bull Rex Gloriae marked the emergence of the King of France as complete sovereign of his kingdom."[134]

The choice of the king to favor Roman law and society's willingness to accept that as a basis of authority signified more than simply institutional preferences; it indicated a staggering shift in beliefs. First, Roman law was radically different from the earlier personalized legal systems of the Gothic and Frankish tribes, and it differed from the particularism induced by feudalism. Lawyers' arguments became based on abstract equity before the law; the law was a text above party and society.[135]

Second, the reliance on written law rather than custom required a profound switch from relying on immediacy of exchange to abstract ties.[136] Written law was suspect because it could be tampered with, unlike sworn oaths or divine justice which manifested themselves through trial by combat or ordeal. Moreover, given that writing was solely the province of members of the clergy, its accessibility to commoners was limited and hence distrusted. The emerging mercantile interests, by contrast, required exactly the abstraction and certitude that were absent in the old feudal order. Written law fit in the context of the burghers' literate and numerate understanding of the world.

Third, the idea of exclusive authority over territorial space corresponded with the definition of property rights in Roman law. The early feudal era, by contrast, lacked such well-defined property rights. The medieval idea of possession, seisin, was embedded in a network of overlapping rights and claims. Moreover, the content of Christian doctrine was biased against private property.[137] Roman law, by contrast, granted to the owner exclusive use and rights. This, coupled with the king's claim to final jurisdiction,[138] led to increased royal preoccupation with the specification of property rights.[139] In addition, Roman law, in contrast to canon law, permitted interest charges.[140] In short, the adoption of Roman law had important ramifications for the conduct of business.

Fourth, Roman law also entailed a different view of what was to count as proof and evidence. It favored written documents and fact finding rather than trial by ordeal or combat.[141] Consequently, Louis IX outlawed trial by ordeal and combat in the middle of the thirteenth century.[142] The Capetian kings also passed ordinances against the private feud, judicial duels, and recognized evidence by witnesses and written charter as proof.[143]

Moreover, against localized customs, Roman law posited that there was only one source of law, the written law emanating from the king. "Against the tendencies which would have subordinated the royal authority to feudal law and custom, the administration more or less consciously set Roman law."[144] Given that the land of the droit coutumier, the North which followed customary law, had about three hundred different customs, standardization was highly important for some measure of legal certitude.[145]

The alliance of bourgeois and kingship had, therefore, an important ideological dimension. The legal framework, and ideological legitimation favored by the king, fit the perspectives of the bourgeois better than the medieval mentality favored by nobility and church. Instead of structuring authority through personal ties and lineage, kings and burghers favored authority structured by territorial boundaries. In sum, both king and burghers favored the adoption of a centralized and formalized legal structure based on Roman law. They were both antifeudal and anticlerical.[146] Both benefited from the existence of an exact locus of authority. The emergence of the sovereign state involved a transfer of loyalties to a secular state at the expense of local dynasts and the church.[147]

I have highlighted these ideological facets of the development of the French state because they explain why the towns would support the king and how towns and kings recognized that they also had an affinity of material interests besides similar ideological views.[148] Moreover, an account based solely on similar material interests of king and towns does not fully capture the content of their coalition or explain why it remained so durable. The development of the sovereign state involved a leap of faith, or perhaps more accurately a loss of faith, for both king and burghers were willing to abandon beliefs in divine justice and many other norms and principles that laid at the basis of the traditional medieval order.

CONCLUSION

The emergence of a sovereign, territorial state in France was not due to changes in the nature of military force. The foundation of the sovereign state had been laid prior to the military revolutions of the fifteenth and sixteenth centuries. Nor could the kings of France claim any specific authority as protectors of the realm, given that the Capetian Dynasty was quite weak compared to some of their rival lords. Indeed, "foreign" policy of the king initially consisted primarily of diplomacy and warfare with the lords within the kingdom.[149] Since these lords de facto provided defense of the common weal in their lordships, people did not see the king as the defender of the realm.[150]

Instead, the king's power grew as a result of support from the burghers for royal policy.[151] Because of the expanding market, townspeople were in search of alternative political institutions more conducive to commerce and their way of life. Royal and bourgeois interests converged on the issues of taxation and administration, and they shared similar belief systems. Regular tax revenue was of great importance for royal policy because it allowed the king to weaken the old feudal order. His increased monetary capability also allowed the king to appease the nobility and clergy through side payments of pensions, tax exemptions, and rents.

In return the king offered burghers communal liberties which freed many people from feudal servitude. In addition, the King's standardization of tax procedures benefited the commercial interests of the burghers. These taxes, furthermore, were levied through local bargaining procedures which allowed both town patriciate and king to negotiate on its incidence level. This bargaining procedure enhanced quasi-compliance. That is to say, by giving the burghers a modest say in the taxation process, the king was assured that shirking would be less than when taxes were raised solely through duress.

Closely related to the king's ability to tax was an antifeudal and anticlerical mode of administration. Remunerated officials continued to be dependent on the king, in contrast to the fragmentary effects of in-kind transfers such as land grants. But the royal policy was also deliberately antifeudal in that the king devised a system wherein his officials, such as tax farmers and bailiffs, had their own incentives to expand the power of the king at the cost of his rivals. Tax farmers were continuously interested in expanding their share of the tax receipts. Moreover, by moving his higher officials around, the king managed to exert control without having his officials captured by local interests. The king guaranteed the loyalty of his officials by generous salaries and pension systems. For the burghers, this system of administration provided the possibility of local input in the decision-making process. Furthermore, it standardized the administration of justice. Although local customs were still taken into account, the administration became increasingly specialized and controlled from Paris. All this provided for more certainty in the mercantile environment of the bourgeois.[152] Finally, the royal administration created career incentives for bourgeois and lesser nobility. Higher nobility and members of the church meanwhile became less relevant to royal administration.

The French king and the burghers also had different sets of beliefs and social ideas than the church and aristocracy. Against the personal ties of feudalism, merchants posed the depersonalized relation of the written contract. Against customary law and trial by ordeal, they posed Roman law with its well-defined notions of private property, codification, interest charges, and trial by evidence. The development of literacy and the spread of knowledge—at the expense of the church's monopoly—were actively encouraged by both king and towns. Both, for example, favored language in the vernacular and the foundation of universities.[153] The king also favored a change in the legal order. He used Roman law with its notion of sovereignty to counteract universal claims by other political actors, particularly the pope. Although the king on occasion utilized feudal theory to justify an enhancement of power, the notion of sovereign authority, circumscribed by territorial markers, was logically different from the personal bonds of feudal authority. The king's authority was increasingly depersonalized and based on his public role as the maker of law with supreme jurisdiction. It is only, then, after France had embarked on a path of sovereign, territorial rule that the king could become the logical protector of the realm and justify higher taxes for its protection.

Given the nature of side payments to the nobility, one might entertain the view that the rise of the French monarchy was based on a political alliance between king and nobility, with the aim of saving the feudal system. I cannot endorse that view. No doubt the nobility did well in terms of the French pension system and tax exemption.[154] Aristocratic privileges continued well into the eighteenth century and were only brought to an end by the French Revolution. Such accounts wish to denote the political outcome of Capetian centralization as "feudal" in order to place this in a theoretical framework of sequential economic stages.

But the strategy of the French king was antagonistic to feudalism as a political mode of rule. That is, the king explicitly sought to reduce political fragmentation of the French realm. He strove to make French politics ultimately subject to royal control and to act as the sole representative of the French kingdom in international affairs.[155] He obtained this objective by pursuing policies that met the approval of the burghers and towns. The many privileges that the aristocracy maintained until the French Revolution were hardly the same as the large political autonomy of the lords before the success of the Capetian kings. Before the Capetian consolidation, some great lords could call their territories *regna*—kingdoms in their own right; after the consolidation, they merely had privileges.

Furthermore, the attempt of some of these accounts to put towns within the feudal order is not convincing.[156] I have suggested in this chapter that towns were basically antagonistic to the feudal aristocracy. What is puzzling is that neo-Marxist accounts admit this but nevertheless wish to place towns within feudalism.[157] The alliance between king and towns is best demonstrated by the fact that during the baronial revolts of 1242 and 1314–1325, the towns remained loyal to the king against the aristocracy.[158] A variety of historians believe that this continued beyond the Capetians.[159] Blockmans suggests that this alliance continued into the fifteenth century, and Chevalier extends it even further until the Wars of Religion of the mid-sixteenth century. Parker notes that even during these wars the towns would not ally with the nobles against the king.[160] In short, I maintain that the political fragmentation of the French kingdom had basically come to an end by the late thirteenth century, in no small part because of the alliance of king and towns.

In this chapter I have tried to suggest which material forces and coalitions gave rise to the sovereign state. I have also discussed the underlying conceptual frameworks of different social actors. These facilitated the formation of a social coalition between burghers and king. But they also suggest how the later conceptual development of the "sovereign state" could take hold. Individuals, of course, did not consciously set out to design the abstract notion of the "state."

But in pursuing their own material and ideological interests, they laid the basis for its development and the later emergence of a system of states. Elsewhere, however, individuals developed other institutional arrangements such as the German city-leagues and the Italian city-states. These were likewise responses to the growth of a market economy, but institutionally they were quite different in nature. For a considerable amount of time, it seemed that they, not the sovereign state, were the wave of the future.

The Fragmentation of the German Empire and the Rise of the Hanseatic League

> All the same, and notwithstanding serious economic setbacks in the late Middle
> Ages, the Hanse was to fight and negotiate, often on all fronts at once, over long
> periods, and with remarkable resilience and success. . . . It could put armies in
> the field. . . . And it could deal, on more than equal terms, with sovereign states.[1]

THE POLITICAL developments of Germany formed the antithesis to that of
France. In France the king allied with the burghers, made side payments to the
aristocracy, and established a considerable measure of centralized and hierarchical control. The German king, by contrast, favored the lords at the expense
of the towns. Forced to fend for themselves, the towns formed city-leagues to
protect their interests against the lords. The result was that Germany's future,
after the middle of the thirteenth century, was determined by a combination of
lordships, independent towns, and city-leagues. Under the nominal authority
of the emperor, lords and towns vied for real control.

The Hansa proved to be the most important of these leagues (see Map 6.1).
It exerted a unifying force beyond, and against, the local jurisdictions of the
lords. This confederation of towns emerged as an alternative institutional solution to the sovereign state and performed many functions that elsewhere were
carried out by sovereign monarchy. The league waged war, raised revenue,
signed treaties, and regulated economic activity.

I have argued in the preceding chapters that the institutional development
of the Late Middle Ages must be explained by the political and social alliances
of kings, lords, church, and towns. Kings and towns in France, for example,
developed a political alliance based on shared interests and similar ideological
perspectives. In Germany political coalitions worked out quite differently despite the fact that German towns had roughly similar interests and perspectives
as their French counterparts. In contrast to the French king, the German king,
who was also the Holy Roman Emperor, opted for a policy against the towns.[2]
Instead he sought support from the dukes and ecclesiastical lords, in order to
pursue imperial control of Italy, and granted them control over the towns. This
strategy proved to be a failure. The German king gradually lost all real authority
to the German lords. The ensuing history of Germany is therefore one of weak
kings and strong feudal lords. The dukes and counts struggled in turn with
towns that sought independence. The explanation of German political development revolves around this axis of lord-town opposition.

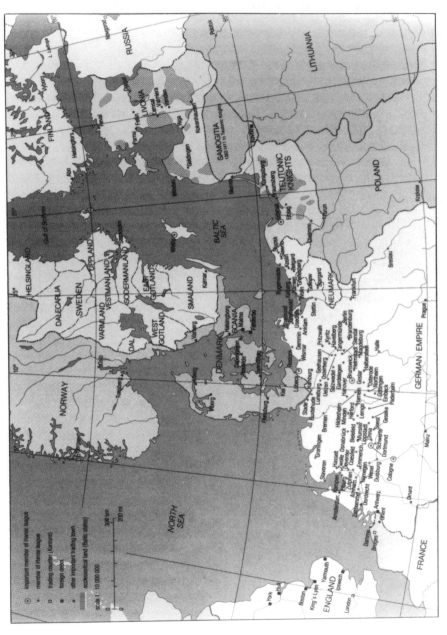

6.1 The Hanseatic League (Source: Donald Matthew, *Atlas of Medieval Europe*. New York: Facts on File, 1983, p. 128.)

Germany thus went through a highly particularized development quite unlike the gradual development of the French sovereign state. The French story is one of centralization and gradual establishment of sovereign authority in a juridical and factual sense. The German story is one of dissipation. It evolved into a confusing pattern of multiple authorities where juridical status and factual independence seldom matched. Although the Holy Roman Empire continued to exist in name until 1806, central authority was not really established until Germany's unification under Bismarck.[3] Power had shifted to the duchies and other lords, and to the cities and city-leagues which sometimes were juridical subjects but factually independent.[4] Although it is true that the empire regained some of its lost power during the Hapsburgs of Austria, the empire in fact remained a set of independent principalities. Even Charles V, who had vast resources under his control and who united the Spanish and Austrian holdings, had to pay large sums of money to these lords to obtain their approval.[5] The Reformation and Thirty Years War simply reinforced the fragmentation that had started centuries earlier.

The German case, more than any other, dispels any notions of unilinear explanations of state development. Since German development was so starkly different from the development of the sovereign state in France, one cannot argue that states developed solely as responses to changes in the overall environment. Arguments that feudal organization "had to" give way to larger territorial states, because of changes in the character of warfare, or because of shifts in belief systems, fail to explain variation in outcomes. Germany, like France, was exposed to the developments in military technology of that time, and individuals also had access to different sets of ideas which could legitimate authority on more abstract bases, such as Roman law. Indeed, the German emperor was one of the first to pioneer and foster the concept of sovereignty and the role of the monarch as ultimate source of law and jurisdiction. Neither of these two variables, military technology or shifts in ideas, can satisfactorily explain the variation in development between Germany and France.

The central question must therefore be, why did the German case turn out so differently from the French? German towns, like the French, opposed domination by feudal lords and the church. Like the French towns, they would benefit from a central actor who could diminish feudal exactions and the incertitude caused by crosscutting jurisdictions. Given the high transaction and information costs involved in conducting long-distance commerce in a highly particularized environment, one might argue that they would benefit even more from an organization that could reduce such costs and uncertainty. And like the French king, the German king opposed control by Rome. So why did not the German king forge an alliance with the towns and create a sovereign state? The question is all the more pertinent since the discussion of the Investiture Struggle indicated that the imperial strategy to control Italy and the pope came with high costs of its own. We must seek the answer in the particular political coalitions that developed following the economic upswing of the eleventh century.

The Northern Renaissance and the Impact of
Long-distance Commerce

As trade expanded throughout Europe, German towns profited immensely,
particularly those on the Rhine, such as Cologne, and the maritime towns on
the North Sea and Baltic, such as Hamburg, Lübeck, and Bremen. The development of trading towns, such as Regensburg and Nürnberg in the south, came
a bit later. The northern towns had access to waterways and were thus in a
strong position to engage in long-distance trade.[6]

These northern towns dealt in high-volume but low added-value goods. Most
of these goods were foodstuffs such as fish, primarily herring, and grain from
the Baltic regions. From farther east came timber, Scandinavian metals, furs,
and honey. More valuable were the textiles shipped from Flanders to the East.
As we will see from the discussion of the Hanseatic League, profit margins were
modest.

Although trade had a significant impact on Germany, it differed from the
impact of trade in Italy. A large number of German towns sprang up, but these
were of modest size (see Table 6.1). There were maybe fifty intermediate-size
towns and only a few with more than 25,000 inhabitants. (Italy, by contrast, had
about thirty towns of more than 25,000 citizens, and commerce allowed its
towns to accrue great wealth.)

The first estimate of the towns' preferences, therefore, does not diverge
much from that of the French towns. Since German towns were of intermediate
size and wealth—Lübeck and Cologne to some extent being the exceptions—
they could not survive on their own. They needed some form of authority to
help pool their resources. And indeed, we will see that one of the main objectives of the city-leagues was mutual defense.

Because the towns' environment consisted of the movement of bulk commodities with relatively low profit margins, the towns could benefit from some
centralizing form of organization in that sector as well. Rather than erode already slim profit margins of 5 to 25 percent by competition, towns had more to
gain from trying to monopolize trade routes.[7] That is in fact what the Hansa
attempted. Moreover, a central authority would have been better at reducing
transaction and information costs, which were the consequence of multiple
feudal tolls, manipulation of coinage, and the variation of exchange rates induced by local particularism. In short, like the French towns, the German
towns would benefit from a central authority.[8]

By looking solely at the particular impact and nature of trade, we can make
a first approximation of what the towns might have preferred. But again, deducing preferences is nothing but an approximation. It cannot account for actual
political outcomes. Lords, church, and emperor had their own agendas. To see
how specific political outcomes occurred, we need to trace these actors' material interests and conceptual perspectives and see how these matched or con-
flicted with those of the towns.

TABLE 6.1
Estimated Population of Some of the Major Northern Towns

Town	Population	Year
a) Members of the Hansa		
Bremen	20,000	1400
Bremen	17,000	1450
Cologne	40–60,000	13th–14th century
Cologne	30,000	1450
Danzig	20–30,000	1450
Deventer	12–14,000	1300
Deventer	10,000	1450
Hamburg	16–18,000	1450
Kampen	12–14,000	1300
Kampen	10,000	1450
Lübeck	25,000	1400
Lübeck	25,000	1450
Rostock	13,000	1400
Stralsund	13,000	1400
Zwolle	12–14,000	1300
b) Some major towns that were not members		
Augsburg	10,000	1400
Augsburg	18,300	1475
Frankfurt	10,000	1400
Nürnberg	13,750	1363
Nürnberg	22,800	1430

Sources: Ennen, The Medieval Town, pp. 187–188; Blockmans, "Princes Conquérants et Bourgeois Calculateurs," p. 175; Du Boulay, Germany in the Later Middle Ages, pp. 115, 161, 167; Lensen and Heitling, De Geschiedenis van de Hanze, p. 68; Holborn, A History of Modern Germany, p. 38.

REASONS AND CONSEQUENCES OF GERMAN FRAGMENTATION

The Feudal Strategy of the German Emperor and the Opposition to the Towns

As we saw in Chapter 3, there was an implicit tension between the emperor's weak domestic basis and the desire for imperial control of Italy. On the one hand, the emperor was confronted by strong dukes and lords who elected the German king, that is, the emperor.[9] The initial success of using ecclesiastical lords only worked until the Investiture Struggle. After that, they too became unreliable.

On the other hand, the imperial position required the German king to expend considerable resources to control the Lombard towns of northern Italy and the universalist pretensions of the popes. A weak basis of support in Germany, however, meant that imperial pretensions would often come to naught. Kings somehow had to acquire aristocratic support at home. But the lords had little incentive to support imperial contenders who might mobilize Italian resources against their independence. Consequently they preferred to choose weak imperial pretenders, as they did after Frederick II (1211–1250) in choosing William of Holland.

Within the cauldron of competing interests, the German kings might have pursued the support of the towns as had the Capetians. The towns were certainly amenable to the idea. As early as the eleventh century some towns had sought an alliance with the king against their lords. Worms, for example, evicted its bishop in 1073 and asked for aid from the king.[10] Similar events took place in Cologne in 1074 and Goslar in 1107.[11] Strasbourg fought its bishop on the field of Hausbergen (1261), and Cologne battled its archbishop again in 1288.[12]

The resistance of these towns against their feudal overlords—be they clerical or secular—looked remarkably like the resistance of the French towns. The German towns were no different from the French. The burghers' material interests and preferred social ideals were antithetical to the feudal social order.[13] Neither the caste system of a warrior elite nor the condemnation of monetary pursuits by the church fitted the towns' preferred conceptual framework. Politically the towns wanted a ruler to defend them against feudal encroachment. Economically they wanted central organization to curtail seigneurial taxation, reduce the amount of tolls, and rationalize the legal process.

The German kings were not ignorant of the advantages of a town alliance. Henry IV sought and obtained urban support against the clergy and the aristocracy during the Investiture Conflict. His son, Henry V, however, sought the support of the clergy and aristocracy and fought his father. Later, when he himself acceded to the throne, he tried to reconcile with the burghers.[14] Frederick I (Barbarossa) also tentatively pursued an urban strategy (1152–1190). But he wavered in his policy, sometimes supporting the towns, then again the lords. His experiences with urban independence in northern Italy had made him weary of communes. Indeed, at the Assembly of Roncaglia (1158), he explicitly tried to recoup the regalian rights of coinage and jurisdiction which the towns had usurped. To do so, he was the first German emperor who explicitly turned to Roman law, with its ideas of hierarchy and the king as the foundation of law.[15] This was to little avail. The Italian towns united to form a league of Lombard communities and gained the support of the pope. At Legnano they soundly defeated the imperial armies in 1176. Towns retained their rights to self-government and the revenue of tolls and taxes.[16] Consequently Frederick Barbarossa became "an opponent of sworn communes and of town leagues, but he was cautious even in the question of urban legal autonomy."[17]

Moreover, Frederick Barbarossa, as one of the first kings in the Hohenstaufen Dynasty, also had to take care not to offend the Welf aristocracy, the enemies of the Hohenstaufen who contested their ascendence to the throne.[18]

The principle of hereditary kingship had been successfully attacked in 1125 and again in 1138.[19] In effect this made the elective principle, and hence the position of the lords, stronger. The king's position in Germany remained precarious, and he could ill afford to antagonize these lords any further.

By the time of the reign of Frederick II (1211–1250), Frederick I's grandson, the imperial situation had become critical. Frederick II also was opposed by an Italian coalition of the independent communes and the pope. The pope particularly feared encroachment by Frederick II on the papal lands after the Hohenstaufen had also acquired Sicily through a marriage alliance with the Normans. The communes, for their part, continued to fight for complete independence.

Because of the continued strength of the German lords, the emperor opted for concessions to them. Frederick II ceded control over towns in Germany to the lords in 1220 and 1232 in exchange for their support for his imperial campaign. Already in 1213, in the "Golden Bull of Eger," he had given ecclesiastical lords full control over the towns in their domains. These were officially sanctioned and fortified in the *Confoederatio cum principus ecclesiasticis*, the "Treaty with the Ecclesiastical Princes" (1220), which were "concessions towards the territorial politics of the higher clergy."[20] Frederick II's *Statutum in Favorem Principum* of 1232, the statute in favor of the princes, contained twenty-three clauses, thirteen of which referred to towns and markets.

> The king promised (1) to build no more castles or walled towns in princely territories. No new (in other words, royal) markets were to compete with the older markets in the princes' hands.(2, 3); . . . Royal jurisdiction in the cities, which had been extended to the detriment of the princely courts, was to be limited to the "ban-mile" of the cities(5,18); . . . The cities were not to admit dependents of lords and princes (12), and royal officials in the cities were not to prevent any such persons returning to their lords (23).[21]

Essentially this meant that Frederick II yielded effective power to bishops and higher aristocracy. "It was the abdication of the German monarchy and the recognition of the princes as the exclusive rulers of their territories and as equal partners with the emperor in the government of the Empire."[22] He thereupon left to pursue his campaigns in Italy and did not return for many years.

Frederick's son, Henry VII, opposed the policy. He favored a reverse strategy. Rebelling against his father, he sought the support of the towns and attempted to build an administration of ministeriales who were recruited from the commoners and lesser nobility. He favored a domestic strategy and was willing to concede the right of self-government to the Lombard communities. In short, his strategy to build up the royal domain and use the towns against the princes looked remarkably like that of the Capetian kings who were pursuing such a policy at that very time. The princes, however, called in the emperor to uphold the agreements of 1220 and 1232. Henry was defeated in 1235 and imprisoned by Frederick II for the rest of his life.[23]

Nevertheless, the imperial strategy of the emperor failed. Frederick II gained initial military successes in Italy, but he could not win outright. He was continually opposed by the Lombard League, which was supported by the pope. Although Frederick II managed to reduce individual towns such as Milan, he could not defeat the league's combined opposition. Indeed, the more successful he was in combating individual towns, the more the usually disjoint Italian towns realized that they had a common enemy. Toward the end of Frederick's reign, the Italian towns had gained factual independence. Simultaneous with the failure in Italy, the German princes expanded their hold on Germany. By ceding regalian rights to the German lords, Frederick II granted them the means to establish secure sources of revenue and troops. An indicator of the failure of this strategy was the fact that the royal domain, at Frederick's death, was smaller than the areas controlled by some of the dukes.[24] The German choice to seek princely support was also unwise since the larger part of royal revenue in Germany came from the towns. The strategy can therefore only be understood in the larger imperial context. The emperor believed that he could still control both Germany and Italy.

The weakness of the imperial position was exacerbated by the Interregnum (1256–1273), the period without a royal successor. The emperorship became wholly dependent on support by the nobles. The election came into the hands of the College of Electors, consisting of three archbishops and four secular lords.[25]

The entire process was formalized in the Golden Bull which the emperor signed in 1356. It maintained the imperial title for the German king, but he had to cede factual control over Italy to the nobles and papacy. Italy became a constellation of independent communes and papal lands, beyond German control. This bull also formally recognized the rights of the German College of Electors. Although the election of emperors was an old practice, it had historically—since the Ottonians—meant the affirmation of the emperor's choice of successor. Since the Investiture Conflict, however, it had increasingly become a real elective procedure. The Golden Bull thus formalized the power that the lords had drawn to themselves over the course of several centuries. The election came to rest in the hands of the archbishops of Mainz, Trier, and Cologne and four secular lords—the Count Palatine, the duke of Saxony, the margrave of Brandenburg, and the king of Bohemia. Two powerful dukes, the dukes of Austria and Bavaria, were not part of the college.[26]

The bull also forbade the formation of city-leagues, symbolizing to the towns what had de facto been the case for more than a century since Frederick II.[27] The towns were left to fend for themselves, without a central authority to unite them against lordly encroachment. The lords ruled Germany. The electors were recognized as independent rulers in their principalities, with regalian rights.[28] Their territories were indivisible, and hence the procedure established territorial integrity. Soon similar rights were taken over by many other lords. The bull was essentially a "Magna Carta of German particularism."[29]

Why did the German kings pursue an imperial strategy rather than concentrate on Germany and establish a sovereign, territorial state there? Could the fragmentation of the German kingdom have been prevented by someone less ambitious than Frederick II? The argument that his rule specifically constituted a turning point can be generalized. No emperor allied with the towns to the extent that the French king did. "Co-operation between the emperor and the cities might have laid the foundations of a modern German monarchy. In England and France the cities contributed immeasurably to the growth of modern national monarchies . . . the princes recognized the danger and forced the emperors into a course of action inimical to the cities."[30] Despite the risks of an imperial policy, there were good reasons to pursue it rather than a strictly domestic one.

First, control of empire meant authority over Burgundy and northern Italy and later also Sicily.[31] These areas were attractive sources of revenue. The economic upswing from the tenth century onward had produced vibrant towns there. Frederick Barbarossa's campaign in northern Italy and the ensuing negotiations at Roncaglia were explicit attempts to recapture many of the regalian rights, and hence revenue, which had been appropriated by the Lombard communes. By some estimates the revenue for the German king in Italy yielded about 84,000 pounds, whereas Louis VII's revenue in France was approximately 60,000.[32] Sicily, too, yielded considerable revenues at that time. Some chroniclers suggested, but we have no exact figures, that the revenue of Palermo equaled that of the English kingdom.[33] Sicily was an important grain producer in the Mediterranean, and the Normans had established an effective administrative machinery there.

Furthermore, the universalist strategy of the papacy and particularly its attempts to control ecclesiastical lordships in Germany required the emperor to respond in a similar fashion. That is, given the strong position of ecclesiastical lords in Germany, the emperor could not surrender absolute authority to the pope without a serious loss of domestic resources and position.[34]

Finally, the emperorship conveyed an important ideological message. Since the middle of the tenth century, the German kings had claimed to rebuild the Roman Empire—a holy empire at that. They ruled as Caesars with the added support of a universalist religious doctrine. Frederick II thus claimed a Caesaro-Papalist standing. He called his birthplace Bethlehem, kept a harem, and his supporters addressed him as the "Messiah."[35] The idea of a peaceful, unified Christian Europe formed the logical equivalent of the perception that the Pax Romana had been beneficial. Hence a German Empire was much preferable to the frequent violence of the feudal era. Although the practical implementation left much to be desired, the social idea still seemed very attractive to many. How could the German kings reverse their policies and claim that authority was now to be limited by territorial parameters? How could the emperors, who for centuries had pursued control over the areas of the old Roman Empire, now claim that they only had jurisdiction within recognized boundaries, and in turn recognize others as equals? It would constitute a reversal of their logic of organization. The conceptual framework of imperial rule was tied to universalist and religious ideas. It was not simply another secular form of rule; it had a particular ideological standing from which the German king could not divorce himself without great cost.[36]

Towns versus Lords

The Golden Bull of 1356 formalized the long process of erosion of royal power. Royal policy had foundered on the strength of the lords, the conflict with Rome, and the failure to adopt a consistent town policy. One can say that from 1250 onward, material power in Germany rested with the lords and the towns.

The growth in power and independence of the dukes, counts, and margraves was further enhanced by the frontier movements of the twelfth and thirteenth centuries. The cultivation and population of areas to the east created new lordships and added areas to already existing ones. These areas, moreover, had never been under royal control. Many new towns were founded. This occurred particularly to the east beyond the Elbe, an area that had no Roman influences.[37] Thus the duke of Saxony founded Lübeck, which was later to become virtually independent and the critical actor in the Hansa. Most of the Baltic towns also originated in this period.

This frontier area consisted largely of non-Christians, so the settlement of new towns and new monasteries was also encouraged by the church. Rome favored the expansion by new monastic and semimonastic orders which answered directly to Rome. The Cistercian order built new abbeys in what is today Hungary and Poland.[38] It was also aided by orders of knights who had taken vows of association and who had fought in the Middle East. The Teutonic Order of crusading knights was thus redirected to crusade against the Baltic people. Its main center was moved from Acre to Venice, and then finally Marienburg—in the north of contemporary Poland.[39] They forced conversion on the Prussian and other peoples and engaged in wholesale expulsion and extermination, after which those areas were resettled by colonists from the west. German ecclesiastical lords similarly recognized opportunities in this expansion and created new bishoprics. In short, Rome, secular lords, and the German clergy all had something to gain from the eastward frontier movement. They all sought to establish villages and towns which would provide revenue, converts, and subjects.

However, like towns in Flanders, Italy, and France, the German towns opposed such overlordship.[40] They sought to expand their freedom, either by paying for chartered liberties or by violent resistance. Even before the eastward expansion, towns had rebelled against their lords in their quest for independence: "residents of the market settlement banded together, swearing an oath, to win recognition, rights, and eventually independence from the bishop, abbot or prince."[41]

As I have said earlier in this chapter, clerical lords in particular were the target of urban resentment. Arguing that they had common enemies, the towns supported the emperor against German ecclesiastical lords during the Investiture Struggle. Thus the citizens of Mainz drove their archbishop out of town and wrote Henry IV: "If God grants us victory we shall both be secure, you on your throne and we in our town."[42]

Because of the variety of lordships and the particularity of urban bargaining with their lords, a patchwork of different urban developments took place. Each town had a variant set of liberties which it had obtained in piecemeal bargaining, and consequently one must be cautious to generalize indiscriminately. Every town had different laws and ordinances. In general, however, one can distinguish juridically three types of towns: imperial towns, free towns, and territorial towns.[43] One should keep in mind that this differentiation was often blurred in practice. In many instances towns were virtually indistinguishable. Even the royal chancery would occasionally address important towns as imperial towns, although they actually were not.[44]

Simultaneous with the growth of urban independence, many lords started to accumulate powers that traditionally had been powers of monarchical rule. They minted their own coins and put their own facsimile on the coins in emulation of the Byzantine practice. They passed laws and claimed final jurisdiction.[45] But although these princes increasingly appropriated some of the royal prerogatives, they initially did not become small sovereign states, and the towns did not ally with these lords.

There are several reasons why towns opposed their lords and sought to obtain their goals by a unique alternative: the city-league. First, these lordships only started to establish themselves as territorial lordships in the late fourteenth and fifteenth centuries.[46] Towns, however, had started to develop in the twelfth century. Indeed, the Hanseatic League, as a federation of towns, already existed de facto in 1292. In other words, most of these lordships were feudal in nature when towns were expanding and sought to regulate their economic environment. The towns thus faced the problem of multiple overlordship and uncertainty. German towns opposed these lords for the very reasons that the French towns opposed their secular and ecclesiastical overlords. They remained feudal lords rather than sovereign authorities. The particularistic pattern of feudal lordships complicated long-distance commerce immensely. The grievances of merchants regarding the numerous tolls on the Rhine—which the English merchants who were accustomed to more centralized authority called the "German madness"—are a case in point.[47] Towns that transacted business across these feudal units were faced with a variety of different legal codes, local tolls, differences in weights and measures, variation in coinage, and sometimes outright robbery, all to the detriment of the burghers' business.[48]

Second, the towns had little affinity with the social ideals of lords and clergy. We have already seen at several junctures how clerical overlordship was considered particularly odious. With its prohibitions on usury, its denigration of monetary practices, and its overall low evaluation of mercantile activities, the church was an obstacle to the burghers' practices. The differences between the belief systems of the bourgeois and those of feudalism and the church, which I discussed in Chapter 4, hold as true for Germany as they did for France. One of those differences revolved around the feudal legal system and the mercantile preference for a more standardized and rational legal environment. Consequently, the German emperor had tried to limit aristocratic prerogatives, in an attempt to attract Flemish merchants, by ordering that traders not be subject to the ordeal, the common procedure in debt cases.[49]

Third, many of the towns to the east were in fact founded by business groups from the older German towns.[50] Although lords might nominally have been the charterers of the new towns, in fact the actual creation, investment, and risks were left up to the entrepreneurs from the westerly towns. Factual control over these new towns was thus from the beginning in the hands of the business entrepreneurs who had run the risks and provided the capital. "In any case— the most important new towns of the twelfth and also of the early thirteenth centuries were created in the main by enterprising burghers of the Old German towns; not until the thirteenth century were agricultural towns founded by local lords, which frequently were of no commercial importance."[51] One can even retrace the structure of the town council (ranging from twelve to twenty-four members) to the corporate arrangements that these entrepreneurs had made prior to establishing new towns. These towns had little incentive to share the benefits of their new trading centers with lords who had taken little monetary risk themselves.

Finally, it is important to remember that towns primarily desired full independence from the old feudal order. In France the towns allied with the king who was useful against the lords. The French king provided certitude in the tax environment, career opportunities, and a set of ideas with which the burghers could identify. Although the king was initially perhaps not the most powerful actor, he was more attractive than alternative providers of protection because he could offer these other benefits. In return, the towns proved to be an important source of revenue and personnel. The political cost of that arrangement was that the king kept the towns divided. The national assembly meant little. French towns sacrificed full independence because sovereign kingship provided them with many benefits. The German towns, by contrast, had no such incentive to sacrifice their liberties.

The German City-leagues

As trade around the North Sea and Baltic started to develop, merchants organized themselves in trading groups such as the Gotland association. Gotland was an island off the coast of Sweden where merchants would congregate to trade with the areas of the eastern Baltic. This community of traders, the universi mercatores, would sail together in convoy and seek joint representation in foreign countries. Sailing together in convoy provided for better defense against deprivations by pirates and lords. By acting together overseas, they found they could obtain better privileges. They elected an alderman and swore mutual aid. In many ways similar to a guild, the associations provided for burial should a merchant die overseas, they acted as information centers regarding alien business practices, and they provided a social meeting place for businessmen.[52] From them originates the first (preserved) treaty of the Hansa with a foreign prince in 1189.[53] Similar associations of traders were generally all called *hanses*, meaning a group of merchants acting together. There were thus hanses from Bruges, Cologne, Deventer, and other trading cities. Their towns of origin, however, were not formally involved. These were private associations.

As towns gained more independence from their lords, they developed their own political institutions. They formed associations similar to the Italian communes. The citizens swore oaths of mutual assistance and started to appropriate and purchase rights and liberties from their overlords. The burghers elected councils which had juridical power within the town. These councils also represented the burghers' interests vis-à-vis other towns. Sometimes such councils decided to act together to pursue common interests and fight common foes. With the emergence of the independent town, we thus simultaneously see the first beginnings of city-leagues.

Burghers formed these leagues with the explicit purpose of defending towns against encroachment by the nobility. Militarily they promised each other mutual aid against the common enemy.[54] They assessed troop contingents which each town had to provide. Economically they sought to reduce the tolls that lords had imposed. This was one of the objectives of the Swabian-Rhenisch League of 1385. They also sought to regulate weights, measures, and coinage.[55] This was an important objective given that in the twelfth century coinage privileges resided not only in the royal mints but also in the hands of 106 ecclesiastical and 81 secular lords.[56] Juridically the leagues defended the towns' rights of self-governance.

There were a considerable number of such leagues.[57] And they varied greatly in composition and objectives. In general, however, one can say that "the cities relied against princely encroachments on leagues for mutual defense."[58] The Saxon League, for example, was formed for the purpose of mutual aid against demands by secular and ecclesiastical lords. This league fluctuated in its membership but over the years included about eighteen towns. Interestingly, the towns also had a provision for mutual aid in case of internal disturbance.[59] If a town's patriciate were ousted by radical elements, members from other towns were obliged to aid the deposed council.[60]

The Swabian-Rhenisch League proved in 1385 that such leagues could muster considerable military might. This league consisted of about eighty-nine towns and could field an army of 10,000. It "held far more power than any prince."[61] Only because of a divergence in interests between towns and a military alliance of several lords was the league overcome in battle at Döffingen in 1388. Prior to that, the league had even successfully fought the emperor Charles IV.[62]

Leagues gradually started to replace the personal associations of merchants. In effect these towns were run by the mercantile patriciate who now used the towns' resources to obtain their goals. The Gotland association thus became the basis of the Hanseatic League. The Hansa in its heyday included almost two hundred towns. It opposed and deposed kings and monopolized trade in the Baltic and the North Sea.

STRUCTURE AND OBJECTIVES OF THE HANSEATIC LEAGUE:
"CONCORDIA DOMI. FORIS PAX"[63]

The Nature of Trade

It is not exactly clear when the Gotland association changed into an association of towns rather than individual merchants. By 1298, however, merchants no longer operated as individual traders but were organized under the representation of their towns of origin. The merchant association was replaced by the league of towns on the Baltic and the North Sea. Merchants were forbidden to operate through private organizations.

Initially the Hansa, like the Gotland association, focused primarily on trade between the German and Dutch towns in the west with the towns on the Baltic.[64] Gradually, with the expansion of urbanization farther eastward, the number of members increased. The Hanseatic merchandise included timber, metal, furs, wax, grain, and fish. Hanseatic trade was thus typified by trade in bulk goods with relatively low profit margins. Mediterranean trade, by contrast, consisted more of luxury goods.[65] Because of the expansion of commerce, the regions around the North Sea and the Baltic proceeded to engage in further division of labor and specialized production.

The calculation of profit margins is a highly complex historical enterprise. But it is worth discussing in some detail because it demonstrates the high transaction and information costs that these entrepreneurs had to overcome to conduct commerce. Analysis of business records suggests a variety of numbers. For example, a study of the records of the Vechinchusen family (which formed a variety of business ventures with others in the early fifteenth century) suggests profit margins of roughly 7 to 18 percent.[66] But other historians suggest more conservative estimates or much higher ones. There are a variety of reasons for this. First, business was highly uncertain. Although profits were possible, we also know that the Vechinchusen group at one point incurred a loss of 55 percent. Moreover, trade routes yielded considerable variation. We now know that on average the west-east trade yielded almost twice the profit margin of the east-west trade. There was also great variation in goods. Cloth or herring could sometimes yield high profits, but that might depend on extraordinary market conditions. Calculation of profit was thus a complex matter for the Hanseatic businessman. Prior to established accounting and recording methods, merchants used a variety of techniques to keep track of their expenses and income.[67] Everything was further complicated by the lack of established exchange procedures, the great variation in coinage, and the lack of standardized measures. For example, if we study the records of Johann Töhner (1345), the profit margin changes dramatically with the exchange rate used. Merchants noted everything in local currency. But was the Rostock mark equal to eleven or twelve great pounds?[68] Measures, furthermore, tended to decrease in size the farther one got from the point of origin. The el might be about 57.5 cm in Lübeck but only 53.7 cm in Riga.[69] (This was one way to get around clerical disapproval of prices that were not just. The prices remained the same between point of purchase and point of sale, but the quantity supplied varied.) In short, merchants engaging in commerce had to be as informed as possible of particular conditions, exchange rates, and measurements. One of the tasks of the league was thus to facilitate the exchange of information between merchants.

As stated, the Hansa resembled the medieval guild.[70] Like the guild, it sought to restrict entry of competition and to control the market. And like the guild, the Hansa tried to aid its members in the pursuit of their common economic interests by lowering information costs. One of the earliest surviving documents of such activity is the public register. The public Book of Debts in Hamburg, for example, recorded debts and contracts and attached a municipal guarantee of their authenticity.[71]

The Hansa further sought to gain privileges for its members in their trade overseas, while denying privileges to nonmembers. It thus received privileges from the English Crown to trade in London. The league initially gained exemptions from customs duties, and later it also received legal protection and exemption from all taxes. Members obtained similar privileges in Flanders.[72] But conversely, the Hansa forbade nonmembers to enter Hanseatic ports.[73] The objective of such policies was the pursuit of monopoly rent for its merchants. During its heyday, the Hansa monopolized all Baltic trade and much of the trade in the North Sea. Its ships sailed even to Portugal and Spain and on rare occasions as far as Latin America.[74] Its main line of operation, however, was the east-west commerce of the northern seas.

Nevertheless, one should not see the Hansa as merely an economic association. Like states, it waged wars, and on occasion it could make or break kings. It could participate in international treaties and send emissaries. Some scholars have viewed it as a major unifying force in northern Europe.[75]

The Relations of the Hansa, Territorial Lords, and Emperor

Many Hansa towns, like hundreds of other towns and villages, were established during the great eastern expansion of the twelfth and thirteenth centuries. Lübeck was founded by the Count of Holstein in 1143. It was then taken over by Henry the Lion, the duke of Saxony, in 1159. Lübeck in turn formed settlements farther east.[76] The knights of the Teutonic Order also founded hundreds of Prussian towns and villages. And yet farther east, the Brethren of the Sword colonized and christianized Lithuania and Estonia.[77]

What held for many German towns also held true for the Livonian, Prussian, and Wendish towns. Many sought increasing independence from their lords. The strife between lords and the king allowed the towns to gain independence by formal and informal means. Lübeck became an imperial city in 1226.[78] This meant it had no territorial overlord and owed allegiance only to the emperor.[79] Decreasing power of centralized monarchy implied increasing autonomy for such towns. Most towns remained technically subject to lords but gradually purchased, or were granted, considerable rights of self-determination.

As said, at first the merchants of the Baltic towns regulated their own interactions. They formed organizations such as the Gotland Association to protect their interests and to negotiate with other states. The merchants of the Baltic thus competed with those of Cologne who had already established a bridgehead in London by 1130. Later, merchants of Hamburg and Lübeck also acquired privileges there, similar to those of the Rhenisch traders, and from 1266 they were known by the word *hansa* to denote a group of merchants.[80] By 1281 the Rhenisch and Baltic towns reconciled and formed a single hansa.

Gradually, however, the town councils took these tasks over from the merchants, as the towns became factually independent from lords and kings. Some towns on the Baltic thus formed leagues just as other towns had done earlier. The Wend towns—Lübeck, Rostock, Stralsund, Greifswald, and Wismar—formed a league in 1284. In 1298 representation of merchant interests through the Gotland association was formally forbidden.[81] It would still take half a century, however, before the first general council of the Hansa towns met in 1356. That year is usually taken to be the founding of the Hanseatic League. The various hansa (merchant associations) were thus over time replaced by the Hansa, denoting the association of towns.

Through Hanseatic institutions, members sought to regulate the interactions between towns within the league, and between the league and other actors. Internally, member towns exercised their own jurisdiction. That is, in matters pertaining only to that town, the town council had final jurisdiction.

The factual independence of towns, however, varied.[82] On one end of the spectrum we find towns such as Lübeck or Hamburg which, although surrounded by the lands of territorial lords, were in fact independent. In general the Hanseatic towns opposed any feudal or monarchical encroachment. Other Hanseatic towns had considerable independence but were allied with feudal lords. This was specifically the case in the alliance of Hansa and the knights of the Teutonic Order. The Prussian towns were directly under the order's territorial control but were granted considerable latitude. In return, before 1406, one-third, and later two-thirds, of customs duties levied in Prussia (the Pfundzoll) went to the order.[83]

Finally there were towns where the Hansa had an establishment, or even Kontor, as in London, which was subject to direct territorial overlordship.[84] Thus London was not a Hanseatic town. The Hansa, however, had a Kontor there and a staple market, the Stahlhof. Although the Hansa had jurisdiction within the area of the Kontor, this was not true for London as a whole.[85]

In short, some towns that were Hanseatic members were also subject to territorial overlords. They did not escape the system of crosscutting jurisdictions which had permeated the feudal era. Other towns owed only nominal allegiance to territorial overlords. These towns established their own juridical and political structures and directed the Hansa's military and economic policy vis-à-vis non-Hansa political organizations.

The Formal Institutions of the Hansa

The most important organ of the Hansa was the Hansetag, or Diet. This was the meeting where all towns were supposed to appear or send delegates to represent them. Nonappearance could result in exclusion from the league.[86] The Hansetag met with varying frequency. At most it met once a year, but usually it met once every several years. The towns that called the Hansetag together were usually Lübeck and the other Wend towns. The Hansa did not have its own officials. Instead town councils, such as Lübeck's, operated on its behalf.[87] The leading towns were also responsible for keeping records of such meetings and maintaining them for future reference. On some occasions the current Hansetag specified the date of the next meeting.

The Hansetage made decisions that affected all towns. The towns voted on membership, a wide range of economic matters, external representation of the Hansa, and military issues.[88] Each town had one vote. To enforce its decisions, the Hansa could levy particular fees on individual towns. Alternatively it could exclude towns from specific benefits. The most severe instrument was expulsion from the league. Even Lübeck, the dominant town of the Hansa, was at one point threatened with such exclusion.

Representation on the Hansetag was an indicator of one's position in the Hansa. The most important towns were virtually always present. Lesser towns or towns that were only marginally involved with Hanseatic business let themselves be represented by other towns. Consequently it is not fully clear who could be considered a member of the Hanseatic League. At its core one might count seventy-seven members. These were members who usually partook in general decision making. Another one hundred towns might have considered themselves associates.[89] Depending on the frequency of participation in Hansa affairs, the Hansa might have included as many as two hundred towns.

The problem for the Hansa was, of course, to get all members to act collectively on affairs that might not pertain to all of them. One solution was to allow decision making on a regional level. Thus many decisions were made by the regional Tage where groups of towns came together. These were towns that shared geographic proximity and often similar interests. As with the membership issue, there is some disagreement regarding the relevant regional groups.[90] These regional groups were then aggregated for representation in the general Hansetag. There were three such groups, called Drietel: the Wendish and Saxon towns formed the first, the Westphalian and Prussian towns the second, and the Livonian towns and Visby the third. Each of these groups had its own treasury and elected aldermen.[91] At other times regional organizations were structured around quarters, that is, four groups of regional associations. In such an arrangement, the Cologne quarter, for example, consisted of the Dutch towns of the Southern Sea (Zuiderzee) and the Prussian and Westphalian towns.[92]

Decision making within the Hansa was further decentralized by granting considerable latitude to the Kontors. These were the main trading offices of the

Hansa. There were four: Novgorod, Bergen, Bruges, and London. The Kontors were run by officials who were elected by the merchants. These officials had juridical and taxing power and could represent the Hansa overseas.[93] The governing body of each Kontor was subdivided in thirds or fourths. Each of these subdivisions represented a regional town group.[94]

Another form of hierarchical control, aside from supervision by the main Hansetag, was the superior placement of some towns over others. Thus, smaller Hanseatic towns, or towns where the Hansa at least had a settlement, were subject to control by a larger sister city.[95]

The Hanseatics were also aware that close ties between individuals diminished freeriding and enabled towns to coordinate their activities more satisfactorily.[96] There were stringent restrictions on marriage with non-Hanseatics, both for inhabitants of the Hanse towns as well as for their merchants abroad. Non-Hanseatics could not acquire citizenship in Hanse towns. The penalty of entering into a business venture with a non-Hanseatic was the loss of two fingers.[97] As a consequence of the closed nature of business and the use of family ties, one finds a considerable number of similar last names among the various town oligarchies throughout the Hansa.

Finally, the drawbacks of the confederative structure were mitigated by the predominance of a few towns. Lübeck, the other Wend towns, and later Hamburg and Bremen were so preponderant that they could organize many of the other towns almost in an ad hoc manner. The regional groups thus usually had several predominant towns to keep the others in line.[98] Lübeck, for example, had a critical geographical position because it controlled the land passage between it and Hamburg. It further had about one-third of the total shipping capacity of the Hansa at its disposal. Consequently, when the Hansa met in 1418 to re-evaluate its institutional machinery, Lübeck became its formal leader.[99]

The Hansa as an Alternative to the Sovereign State

The Hanseatic League was undoubtedly the most powerful of the city-leagues and is an interesting case because it suggests an alternative logic of organization to that of the sovereign state. It was an identifiable political unit which not only connected east-west maritime trade but also made inroads into the European continent on the north-south dimension.[100] It is wrong to see the Hansa as merely a loosely bound interest group. As Wernicke and Dollinger have pointed out, the weight of contemporary evidence belies that position. Wernicke and Dollinger argue that the Hansa had the ability to send emissaries, sign treaties, collect revenue, and enforce Hansetag decisions.[101] Lensen and Heitling concede that although the Hansa was a confederation that did not have a founding constitution, it could raise an army, conduct foreign policy, decree laws, engage in social regulation, and collect revenue.[102]

The political institutions I discussed above demonstrate that the Hansa had a variety of fora where decision making was formulated. Although it is true that the Hansetag met on an irregular basis, this practice was not so different from early state administration. There, too, the ad hoc character of government was more rule than exception.

It will also not do to argue that the Hansa had no well-established sources of revenue and hence cannot be construed as a true political organization. Although the Hansa did not have an established system of direct taxes, it did have a variety of other means to obtain revenue. It levied general fees for specific purposes, such as the arming of the fleet in 1407.[103] It also obtained revenue through Kontor fees. Another important source of income were the tolls levied on the ships entering and leaving harbors. These were the Pfundzolls, and they were particularly levied in times of war.[104] In 1557 the Hansa established yearly dues and individual town assessments. Part of the revenues could be earmarked for specific Hansa expenses. When a particular town had incurred expenses, for example, by fitting out a certain number of ships for war, then the Hansa permitted it to levy specific tolls to recap its outlay. It developed a constitution with a precise enumeration of duties, and there was even discussion of creating institutional arrangements similar to those of the Dutch states.[105]

In an external sense, that is, vis-à-vis other actors, the Hansa behaved in many ways like any state. It had military capability and fought wars with Sweden (1567–1570, 1630s), England (1470–1474), Holland (1438–1441), and Denmark (1370, 1426–1435, 1616). After the Peace of Stralsund (1370), in which it defeated Denmark, it controlled the royal succession and took control over the castles that controlled the Sound.[106] It also equipped warships to deal with pirates, of which the Vitalienbruder were the most prominent and required concerted naval effort to control. Towns were individually assessed to provide troops and so-called peace-ships. Each ship had to have a certain number of lances, bowmen, and crew.[107]

The most used method of coercion, however, was the economic blockade. Since the Hansa had a virtual monopoly on many bulk goods, they could bring recalcitrant towns, or lords who refused to grant concessions, to their knees. The various blockades of Bruges, directed against the Count of Flanders, and those of Norway directed against the king, were but two successes.[108] Such blockades could take the form of forbidding provision of essential supplies. Bergen, for example, was cut off from food supplies until it yielded. But blockade also meant the loss of a consumption market. A threat not to buy from that location was every bit as effective as one curtailing supply.

Like independent monarchs, the Hansa signed treaties which bound its members.[109] Heads of the Kontors could be empowered to negotiate on the part of the Hansa, or the various towns concerned could jointly send an embassy. Later special delegates, the syndics (syndikus), were given authority to represent the league. The syndikus made its appearance particularly in the later part of the sixteenth century.

The towns of the Hansa also demonstrated many cultural similarities, such as language. Low German was the language understood and spoken in towns from Holland to Novgorod.[110] One might even argue that the Hansa evinced more homogeneity than states such as France which only managed to overcome some language barriers by the nineteenth century. This, in short, strengthens the argument that there is no a priori reason why the Hansa should not be perceived as a viable way of organizing economic and political activity in the absence of a central authority.

It is true that the individual towns maintained considerable autonomy and pursued their own specific interests. For example, some of the more important towns acquired considerable territories. This was partially due to deliberate town policy. They strove to acquire territory with strategic value to control incursions by lords and to gain cheap supplies. This was also partially due to investment by affluent merchants in the surrounding countryside. Thus Lübeck had about 240 villages and Hamburg almost 100 under their control.[111]

It is also true that the members of the Hansa exercised autonomous jurisdiction within their own cities. As a result there were a variety of legal codes throughout the league. Merchants, however, tried to deal with this legal variation by accepting merchant law side by side with urban law. The law between merchants was administered by the commercial courts of the towns. Interurban legal questions were dealt with by the Hansa. Many towns also adopted the laws of their mother towns, although this was not done in a very systematic way.[112] Wernicke argues that through reciprocity between towns, bilateral treaties, and intervention by the Hansa, "the Hansa towns created a relatively coherent legal system."[113]

It would therefore be incorrect to assume that the individual town was the actual political unit with which we should be concerned.[114] This was not the development of territorial city-states as in Italy. The town itself was not the final authority in many affairs. Where inter-Hanseatic problems arose, the relevant forum was the regional Tag. Larger issues were brought before the general Hansetag. In short, the town's jurisdiction was independent as far as its demarcation from territorial lords was concerned. When issues pertaining to other Hansa towns were at stake, the league had final say. A simple majority sufficed to make decisions in the Hansetag even for those not present.

Conclusion

Medieval towns favored different principles of rule. The walls of the towns not only served defensive purposes but physically demarcated the towns from different orders. The towns were, in Postan's words, islands of urban law in a feudal sea.[115] They introduced new concepts such as freedom for their citizens, equality before the law, the right to make law, and new regulations on property and investment. Most importantly, they introduced a concept of territorial law rather than personal law. "The development of autonomy occurred simultaneously with the transition from the personal to the territorial principle in law. No longer were old relationships of a personal nature to decide the legal standing of the individual, but the judicial area of the place he was living in."[116]

But townsfolk, of course, did not remain behind their walls. Trade between the towns required them to regulate their interactions. Germany, however, lacked political entrepreneurs such as the French kings who established the beginnings of sovereign rule against rival principles of order. Against the particularistic bonds of feudalism and the universalist claims of church and empire, the French monarchs claimed their authority to be territorial, confined by recognized borders, and supreme to any authority within those borders. They represented their subjects externally and established internal hierarchy.

In Germany the reverse took place. The kings perceived their interests to lie with a universalist order, and more specifically with the control of Italy and the pope. They attempted to follow through on their imperial claims by conceding control over the towns to the feudal lords. No alliance of burghers and king materialized, and in its absence the possibility of a sovereign state evaporated.

Towns responded by forming city-leagues, which could represent the towns, organize them for war, and bring some regularity to trade. The Hanseatic League performed just such functions. Preferably, the league would extend political control over its entire sphere of economic interaction. In a sense its logic resembled that of an empire; "imperial expansion tends to incorporate all significant economic needs within the domain itself."[117] It lacked a clear hierarchical authority and formal territorial borders. It attempted to construct political institutions to organize its long-distance commerce, wherever that went. Ultimately, however, that system of rule was destined to come into conflict with the logic of a state system.

The Development of the Italian City-states

From this it has resulted that they far surpass all other states of the world in
riches and in power. . . . For they scarcely if ever respect the prince to whom
they should display the voluntary deference of obedience or willingly
perform that which they have sworn by the integrity of their laws,
unless they sense his authority in the power of his great army.[1]

WE HAVE seen that whereas a sovereign, territorial state developed in France,
Germany fragmented into lordships and city-leagues, of which the Hansa was
the most prominent. Although Italy, too, was affected by the economic expansion of the eleventh century onward, the new institutional arrangements that
developed there differed from those of France and Germany. Italy gave rise to
yet another form of political organization: the city-state. To reiterate, the ultimate cause for the demand for new systems of rule came from the increase in
commerce. However, the outcome of these demands differed because of the
variation in the type of political coalitions that formed in response to that overall environmental change.

Unlike the situation in France, no aspiring central actor managed to form a
social alliance with the burghers in Italy. And unlike the situation with the
German towns, the divergent interests and variation between the Italian towns
prevented them from forming city-leagues. This chapter, therefore, centers
around two main questions. Why did a royal-urban alliance not materialize in
Italy? And why did the independent cities not form leagues as the members of
the Hansa did? To answer these, we must again start with an analysis of the
specific nature of the commercial revolution, this time in Italy (see Map 7.1).

THE IMPACT OF ITALIAN LUXURY TRADE

Throughout this book, my main argument has been that the economic expansion in the Late Middle Ages led to increased urbanization and the founding of
new towns. Townsfolk used their newfound power to form political coalitions
to restructure the old feudal system. Conversely, rulers sometimes saw in the
towns a novel way of acquiring revenue and support. In France a royal-urban
alliance developed. In Germany, by contrast, the emperor opted for a feudal
strategy and towns pursued an independent course. Italy, too, was highly affected by the economic upswing of the eleventh century. Urban growth in

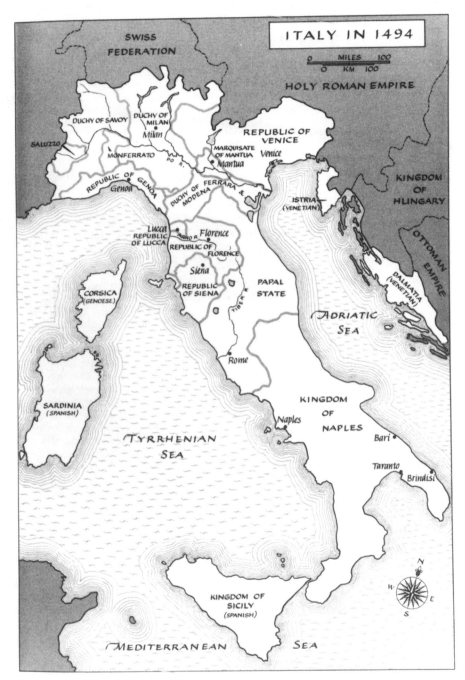

7.1 The Italian City-states in the Late Fifteenth Century (Source: Lauro Martines, *Power and Imagination*, New York: Vintage, 1979, p. 5.)

TABLE 7.1

Estimated Population of Italian Towns

Town	Population	Year
Bologna	50,000	1348
Bologna	40,000	1370
Florence	50,000	1200
Florence	74–100,000	1300
Genoa	80–100,000	1300
Genoa	100,000	1348
Genoa	100,000	1400
Genoa	117,000	15th century
Lucca	20,000	1300?
Milan	>100,000	1288
Milan	>50,000	1348
Milan	125,000	1400
Padua	33,000	1320
Pavia	30,000	1250
Pisa	20–30,000	1300–1350
Rome	35,000	1200
Siena	20–30,000	1300–1350
Siena	>50,000	1348
Venice	80,000	1200
Venice	100–120,000	1300
Venice	90,000	1328
Venice	100,000	1348
Venice	110,000	1400
Venice	150,000	1423
Verona	30,000	1320

Sources: Schumann, *Italy in the Last Fifteen Hundred Years,* p. 103f (he also suggests that around 1300 Paris had about 50–60,000 inhabitants; London 35,000; Cologne 30,000; but that Venice, Milan, Genoa, Florence, Naples, and Palermo all had more than 50,000); Abu-Lughod, *Before European Hegemony,* p.125; Scammel, *The World Encompassed,* p. 155; Braudel, *The Perspective of the World,* p. 133; Ennen, *The Medieval Town,* p. 189 (She also notes that Naples had about 50,000 inhabitants and that the two most important Sicilian towns, Palermo and Messina, each had 44,000 and 27,000 respectively); Hohenberg and Lees, *The Making of Urban Europe,* p. 11; J. C. Russell, "Population in Europe, 500–1500," pp. 34–35; Dodgshon, *The European Past,* p. 229; Mundy and Riesenberg, *The Medieval Town,* p. 30; Heer, *The Medieval World,* p. 78; Brucker, *Renaissance Florence,* p. 51.

terms of revenue and population resumed in this period. "The increase and movement of rural folk took many of them into the budding towns and older urban agglomerations. Such movement was well under way by the beginning of the eleventh century and would continue, on a massive scale, down to nearly 1300."[2]

Many towns of considerable size emerged, which were far larger and wealthier than their French or German counterparts. Italian towns dwarfed other European urban centers. Venice, Florence, Milan, and Genoa were all much larger than any of the German cities or French towns. Only Paris came close in number of inhabitants. Cologne, the largest German town, had roughly 35,000 inhabitants, and only a few other German towns had more than 20,000 citizens. Early medieval Italy, however, had at least twenty towns with 20,000 or more inhabitants (see Table 7.1).[3] As a consequence, the division of labor advanced here more than anywhere else.

Each of these cities could thus field considerable armies and navies on its own. A contrast with the German city-leagues is illuminating. The Swabian-Rhenisch League of 1280, for example, could form an army of approximately 10,000 men.[4] This army could compete with any of the German dukes, but to do so it had to unite eighty-nine towns. Italian towns, however, could raise such numbers by themselves. The Florentines could raise an army of 12,000 in this period.[5] By 1295, Genoa had 200 galleys and 40,000 men at its disposal.[6] Consequently, one of the main reasons for towns to choose either a central monarchy or league was absent in Italy. Unlike the individual German and French towns, the Italian cities could defend themselves.

The nature of Italian trade also differed. The Hanseatic towns traded in large quantities of relatively cheap commodities. Although the Italians also engaged in bulk trade, such as grain for the towns, they focused particularly on luxury goods. These were expensive commodities of relatively small quantity. This commerce created a different incentive structure for the Italian towns.

> The Baltic, by the very nature and sheer volume of the goods it provided, could support a whole galaxy of entrepôts. But in the Mediterranean a traffic in small quantities of immensely valuable commodities was already in the 1300s contested between Venice and Genoa alone. . . . And so there emerged an imperial pattern soon widely emulated, in which a trade considered vital or particularly valuable was conducted as the carefully defined monopoly of a single port.[7]

The German towns could benefit from some form of centralized organization which would maintain their relatively low profit margins and diminish the effects of feudal particularism. Given the German towns' low profit margins, the transaction and information costs that they incurred were more problematic than they were for the Italians. The German towns preferred to cut costs and keep competition among their members to a minimum, while at the same time they sought to monopolize their trade vis-à-vis outsiders. The Italian towns, however, faced a predatorial market where fortunes could be made by eliminating rival towns. One of the most important factors preventing urban collusion,

I would argue, was the specific nature of the Mediterranean market. The trade of the Italian towns was small-volume, luxury trade.[8] Profit margins in the northern seas ranged around 5 to 15 percent, very occasionally 25 percent,[9] whereas those of the Venetians and Genoese could reach 150 percent.[10] A few galleys of spices might have represented a fortune. Consequently the German towns had an incentive to collude, to negotiate higher prices, reduce risks, and maintain the slight profit margins that existed. The Venetians and Genoese, by contrast, were locked in a life-and-death struggle to control ports of access in the Black Sea and the Mideast.

The maritime technology of the Venetians and Genoese reflected this kind of trade. The labor-intensive galleys were equipped to move relatively small loads, and few ships were needed. Each ship, moreover, had considerable defensive capability of its own in contrast to the bulky, labor-extensive cogs and hulks of the northern waters. The Venetian galleys were manned with freemen, who could double as troops. They were complemented by about thirty to forty professional soldiers, usually crossbowmen, making a complement of about two hundred to two hundred fifty men per ship. Such ships sailing together with two or three others from the same town were highly invulnerable to pirates. The security of Venetian shipping was reflected in the low insurance rates of individual ships.[11] This protection rent thus benefited the Italian maritime cities.

Genoese ships were different but had roughly a similar effect. The Genoese mixed the military ability of its landed aristocracy (which Venice did not have) with enforced galley slaves. Genoese trade was closely tied to the use of force. Trade, piracy, and territorial expansion were intertwined.[12] Because of its defensive capacity, individually or in small contingents, Genoese ships proved unattractive targets.

Without knowing about the internal politics of the Italian towns, one can, therefore, infer that there were two a priori reasons why towns might not have preferred a central monarchy or a city-league. First, they were strong enough to defend themselves from lordly control. And second, their economic environment suggested mutual competition rather than alliance.

But this can only be a first estimate of the actual political outcome. As I have argued before, the towns' preferred objectives need not have materialized in practice. Outcomes also depend on the agendas of other social groups and political actors. For example, in the German case, the choice for an imperial strategy forestalled a royal-burgher alliance. Furthermore, the question of why these cities did not band together during their period of decline remains. Why, for example, did not we see the formation of city-leagues in the face of foreign incursions during the late fifteenth and sixteenth centuries? And finally, why did the city-states not transform themselves into sovereign states such as France? Although the character of the economic environment provides us the context in which these towns pursued material gains, it cannot provide us with answers to those questions. Once again, we need to retrace the actual preferences and bargains that were struck between towns and relevant political actors.

CENTRIFUGAL FORCES IN THE ITALIAN KINGDOM AND THE
ABSENCE OF A ROYAL-URBAN ALLIANCE

The Historical Origins of the Independent Communes

The Frankish Empire, which had replaced the Byzantines as the protector of
the papacy, broke up after Charlemagne's death in 814. Four kingdoms were
established: the kingdom of Italy, the West-Frankish kingdom, the East-Frankish kingdom, and the kingdom of Burgundy. As in the West-Frankish kingdom
(later France) and the East-Frankish kingdom (later Germany), the Carolingian
lineage died out in Italy. Subsequently, central control in northern Italy
declined.

The papacy lacked the ability to enforce centralized rule without a strong
secular force to back it up. It soon become the pawn of opposing factions, which
supported and deposed popes at will. One faction even went so far as to dig up
and put on trial the body of a deceased pope.[13]

The local lords stepped into this power vacuum. The effect of Carolingian
decline was thus similar to that in the West-Frankish kingdom and the East-
Frankish kingdom; power shifted to local counts, bishops, and dukes.[14] The
bishops were particularly successful in their usurpation of royal powers. They
assumed regalian rights of jurisdiction and control over weights and coinage.
The bishops were well positioned to do this because of the continued urban
character of Italy. Since the bishopric was an ecclesiastical office designed
around an urban seat, from where the bishop controlled the surrounding diocese, he was well suited to take over many of the royal administrative tasks.
Moreover, Italy continued to have a strong urban character even after Roman
decline, because trade remained significant.[15] The ascent of the Muslims did
not alter this.[16]

As towns grew, secular and ecclesiastical lordship became less tolerable.
By the tenth century, some burghers rebelled—particularly against ecclesiastical control—in a manner strikingly similar to the developments in France
and Germany. Around the middle of the eleventh century, townsfolk started
to organize themselves in a formal sense. They formed communes, sworn
associations for the exercise of public authority. The first of such formal associations originated in 1081 in Milan and Parma.[17] Many others soon followed.
The communes specifically aimed to diminish the powers of all outside interference.[18]

Often these communes took over the powers the bishop had held. That is,
the powers of jurisdiction, the levying of tolls, and control over weights and
coinage were now seized by the urban governments.[19] Genoa, for example, had
these rights explicitly ceded to it by the emperor Frederick Barbarossa in
1162.[20] Genoa also obtained exemption from imperial taxation and the right to
make war and peace and conclude alliances. To demonstrate how the towns
usurped the powers of the bishop, one need only realize that the towns used
the boundaries of the diocese itself to delineate the area of urban rule over the

surrounding countryside.[21] These communes claimed independence and ruled as sovereign powers.[22]

It is not clear to what extent the communes modeled themselves after Roman imperial government.[23] Nevertheless it seems that there were parallels. The communes were first governed by consuls—clearly a reflection of the Roman office—and later by the podesta, who resembled the old office of dictator. Furthermore, Roman law was a critical source of legitimation of the communes' sovereignty.[24]

In summary, Italy managed to maintain a strong urban character even after centralized rule declined. Local power-holders, particularly bishops, assumed regalian rights. Around the middle of the eleventh century, the urban centers rebelled against this lordly control. Influenced by old Roman models of government, they freed themselves from ecclesiastical and lordly control and exercised regalian rights themselves.

Urbanized Nobility and Factionalism in the Commune

The relationship of nobles to burghers differed in northern Italy from that in France and Germany.[25] In both France and Germany, the economic, political, and cultural interests of the nobility were antithetical to the burghers' interests. This was not the case in most Italian towns.

Unlike the urban communities of northwestern Europe, many Italian towns can trace their origins to Roman foundation.[26] Florence, for example, expanded from its Roman core. Even towns that emerged after this period still developed earlier than in the rest of Europe. Venice did not have Roman origins and was founded in the ninth century as a port of trade with Byzantium.[27] As a consequence of their historical development, the Italian towns contained a resident nobility. Many German and French cities, by contrast, did not originate from Roman foundations and were only founded in the twelfth and thirteenth centuries by the merchants in response to the upswing in trade.

In Italy the landed aristocracy were involved in trade and finance: "there was no stage at which noble descent was incompatible with trading."[28] The absence of runaway serfs in the towns demonstrates the lack of controversy between urban and rural economy. The aristocrats surrendered their residences in the countryside and moved to the city.[29] As Hibbert has noted, the nature of the Italian town differed from that in northwestern Europe.[30]

The divergent social composition of the towns in northwestern Europe from that in Italy is thus demonstrated by the physical location of the mercantile quarters. In northern Europe the free citizens did not establish residence in the area or villages controlled by a lord; instead they set up residence outside the old fortification, hence suburbs, or formed new towns altogether.[31] They soon built town walls and thus physically differentiated themselves from those living under lordly control. Such demarcation did not occur in Italy. Most towns simply expanded beyond their old Roman confines and incorporated the older part of the town. Furthermore, in northern Europe aristocrats were forbidden to settle in the city, whereas in Italy they were often obligated to do so.[32] Italian social development was thus quite different from that of France or Germany and had important political consequences.

> The townsmen of north-western Europe, and of the eastern towns they helped to found, were hostile to the aristocracy and the feudal system, and turned naturally to the monarchy as their protector and ally. But in Southern Europe, particularly in Italy, towns were the centres of aristocratic landed properties, and the nobility were drawn into the life of the city and took to trade, particularly overseas trade, at an early date.[33]

Why was the gap between the Italian nobility and the burghers less pronounced than in France and Germany? There are several reasons. First, noble-burgher coalitions formed the communes from the very beginning. The lesser aristocracy in particular allied with the commoners against ecclesiastical rule.[34] These lesser nobles, below the level of counts, sought to gain from the bishop's loss of power.

Second, Italy arguably was less feudalized than France or Germany.[35] As we saw, feudalism was to a considerable extent a Germanic practice, going back to the allegiance of chieftain and retinue.[36] Despite the Lombard and Frankish presence, feudalism proper never quite took root to the same extent as it did in northwestern Europe. The Roman influence predominated. (For the same reason, feudalism was less strong in southern France.) Consequently, military and mercantile pursuits were never completely distinct enterprises. Although the man at arms might have denigrated the commoner, he was astute enough not to forego profit when the opportunity arose.[37]

Third, the nature of Mediterranean trade offers a further explanation of why nobles made this urban transition. The luxury goods traded in the Mediterranean were obtained through long-distance commerce. Thus, luxury trade in products unobtainable in Italy would not encroach upon the agricultural production of landed nobility. The import of spices, for example, would not hurt domestic grain production. Moreover, much of this trade depended on the successful marriage of military power—the domain of the landed knight—and maritime capability.[38] That is, both interests were mutually reinforced. Genoa's trade, in particular, melded force and economic interests.[39] Venice, too, was not averse to military involvement. It managed to divert the Crusaders to Constantinople and overthrow the Byzantine Empire in 1204. Its expansion throughout the eastern Mediterranean offers further proof.

This urbanized nobility provided Italian towns with some unique traits. For example, one consequence of the noble presence was internal factionalism. Although there are few generalizable categories that hold true for all Italian cities, such cleavages played a very real part in the lives of most Italian town-dwellers.[40] Nobles were conspicuous by their military lifestyle. They were thus sometimes denoted as milites (the Latin description of a mounted knight) to distinguish them from the pedites (those on foot, hence commoners). Sometimes they were simply described as magnates ("the great") to distinguish them from the popolani (*populus* meaning "the people").[41] Hence, one cleavage was that between noble and commoner, however wealthy the latter might have been. As with the aristocracy in Germany and France, these nobles placed high value on their bloodline to distinguish themselves from commoners.[42] This was one source of perennial tension in the Italian cities. In the two years following 1293, the Florentines exiled just under half of their nobility.[43]

Nobles also feuded among themselves. Families might clash because of economic competition or perceived offense to a family member. Another split divided urban nobility and landed nobility, although it was virtually impossible to distinguish where one group began and the other ended.[44] Rather than compress into nuclear families, the common result of urbanization, noble families actually extended in the city.[45] Families that were not blood related might even assume a similar last name to fortify their allegiance. Such extended families used their sons as business agents, at home and abroad.[46] These family clans formed armed companies, the consorterie, to defend themselves from rival families.[47] They often lived in adjoining houses, with their own parish church and the ubiquitous tower into which they could withdraw in times of danger and pelt the streets below.[48] Blood feuds between different clans were not uncommon.

Other divisions proliferated, particularly during the twelfth century. The cause was increasing division of labor in the growing cities. Although the difference between the nobles (magnates) and the upper class of the commoners (popolani grasso) was sometimes minute, economic differences between burghers could be quite large.[49] The popolani grasso (traders and established middle class) were distinguishable from the popolani minuto (guildsmen), who in turn were differentiated from the capette (urban proletariat). Many of these factions not only regulated economic activity but also formed cohesive social units with their own guard. The guild, for example, regulated marriage ages and entry into the profession and formed a military company.[50] Economic differences thus crystalized in social and cultural differences. All of these groups provided themselves with the military means of defense.

These social cleavages might overlay or crosscut geographic divisions within the city. Cities were often divided into quarters, or contrade (neighborhoods).[51] Bologna thus had four quarters which were subdivided in seventy-two contrade. The latter were often centered around a chapel. These, too, might be cohesive units with their own armed force.[52] The differences between the various contrade and quarters were often reinforced by rituals that enhanced the competitive character of the geographical areas.[53]

In short, Italian towns were quite different from those in northwestern Europe. They had two particularly unusual characteristics. First, landed nobility had become urbanized and engaged in mercantile pursuits. Second, Italian towns were rife with factions. The political organization of these factions paralleled that of the city government. Such factions, too, appointed consuls and had their armed forces. The towns of the Hansa, by contrast, were dominated by a mercantile patriciate which ruled through town councils. These towns were politically and juridically relatively homogeneous, partially because they accepted the law codes of their mother towns. The dispersion of families throughout the Hansa towns also aided social homogeneity across the various member cities.

The Influence of Foreign Actors on the Divisions between and within the Cities

Historically, foreign powers had played an important role in Italy even before the emergence of the independent communes. Their continued interference throughout the later Middle Ages and Renaissance exacerbated the internal rifts within the communes. These powers also divided the communes among themselves, thus preventing any unified opposition. Conversely, the competing interests of the cities sometimes welcomed and enabled foreign encroachment. Some cities allied with foreign powers in order to overcome their external competitors.

As we have seen, the German king tried to establish a strong authority in northern Italy and the papal states. Consequently, the Ottonian Dynasty controlled papal elections with a heavy hand at least until the Investiture Conflict. At virtually the same time, however, a new power, the Normans, established themselves in the south. When the Byzantines were gradually evicted from Sicily by the Muslims of the Aglabid Dynasty (902), they turned to mercenaries. They recruited the Normans, Viking descendants who had settled in France.[54] As elsewhere, the Norman warriors proved to be highly successful. Their military prowess, however, was matched by their unreliability. In 1043 the Normans turned against the Byzantines and evicted them from Italy. The Normans then went on to take Sicily from the Muslims.

The pope saw in these Normans possible new secular allies against the German king. Consequently, in the direct aftermath of the Investiture Conflict, Pope Gregory sought support from the Normans against the Germans who were marching on Rome. The Normans provided the pope with the help requested, and German conquest was forestalled. However, once again the Normans proved to be less than reliable allies, and they sacked Rome themselves.[55] They then retreated to their southern holdings and concentrated on the formation of a strong feudal state. They divided property holdings into allods of the church (free holdings), feudal fiefs (held by vassals), and a royal domain. As a consequence, the towns became subjected to feudal domination and their independence was prevented.[56] This is part of the reason why only the northern towns would become independent and develop into prosperous city-states.

Under the Hohenstaufen (1138–1254), the German emperors renewed their interest in Italy. Frederick I succeeded in marrying into the Norman dynasty (1177). And in 1198, his grandson, Frederick II, was crowned king of Sicily. From then on the Norman kingdom of Sicily was in German hands, and the Germans continued the Norman feudal strategy.[57]

Needless to say, with the German Hohenstaufen seeking to enforce imperial privileges in the north and factually holding on to the south, the papacy felt extremely threatened. The revenues of Sicily, a major grain producer at the time, added moreover to the imperial cause.[58] Consequently, the pope sought alliances with the communes in the north and sought to weaken the imperial position in the south. Some communes sided with the papacy and thus became part of the anti-imperial party, the Guelphs, whereas others, the Ghibellines, sought to gain imperial favors.[59] The formation of these two parties dates from roughly 1240, when Frederick II was a major actor in Italy.[60]

The pope now turned to Charles of Anjou, the brother of the French king, to challenge the German hold on Sicily after the death of Frederick II in 1250. In 1254 the direct heir to the Hohenstaufen line died, so the pope, as nominal suzerain,[61] offered the lands to the French House of Anjou.[62] The pope further offered Charles the revenue of a tithe in France to cover expenses. The Angevins indeed took Sicily, and Charles had all German contenders, of all ages, killed or imprisoned for life. The Sicilian population, however, did not take well to French domination. On Easter of 1282 a rebellion broke out, and within a day about two thousand Frenchmen had been killed. This rebellion was supported by the Aragonese who had married into the Hohenstaufen lineage and thus laid claim to the Hohenstaufen heritage.

The result was that the French withdrew to the mainland and established the kingdom of Naples.[63] The Spanish, the Aragonese, now held the kingdom of Sicily. The German emperors still had nominal claims on the north, although de facto the communes ruled as sovereign.[64] The middle of Italy was still held by the papal state which would ally with any foreign actor and/or the communes to oppose German imperial pretensions.

A multitude of foreign intrusions thus occurred. These had important consequences for the communes and their subsequent development to that of city-states. External forces divided the communes. The already vacillating urban strategies to ally with either pope or emperor were further accentuated with the French entry into the south. *Guelph* therefore became a term representing support for the pope as well as the French against the emperor.[65]

Foreign involvement also heightened the factionalism within the towns. Each faction was willing to sacrifice communal peace and independence for its own gain.[66] As a rule, one can argue that nobles favored the imperial strategy, perhaps hoping for feudal favors, whereas the merchants favored the Guelph party.[67] But because of the interchange of burghers and nobility, the generalization is very rough.

In short, external pressure led to conflicts between towns and increased factionalism within the towns. Towns had to contend with the internecine struggles between the various noble clans, between nobles and commoners, and between the different classes of commoners. Any one of such groups had different preferences as to which external power might be the ideal ruler.

The Conflicting Interests of King and Towns

These external pressures illuminate why the German king could not profit from the urban revival as did the French king. By shifting their allegiances between the foreign powers that tried to dominate Italy, the towns were able to improve their negotiating position or gain independence outright.[68]

But there were other reasons as well. First, the communes united both noble and mercantile interests. The communes had early on freed themselves from ecclesiastical lordship. The main factor that drove French towns to seek royal support, freedom from lordly control, was thus absent in Italy.

Furthermore, as I discussed at the beginning of this chapter, the Italian towns were far stronger than their French or German counterparts. Venice, Florence, Milan, and Genoa were all two to three times the size of Cologne, the largest German city. All the other German cities were far smaller. Likewise, the French towns were of limited size—the exception being Paris which was slightly smaller than Genoa at the time. Since each of the Italian towns had considerable strength of their own, they did not need allies for military protection.

Third, as an outsider, the German imperial position was always suspect. In France the towns could hope that the king would protect their interests because they in turn provided him with his source of revenue. But the Italian towns had little reason to expect that behavior from the German emperor. The kingdom of Italy might simply serve as a revenue basis for the emperor's imperial pretensions in Germany or elsewhere. Additionally, Frederick I tried to reimpose feudal obligations. Feudalism, however, was a mode of organization based on "a web of personal relations." Hence such obligations were not useful for abstract corporate entities.[69] In a system of personal bonds, possession over time might suffice to uphold title; but in an urban system based on market exchange, more clearly defined property rights are necessary.[70]

Moreover, during the period of weak German kingship, in the decades preceding the Hohenstaufen, the towns had managed to gain power and free themselves from these feudal obligations. When Frederick I sought to reimpose them, it was too late.[71] The towns were unwilling to relinquish their acquired liberties.

Finally, as in Germany, the Italian towns could unite when absolutely necessary. Despite the rivalry between the communes, and the internal factionalism, the towns occasionally realized that their convergence of interests dictated united action against the emperor in times of crisis. They formed the Lombard League in 1160 and renewed it several times in the face of imperial pressure by Frederick I (1152–1190) and Frederick II (1211–1250). It formed a mutual defensive alliance and set troop contingents to be borne by the independent towns.[72] This league dealt Frederick I a crushing defeat at Legnano in 1176. And although Frederick II had more success in the field, he, too, could not gain an outright victory.

We should also not forget the role of the pope in bringing such towns together. Given the disparity of interests between the cities and their different domestic coalitions, they could face serious collective action problems, which now were partially overcome by the willingness of the pope to help organize such leagues. Indeed, Hay and Law blame the lack of centralization in Italy basically on the pope's strategy of opposing any secular lord who sought to establish such authority.[73]

As a response, the German emperors turned toward their holdings in southern Italy. They kept these in feudal form.[74] This was partially due to the fact that urbanization was less advanced in southern Italy and partially due to the agricultural nature of Sicily.

In short, German imperial policy failed in the north and reinforced urban independence, whereas in the south it successfully reinforced a feudal monarchy, with little urban independence.[75] An alliance between king and northern towns was precluded because the king had little to offer the towns. The towns themselves had eliminated lordly repression; they had long since exercised regalian rights such as jurisdiction, coinage, and taxation; they did not need any external military ally to defend them; and they objected to reintroduction of feudal obligations by the emperor. Moreover, the diversity of urban political regimes made any coalition difficult. Finally, the continued influence of outside powers—the Germans, French, Spanish—meant that towns could switch sides when necessity dictated.

City-state Rather than City-league

Many of the factors that made a royal-burgher alliance impossible also worked against the creation of city-leagues. The factionalistic interests that divided the towns internally, and the variation in regimes across the towns, negated any attempts at a more permanent form of cooperation. But perhaps most important was the predatorial market environment which led towns to compete rather than unite.

Concentration of Power: The Ascent of the Signoria

Between the late twelfth century and the early fifteenth century, internal factionalism and external involvement led to changes in the type of government of the Italian communes. The consular government of the early communes disappeared. It was replaced by more autocratic forms of rule.

The communes, from their very origins in the eleventh century, all had to contend with debilitating internal strife. Nobility of birth demarcated aristocrat from commoner. Money demarcated wealthy from poor. Across these divisions there were rivalries between noble clans and geographic divisions of the contrade. The original communal government, the rule by two consuls, proved inadequate to control this cauldron of competing interests. These consuls were often aristocrats (milites) and hence not necessarily neutral. Since none of these factions trusted the other with strong powers of authority, they not only kept the consularship weak but each also formed armed companies of its own.

Starting in about 1170, the communes turned to an alternative form of government—the rule by the podesta. The podesta was an outsider brought in to fulfill executive powers, particularly police functions.[76] He was basically an entrepreneurial captain with military skills. He was thus often an aristocrat and was accompanied by a small armed retinue. The podesta was a temporary position, normally lasting between six and twelve months, after which the podesta was responsible to the communal council for the actions undertaken during his command.[77] The position in this regard resembled the Roman dictatorship, which gave absolute power for six months, with accountability afterward. The podesta was thus meant to be a neutral arbiter to control the many armed factions in the city.

Podestal government, however, was a double-edged sword. On the one hand, the captain had the task of maintaining the peace. Hence he had to control the exercise of violence by the armed noble consorterie, and the guilds which likewise possessed armed companies. On the other hand, he also had a personal incentive to increase his position within the city. The neutralization of other powers left him with a possible monopoly of violence. Hence, the podesta often ended up dominating the very groups that had brought him in.

From roughly 1270 onward, the temporary podesta transformed into the permanent signoria. The signoria, the rule by an aristocratic leader, had several sources of support from which to choose.[78] A captain might form an alliance with the leading powers in a city. Fellow aristocrats or moneyed men from the upper class might enlist his support against their internal rivals. Other captains enhanced their standing by gaining external support. Foreign powers could prove to be useful allies for aspiring despots.[79] Furthermore, as the conflicts between cities increased, the military capabilities of these professional soldiers became more important. The commercial and military struggles between Genoa, Pisa, and Venice rose to a serious pitch during the thirteenth century. Also, as cities started to expand beyond their contado, the area surrounding the city, they automatically encroached upon the territories controlled by other cities. The rivalry between Florence and Lucca was of this nature.

The career of Castruccio Castracani in Lucca provides an illustrative example of how this office might evolve.[80] Lucca had been involved in a period of warfare and hence required the services of a skilled military professional. Furthermore, aristocrats had previously backed a Pisan takeover, since they favored Pisan aristocratic rule rather than independence under the popolo. The city was thus in intense turmoil and called in a strongman from outside in the hope that an outsider would have less affinity with particular factions. Castracani, however, expanded his position by making alliances with specific groups and by controlling internal violence. He also obtained imperial support against Florence, which was Guelph. The emperor therefore granted him the ducal title. With internal and imperial support, Castracani managed to expand the territory controlled by Lucca. This generated trade benefits and a larger revenue basis which he used to strengthen his position with the mercantile groups.

Basically, seigneurial rule in the form of an autocratic ruler meant the triumph of the nobility.[81] However, this did not necessarily mean a loss to mercantile interests. The popolani grasso, the moneyed class, would sometimes support such strongmen in order to control the lower commoners and the guildsmen.

But not every city moved toward absolute rule by a single aristocrat. Signoria could also mean the rule by a few. Some cities, about seven, such as Venice and

Florence (the latter with some interruptions), maintained a republican oligarchy. Venice managed to maintain republicanism by concentrating government in the hands of a fixed number of influential families. The last modification of the Venetian nobility occurred in 1382 and included between 2,000 and 2,500 citizens, with only minor changes in the next centuries.[82] This might have been due to Venice's greater homogeneity. More than in other towns, mercantile pursuits dominated every other economic interest. In Florence other factors were at work. Here, too, social forces moved away from popular government. In 1328, Florence established a rule by the thirty. In the 1420s, the core of the regime was made up of sixty to seventy families. The new constitution of 1494 included 3,000 out of 90,000 citizens in the political class.[83] Nevertheless, it did not evolve into a dictatorship, and oligarchical government was kept in check.[84] Oligarchical government was sporadically alternated with popular and dictatorial regimes. The nouveaux riches, the continuing influx of new wealthy, also worked as a stabilizing factor. Any group excluded from power could find in these up-and-coming individuals, who were themselves yet without political power, valuable allies to alter the existing power structure. The result was continual compromise.[85]

But one should not confuse these developments as democratic forms of government. Even the republics did not enfranchise more than 2 to 3 percent of the population.[86] Authority thus always rested on the specific elite coalitions in each town.

The Divergent Interests of the Towns

The development of the cities toward oligarchical republics or despotism proved, therefore, another barrier to league formation. These differences in types of government reflected whether trade or landed interests had gained the upper hand. The preconditions for republicanism, such as a sound commercial base, a vibrant bourgeoisie, and a defeated nobility, were increasingly difficult to meet for many Italian cities.[87] Consequently, there was little conformity of interests across towns. The turn to more despotic regimes reflected a move toward a greater reliance on landed interests as compared to the mercantile interests of the republics, such as Lucca, Siena, Florence, Genoa, and Venice.

Among the towns of the Hansa, by contrast, there was a stronger political and social homogeneity. In all towns a mercantile patriciate dominated. Indeed, as we saw earlier, one of the functions of the city-leagues was to maintain such elites in power. Towns that overthrew their town councils could be excluded or, worse, provoked military and economic retaliation by the other members. Landed aristocracy was not integrated into the towns. Furthermore, social mobility between the towns was high. The genealogy of many commercial families can often be traced across several Hansa towns. In Italy, however, social mobility was low. Migration was discouraged by tough citizenship requirements. New arrivals only obtained citizenship rights after many years of residence, and they had to meet certain requirements, such as owning property in the city.[88]

Each city was also adamant in asserting its own particular social and cultural heritage as opposed to that of other towns. Migration to another town was not taken lightly but required a conversion to the particular rules of order and local customs, the regimento.[89]

Furthermore, political reasons that might necessitate a united front by the towns were absent in Italy. German towns had formed leagues with the explicit intent to curtail encroachment by secular and ecclesiastical lords. In Italy the nobles had since long acquired mercantile interests—partially because of the Italians' mixture of trade and warfare—and thus the urban-rural rift was less pronounced. The bishops had early on been subjected to the control of the communes and thus constituted no threat.

With the exception of the Hohenstaufen, there was no outside force, prior to 1500, that could effectively challenge the independent cities. And when there was a serious challenge to the autonomy of the cities, they formed temporary unions. The repeated formation of the Lombard League against the Hohenstaufen, particularly Frederick I and Frederick II, proved that an external military threat could provide sufficient impetus to form a temporary alliance. A permanent league, however, would need more than a military threat to be viable in the long run.

Nor was the pope a threat to urban independence. Despite the fact that the communes gained their independence at the expense of the bishops, there was little conflict between the papacy and the communes. Both were allies in their opposition to German imperial rule. Moreover, the financial organization of the communes proved to be valuable for papal financial interests as well. Although knightly orders were useful for collecting and transporting revenue, as the Templars did for the French king, the papal administration soon realized that their financial needs were best served by merchant bankers. Members of the clergy would thus take out loans from these merchant bankers, even though the clergy would occasionally balk at tacit interest charges.[90]

As I already mentioned, a contributing factor to the lack of any urban alliance was also the sheer size of the Italian towns. The towns could individually muster considerable military and economic strength. At the end of the fifteenth century, when Venice had started to acquire considerable territorial holdings beyond its original city confines, Venice and the terra ferma had a population of almost 1.5 million.[91] This was comparable to Burgundy's population and the Dutch Republic's population in the sixteenth century.

Economically, the revenues of the cities matched or even outstripped those of far larger states. The Della Scala signoria, which controlled Parma, Lucca, and Modena, is estimated to have had a yearly revenue of 700,000 florins in the early fourteenth century. English revenue was about the equivalent of 350,000 florins. Florence in 1336 and 1338 had a yearly revenue of 500,000 florins and Siena, in 1315, a revenue of 250,000 florins.[92] These revenues came from direct taxes (particularly from the forced loans, the prestanze) and indirect taxes. In 1423 the Venetian budget was about 750,000 ducats, whereas that of France was 1 million ducats. The English and Spanish budgets were about 750,000

146

CHAPTER 7

ducats.[93] If one considers the revenue of the Venetian Empire, that is, Venice and its territorial holdings in Italy and the Adriatic, the total rises to 1,615,000 ducats. And one must keep in mind that this was raised by a population of 1.5 million, whereas the population of France was ten times that number. The revenue of the Genoese commercial colony of Pera was almost equal to that of Genoa itself and was ten times that of Lübeck.[94] In short, the cities were large enough to go it alone. They needed neither king nor alliance to defend themselves.

Moreover, as I discussed at the outset of this chapter, the nature of Italian long-distance trade did not favor collusion as it did with the Hansa. Instead it favored competition wherein fortunes were made by relatively few ships of individual towns. Maritime technology enhanced the ability of individual towns to work alone rather than form large convoys.

Consequently, the history of Italian trading towns is filled with conflict. In 1204 Venice managed to divert the Fourth Crusade to Constantinople and take the city. It claimed Crete and three-eighths of the city and Byzantine Empire and obtained a monopoly on the Black Sea trade by excluding Pisa and Genoa. It thus gained access to the ports that formed the endpoints of the caravan routes that crossed Central Asia. Half a century later, the Genoese supported the Byzantine emperor in retaking the city, after which it was Genoa's turn to obtain a monopoly on the Black Sea trade. In 1284 Genoa defeated the Pisans in a brutal war.[95] In the War of Chioggia (1378–1381), Genoa almost succeeded in taking Venice itself. Venice ultimately won and embarked on a policy of conquest, taking Treviso (1389), Vicenza (1404), Verona and Padua (1405), Bergamo (1428), and additional towns. Others were not to be outdone. Florence, for example, captured Prato (1350) and Volterra (1361) and managed to obtain a port by conquering Pisa (1406). The policies of Florence and Venice were nothing new; "the two republics extended their dominions to pre-empt rivals, to protect earlier gains and to defend their trade routes."[96]

To sum up, each Italian city had material reasons to see itself as a sovereign entity. At the end of the fourteenth century, the Florentine Republic introduced new concepts to denote the entire city and its centralized authority. Florence also introduced the crime of lesae-maiestatis, offenses against the government and unofficial head of state, the Medici.[97] The city-states thus claimed similar status with any sovereign state. Cities legitimated their power as independent authorities and were unwilling to cede their independence to some form of federation with other cities. Consequently, other cities were perceived as rival entities, which if possible, were to be subjugated.

CITY-STATE AND SOVEREIGN, TERRITORIAL STATE COMPARED

Rather than form city-leagues, the individual Italian towns sought expansion by annexation of rivals. Between 1200 and 1450, the Italian landscape changed from roughly two hundred to three hundred independent communes to a handful of territorial city-states. In the north, Venice, the Papal State, Milan, and Florence gradually came to dominate the others.[98]

Reasons Behind the Territorial Expansion of the City-state

One reason for the expansion of the city-state was the town elites' renewed interest in territorial holdings. In cities where the podesta had changed to signoria, and then finally to princely authority, the landed interests of the aristocracy serves as a partial explanation. The princely territories, such as Milan and Ferrara, consisted of many small feudal estates with considerable powers of their own.[99] Their revenues were based on indirect taxes rather than on the direct tax of property; they did not distinguish public and private revenue; and the princes themselves were not subject to the rule of law. In other words, these princes had essentially set themselves up as despots serving the landed interests of the privileged.

But even in more mercantile cities such as Venice, with only a small number of landed aristocrats, there was a turn toward a territorial policy. An explanation of Venice, as a least likely case to expect territorial holdings, thus illuminates why towns turned to expansionism.

Starting in the fifteenth century, Venice increasingly encountered impediments to its trade. The renewed Turkish expansion under the Ottomans drastically curtailed the Venetian position in the eastern Mediterranean. The Black Sea, certainly from 1453 on, became inaccessible because of the fall of Constantinople. Furthermore, Portuguese and Spanish competition increased at the end of the fifteenth and throughout the sixteenth century. The Iberians utilized different maritime technology. The opening of Atlantic commerce favored larger ships which were driven solely by sail. The start-up costs for such new technology proved too high for the Venetians.[100] This presented yet another reason to invest in landed property closer to home rather than in increasingly risky trading ventures. The economic hazards and already accumulated wealth led to the development of rentiers rather than mercantile entrepreneurs.[101]

Another reason for the decline in the number of independent cities lay in the economic and political rivalry we have discussed. Within the framework of those rivalries, Genoa fought and defeated Pisa. Florence tried to get territories from Siena and in turn subjugated Pisa to get a harbor.[102] Venice annexed Vicenza. Milan gained suzerainty over Genoa. Even the Papal State followed similar methods of expansion. The continual cycle of urban warfare thus eliminated those who were unable to meet the challenges of their larger predators. There was thus "incessant warfare between the Italian cities."[103]

In the process, the cities might ally with a strong external force. In 1312, Pisa, threatened by Florence, supported the empire, whereas Florence was Guelph. Later, when Siena and Lucca felt Florentine pressure, they, too, favored imperial intervention.[104] The duke of Milan gained the support of the Habsburgs to get control over Genoa.[105] The aristocrats within Genoa thereupon sought support from France, which by the end of the fifteenth century wished to curtail Habsburg encirclement. Foreign powers thus played no small role in reducing the numbers of competing Italian cities.

In short, the ascent of the signoria, tougher market conditions, competition between towns, and foreign intervention all played a role in diminishing the number of independent city-states. In many ways, the remaining city-states started to resemble sovereign, territorial states.

The Fragmented Sovereignty of the Italian City-states[106]

Although the city-states expanded, they never made the complete transition to sovereign, territorial statehood. Although the difference between city-states and sovereign states is difficult to portray,[107] city-states were not simply small sovereign states.[108] First, internal hierarchy in the city-states was more diffuse than in sovereign, territorial states. The towns that were annexed by more powerful cities maintained much of their previous independence. They continued to exercise their own sphere of jurisdiction.

> In this sense, the general political orientation of the new states, whether principalities or republics, did not break with the old ways. Especially in matters of local government, old communal institutions, such as statutes, councils and offices, were maintained besides those of the central power. Legally or practically, large responsibilities were left to cities.[109]

Moreover, the large number of towns, which traditionally had been independent, made centralization difficult.[110] A similar point can be made about the incorporation of rural areas. The dominant city was slow in granting these subjects citizenship.

Furthermore, none of these city-states developed formal kingship. Despots called themselves dukes or princes, but not kings, although they basically exercised regalian rights.[111] The government of the city-state was always tied to some faction. The French king, by contrast, could claim to be a mediator of these social tensions. The interests of the king coincided with those of the realm. Aggrandizement of the realm by increasing revenue through trade (mercantilism) or territorial expansion benefited the king as well as his subjects. The Italian aristocrats were not mediators. The city-state never resolved factionalism.

> One cannot help wondering how such far-ranging supremacy can possibly have been established and maintained on such a narrow foundation—particularly since power inside a city-state was always being challenged from within. . . . And all this for the benefit of the handful of families . . . who held . . . the reigns of power. These families moreover fought bitter feuds among themselves.[112]

In summary, the political organization of city-states remained one of a dominant city and subject towns. The previously independent communes retained a large amount of independence and were not fully integrated into the city-state. Hierarchy within the city-state was always contested. Sovereignty remained incomplete.

City-states, however, did develop the other characteristic similar to sovereign states. They did define authority by territorial boundaries. Unlike the Hansa, which lacked such territorial specificity, the Italian cities could agree on specific borders delimiting their claim to control.

Conclusion

This chapter focused on three matters. First, it examined why no sovereign state emerged in Italy. That is, it focused particularly on why no centralized kingship managed to reassert itself. Second, it analyzed why the cities formed independent city-states rather than city-leagues. And third, it briefly compared the city-state to sovereign statehood.

The strong impact and particular nature of long-distance trade are the primary reasons why no central authority emerged, be it a king or confederacy. The large urban population, made possible by this commerce, and their considerable economic and military resources diminished the necessity for a royal protector or town alliance. Moreover, the specific nature of this trade made towns prefer competition rather than central control. The Hansa's low-value, high-volume trade yielded low profit margins. Collusion was one way to obtain a higher price for Hansa commodities. The great profits of Mediterranean trade, by contrast, were primarily from low-volume, high-value commerce. Individual towns sought, and Genoa and Venice often obtained, monopolies of particular trade routes.

A royal-urban alliance was furthermore unnecessary because the landed aristocracy resided in the towns and pursued mercantile interests. Italian towns were not under external lordly pressure, as were French and German towns. Foreign powers also played an important role in Italian politics. On the one hand, these powers consciously sought to divide the communes. But on the other hand, communes could also form alliances with these actors to maintain their independence.

Similar reasons prevented the towns from forming city-leagues, as the German, Dutch, and Baltic towns did in the Hansa. The factionalism in the Italian towns gave rise to a wide variety of institutionalized preferences. In some towns, landed aristocrats dominated; in others, the upper middle class; and in yet others, the artisan guilds. The variety of social conditions and different forms of government thus reflected a disparity of interests, quite unlike that of the city-leagues. The communes also perceived themselves to be culturally distinct from each other. Each commune had its *regimento*, rules of order, which regulated citizenship and social and political activity. Each commune also developed the concept of sovereignty and thus saw no legitimate reason why any authority, be it pope, emperor, or town confederacy, should stand above the government of the city.

In many ways the city-state resembled the sovereign, territorial state. Like the French monarchy, the city-state developed notions of sovereignty and the public realm. Roman law figured prominently. And like the sovereign state, the city-state had territorial parameters. Nevertheless, there were differences between the two. The city-state did not integrate its surrounding countryside and the subjected towns. This shows, for example, in the lack of citizenship privileges for the inhabitants in these subjected areas. Not all members within its territorial parameters were thus full members of the city-state.[113] This lack of integration of different interests likewise shows in the inherent factionalism of many Italian towns. In France, the king could claim to be a mediator of interests, since he stood to benefit from the overall welfare of the kingdom. The Italian city-state lacked such a political actor. The government was simply perceived as the extension of a specific factional interest. As we will see, this proved to be an institutional weakness in the long run.

PART III

Competition, Mutual Empowerment, and Choice: The Advantages of Sovereign Territoriality

The Victory of the Sovereign State

> Sovereignty simultaneously provides an ordering principle for what is "internal"
> to states and what is "external" to them. It presumes a system of rule that is
> universal and obligatory in relation to the citizenry of a specified territory but
> from which all those who are not citizens are excluded.[1]

IN THE preceding chapters I have argued that the economic transformation of
the Late Middle Ages inspired individuals to create new forms of organization
in western Europe. Universalist empire, Roman theocracy, and feudalism gave
way to the sovereign, territorial state, the city-league, and the city-state.

These new institutional forms differed from each other in their degree of
internal hierarchy and in whether or not their authority was demarcated by
territorial parameters. Sovereign, territorial states contained a final locus of
authority. Although my main emphasis has been on France, the same was true
for other states such as England. Sovereignty need not imply absolutism. Even
Hobbes recognized that sovereignty could take the form of parliamentary rule.
But within sovereign states there existed a final decision-making structure
which brooked no outside interference and which gradually claimed a monopoly on violence and justice. In addition, the sovereign state confined itself territorially. That is, sovereigns claimed hierarchy within borders and recognized
no higher authority.

The city-league formed the antithesis of the sovereign, territorial state. Because of its confederated nature, its locus of final decision making was ambiguous. Did it reside with individual cities or with an executive body of the league
of towns? Confederation, as in the case of the Hansa, left this highly unclear.
Moreover, the city-leagues were nonterritorial in character. Although individual towns were surrounded by city walls, the leagues were not only noncontig-
uous, they lacked borders altogether. They were functionally but not territorially integrated for mutual defense of liberty and commercial interests. In short,
unlike the sovereign state, the Hansa did not differentiate its authority by territorial specification, nor did it recognize a final locus of authority, either internally or externally.

The city-state formed an intermediate category of institutional structure.
With the sovereign, territorial state it had in common a strict demarcation of
jurisdiction by fixed borders. Also, externally the dominant city acted as the
focal point for interunit contacts. But like the city-league, the city-state was
internally divided. Given that the city-state consisted of one city dominating

TABLE 8.1
Two Dimensions of Hierarchy and Fixed Territoriality

		Internal Sovereignty	
		Fragmented	*Consolidated*
Territorial	*Borders*	Italian city-states	French state
Demarcation	*Lack of borders*	Hanseatic League Feudalism	Universalist Empire Universalist Theocracy

other towns, the latter always contested the rule of the leading center. Sovereignty in the city-state, to use Tilly's terminology, was fragmented.

These two facets of organization, internal hierarchy and territorial demarcation, can be used to examine all the systems of rule discussed so far (see Table 8.1).

As I have already argued, feudal organization, with its crosscutting and overlapping jurisdictions, lacked both a clear center as well as territorial borders. Empire and church both claimed final decision-making power but lacked clear territorial specification of their authority. In theory all other political actors were their subjects.

It is clear that the Hansa, the Italian city-states, and the French state all cued in to the new market opportunities created by the transition from local in-kind trade to long-distance monetarized commerce. Yet from these three synchronic alternatives, only one survived. By the middle of the seventeenth century, the city-league no longer proved to be a viable competitor to the sovereign state. The Hanseatic League basically ended in 1667, when the last diet convened. And although the decline of the city-states proved to be less dramatic, they, too, gradually fell by the wayside.[2]

What happened in the three centuries preceding Westphalia that allowed sovereign states to become the constitutive elements of a global state system?[3] The historical literature on the rise and decline of specific types of units often emphasizes the importance of unique and critical developments. Particular policies, changing fortunes in war, shifting trade routes, and idiosyncrasies of rulers all provide plausible explanations. For example, the changing location of the herring schools, the silting of the harbor in Bruges, or the opening of the transatlantic routes are sometimes presented as explanations for the waning of the Hansa.[4] Likewise, some believe that the discovery of African circumnavigation struck the fatal blow to the Italian city-states.[5] Others see the influence of the guilds or the pursuit of landed interests as reasons for their decline.

No doubt many of these observations are pertinent and contribute to the explanation of why the Hansa and the Italian city-states drew to a close. But can we elicit general lessons from their demise? That is, although the descent of the Hanseatic League, or of Venice and Florence, are interesting in their own right, the broader and theoretically more challenging question is, why did they die out as institutional alternatives to the sovereign state? The diminishing fortunes of the Hansa and Venice do not fully explain why city-leagues and city-states, as particular logics of organization, should have disappeared. After all, sovereign states have also risen and declined, but that has not led to the disappearance of the sovereign state as an institutional form. Quite the contrary. We need, therefore, to go beyond the historically particular to theorize about the general implications of certain institutional arrangements.

This chapter suggests that organizational types have particular properties, which in the case of city-states and the Hansa contributed to their decline. I shall use the Hansa and the Italian city-states as institutional cases from which we can deduce certain general consequences. To be specific, we need to examine what consequences the presence or absence of internal hierarchy and territorial demarcation had for the survivability of those types of institutions.

The sovereign, territorial logic of organization replaced the alternative modes of authority in Europe because of several major factors. Institutions that internally had a final decision-making authority were in a better position to overcome the feudal remnants of economic and legal particularism. The king's interest in rationalizing and improving the overall economy coincided with the interests of the mercantile elements in society. Such institutions were, competitively speaking, more effective and more efficient in curtailing freeriding and defection, and hence they were better at mobilizing the resources of their societies.

But there were additional reasons why sovereign, territorial institutions spread. Given the existence of a final decision maker, sovereigns could credibly speak on behalf of their constituencies. One knew that the kings, or the kings-in-parliament, could force their subjects to follow through on agreements they had reached. Moreover, because of their territorial character, states were compatible with one another. Their respective jurisdictions could be precisely specified through agreement on fixed borders. So not only could sovereigns speak on behalf of their subjects, they could also precisely specify who their subjects were. And by extension, perhaps even more importantly, borders enabled sovereigns to specify limits to their authority. City-leagues in particular were unable to do so, and hence they were difficult to incorporate in a system of states. Sovereignty, therefore, also spread by mutual recognition.

Finally, institutional selection occurred by mimicry and exit. Attractive institutions were copied by political elites.[6] In addition, societal actors voted with their feet. They left institutions that were less to their liking and sought entry into those that best met their interests and belief systems.

THE CONVENTIONAL EXPLANATION:
DARWINIAN SELECTION BY WAR

For some, institutional selection in international politics occurs primarily, perhaps even solely, through war. Given the anarchical nature of the international system, force is viewed as the final arbiter regarding the viability of any institution. In this Darwinian milieu those less able to defend themselves are annihilated. The small fall prey to the large.

One body of literature that has closely studied how war operates as a selective mechanism is the hegemonic rivalry literature.[7] It argues that dominant actors in the system are periodically challenged and defeated. Thus, Spain gave way to the Netherlands and England. In turn, the Netherlands lost its position to England. But a closer look at this literature reveals that it focuses on a different set of issues than the one with which we are concerned. The hegemonic rivalry literature largely focuses on rank order change between similar types of units. It explains, in Gilpin's terms, rank order, or systemic change.[8] War determines position. My work, however, focuses on the selective process between dislike units. Specifically, why did sovereign states prove to be superior to city-states or city-leagues?[9] This form of selection is constitutive rather than positional. To use Gilpin's terminology again, it is a systems change, a change in the character of the constitutive units of the international system.[10]

Despite the fact that hegemonic rivalry literature and long-cycle literature pay little attention to the type of competing units, it is still worth examining whether their causal explanation might also hold true for competition between different forms of organization. That is, could selection between dislike units be explained by success in war? Because of the predatorial nature of the international realm, all units have to be able to wage war in order to survive. Accordingly, if particular forms of organization fall by the wayside, this must be explainable by their inability to wage war as effectively as their rivals. It is simply a matter of Darwinian survival of the fittest.

There are several variations to this type of explanation. One variant compares sovereign states to the preceding feudal mode of organization. According to this explanation, sovereign states could raise more revenue and larger concentrations of troops than their feudal predecessors. In short, efficiencies of scale made sovereign states superior in waging war.[11] The problem with this type of account is that the synchronic alternatives to the sovereign states, that is, city-leagues and city-states, were also superior to feudal forms of organization. As we have seen in the past few chapters, the ability of states to develop new military technologies, hire mercenaries, and use artillery were also part of the repertoire of the states' rivals. The Hansa had the ability to raise considerable numbers of troops and to equip large fleets. Its successes against Denmark, England, Holland, and Sweden attest to that. When Lübeck aided Denmark against Sweden in the sixteenth century, it did so with some of the largest and most advanced ships of the time.[12] City-states were even closer to the cutting edge of military developments. Italian military engineers were eagerly sought after. For example, Italians were hired by the English Crown to build its fortifications against the Scots.[13] The city-states also institutionalized the condotierri, the professional captaincy with its specialized military entourage. In short, the question remains as to why the sovereign state proved to be superior to these synchronic rivals, not why it was superior to feudal organization.

A second variation correctly compares the sovereign state to its synchronic rivals and argues that the state surpassed city-leagues and city-states because of its command of a larger territorial space and greater population. The successful invasion by France of the Italian peninsula in 1494 is thus explained in this fashion.[14]

This argument is more powerful than the first, but again success or failure does not depend simply on efficiency of scale, whether construed in terms of territory or size of population. As previously shown, some Italian city-states could muster equivalent amounts of resources for long periods of time. Although it is true that France had a population ten times larger than that of Venice, Venetian revenue in the middle of the fifteenth century was 60 percent higher than that of the French Crown. In a day and age before the levée en masse, when revenue bought troops and fleets,[15] revenue mattered more than population size.[16]

If some forms of organization failed because of comparatively inadequate territory and population, how, then, could the Dutch success against Spain or France, or the rise of the Portuguese, be explained? The Dutch Republic and Portugal each had populations of about 1.5 million—comparable to Venice— yet they succeeded in becoming leading powers of the international system of the early sixteenth and seventeenth centuries.[17]

Another perplexing puzzle to solve is why many small sovereign, territorial states continued to survive.[18] The continued existence of many small German principalities is the most stark example. Furthermore, one may ask why the Hansa disappeared whereas some of the individual towns that had been members continued as independent actors in the international system. The traditional story that the militarily strong simply annihilated the weak does not hold. Weak individual German cities continued to operate in the international state system—as it took form after Westphalia—whereas stronger city-leagues disappeared.

If size and population are only crude and sometimes incorrect predictors of the ability to raise resources for warfare, what does explain the success of the sovereign state? I submit that competitive success lies in the particular institutional makeup of different forms of organization. What was it about the Venetian institutional arrangement, or for that matter of the Dutch Republic, that made such territorially small units such powerful actors?[19]

Warfare is thus an important selective mechanism, but success in warfare is only an indicator which itself needs to be explained. No doubt there are many variables that matter. The organizational skills and training of the Dutch armies under Maurice of Nassau propelled the Dutch to the forefront of military prowess. The success of the Swedes might not be explainable without the specific abilities of Gustavus Adolphus. The legendary capabilities of the Swiss pikemen derived, to considerable extent, from their village independence and poor countryside.[20] One variable, however, namely the nature of institutional arrangements, has often been neglected.

The analysis developed in this chapter suggests that the different institutional logics of city-states, city-leagues, and sovereign states had long-term consequences for their ability to raise revenue and troops for war. That is, the institutional choices of individuals in the Late Middle Ages produced long-term consequences for the ability of some of these units to compete. The argument that in the sixteenth and seventeenth centuries sovereign states were able to wage war more successfully than their institutional rivals is thus correct, but it tends to beg the question, why could they do so?

The long-term effects of the different logics of organization were also weighed by actors in terms of systemwide organizational outcomes. That is, some forms of organization were more preferred partners than others. We can thus solve the puzzle of the survival of small states by analyzing why they, unlike other forms of organization, might be more acceptable to their fellow actors in the international system.

Given that the French state and Hanseatic League were the most distinct cases, the consequences of these two different ways of structuring political order provide us with the clearest insights. By concentrating on these logics of organization, we can draw conclusions that can then be applied to the Italian city-states.

ADVANTAGES OF SOVEREIGN TERRITORIALITY OVER THE CONFEDERATED CITY-LEAGUE

Selection in international politics occurs basically through three mechanisms. First, selection operates through Darwinian survival of the fittest. The intentionality of the agents who have created and continue to favor particular institutions is largely irrelevant. As in biology, some species are more adept at surviving in their new environment whereas less-suited species die out. Similarly, not all institutions that are created following changes in their social environment will be equally successful in the long run. Thus, city-leagues proved to be less effective and less efficient than sovereign, territorial organization on a variety of dimensions.

Second, I will argue that selection occurs by mutual empowerment. Here social selection differs from the unintentional biological process. Unlike what happens in natural selection, individuals create their own environment by preferring and tolerating only certain types of institutions. Sovereign, territorial actors had reasons to prefer similar systems of rule elsewhere. Although this process is thus less structural than Darwinian selection, the iterative choices of individuals limit the opportunities and possibilities for others. In that sense a structural situation is created as well, albeit from a more sociological perspective.

Third, selection also occurs by deliberate mimicry and exit. Political elites copy institutional forms that they perceive as successful. At the same time, social groups switch their allegiance to those types of organization that better meet their interests.

Selection by Darwinian Pressure: The Advantages of
Internal Hierarchy

STANDARDIZATION AND CERTITUDE

One advantage of sovereign authority was the existence of an actor, whether a king or king-in-parliament, who could tackle the legacies of feudal particularism. Sovereigns had a vested interest in rationalizing the overall economy because it led to higher revenues and larger military capacity. "It was in the common interest of the king and the middle class to remove the barriers, physical and feudal, which obstructed internal trade."[21]

One of those feudal barriers to trade was the lack of standardization. Medieval measures and weights were of a mind-boggling variety. Ronald Zupko notes that in late tenth-century England there were fifty major measures. By the Late Middle Ages this had increased to several hundred major measurements with 25,000 local variations.[22] The situation in the rest of Europe was no better.

This multitude of measurements had several causes. It sprang first of all from seigneurial control over measurements. After the decline of the Carolingian Empire, many of the lords had taken over the rights to issue specific measures and weights. Such lordships were reluctant to surrender their authority because control over measures provided income through, for example, charges for use of scales. Moreover, many of the payments to the lords were still in-kind, and hence manipulation of such measures yielded direct benefits. Lordly monopoly over the only legal measures and scales also provided a means of social control. A second cause for this diversity was that measures were representational rather than abstract. Measures often reflected human body parts (the foot, the ell(bow) or particular structural contexts of human labor.[23] A third cause lay in the odd duality of measurement. There were different measures for buying and for selling.[24] We have also seen, for example, in the case of the Hansa, that measures became smaller and lighter the farther the point of origin of the product. Merchants thereby obtained profit, while circumventing the church's demands for a just price; prices might remain the same, but the quantity delivered diminished. Modern consumers will unfortunately recognize that practice as alive and well.

Furthermore, some authorities were competent in setting standards, others had rights to enforce them, and still others had rights to lease public weights and measures to private actors. Needless to say, this proliferation of measures was hardly conducive to commerce, and the bourgeois sought means to overcome this variety. What kinds of institutions managed best to overcome the consequences of feudal decentralization?

The Hansa did not manage to standardize a system of measurements. The confederated nature of the league left considerable autonomy to the towns, and they were unwilling to relinquish their authority regarding weights and measures. Attempts to introduce particular measurements of volume, for example, by using the size of the Wismar or Rostock barrel as an indicator of a particular quantity, proved to be illusive.[25] Many towns continued to use their particular customary measurements. At one point the Hansa tried to induce standardization by requiring the regional groups, the quarters, to follow the measurements of the dominant town of that group. The Dutch, Prussian, and Westphalian towns, for example, were thus supposed to follow Cologne.[26] This was to little avail. The Rostock barrel did make some inroads as a measure of volume but only for certain products. All in all, the process of standardization was of dubious success. "But with the other measures such standardization was not achieved. . . . The same must be said for measures of length. . . . With regards to measures of weight, there was no standardization either."[27] Merchants of course made the most of local control over measures. In other words, cheating was not beyond Hanseatic traders. They would, for example, use a smaller barrel or a double-bottomed barrel but put the Rostock benchmark on it. The common saying was that the Dutch preferred to sell wood rather than butter, because of their use of extremely thick barrels.[28]

Enforcement of Hanseatic decisions rested with municipal councils. But such councils were often dominated by the very merchants who were responsible for their violations. Enforcement of standardization therefore remained problematic. The German cities lacked a sovereign authority who could exercise such justice. Although all towns would have benefited from standardization, they had individual incentives to freeride.[29]

In France, kings took it upon themselves to attempt to standardize measures as early as the twelfth century. Philip Augustus tried to standardize measures for the water merchants of Paris.[30] Attempts to introduce some standardization throughout the kingdom date from Philip the Long (1316–1322) and started again after the Hundred Years War with Louis XI (1461–1483).[31] Their policies were pursued by many successive kings. Louis XII tried reform in 1508. Francis I issued an edict in 1540 claiming royal control: "But the supreme authority of the King incorporates the right to standardize all measures throughout his kingdom, both in the public interest and for the sake of promoting commerce, among his subjects and with foreigners."[32] Henry II decreed in 1557: "All lords in the city, suburbs and environs, who hold the privilege of measures, are obliged to furnish the names of their weights and measures. . . . Old standards not harmonizing with our measures, shall be broken up. . . . All shall be required to regulate their measures according to ours."[33] Charles IX, Henry III, and Louis XIV all continued with these attempts to control and standardize measures.

The royal attempts met strong opposition. The actors who opposed standardization were the old enemies of the bourgeois: clergy and nobles, who opposed this loss of seigneurial control.[34] At the outbreak of the French Revolution there were thus still hundreds of different measurements throughout France, particularly in agricultural areas. In the towns, by contrast, standardization was more successful.[35] Robin Briggs's overall assessment is that by the beginning of Louis

XIV's reign, considerable strides had been made in economic regulation and codification of customs.[36]

Despite the fact that standardization of weights and measures did not succeed as far as the burghers wanted, this was not perceived to be a problem endemic to the type of rule in France. Indeed, here the merchants and traders preferred more authority for the king rather than less. The Cahiers de Doleances, the letters of grievances sent to the court before the revolution, clearly indicate that people thought that the only authority that could end this haphazard system was the French king.[37] There were literally hundreds of petitions for standardization—most of which demanded standardization on a national level.[38] Moreover, although the king had only limited success in changing this situation, he did manage to institutionalize methods of converting different measures. Kings tried to draft tables of conversion to make it easier for commoners and traders to deal with the plethora of measurements. The Hansa lacked an actor that could enforce such standardization on relatively independent towns.

As if this plethora of measures and weights was not enough to give merchants considerable grief, they also had to contend with a large assortment of coinage issued by the same particularistic authorities. The private accounts and letters of Thomas Betson, a Merchant of the Staple of the late fifteenth century, gives new meaning to the term *transaction costs*.[39] How did the various institutions fare in reducing this assortment?

The French state fared better than the Hansa in centralizing the minting of coin.[40] The league did not manage to standardize a particular coinage, and many towns continued to mint their own. "They [attempts at reform] remained without significant success until the great coin reform movement of the 16th century, and then only in a very limited way. In France, by contrast, the Crown, since Louis IX, had successfully curtailed the coining privileges of the lords, and took coining back into its control."[41]

Although a few towns adopted the Lübeck coinage, many others adopted different standards.[42] Such diffusion of coinage dated from the decline of the Holy Roman Empire. Historically the issuance of coinage was a regalian right, only to be exercised by the highest authority. Consequently, during the Roman Empire and the Carolingian period, the issuance of coinage occurred only under strict supervision of imperial administration. Although the German emperor tried to maintain such control, this became increasingly impossible in the face of his failed Italian strategy and his surrender of Germany to the feudal lords. From then on, coining passed into the hands of dukes, to many of the counts, even to the level of viscounts, and to individual towns. "The number of issuers in the thoroughly fragmented Empire of the thirteenth century seems as infinite, and many of them as insignificant, as the wave of 'feudal' denier [penny] strikers in Post-Carolingian France."[43] The surrender of such regalian rights was formally acknowledged in the Golden Bull of 1356 but had in fact started a good deal earlier. By the sixteenth century the situation had gotten worse. By then there were roughly 2,500 local and regional authorities, and although not all of these minted, the chaotic currency and money conditions continued to greatly hamper German commerce.[44]

The diversity of mints thus had two consequences. First, merchants and tax collector had to develop some way of comparing different currencies. In addition to other currencies, the Hanseatic merchant had to contend with Lübeck, Pomeranian, Prussian, and Rigan marks, Brandenburg thalers, Rhenish guilders, Flemish pounds, and English pounds sterling.[45] Second, the actual value of the coin might vary depending on its regional place of origin. Different coiners used different metal contents.[46] Needless to say, this lent itself to considerable abuse by the minter.

In France, coinage became regulated by the king.[47] Louis IX decreed in 1265 that royal coin should be good throughout the realm, whereas baronial currency was only to be used within their domains and had to be of equal value. "The barons needless to say were outraged at this systematization."[48] Philip V's economic program of 1321 tried to repress the unpopular currency issued by the nobility and revalued the royal coinage.[49] Even prior to that, by 1300, the French kings had reduced the number of vassals claiming the right to issue coin from three hundred to about thirty who actually minted their own currencies.[50] The kings managed to standardize metal content and institutionalized a system based on the pound, the shilling, and the penny (livre, sol, denier), a system that originated first in the Carolingian Empire. The king thus reduced the number of mints in the kingdom and thus increased certitude in transactions. "So that in the later Middle Ages the only effective non-royal coinages in France were those issued by a handful of the greatest, near-autonomous princes . . . such as the duke of Brittany and the duke of Guyenne who was also the king of England."[51]

One might counter at this point that increased hierarchy also has a negative consequence. Central control over coinage should also lead to debasement. It is true that the French king, just as feudal minters, would debase coinage to obtain revenue.[52] But the king was not unconstrained. Continued debasement would lead to lack of confidence in such currency and raise the ire of merchants.[53] Empirical evidence suggests that the general tendency was the more consolidated the central government, the less debasement of coinage.[54] Furthermore, it could be argued that the level of tolerance toward debasement is at least equal within all systems of rule, whether league, city-state, or territorial state, because capital always had the option to exit. French kings had an interest in establishing exchange rates to prevent such flight from occurring.[55] The burghers at times could put a halt to debasing.[56] In any case, on the issue of variation in minting, the French king brought some standardization to the multitude of mints and coinage types.

Likewise, French royal justice centralized the legal system more so than the Hansa. The Hansa continued to exist with a variety of legal codes on the municipal level.[57] Since the enforcement of Hansa decisions had to be carried out by the individual town councils, implementation varied greatly. Furthermore, the

Hansa did not have any formalized system for determining whether particular issues called for municipal, regional, or Hanseatic decisions. Part of this was due to the absence of a formal constitution for much of the Hansa's existence.[58] The members of the Hansa refrained from drafting such a constitution because they believed that a formal list of membership, which would consist of the signatories to that constitution, would prompt states to cut deals with individual towns and encourage freeriding. Paradoxically, then, the Hansa feared that a formal organizational listing would dilute its power to act as an organization for all the towns.

In France, by contrast, one of the tasks that kings early on reserved for themselves was the right of adjudication. Going back to feudal claims of arbitrator and judge, the newfound power of the kings transformed these ancient rights into factual exercise of royal power.[59] At the highest level, justice was meted out by the royal high court, i.e., the Parlement. Thus Philip Augustus (1180–1218) argued that the king was the highest legislator. Louis IX outlawed trial by combat in 1258.[60] Kings also started to enforce property rights and contracts under the motto *pacta sunt servanda*.[61] In short, the king rationalized juridical procedure.[62]

Finally, as discussed in Chapter 5, the French king institutionalized the means of raising revenue. The two largest taxes were the royal taille—from the 1460s responsible for about two-thirds of revenue—and the gabelle, the salt tax.[63] Although these might have had some negative influence on the level of business, they were at least standardized and could thus become part of the regular business calculations of those engaged in commerce.

The ad hoc nature of Hanseatic revenue precluded such business certitude.[64] The incidental tolls and customs, which the Hansa allowed some of its towns to raise, duplicated the very problem that feudalism had previously posed for mercantile pursuits.[65]

To sum up, the Hansa proved to be less efficient in reducing transaction costs and providing collective goods than the sovereign state. It did not manage to provide standardization of weights and measurements, enforce centralized justice, establish a general system of coinage, or establish a regular means of raising revenue for a general fund.

PREVENTING FREERIDING AND THE KING AS PUBLIC ACTOR

The confederated nature of the Hansa led to continuous freeriding and defection. There were always incentives to disavow the edicts of the diet. Defection from international agreements, for example, by engaging in piracy, led to deterioration of relations with trading partners such as England. The gains accrued to the individual town and merchants engaging in that particular practice. But the costs were borne by the entire Hansa. Although there were means of dealing with defectors—the most serious was exclusion from the Hansa—these mechanisms did not always work. Enforcement still required detection of the perpetrator—not easy to come by on the high seas—and a majority of Hansa members voting for punishment of the defecting party.[66]

Such defection also included reneging on contributions to military campaigns and individual bargaining with non-Hanseatics. For example, the Saxon
towns did not wish to contribute to the military defense of the Wend towns.
When the Wend towns fought the Danish in the 1420s, members of the Saxon
group agreed to send help. However, they procrastinated in sending troops
until Lübeck had effectively defeated the Danes by itself.[67] Likewise, the
Dutch towns on the Zuiderzee were unwilling to support campaigns against the
Hollanders who were not members of the Hansa.[68] Similarly, when the Hansa
was at war with the two Dutch provinces of Holland and Zeeland in 1438, the
Prussian regional diet continued to authorize voyages to those areas.[69]

In economic matters, towns such as Hamburg and Elbing were all too willing
to defect from Hansa stipulations that no privileges were to be granted to English traders using the Hansa ports on the Baltic and the North Sea. Hamburg
granted English traders special privileges from 1568 to 1577.[70] It finally withdrew these privileges when threatened with exclusion from the Hansa. Elbing
was eager to give the English a base in Prussia. Likewise, Danzig became a
major port for English trade in corn and flax.[71] Cologne was yet another town
willing to pursue its individual interests in trade with England at the expense
of the Hansa. The effect of all this was a gradual erosion of Hanseatic trade
hegemony. In 1570—well after the peak of the Hansa—Hansa merchants still
shipped 25 percent of English trade. But by 1600 this had been reduced to 3 to
4 percent.[72]

Defection and freeriding in the Hanseatic League were driven by mutual
distrust between the towns and the decentralized institutional arrangements of
the Hansa. Although the league had towns, such as Lübeck, that could sometimes override collective action problems, other towns did not view Lübeck's
interests as necessarily compatible with their own.[73] The Prussian towns, for
example, distrusted the treaty that the Wend towns, primarily Hamburg, Bremen, and Lübeck, had signed with the Danish king in 1435.[74] Although the
Wend towns had actually negotiated the treaty on behalf of all the Hansa, the
Prussian towns believed that the Wend towns had only sought to further their
own particularistic interests.

Sovereign actors capitalized on this mutual distrust. The Danish king only
recognized the treaty for ships flying the flag of the Wendish towns, in the
hopes of creating a rift. The king exacted tolls on the Prussian ships that crossed
through the Sound but took care not to demand tolls from Wend ships. Similarly, England was eager to close deals with individual Hansa towns and thus
circumvent the protectionism of the entire league. When obstructed from access to Bruges, where the Hansa had a major trading office (Kontor), the English moved their trade to Antwerp which was a relay station for trade with
Cologne, thus fostering competition between Cologne and other Hansa
towns.[75]

The centralized role that the general Hansetag might have played was further eroded by the regional Tage. Although the regional Tage represented one

way of coordinating policy in a more manageable geographical size and issue-specific manner, regional interests tended to erode the general policy of the league. When English merchants began to make inroads into the eastern Baltic, they were welcomed by the Prussian towns which wanted to sell grain to the English. The Wend towns, however, opposed this since they had made money as middlemen between England and the Prussians.

In France, by contrast, the interests of the subjects of the realm and the interests of the king largely coincided. What was good for France was good for the royal coffers. The king, as a political entrepreneur, has his own reasons to provide collective goods and control freeriding. "Making peace prevail, therefore, served a variety of interests: those of merchants, the fiscal advantage of princes and the presumed obligation of the latter to pursue the common good."[76]

This is most clear in the activist policies of the French Crown from the later fifteenth century on through the mercantilist era. Aside from seeking to improve economic efficiency by the standardization and regulation which I have already mentioned, the crown engaged directly in manufacturing and commerce.[77] Louis XI (1461–1483) is thus regarded as the "father of French mercantilism" and was "Colbertian before Colbert."[78] He tried to standardize measures, attract foreign craftsmen, and protect domestic industry. In the sixteenth century, the French Crown also engaged in saltpeter mining and industry that was relevant for the manufacture of munitions.[79] It also protected by means of patents the profitability of new inventions. By the seventeenth century, mercantilism had come into full swing with the policies of Colbert (1661–1683). The crown regulated the movement of bullion, tried to reduce imports, and fostered internal efficiency by reducing the large number of tolls.[80] It also engaged in a sustained effort to improve land transport.[81] No doubt royal absolutism was not always appreciated, certainly under Louis XIV's imperialist policies. But in general, "many towns also profited from the slow and difficult unification of the realm."[82]

Most noteworthy, perhaps, defense became defense of the realm.[83] The standing army, since the late fifteenth century, thus became an instrument of the state rather than an instrument for the defense of the king's private property. The king's ambitions and the fate of France were closely tied, and the army was no longer based on the system of feudal service owed the king in exchange for grants of land.

The development of the king as protector of the realm was closely tied to the dissociation of the realm and the royal domain.[84] For the Franks, "the kingdom of France was the king's thing; . . . there was no 'public thing'; the state belonged to him."[85] With the later Capetians, the royal domain, which had originally been synonymous with private property, became an unalienable entity. Unlike a feudal estate, it could not be estranged by inheritance or sold. Hence the argument that the English king could not acquire part of France even if the French king so wished. Through the subtle transition from royal domain, which was simply the personal holdings of the king, to the public realm, the quality and functions of the king had changed.[86] The private domain became the public state.

The king had two bodies—the person was gradually distinguished from the office. Whatever might happen to the individual as king did not affect the status of the crown. Although this was originally justified within the medieval mentality which perceived duality as pervading many physical phenomena, it was increasingly grounded in Roman law, wherein the king was the fountain of law. Ecclesiastical kingship was transferred to law-centered kingship, thereby opening the way to national states and absolute monarchies.[87] Salisbury could, therefore, already plausibly argue in the twelfth century that the king "is, and acts as, a persona publica. And in that capacity he is expected to consider all issues with regard to the well-being of the res publica, and not with regard to his privata voluntas."[88]

Although this theory was especially articulated in England, similar ideas took root in France. Louis VII (1150) argued that the magnates owed service "to realm and Crown." Philip Augustus asked for military support "for the defense of our head as well as of the crown of the realm."[89] In short, the king acquired public status. The Hansa, by contrast, lacked a theory legitimating sovereign power. This was partially due to the absence of clear internal hierarchy and diffuse demarcation from non-Hansa authorities.[90] There simply was no clear center that could operate as a sovereign.

There were thus specific reasons why social groups perceived that the king might have the interests of the realm at heart. The king benefited from the overall welfare of the state, whereas the leading towns of the Hansa did not necessarily gain from the overall welfare of the league. Individual towns rightly perceived that the disparate members had various interests which were not always served by the actions of the diet.

In short, sovereign, territorial rulers were recognized as political entrepreneurs who had vested interests in decreasing the remnants of feudal economies. In standardizing coinage, reducing the number of weights and measures, and creating more legal certitude, they reduced transaction and information costs. The greater degree of internal hierarchy was also more suited to control freeriding and defection. This in turn affected their ability to wage war more effectively than city-leagues. Arguably, the Hansa of the seventeenth century was less able to wage the type of war that the French state could engage in at the time. But this was due to the organizational flaws of the Hanseatic League, not to any inherent lack of size or population. Scholars of the Hanseatic League repeat the same theme. There was "no effective governing body to coordinate the Hansa's interests."[91] Consequently, when sovereign, territorial rulers started to increase their powers, they could prey on individual towns and regions that lacked united opposition.[92]

Nevertheless, the demise of the Hansa was long and protracted. There was no decisive battle that sealed its fate. Decline was relative, not absolute. Indeed, the tonnage of Hanseatic shipping was 50 percent higher in 1600 than it was in 1500. This tonnage was equal to the total owned in the Mediterranean and larger than that of England. But the Hansa had lost ground relative to the Dutch who by 1600 had a fleet of almost three times the tonnage of the Hansa.[93] Overall there was an economic revival after 1550, and the Hansa tried to remedy some of its institutional defects by agreeing on yearly assessment and a constitution in 1557. Like the Italian city-states, it lingered for a long time.[94] By some accounts even the Thirty Years War did not ruin the Hansa's economic prospects.[95] But there were other forces at work as well. The European world was gradually shifting to a system of sovereign, territorial states, and in that system the Hansa had no place and its towns lost their desire to maintain the league. Consequently, the last Hanseatic diet convened in 1669.

Selection by Mutual Empowerment: Credible Commitments and Territorial Jurisdiction

International exchange requires a modicum of domestic stability on the part of the contracting parties and at least some expectation that each will adhere to the terms of the agreement. Internal stability is required to guarantee that the negotiating partner can indeed commit the individuals on whose behalf he or she is negotiating. The direct correlate of that condition is that the party that is committing itself to particular agreements can be expected to continue the terms of the bargain over a period of time. In short, can the other party engage in iterative behavior over time?[96]

The Hanseatic diet did not clearly specify on whose behalf it was negotiating or to what extent its members were bound by the terms of certain agreements. Because of this, as well as the Hansa's inability to curtail defection, the league was an unattractive partner to international agreements. An illustrative example is provided by the conflicts and negotiations between England and the Hansa. The Merchant Adventurers, an English association of traders, argued in 1551 that privileges for the Hansa should be rescinded because "none of their charters named particular individuals or towns so that there was no way of knowing who ought to enjoy the pretended privileges."[97] This was also perceived to be greatly detrimental to the king, and the Merchant Adventurers claimed that the crown lost 17,000 pounds sterling in customs duties because nonleague members enjoyed league privileges. One of the primary demands of the Privy Council in the negotiations of 1560, in the "Moderatio in commercio," was that the Hansa provide an explicit list of the members entitled to such privileges.[98] Nevertheless, by 1589 the problem still was not resolved and once again the English insisted that the Hansa provide them with a specific membership list.[99] The English Crown wished to know which ships docking in English ports could legitimately claim the benefits that would follow from the treaty. Otherwise any trader could claim affiliation with the Hansa. The league, however, refused to provide such a list.[100] It feared that such a list would make individual towns the target of English encroachment. A state might provide benefits to individual towns and thus encourage their defection from the league, or conversely, it might impose costs on some others, hoping that the league as a whole would not take action.

The Hansa furthermore argued that it could not be held responsible for infringements of treaties by individual towns.[101] Although the Hansa claimed that privileges were obtained for all its members, and thus acted as a legal body, it suspended such uniform legal status when costs were imposed. The Hanseatic diet absolved itself from responsibility for towns that violated agreements, yet at the same time it argued that benefits negotiated by representatives of the Hansa should fall to all members. The problem was that agreements were negotiated and ratified with the Hanseatic diet, but enforcement depended on the further ratification of the individual town councils. Thus, when the Prussian towns refused to sign the 1437 treaty, England wanted to suspend privileges for them. The Hansa, however, claimed that privileges should be given to all Hansa towns, including the Prussians, regardless of their individual position on the treaty.[102]

Even when agreements could be obtained, the Hansa was not able to prevent individual towns from defecting from agreements once they had been reached. The drawn-out trade wars with the Hansa and England were thus driven by the continued defection of Hanseatic towns.[103]

This also meant that territorial lords were able to gain concessions by negotiating with individual towns directly. During the conflicts of the fifteenth century, Cologne pursued several negotiations on its own, despite the fact that external representations were supposed to be handled by delegates of the Hanseatic diet. When England obtained privileges from Hamburg, against the wishes of the Hansa, Hamburg claimed to be a free city "which had the right to adopt any policy."[104] In addition, this lack of committed membership highly complicated the nature of warfare. If a state went to war with the Hansa, this did not automatically mean that one was at war with all the Hansa members. For example, the Dutch towns that were Hansa members tended to excuse themselves from fighting Holland and Zeeland.[105]

In sovereign states, by contrast, the responsibility for redress of violations by subjects was put on the shoulders of the sovereigns.

> They strictly controlled all "letters of mark" and reprisals against foreign merchants, and in their place substituted due process of law, or agreed procedures. By means of registered obligation they also tried to guarantee the authenticity, validity and execution of trading agreements. In lands ruled by custom the contracts were enforced by the affixing of public seals.[106]

Sovereign authorities thus took it upon themselves to regulate trade. Without sovereign assistance, merchants had to rely on self-help. When a merchant had been defrauded by an alien, it was standard practice to take revenge, by violent means if necessary, on other aliens from the same place of origin as the perpetrator.[107] The result was not uncommonly a spiral of mutual retaliations. Sovereigns, however, started to create focal points for institutionalized redress. Only their subjects would obtain benefits from such regulation, and likewise they would punish members of their own society who violated agreements. Defectors were subject to royal jurisdiction, and hence, unlike the Hansa, there was a clear enforcement mechanism to prevent freeriding. Sovereign authorities provided specific loci of authority through which cooperation could be organized. From the early Middle Ages on, kings started to reserve the right to represent their subjects in foreign affairs.[108] The provision of such trade regulation was one of the facets that made sovereign, hierarchical authority attractive.[109]

In correlation to the king's claim to represent the subjects within a given territorial space, the exercise of private external actions was curtailed. Admittedly this was not a sudden process. As Thomson notes, private subjects who were nominally subject to a sovereign continued to exercise violence for many centuries.[110] Piracy, for example, was a recognized means of foreign policy, and blurred all distinction between private and public violence.[111] Increasingly, however, such practices became incompatible with sovereign authority. Such a system of rule implied that there could only be one principle source of foreign relations.

The inability of the Hansa to credibly commit had several consequences for the league's survival. Because the league could not control defection, it could not credibly consign itself to long-run agreements with joint gains.[112] Game theory corresponds here with some of the sociological literature. Institutions originate where repetitive behavior occurs between two actors. The more this repetition occurs, the more the actors expect a typical pattern of behavior from the other. Social roles develop which signal what type of behavior one may expect. When these roles are passed on to actors not immediately involved in the initial interactions, these roles become externalized.[113] Actors should, therefore, prefer those types of institutions that clearly indicate the type of behavior one might expect from that actor. In short, political elites should prefer systems of rule in their environment that can commit their members. The representatives of the Hanseatic Diet were often not able to give such guarantees.

MARKET VERSUS TERRITORIAL STATE

The Hansa and the sovereign state were ultimately driven by different principles regarding their preferred extension of political order. The nonterritorial Hansa resembled, in a way, the imperial form of organization. Although it lacked the central authority of imperial control, it shared with the classical empire the objective of having the widest possible extension of political control over its sphere of economic interactions.[114] Commerce would be organized by incorporating as many towns as possible in the league. Political control would thus ideally correspond with this sphere of economic extension.

Sovereign states, by contrast, are delimited by explicit territorial parameters. Although states might very well seek expansion, their claim to authority is limited by their recognition that authority only extends to their borders. They can coexist with similar types of units in segregated territorial spaces and yet interact extensively across these borders. Although certain border areas, provinces, or previously held areas might be in dispute, states are not logically predisposed to extend their political control to other areas. Sovereignty is based on the principle of juridical equality.[115]

Imperial modes of organization, such as Frederick II's claim to universal rule or that of the Roman theocracy, did not recognize formal borders as limits to their extension. Although the Hansa of course made no claim to world rule, it, too, did not limit its political authority by formal borders. It tried to extend its control transterritorially, and thus "it had no territorial boundaries, but spread out over wide areas on both land and sea."[116] In non-Hansa towns where the league had important trading interests, it would seek special privileges and rights of jurisdiction over its members within the given areas of such towns.[117] In London, for example, the Hansa controlled the Steelyard area and had jurisdiction there. Until 1556 the Hanseatic traders paid fewer duties in England than English citizens engaging in trade.[118] The territorial contiguity of the state with its fixed borders was thus at odds with the nonterritorial character of the Hansa.

Moreover, league membership included towns within sovereign states, thereby reintroducing the feudal problem of crosscutting jurisdictions. Thus, when England seized a large fleet of Hanseatic ships, the ships from the Dutch town of Kampen were released with the other ships from the Burgundian Netherlands, with which England had no quarrel. However, since Kampen was also a member of the Hanseatic League, and since the league's ships were not released, England could have decided otherwise.[119] Towns could simultaneously be subject to a territorial lord, albeit sometimes nominally, and subject to the dictates of the league. Thus the Dutch towns on the Zuiderzee, of which about twelve were members of the Hansa, had to divide their loyalties between the Hansa and the Dutch towns of Holland and Zeeland, who often fought the Hansa.[120]

Consequently, the Hansa did not fit well within a system of sovereign states. This clarifies its precarious position at the Peace of Westphalia where the league sought representation.[121] The league had considerable difficulty obtaining standing at the conferences in Osnabrück and Münster. The German princes particularly wished to deny the Hansa legal standing. They argued that "1. The Hanseatic cities are either intermediate cities, who are represented by their lords, or imperial cities, and in that capacity naturally represented at the conference. 2. The Hansa cities were not mentioned in the religious treaty of Augsburg of 1555. 3. One does not really know what the Hansa in essence is."[122]

Although the Hansa was eventually mentioned in the final draft, the towns were only consulted on the issue of repayments. Because its nonterritorial logic of organization did not mesh with that of the state system, and because the league could not bind all its members to the agreements, the Hansa was not acceptable as a player in international politics.

The issue of Hanseatic recognition was not simply a matter of material resources. If it were, why would the independent imperial cities gain standing?

The individual cities certainly did not have more resources than the league. The answer is that imperial cities, such as Lübeck, could be regarded as small states. Individual towns such as Lübeck, Bremen, and Hamburg could therefore participate in the Peace negotiations. The issue was whether the league as an organization of towns could participate in the new order of international politics which was hammered out during the negotiations in Osnabrück and Münster. The answer was negative. Scarcely twenty years later the Hansa dissolved itself.[123]

Selection of particular types of units thus also proceeds by empowerment. International actors determine who is to count as a legitimate international participant. The Peace of Westphalia made the territorial lords of the basically defunct Holy Roman Empire full participants in the international system.[124] The ministates were acknowledged as legitimate participants in the international realm and would continue to play that role into the nineteenth century.[125]

Selection by Directed Adaptation: Mimicry and Exit

Students of organization theory and scholars of international relations have been vexed by a similar question: Why are institutions similar, or at least why do they become similar over time? One explanation, quite analogous to my own, suggests that institutional isomorphism occurs through competitive pressures and noncompetitive mechanisms.[126] We have just discussed how the first operated in early modern Europe. The latter process explains how less efficient organizations can continue to persist. I have already suggested one noncompetitive mechanism in international politics—the mechanism of mutual empowerment.[127] A second process consists of agent-driven choices. Political entrepreneurs copy institutions that they perceive to be successful in reducing uncertainty and achieving objectives such as a larger revenue and increased military capacity. Copying thus increases one's chances at relative success. It also enables such elites to be recognized as equals within the state system, by mutual empowerment. In a material sense, they are then more suited to pursue long-run gains through treaties. From an ideological perspective, they are perceived as the equals of the leaders. Social actors at the same time vote with their feet. They prefer to exit the less successful system and switch their loyalties to that system of rule that is more likely to meet their goals.

Thus, the German lordships, once they perceived the revenue and strength of sovereign state competitors, started to copy that kind of institutional makeup. Like their royal counterparts, they established hierarchical control within their borders. Within these principalities, weights and coinage were increasingly standardized, and princely adjudication became the norm.[128] In effect, these lordships became increasingly like miniature sovereign states. After the Peace of Westphalia, they were officially recognized as such.[129]

Furthermore, as I discussed above, there were advantages to sovereign statehood. Externally, states could credibly commit themselves and engage in long-run iterative relations. As the advantage swung in favor of sovereign states, only similar forms of organization were recognized. Domestically, sovereigns proved to be better at reducing transaction costs and providing for collective goods. As a consequence, sovereign states eventually managed to raise more revenue than their alternatives. For example, although French revenues in the second half of the fifteenth century were not vastly larger than those of city-states, they increased dramatically in the sixteenth century.[130] The Hansa, despite its attempts to levy an annual tax on each town, succeeded far less in mobilizing such resources.[131]

All of these factors suggested to the German lords that sovereign, territorial statehood was the most preferable form of organization.[132] The Hansa similarly tried to copy institutional forms that were more successful. In the sixteenth century they pursued closer cooperation with the emperor, in an attempt to create the royal-urban alliance that had faltered centuries earlier. By then, however, the emperor lacked the power to override the territorial lords of Germany.[133] The Hansa also entertained the idea of forming a tighter association incorporating all German cities or even forming a government along the lines of the Dutch Republic.[134] Although this would still have left the towns considerable autonomy, the tighter association would have allowed closer cooperation and have prevented defection. The idea failed because of the towns disparate interests. In short, the Hansa could not be transformed into a territorial state with a sovereign.[135]

Towns, perceiving the benefits of territorial entities, increasingly defected from the league. This went beyond freeriding. They allied with local lords, now increasingly acting as sovereign, territorial rulers. The estates basically agreed with the princes to construct states made up of contiguous territories.[136] The tasks of organizing long-distance commerce were increasingly taken over by states and their consular services, thereby making the Kontors and offices abroad less necessary.[137]

Some Hansa towns simply failed to appear at the diets or refused to pay their dues.[138] Rather than remain part of the transterritorial league, towns were incorporated within the borders of existing sovereign states or became small territorial states in their own right. Hamburg, Bremen, Lübeck, and other German cities became independent actors and signed treaties just like any other state.[139] Although these were later incorporated into the united Germany after 1870, Bremen, Hamburg, Danzig, and others maintained some residue of independent decision making as Länder (in the Federal Republic) or free cities, even after 1870.

FRAGMENTED SOVEREIGNTY IN THE ITALIAN CITY-STATES

The previous discussion of the Hansa and France presented the starkest contrast between two distinct logics of organization. The sovereign state had two specific traits: external, territorial definition and internal hierarchy. The Hansa lacked both those elements. The city-state demarcated itself externally from other authorities by territorial borders—therein it resembled the sovereign state.[140] Internally, however, it lacked a clear sovereign. Although the dominant city monopolized external contacts, internally its jurisdiction over the subject towns was always contested. Sovereignty, in other words, was fragmented. Given that we have discussed the consequences of such institutional facets above, we can now briefly apply these insights to the Italian city-states.

Darwinian Selection: The Consequences of Contested Sovereignty

As seen, medieval commerce was bedeviled by a variety of measures, weights, and coins, irrational means of trial, and a bewildering collection of local customs. This feudal particularism was combatted internally by the king, who also tried to become the external focal point for transnational interactions. The surviving mercantile manuals of Mediterranean commerce reveal that Italian merchants had to combat problems similar to those of their northern counterparts, internally as well as abroad.[141]

However, unlike in the sovereign state, hierarchy in the Italian city-state was ambiguous as "power inside the city-state was always being challenged from within."[142] In this it resembled the city-league. This fermentation within the Italian cities and city-states left them, in the long run, in a disadvantageous position vis-à-vis their territorial counterparts in rationalizing their economies.

The lack of a clear sovereign authority in Italian city-states was due to several causes. First, the formation of the Italian states occurred through the annexation of other towns by dominant cities. Thus the two hundred to three hundred independent communes of the thirteenth century were amalgamated into roughly a dozen small states by the end of the fifteenth century. All these towns, however, had considerable autonomy before such incorporation, and many did not relinquish their local autonomy even within the framework of a larger city-state. "Large responsibilities were left to cities—a distribution of power that some historians have called a diarchy."[143] Although the dominant city would appoint a governor or local elites to subjected towns, any attempts to bring them fully under the dominant city's rule were negated by the towns' long history of independent development.

From the angle of the dominant city, subject cities were looked upon as vanquished areas at the disposal of the victor. "For a long time the relationship of Venice and its dominions was probably that of a conquering city-state and a conquered exploited empire. It was not that of a capital and provinces."[144] The Venetian relation to its Terra Ferma (the mainland) was not unique. The organization of the Florentine city-state was similar.

> Moreover, it never occurred to the Florentine republicans to adopt one measure . . . namely transforming their city-state into a territorial state. . . . For them, Florence existed for the sole benefit of some three thousand privileged Florentines; and the Florentine dominion existed solely to be governed and exploited by the Dominante,

the "Dominant City." Having refused to enfranchise the vast majority of their compatriots . . . they were not surprised when every one of the subject cities surrendered to the Imperial Army in 1529–1530 the moment it was abandoned by its Florentine garrison.[145]

This attitude and lack of integration are thus evident in the slow extension of citizenship by the dominant city to its subject towns and rural areas.[146] Even in later centuries citizenship was only conferred on the leading elites of the subject towns rather than the towns as a whole.[147] In short, the subject towns had little incentive to acknowledge the sovereign authority of the dominant city.

Second, hierarchy of authority was also less pronounced because of endemic factionalism within the dominant city itself. Town government continually fluctuated between despotic, oligarchical, and democratic regimes. Each of these would use government to serve its particular ends. Unlike the French system, where increased centralization benefited the towns, and paid off the nobles and clergy, the Italian system was set up in a more exclusive manner. The exercise of sovereign authority was thus always inclined to further particularistic rather than collective ends.

Moreover, various factions claimed for a long time the legitimate right to exercise violence. In France, by contrast, the king came to be the common provider of protection. He embodied the national interest. His private interest in expanding the welfare of the realm coincided with the interests of individuals within the realm. In the Italian case, no actor could be plausibly identified as an unbiased provider of collective goods. Just as in the case with the leading towns of the Hansa, the provision of public goods was tainted with particularistic interests. What was touted as being for the good of the city-state in reality most often benefited only the dominant city or often only the elite of that city.

A disproportionate share of the tax burden was placed on the surrounding countryside and subject cities.[148] Legnano, subject to Verona, constantly contested its taxation and duties. Later it was Verona's turn to protest domination by Venice on similar grounds. Although the share of tax on trade declined dramatically in the course of the seventeenth century, the amount of taxes provided by the Terra Ferma went up dramatically.[149]

In the previous discussion of the Hansa and the French state, I suggested that because of its confederated institutional nature, the Hansa was less successful in rationalizing the economy, preventing defection, providing for collective goods, and reducing transaction costs. The fragmented sovereignty of the Italian city-states had difficulties dealing with these problems as well.[150]

Standardization of weights, measures, and coinage seems to have come relatively late to the Italian city-states. Venice attempted to suppress local mints, but by 1490 there was still a prevalence of local patron saints on coinage, indicating that such mints were still operative.[151] Subject towns had previously exercised these regalian rights themselves, and they were unwilling to give up their control. Consequently there continued to be a large variety of coins, which differed in name and intrinsic value.[152]

Despite the presence of Roman law, many towns judiciously guarded their privileges. They raised their own revenue and levied their own customs duties. Consequently, economic integration proceeded slowly. In Florence, internal trade barriers continued to exist, despite efforts by the Medici to curtail these in the sixteenth century. Venice was remarkably late in eliminating internal customs barriers (1794).[153] Although the evidence is anecdotal, in general there was "no planned action to create a more economically integrated region with deliberate policies to favour freer patterns of internal flows of goods."[154]

Given their inferior status and the burdens placed upon them, the subject cities were eager to defect when such an opportunity arose. Pisa preferred domination by the French king to that of Florence. The Sienese likewise preferred the French or Ferraro to domination by Florence. Venice destroyed one of its subject cities, Adela, in 1509 for prematurely admitting the French.[155] Subject cities welcomed foreign invaders. There was little if any identification with the dominant town. *Patria* or *Nazione* referred only to the city of birth.[156] Subject cities referred to Venice as the city of "The Three Thousand Tyrants."[157] For these reasons the capital cities kept their subject towns heavily garrisoned.[158]

In short, city-states looked internally somewhat like city-leagues. There was an absence of a central actor who had incentives to further the overall interest of the city-state. The dominant town exploited the subject cities as it saw fit. Conversely, subject towns judiciously guarded their autonomy and were willing to defect from the city-state whenever the opportunity presented itself. Consequently, rationalization and standardization came relatively slowly to the Italian city-states. Although such processes took a long time in France as well, there were at least political entrepreneurs who had vested interests in furthering the consolidation of a more unified national economy and social groups which benefited from the process.[159]

Mutual Empowerment: Fixed Boundaries and Transnational Focal Points

I can be short on this point. City-states behaved no differently in international affairs than sovereign, territorial states. Externally the city-states resembled sovereign states rather than city-leagues. Because their authority was bound by specific territorial parameters, they were able to participate as equals with states. The dominant Italian actors had recognized the territorial status quo among themselves after the Peace of Lodi in 1454, and they made elaborate lists identifying which towns were allies (amici and collegati) of specific dominant towns. There were thus circumscribed spheres of jurisdiction. It has been argued that Venice started the first systematized diplomatic service in history.[160]

Moreover, the dominant city monopolized the foreign relations of the subject towns.[161] As far as the other actors in the system were concerned, the city-state provided a clear focal point for negotiations. With the league, by contrast, it was ambiguous whether individual towns or the Hanseatic Diet were the most appropriate channels for diplomacy. That was not the case with the Italian city-states.

City-states, therefore, survived for a long time within the state system. The diplomatic role of Venice, for example, lasted well past its relative economic decline. Like the German principalities which converted themselves into miniature states, the Italian city-states were logically compatible with the state system, as it emerged after Westphalia. Again, this was not a reflection of their material power or geographic size.[162] Instead this was the result of their empowerment as equivalent actors on the international scene, because of their external similarity to sovereign, territorial states.

Institutional Mimicry and Exit

The benefits of sovereign authority were not lost on the rulers of the Italian city-states. Especially after the incursions of the French and Spanish, which began in the later part of the fifteenth century, political leaders tried to restyle the city-states into sovereign, territorial states. In Florence, for example, the Medici began to perform many regalian tasks during the sixteenth century. They tried to regulate the manufacture of goods, stabilize the metal content of coins, bring internal peace, centralize jurisdiction, and provide more certitude in the tax environment.[163]

The success of these initial efforts is unclear. Economically the subject cities seem to have declined after annexation by the dominant city. Although the differences between subject towns and dominant city were lessened, even the Medici did not grant them equal status. As said, only leading citizens of subject towns obtained citizenship, and internal barriers remained in existence.[164] Even by the beginning of the eighteenth century, there had been little progress in eliminating economic localism.[165] And although the Venetian Council attempted to bring Venetian statutes "in conformity with the principles of clarity, simplicity and rationalization . . . the terra ferma continued to be ruled according to Roman law codes very different from the law observed in the metropolis."[166]

The Venetian government moreover remained locked in a system in which only noble families who had centuries before been entered into the Golden Book were allowed to participate. Only after 1646 were 127 new families admitted. Even so, the absolute size of the patriciate had only increased by 100 members when the patriciate was closed again in 1718. Only in 1775 was it reopened again, at which time membership could be purchased at a very high price. As a consequence, the patrician ruling class declined from 2,500 members in the 1550s to 1,100 in 1797.[167]

Few families from the mainland gained any influence in Venetian government. Moreover, administration continued to be the privilege of noblemen rather than of "men raised from the dust," as in France and England. Hence, unlike the government of the French king, commoners and lesser nobles gained little access to the system.[168] Consequently, there was little room for the development of the notion of a sovereign as a neutral arbiter who could advance the interests of a variety of groups. Government was closed and operated for the benefit of the few who had consolidated their positions centuries earlier.

The implications of this imperfect territorial integration have yet to be uncovered. For example, despite this type of government, Venetian coinage was relatively stable, and it is unclear how far mainland economies were sacrificed for Venice.[169] There were cases wherein Venice forbade mainland production of, for example, silk, because the Venetians wished to restrict competition with Venice proper.[170]

In any case, it is clear that Venice never fully integrated the Terra Ferma. And although many city-states tried to centralize government in the eighteenth century, they failed. "Nobles and ecclesiastics, cities and communes . . . resisted, in the name of their legal and customary rights, the encroachments of the central administration."[171] They clung to their historically developed, local, and particularistic self-rule.

Continued local particularism and the turn from mercantile pursuits to landed interests brought the Italian economy full circle. Refeudalization occurred throughout Italy. Some believe this happened because the nobility was always involved in Italian commerce.[172] The bourgeois movement in northwestern Europe, by contrast, had separated itself from this aristocratic mode of life. In Italy, that avenue always remained open. Whatever the explanation might be, the turn to landed pursuits accompanied by considerable autonomy became a reality. Like the feudal aristocracies of the past, leading families claimed illustrious genealogical ancestries.[173] Even the confusing crosscutting jurisdictions that we know so well from feudal France returned. "The notion of borders between political entities vanished as well . . . since many of the same feudatories held contiguous domains on both sides of what was supposed to be the border."[174]

Only after the second half of the eighteenth century did centralization achieve some measure of success. Intellectuals looked abroad to foreign rulers such as Frederick and Catherine the Great and argued that only princes (that is, sovereign authorities) could be effective agents of reform.[175] In summary, the city-states slowly transformed themselves into sovereign, territorial states. Nevertheless, even then the unification of weights and measures was not completed. That only occurred under Napoleonic occupation in 1807.

I argue, therefore, that city-states, unlike city-leagues, were compatible with a system of sovereign states. Consequently they survived with the German principalities for many centuries after Westphalia. They acknowledged territorial delimitation of their political control and a final locus for external interactions.

However, because of their imperfect territorial integration and absence of a fully articulated sovereign authority, they proved to be less competitive than their sovereign, territorial counterparts. Local autonomy and factional interests prevented an effective and efficient mobilization of the city-states' resources.[176]

Although attempts were made to transform city-states from a system in which dominant cities exploited their subject territories to one that was territorially integrated, such efforts largely failed. Historically developed privileges, and the intransigence of elites in the dominant cities to relinquish their position, made such development impossible. By the end of the eighteenth century the city-states looked for alternative models of rule. The model they turned to was that of the consolidated, sovereign state.

THE GENERAL NATURE OF INSTITUTIONAL SELECTION

The prevalent view that war is the all-decisive selective mechanism needs to be amended. Warfare did not obliterate the alternatives to the state. There were no decisive battles to end the Hanseatic League or the Italian city-states. Although it is true that the Thirty Years War (1618–1648) devastated many individual towns, it was not the war that led to the demise of the Hansa. That process had started much earlier. Similarly, one cannot argue that the Spanish and French invasions after 1494 ended the existence of the city-states. Some city-states went through an economic revival in the late sixteenth century. They continued to exist until the Napoleonic era. War, therefore, was not the dramatic decisive selective mechanism. The city-leagues and city-states were not like the Incan Empire crumbling before the Spanish.

Success in war, however, may indicate the effectiveness and efficiency of types of organization. Although Venetian defeat at the hands of the French was not such that Venice disappeared as an institutional type, it did prove that some forms of organization were institutionally superior. Sovereign states were better, in the long run, in raising more revenue and larger numbers of troops.[177] War did not work as an evolutionary process that selected among types of units, but it did indicate to political elites and social groups which type of organization was the more efficient, and they subsequently adopted the most competitive institutional form.

Moreover, the ability to wage war needs to be explained. I have suggested that size and population are at best imperfect predictors of military power. The argument that the Italian city-states had to give way to territorial states because they were too small neglects the rise of Portugal and the Netherlands which were no larger in terms of territory or population. Instead, I have advanced the argument that the ability to wage war was a function of institutional arrangements. Organizational types that were fraught with freeriding and factionalism, that had problems rationalizing their economies and reducing transaction costs—in short, those that could not make the transition to consolidated national economies—were less effective and less efficient in mobilizing resources than sovereign states.[178] The ability to wage war operated as an intermediate cause of selection but was ultimately propelled by the consequences of particular institutional logics.[179]

Selection was thus partially driven by competitive efficiency. It also advanced, however, by the process of mutual empowerment. Sovereign actors only recognized particular types of actors as legitimate players in the international system. Because the Hanseatic system of rule proved to be incompatible with that of territorially defined states, and because it was less able to credibly commit itself to international treaties, it was not considered to be a legitimate player in international relations.[180] As I mentioned, it was barely recognized in the Peace of Westphalia. Yet very small entities, which were organizationally compatible with sovereign states, were considered to be legitimate. The miniature states of Germany and Italy continued in the international system until their respective unifications.[181]

During this process of competition and empowerment, social and political actors engaged in institutional learning. First, actors tried to create institutions that corresponded with their belief systems and best met their economic and political interests. This occurred with the formation of new institutions during the Late Middle Ages in response to economic expansion. Over time some of these institutional choices proved to be better than others, and the lesser ones were structurally weeded out by competition and the process of mutual empowerment. There were good reasons to prefer systems of rule that could make credible commitments and systems that would not encroach upon one's own jurisdiction.[182] Simultaneously, social actors instrumentally switched their allegiances to their newly preferred form of organization, and political entrepreneurs copied the more successful institutional logic.

The gradual institutionalization of a system of sovereign states thus imposed a certain nonhierarchical order on transnational interactions. The old possibilities of political control over the primary market (the empire) or of leaving social actors to fend for themselves (a self-help system) were replaced by diplomatic focal points. Sovereigns spoke on behalf of their subjects. To use Nettl's words, they became gatekeepers for international transactions.[183]

This description should not be understood as introducing an element of teleological development into my view of institutional evolution. I continue to maintain (like Gould) that evolution is adaptation, not progress. Although attrition of the less competitive occurs, this only leads to the development of the "most competitively efficient" institution for that particular environment. Efficiency is thus historically contingent. Selection occurs among the synchronic rivals that emerge after a broad environmental shift. Had the institutional form of the sovereign state not emerged—and it did not outside Europe—then the selective process might have operated between city-states and city-leagues. Moreover, with another dramatic transformation, the contemporary "winner" of this process of selection and empowerment—that is, sovereign, territorial authority—might prove to be susceptible to change itself.

CONCLUSION

The evolution of the state and the development of a state system were mutually reinforcing processes.[184] On the one hand, the emergence of sovereign states had direct consequences for the other types of institutional arrangements in the system. The system selected out those types of units that were, competitively speaking, less efficient. In other words, the competitive nature of the system determined the nature of the constitutive units. At the same time, sovereign states preferred similar modes of organization in their environment. Actors intentionally created a system of sovereign, territorial states. They preferred a system that divided the sphere of cultural and economic interaction into territorial parcels with clear hierarchical authorities.

The entire process can thus be seen in micro-macro or agent-structural terms. In the first phase the variety of units form the elements of a system. Because of competitive pressure between these dislike units, and through mutual empowerment as well as individuals' choices, the system is gradually transformed into a network of similar actors. At that point the system imposes structural limits on the type of units that are possible and will be recognized by the other actors as legitimate forms of organization in international politics. With that in mind, we might sensibly speculate on the development of the state in the future.

PART IV

Conclusion

Character, Tempo, and Prospects for Change
in the International System

> Even the notion of "international relations" seems obsolete when so many of the
> interactions that presently sustain world politics do not unfold
> directly between nations or states.[1]

THE DYNAMICS OF CHANGE IN THE INTERNATIONAL SYSTEM

As we head toward the end of this millennium, we are witnessing profound
changes in the international system. There seems to be a general consensus that
the bipolar, postwar era has come to an end. But the contours of the future are
far more difficult to discern. There is talk of a new tripolar constellation composed of the Pacific-Rim, North America, and Europe.[2] Others suggest a recon-
figured bipolar world divided into Pacific and Atlantic regions. American hegemony, once a foundation for the stability of international regimes, can no longer
be taken for granted, its power and its purpose increasingly ambiguous in a yet
emerging system. Whereas some see an ailing superpower, others see continued American dominance, for better or for worse.[3]

Indeed, the very future of the sovereign state may be questioned. Global
ecological problems, international financial transactions, unprecedented
human migration, the potentially disastrous effects of nuclear force, and growing economic interdependence cast doubts upon the sovereign, territorial state
as the system of rule most appropriate to deal with such issues.[4] If nuclear
weapons have made the territorial state less relevant, then the same might be
said of financial institutions which move vast amounts of capital worldwide in
the blink of an eye. "Modern global banking, and the new international economic realities it has created, challenges the world's political systems."[5] Such
international financial intermediation has multiplied a hundredfold in less than
twenty years.[6] "Offshore production" and "joint ventures" can barely capture
the nonstate centric nature of modern manufacture. Multinationals know no
boundaries. Trade has also increasingly become the movement of services
rather than exclusively that of material commodities. Such phenomena require
social scientists to rethink the nature and causes of change. To what extent can
the previous discussion of European history aid us in understanding the consequences of such processes? Specifically, is the decline of the sovereign, territorial state as imminent as some suggest?

I have written this book because I believe that an analysis of the emergence
of the state system and its continued existence suggests one way to think about

contemporary changes in a systematic manner. Historical analysis indicates that institutional evolution proceeds in two stages. In the first stage a dramatic change in the overall environment leads to new political coalitions. Such coalitions will favor institutional arrangements that correspond to the coalitions ideological preferences and material interests. In the second stage the different types of institutions exert competitive pressure on each other, and particular arrangements will emerge as more effective and more efficient than others. Some forms of organization are also more compatible with others and hence become preferred systems of rule. A brief synopsis of some of the main arguments might be helpful.

Generation

In response to the economic changes in the Late Middle Ages, three new modes of organization emerged: the sovereign state, the city-league, and the city-state. The expansion of trade offered opportunities to individuals for new means of livelihood and new possibilities of structuring authority. The growth in commerce also changed the relative power of the towns. Given these new opportunities and given the increase in their relative power, the burghers tried to form political coalitions that better met their interests and belief systems. Depending on the nature of coalitions, different institutional outcomes resulted.

I therefore argue that in its simplest form, expanding trade led to political coalitions that preferred a variety of new institutional types. France, the Hansa, and the Italian city-states were examples of the new systems of rule. Neither changes in military technology nor particular ideological perspectives provide for an adequate explanation of the variation in these three types. All three had access to modern technologies of warfare. All three had access to similar ideas of social order, Roman law, and religion.[7]

The nature of expanding trade provides the first estimate of the preferences of social groups and political elites. The advanced nature of trade in Italy made a high level of urbanization possible. Towns were of considerable size and did not need to rely on a central actor or league for protection. Moreover, Italian commerce was based particularly on goods of high added value and of relatively small volume. Towns had the motivation and the capability to try to monopolize trade routes by themselves.

Germany was less urbanized than Italy. Consequently, towns had to pool their resources for mutual aid against feudal and ecclesiastical exploiters. The trade of the northern German towns was largely in bulk goods, large in volume but low in added value. To acquire a monopoly on this trade, the Germans thus had to come together or seek assistance of a central actor who could defend their interests and unite them.

France, short of Flanders, was not very urbanized. Trade was largely local in nature and usually of low added value. The French towns thus had similar interests to the German towns. They would benefit from a political organization that could unite their resources, limit feudal exactions, and diminish the effects of feudal particularism.

But although both German and French towns desired an actor who could provide protection, reduce transaction and information costs, and establish more standardized jurisdiction, the German and French cases worked out quite differently. The primary explanatory variable, the expansion of commerce, provides for only a *partial* explanation.

Different institutional results occurred depending on the nature of social bargains that emerged in response to the new economic environment. Environmental change was mediated by the specific interests and calculations of individuals. In France a social coalition emerged between king and towns based on royal taxation, central administration, and a shared conceptual framework. In Germany, by contrast, the king—the Holy Roman Emperor—turned his attention to Italy, which proved disastrous. The king failed in his Italian campaigns, and the result was German fragmentation. Feudal lordships took effective control. Urban leagues formed in opposition to these feudal principalities in order to maintain urban independence and foster a more favorable economic environment.

The Italian case differed from the other two. In Italy, feudalism had never advanced as much as in France and Germany. The Italian towns were older, dating from Roman times, and had always included the aristocracy. Italy, therefore, did not experience the traditional rivalry between town and aristocracy. Instead, the nobility engaged in mercantile pursuits. The danger for urban independence came thus from the pope and the emperor. Combined noble and burgher resistance thwarted such attempts at centralization. City-states were the result.

Selection

In the long run, however, sovereign states displaced city-leagues and city-states. States won because their institutional logic gave them an advantage in mobilizing their societies' resources. Sovereign authority proved to be more effective in reducing economic particularism, which raised transaction and information costs, and it created a more unified economic climate. Central administration provided for gradual standardization of weights and measures, coinage, and jurisprudence. Undoubtedly this was a lengthy process, as the historical development of France indicates. But there existed an institutional arrangement in which the dominant political actor, the king in France, the king-in-parliament in England, had vested interests in limiting defection and freeriding and in furthering the overall economy. The greater autonomy of urban centers in the Hansa and the Italian city-states made such objectives more difficult to achieve.

Internationally, sovereign authorities were also better at credibly committing their members. They provided a clear and final decision-making authority which could bind their subjects. The reverse was true for the city-league. Because of the continual defection of the Hanseatic cities, the league was less attractive as a partner in international treaties.

Finally, states were predicated on a different logic than city-leagues. States explicitly recognized spatial limits to their political authority. The league, by contrast, was a nonterritorial form of organization which sought political control over its entire market. In view of this noncompatibility, states only empowered like-types. This empowerment therefore was not simply based on intellectual affinity but also on solid utilitarian reasons.

Because the state was more successful on these dimensions, it became increasingly attractive to other political entrepreneurs and social groups. Lordships started to mimic sovereign statehood. German princes styled themselves after the French court. Towns started to defect from the league and joined states.

The decline of the city-states was less stark than that of the leagues. Externally, city-states were compatible with a state system because they did define their authority by spatial parameters. City-states thus continued to function within the state system and signed treaties as equals of states. Internally, however, city-states did not transform themselves into full-fledged territorial units with a distinct locus of sovereignty. The dominant cities of the various city-states did not integrate their annexed territory and subject towns. This was due first, to the subjected towns themselves. As formerly independent and powerful, the towns could sometimes only be brought to heel by dominant cities through acknowledgment of their local autonomy. Second, the elites in the dominant cities were reluctant to relinquish their hold on power by granting other elites, from the subject areas, access to government. A striking example was the closed Venetian patriciate.

As a consequence, the dominant cities found it difficult to fully establish a centralized system of government. The *dominantes* could not override local privileges and law, and the subjected cities had no incentive to be second-rate members of the city-state. Central authority was always contested. There was no political actor who could rise as the logical and uncontested provider of collective goods. In that respect, the city-state resembled the city-league. Whoever held power in the city-state was suspected of furthering particularistic interests rather than the general good.

The evolution of the units in the international system should not be perceived as progress but as adaptation to the environmental demands created at specific critical junctures.[8] Although there is selection among the different responses to the new environment, this is not to be understood as a teleologically progressive development across different environments. Instead, selection operates only among the synchronically existing alternatives.[9]

Punctuated Equilibrium, Path Dependency, and Learning in International Relations

Borrowing from Stephen Jay Gould's theory of biological evolution, this book has argued that fundamental change occurs only sporadically.[10] At particular critical junctures, the environmental conditions change to such an extent that a reordering of the constitutive units of the international system takes place. Unit change in the international system is inevitably a multidimensional phenomenon. It involves more than simply the reordering of material interests. Individuals put forward rival conceptual perspectives on how social arrangements should be structured and what should count as legitimate order.

Once such change has occurred, a period of relative stability sets in. Institutional arrangements follow the paths that were laid out in those times of reordering. Once they have established a particular form of organization, political actors and social groups are reluctant to surrender their positions. Change will only occur if the contenders' relative position becomes strong enough to allow the formation of new political coalitions that can effectively challenge the old order.

Paths of institutional organization, however, are not irreversible. German lordships started to style themselves after the French court and usurped many of the regalian rights previously reserved for the emperor. Likewise, Italian dukes started to emulate the French court in their city-states and attempted to rationalize adjudication and standardize measures. The Hanseatic towns started to defect from the league, once the league could not effectively press its members' interests vis-à-vis the territorial states. In short, both political leaders and social actors might switch their institutional preferences.

This discussion, consequently, has implications for understanding institutional learning. From one perspective, institutions are seen as the outcome of individual preferences. Institutions are rational because they are the deliberate constructs of political entrepreneurs and members of social groups that benefit from those institutions. They are efficient because individuals try to choose institutional arrangements that best further their material interests or correspond with their ideological preferences.

From an alternative perspective, institutions are efficient and rational because the inefficient types have been selected out by structural requirements. Efficiency is thus measured not by individual choice but by Darwinian selection over time. This type of account is functionalist in that the institution is perceived to fulfill certain demands of the environment.

Following the previous historical account of European state emergence, it appears that a variation of both processes occurs. In round one, individuals choose particular arrangements, such as states, city-leagues, or city-states, based on their material and conceptual interests and on the political coalitions that are possible. Note that individuals might have preferences, but these need not necessarily be fulfilled. For example, the German towns might have preferred a central provider of public goods, but because of the emperor's preferred strategy toward Italy, the towns' desired coalition did not materialize.

In round two, some institutional solutions prove to be more adept at responding to a particular environment. The different institutions exert competitive pressure on each other. Some of these prove to be better at creating a favorable economic climate and credibly committing to international agreements. Moreover, the underlying logic of different organizations need not be mutually compatible. In short, selection by the structural environment occurs.

Simultaneously, political and social actors respond to these successes by switching their allegiances or constructing similar forms of organization. After perceiving the structural success of an institutional type, people then make an instrumental choice for that form of organization. Institutional learning thus has structural as well as instrumental dimensions.

POSSIBLE SCENARIOS FOR CONTEMPORARY CHANGE

As I suggested at the outset, we should not discount the possibility that the international system is undergoing a major transformation under our very eyes. According to some, the sovereign state is in decline and the changing nature of the international economy may be one cause.

By contrast, other scholars of international relations, and neorealists in particular, have argued that economic interaction is secondary, if not irrelevant, for understanding the international system in a structural sense. They suggest that although contemporary economic interdependence might be high, it is subject to the interests of the state. Their focus remains state centric, and it emphasizes the importance of security and self-help. If states desire, they can extricate themselves from this economic interaction at any time.

This dismissal of contemporary economic interaction is too simple. Economic interdependence now differs in substantial ways from that of the prewar period. In the productive sphere we see an increasing number of microeconomic linkages. Offshore production and joint ventures indicate that it is increasingly difficult to discern where the interest of the multinational producer and that of the state overlap.[11] Nor can the transfer of services and know-how, and changes in the provision of services, be perceived as business as usual. The standard mercantilist policies that were used to regulate these international transactions are no longer acceptable.[12] Trade no longer seems to follow the flag.

Given this change in economic milieu, there is no a priori reason why social actors and some political entrepreneurs would see the organization of international relations through a system of states as their most preferred institutional arrangement.[13] Multinational corporations and financial institutions might have very good incentives to seek new forms of organizing international behavior in response to new economic opportunities. Likewise, political entrepreneurs might benefit from, for example, increased authority for supranational organizations. If increased global competition has made traditional protection harder to sustain, then supranational organizations might provide political leaders a convenient means to extricate themselves from sheltering these domestic constituencies—"blame Brussels." Alternatively, political entrepreneurs might use such organizations to distribute costs over a larger electorate while at the same time benefiting domestic interest groups.[14]

Similarly, there is no reason to assume that social actors, for example, multinational companies, believe that a territorial state is the optimal way of organizing economic behavior. Indeed, by some accounts such actors are one of the driving forces behind current European integration. Conversely, the integrative effects of some political forces seem to be counterbalanced by the disinte-

grative effects of forces such as ethnicity and religion. Even relatively successful regional organizations, such as the European Community, sometimes
appear to be mere extensions of state interests rather than true supranational
bodies.

What expectations might we have for contemporary challenges to the state
system in view of the argument of the past chapters? Let us first look at two
scenarios that might evolve because of changes in the overall economic environment. I then ask whether a third scenario might emerge, in which reidenti-
fication with ethnic and religious communities challenges the principle of sovereign, territorial authority.

Self-help

One possibility is that there will be relatively little change in the nature of
formal political institutions but considerable change in how social actors order
international transactions themselves. Private actors might place a greater reliance on self-help mechanisms.[15] Medieval traders, faced with a plurality of
political authorities, placed considerable stock in their own means of curtailing
defection and reducing transaction and information costs. The new alliances
between transnational companies, which are based on division of production
and involve transaction-specific investments on both sides, are based on similar
calculations. That is, whereas translocal production and commerce previously
involved a greater measure of state intervention, modern contracts—based on
mutual hostage taking, self-enforcing agreements, and an even share of transaction-specific investments—should require less political oversight.

No doubt many transactions, such as global financial flows and joint ventures, fall outside the direct purview of the state. But although this diminishes
the scope of state authority, it has not yet altered the formal institutional arrangements of international activity. As David Held points out, too often general environmental shifts are presented as causes for the decline of the state
without distinguishing the de iure and de facto sides of sovereignty.[16] Although
the abilities of the state vis-à-vis society might have changed, the institutional
principle of sovereign, territorial rule as the foundation of the international
system has not. As I have argued at the outset of this book, from an international
relations perspective, the question is how the emergence of the sovereign, territorial state has altered international conduct, not how the role of government
has changed. In short, the growth of self-help might be a precursor to alternatives modes of institutional structure, but as of yet it posits no challenge to the
sovereign state system.

The European Community: Regionalization and
Crosscutting Jurisdictions

Arguably the greatest deviation from sovereign rule has come in regional associations, particularly in the European Community (EC). Although the EC does
not present a move away from a territorial conceptualization of authority, it

cannot be simply construed as a larger sovereign entity. That is, the EC recognizes territorial, legal limits to its authority—the borders of its member states. However, in the sense that there is a move toward a crosscutting set of jurisdictions at the national and supranational levels, there is a change in the locus of authority. Sovereignty is no longer defined as a strict external delimitation from other claims to authority. The European Court, for example, has handed down decisions against certain policies practiced by national governments. The EC is thus sui generis.[17] It is neither the simple extension of states nor is it a full-blown alternative that can completely act against state preferences.

Developments in the EC square quite well with our observations about change in general. Change in the EC has not been a continual process. After a dramatic start in the late 1950s, European integration slowed down in the 1960s and reached a virtual standstill in the 1970s. Then in the mid-1980s, with the publication of the White Paper, there was a sudden flurry of support for European integration on some issue areas.

This has not been a purely functional response. As Geoffrey Garrett points out, one cannot simply argue that European trade as a percentage of Gross Domestic Product has increased from 40 to 60 percent and that hence integration was inevitable.[18] Particular institutional types need to be explained by political preferences. European integration can thus be partially understood by focusing on elite bargains, both at the intergovernmental level and between social groups. Sandholtz and Zysman, for example, attempt to explain recent inroads in European integration by the political bargains struck by community institutions, industrial elites, and governments.[19]

Consequently, integration has varied per issue area. The presence or absence of transnational coalitions has depended on the nature of the good in question. Within the EC, domestic control over tax issues has remained intact, whereas on some other issues, such as trade policy, states have been more inclined to surrender their control.[20]

It is therefore incorrect to argue that the EC is nothing but the extension of state preferences. In regard to some matters, states cannot extricate themselves easily from the EC process. Indeed, EC members might construct international agreements in such a way that national governments cannot defect too easily. Institutions may thus be deliberately designed to prevent actors from wavering, which thereby may provide both credibility to group commitments as well as protection to individual governments from irate domestic constituents.

Whether such a form of organization is viable in the long run is an open-ended question. The nonsovereign logic of the Hansa proved to have serious flaws. To some extent we might see the contours of such problems re-emerge in the EC. For example, the foreign decision-making power of the EC administration will inevitably be questioned as long as individual member states claim the right to defect from EC agreements.[21] It remains to be seen whether supranational institutions within the EC can credibly commit their members and whether the EC can prevent freeriding.[22] There are incentives for state elites within the EC to prevent the uncertainty of divided sovereignty, and there are incentives for the other actors in the international system to force the EC to resemble a sovereign logic of organization.

In short, in certain respects the EC has diminished the sovereign state as the locus of decision making. Although this erosion has been tentative, as EC organs have obtained final decision-making authority only on specific issue areas, the EC is certainly not just an extension of state interests. Conversely, it is also not simply a state writ large, and it seems unlikely that the EC will form a superstate in the near future. Nevertheless, we cannot dismiss the possibility of such organization, composed of an internally fragmented sovereignty but which is essentially territorial, because of our lack of historical imagination. The move toward more supranational decision making within the EC seems quite compatible with the overall methodology for understanding unit change which I advanced in respect to the feudal-state transition. Political entrepreneurs and social elites have formed coalitions to create new institutional arrangements to respond to the growth of intra-European trade and the increase in global competition. Two possibilities exist. First, if the EC is successful, this form of organization may yield similar arrangements elsewhere because of institutional mimicry and competition. Or the EC will be forced to take on a more consolidated logic, because it currently lacks a clear focal point through which to conduct international affairs.

Alternative Identities and Institutional Isomorphism

The establishment of sovereign, territorial authority involved a resolution of the struggle between that mode of authority and the translocal rule claimed by the church.[23] Religious organizations base their rule on the community of the faithful—wherever they may reside. The king's assertion of secular and sovereign power over the church achieved its first measure of success by the close of the thirteenth century. But the principle that the secular ruler determines the public character of religion was only resolved by the Treaty of Augsburg in 1555. Through the adage *Cuius regio eius religio*, political elites established the principle that the territorial unit would publicly adopt the religion of the ruler. This principle was again affirmed at the end of the Thirty Years War.

But although the state system has spread globally, the tension between transnational religious affinity and territorial rule has not been resolved everywhere.[24] One of those tensions appears in Islamic religion. By some accounts, the Muslim community of faith is fundamentally at odds with the Western concept of sovereign, territorial rule. Bernard Lewis, for example, notes how the principle of dividing the Islamic world (Dar al-Islam) from the non-Islamic (Dar al-Harb) suggests an incompatibility with the principle of sovereign territoriality. But other Islamicists argue that the tension between the two might be overstated. Both in theory as well as practice, Islamic doctrine and the modern nation-state have proven quite compatible.[25]

Nor have ethnic movements eroded the state system in any fundamental way. It is true that they have destabilized existing sovereign, territorial states, but successful secessionist efforts have subsequently reconstituted themselves as new states. Ethnic movements have not essentially been at odds with the principles of territorial demarcation of rule and of a final locus of authority in external affairs.

What ethnic movements have changed is the chronological order of state and nation. European states claimed sovereignty and territoriality, although fully aware that they were hardly homogeneous ethnic units. Medieval France consisted of Acquitanians, Bretons, Normans, and other descendants of the great migrations at the end of the Roman Empire. It was centralized authority that installed vernacular French against translocal Latin. States made nations. Contemporary claims reverse that order. But as new sovereign, territorial units, they are not antithetical to the state system.

Sovereignty Challenged; Sovereignty Reaffirmed

The foregoing analysis of unit change in the international system provides reasons to expect that in many respects the contemporary state system is becoming more firmly entrenched rather than declining, save perhaps in the case of the EC. The causes of the longevity of the state system should be noted. I argue, in particular, that a system based on territorial demarcation and mutual recognition actually creates a systematized pattern of interaction in international affairs.

Moreover, since the generation of units depends on political entrepreneurs and social groups to form new coalitions which can unseat the dominant ones, unit transformation is an infrequent process. Political elites in power have few incentives to alter existing institutions and experiment with new systems of rule. What held true for the medieval nobility, which was reluctant to surrender its powers to emerging burghers and centralizing kings, holds equally true for political leaders today. African leaders, for example, who have inherited a state system that was clearly imposed, have shown relatively little desire to reconstitute their authority on grounds other than sovereign territoriality.[26]

Institutions are also unyielding because change involves considerable investments in learning and start-up costs.[27] After political institutions formed in the thirteenth and fourteenth centuries, the process of selection, adaptation, and mimicry took a considerable amount of time. But once the state system had established itself, experimentation with new institutional forms of organization became incredibly costly. Network externalities thus create obstacles to unilateral attempts at institutional innovation.

Finally, given that the state system has also been produced by mutual empowerment, there are barriers for any nonsovereign form of organization that wishes to be recognized as a legitimate participant in international relations. Disaffected ethnic and religious groups seldom claim that they wish to create a form of organization that is universalistic or based on translocal affinity. Instead they wish to form a territorial and sovereign state of their own. That is, they wish to become states. New forms of identification, or previously neglected ones, may be recast within the mold of the system to become accepted within the larger community and its corresponding pattern of interactions.[28] Consequently, I agree with Giddens that international organizations strengthen rather than weaken the existing state system. The extension of the European state system to a truly global one has only enhanced this process. De iure the state system is alive and well.

Nevertheless, we should not predict the probability and direction of change from this set of observations. In the long run, history sides with no one. If there is one lesson to be drawn from this book it is that all institutions are susceptible to challenges and that existing institutions are not necessarily the most efficient responses to such challenges. The sovereign, territorial state emerged because it happened to be better than its alternatives, not because it was the result of some necessary unilinear process. We should furthermore recall that the fullest articulation of feudal organization and the church, both in a theoretical and practical sense, occurred shortly before their demise. Such articulation seems to occur exactly when institutional challenges arise. Changes in communications, economics, and the environment challenge the scope of state authority and thus create incentives for actors to alter the existing institutional arrangements.

Thus far, new institutional arrangements have only emerged in a modest fashion. Of all regional organizations, the EC has been most manifest as an alternative institutional form. Yet even its development is sometimes abruptly halted by state interests, as occurred during the French walkout in 1965 and as evident in the difficulties of implementing the 1992 project. But the EC is perhaps less important as an example of an alternative institutional arrangement than as an example of how the process of institutional change might occur. John Ruggie is right.[29] The medieval trade fairs in themselves did not create novel structures of political authority. But in introducing and facilitating trade, they helped monetarize exchange relationships and struck at the core of a feudal society largely centered on in-kind transfers. Economic and environmental forces in and of themselves thus do not indicate the nature of future institutional evolution. Indeed, I agree that there are serious impediments to changing the de iure nature of the state system. But such forces do provide incentives and sets of ideas for actors who are unwilling to make do with the present.

Many arguments within the international relations literature focus on the issue of order in the system. For neorealists, the system is anarchical and order is derivative of the distribution of capabilities. Scholars of the Grotian school argue, by contrast, that the system is permeated with shared rules and principles between states. Anarchy is mitigated by the existence of an international society. Neoliberal institutionalists share elements of both views. Although they concede that state interests drive international affairs, international institutions can affect conduct beyond a purely short-run utilitarian calculus.

We forget that the *character* of the units in the system creates patterns of conduct.[30] Transnational claims of jurisdiction by church and empire differ from sovereign, territorial organization which recognizes other states as juridically equivalent. Fragmented sovereignty and crosscutting jurisdictions raise the costs of international transactions and divide loyalties in unpredictable ways. I have attempted, therefore, to supplement the focus on governance between sovereign states with an analysis of why it is that states do the governing. As in all social sciences, the account provided here is only a partial one. Across history and in different locations, a variety of contextual changes and political coalitions need to be taken into account to adequately explain how different institutions have emerged at different junctures. What I have done is suggest a method for examining such processes. Although the answers may only provide a partial look at a complex reality, no doubt this is an era in which we must continue to ask such questions.

INTRODUCTION

1. Stephen Jay Gould, *The Panda's Thumb* (1980), p. 28.

2. To understand my argument, it is critically important to recognize that this book is not an account, nor a critical evaluation, of general theories of state emergence. A discussion of "the origins of the state" means widely different things within anthropology, sociology, political science, and economic history. Depending on the focus, a widely divergent chronology and different accounts of the origins of the state emerge. Much of the anthropological and sociological literature, for example, is concerned with the rise of formal political organization as compared to tribal or kinship associations. Thus citystates, empires, and leagues are all considered to be forms of states, that is, formal governments. From that perspective, European states emerged very early. See, for example, W. G. Runciman, "Origins of States: The Case of Archaic Greece," *Comparative Studies in Society and History* 24 (July 1982), pp. 351–377. For many others, explaining the emergence of the state means accounting for the development and expansion of government. For example, analyses of when formal administrative procedures were installed, or when governmental revenue reached a certain level, are of this type. Or statehood is equated with the nation-state, a phenomenon attributed to the eighteenth century. I do not use the term *state* in those meanings.

3. Indeed, the very term *international* presupposes a differentiation between domestic and international affairs—a distinction that only became meaningful after sovereign authority had become a constitutive principle of the international order. Diverse conceptions of the state are described by J. P. Nettl, "The State as a Conceptual Variable," *World Politics* 20 (July 1968), pp. 559–562. The state can be seen as an aggregate set of functions, as an autonomous actor vis-à-vis society, or as a unit in international relations. In this work I am concerned with the last of these meanings.

4. See Benn's definition of sovereignty. He notes seven different meanings, but they basically narrow down to the notion of internal hierarchy and external demarcation by borders. Stanley Benn, "Sovereignty," in *The Encyclopedia of Philosophy* vol. 7/8 (1967), pp. 501–505. Hinsley's definition is similar: "at any rate, the idea of sovereignty was the idea that there is a final and absolute political authority in the political community . . . and no final and absolute authority exists elsewhere." F. H. Hinsley, *Sovereignty* (1986), p. 26.

5. Two essays that discuss the material and conceptual implications of sovereignty are: Friedrich Kratochwil, "Of Systems, Boundaries, and Territoriality: An Inquiry into the Formation of the State System," *World Politics* 39 (1986), pp. 27–52; and J. L. Holzgrefe, "The Origins of Modern International Relations Theory," *Review of International Studies* 15 (1989), pp. 11–26. Hinsley also notes this conceptual aspect: "Although we talk of it loosely as something concrete . . . sovereignty is not a fact. It is a concept which men in certain circumstances have applied." Hinsley, *Sovereignty*, p. 1.

6. For example, Rosecrance suggests that interdependence has fundamentally altered states' objectives. Richard Rosecrance, *The Rise of the Trading State* (1986). For an early view that nuclear weapons would change the nature of territorial states, see John Herz, "Rise and Demise of the Territorial State," in *The Nation-State and the Crisis of World Politics* (1976), pp. 99–123. John Ruggie draws attention to the ecological

problematique in his *Planetary Politics: Ecology and the Organization of Global Political Space*, forthcoming. For the impact of international financial markets, see Ralph Bryant, *International Financial Intermediation* (1987).

7. The literature here is vast. To name but a few contemporary examples that have put the historical and future development of the state back on the agenda, see, for example, Charles Tilly, *Coercion, Capital, and European States, AD 990–1990* (1990); Peter Evans, Dietrich Rueschemeyer, and Theda Skocpol, eds., *Bringing the State Back In* (1985); John Hall, *States in History* (1986). Several recent sets of essays have probed the possibility of change in the current system, for example, James Caporaso, ed., *The Elusive State* (1989); Ernst-Otto Czempiel and James Rosenau, eds., *Global Changes and Theoretical Challenges* (1989); James Rosenau and Ernst-Otto Czempiel, *Governance Without Government: Order and Change in World Politics* (1992).

8. I use Gilpin's definition of systems change. Systems change is a transformation in the nature of the constitutive units. An example of such a change is the decline of empires in favor of feudal organization. Robert Gilpin, *War and Change in World Politics* (1981), pp. 39, 40.

9. In methodological terms, the previous focus has been on explaining by the method of agreement. That is, the previous literature focused on locating the critical, similar, independent variable that could explain the similarity in outcome—the emergence of the state—in a variety of contexts. However, since some of the independent variables correlate, for example, the growth of the economy and the change in military technology, there is no unique explanation. I submit that comparing by difference is more fruitful. Given a similarity of some independent variables, which variation among the other independent variables might account for the different outcomes? See Skocpol's discussion in Theda Skocpol, ed., *Vision and Method in Historical Sociology* (1984), pp. 378, 379. Similarly, Given has argued that history has paid little attention to the merits of a variation finding strategy to explain phenomena across two or more cases. James Given, *State and Society in Medieval Europe* (1990), pp. 36, 251.

10. This is not simply due to material resources. Indeed, as Braudel argues, initially the balance swung against states in favor of the cities. As will be clear from my case studies, these alternatives could for many centuries raise armies and extract taxes on a par with any state. Fernand Braudel, *The Perspective of the World* (1984), p. 91.

11. Zolberg makes a similar argument for the integration of internal analysis and the study of competitive dynamics between units. Aristide Zolberg, "Strategic Interactions and the Formation of Modern States: France and England," *International Social Science Journal* 32 (1980), pp. 687–716.

12. I am interested in the de facto emergence of sovereign states and the gradual empowerment of the idea of sovereignty. I am, of course, fully cognizant of the fact that the theoretical articulation of the idea only occurred with Bodin (several centuries after the first claims that kings were sovereign in their own realm). Hinsley even argues that the idea was only fully articulated with Vattel in 1758, because only then was the idea of a Christian community abandoned. F. H. Hinsley, "The Concept of Sovereignty and the Relations Between States," in W. J. Stankiewicz, ed., *In Defense of Sovereignty* (1969), p. 283.

13. Because of the variant impact of trade, in terms of volume and added value, the European towns did not all have the same preferences. This will provide a first estimate of the type of coalitions one might expect.

14. In this sense institutional selection differs from the purely environmental selection within, for example, biology or unrestrained market competition. Selection also

occurs because actors consciously seek to establish and favor compatible types of organization. That is, states empowered only like types. Additionally, one might speculate that the existence of other territorial states strengthened the positions of sovereigns domestically. Political elites might benefit from decreasing the set of plausible institutional alternatives from which their citizens might wish to choose. Furthermore, the existence of other sovereign states might serve to enhance the domestic legitimacy of the political leader claiming sovereignty at home.

15. Note that I have only argued that the sovereign state proved to be superior to European city-states and city-leagues. I am not explaining why the European state proved superior to forms of organization outside Europe, such as Imperial China or Japan. Tilly would argue that it was due to the superior war-making capacity of the national state. My own explanation for the worldwide spread of the European mode of international organization would lie closer to that of Hall and Baechler. See Jean Baechler, John Hall, and Michael Mann, eds., *Europe and the Rise of Capitalism* (1988). That is, once a competitive state system emerged, rather than an imperial organization, the competitiveness between states led to further economic and technological development. Furthermore, I would hypothesize that imperial systems were also incompatible with sovereign, territorial states. On this, more work would be needed, but my estimate is that rule that legitimates itself as religiously sanctioned cannot accept other political authorities as equals. Yet as Kratochwil argues, territorial sovereignty implies exactly that states are equal. Kratochwil, "Of Systems, Boundaries, and Territoriality," p. 35. The preference for compatible institutions also explains the global extension of the principle of sovereign territoriality by the European states. That is, nonsovereign forms of organization were deliberately transformed.

16. See particularly the essays by Stephen Krasner, "Approaches to the State: Alternative Conceptions and Historical Dynamics," *Comparative Politics* 16 (January 1984), pp. 223–246; and "Sovereignty: An Institutional Perspective," in Caporaso, *The Elusive State*, pp. 69–96, for the application of Gould's idea of punctuated equilibrium.

CHAPTER 1

1. Joseph Strayer, *On the Medieval Origins of the Modern State* (1970), p. 27.

2. Gilpin, *War and Change*, p. 41.

3. This work is large in volume and varies in its epistemological position, degree of criticism, and substantive argument. See, for example, the essays in Caporaso, *The Elusive State*; Czempiel and Rosenau, *Global Changes and Theoretical Challenges*; John Ruggie, "Continuity and Transformation in the World Polity," in Robert Keohane, ed., *Neorealism and Its Critics* (1986), pp. 131–157; Anthony Giddens, *The Nation-State and Violence* (1987); Richard Ashley, "The Poverty of Neorealism," in Keohane, *Neorealism and Its Critics*, pp. 255–300; Alexander Wendt, "The Agent-Structure Problem in International Relations Theory," *International Organization* 41 (Summer 1987), pp. 335–370.

4. As Zolberg states, "thus while recent decades have witnessed, on the one hand, an abundance of theories concerning international relations and, on the other, a proliferation of comparative analyses dealing with the regime or the state, very little effort has been directed towards the interface." Zolberg, "Strategic Interactions and the Formation of Modern States," pp. 688–689.

5. Kenneth Waltz, *Theory of International Politics* (1979), pp. 88, 104; and his "Reflections on Theory of International Politics: A Response to My Critics," in Keohane, *Neorealism and Its Critics*, p. 323f.

6. For Durkheim's distinction between mechanical and organic solidarity, see Emile Durkheim, *The Division of Labor in Society* (1933); Emile Durkheim, *The Rules of Sociological Method*, Steven Lukes, ed. (1982).

7. International relations is thus driven by a transhistorical logic. "Through all of the changes of boundaries, of social, economic, and political form, of economic and military activity, the substance and style of international politics remain strikingly constant. We can look farther afield, for example, to the China of the warring states era or to the India of Kautilya, and see that where political entities of whatever sort compete freely, substantive and stylistic characteristics are similar." Waltz, "Reflections on Theory of International Politics," pp. 329–330. See also Waltz, *Theory of International Politics*, p. 66.

8. Waltz explicitly responds to Ruggie on this point. He says in regard to Ruggie's emphasis on dynamic density that "the account, however, tells us nothing about the structure of international politics." Furthermore, he adds, "Ruggie would lower the level of abstraction by adding . . . characteristics of units and of unit level processes." Waltz, "Reflections on Theory of International Politics," pp. 328, 330.

9. Game theorists, for example, have explored the conditions under which cooperation or conflict arise. The number of actors, the particular payoffs that actors expect, and the shadow of the future all influence the probability for conflict or cooperation. The character of the unit is largely irrelevant to the logic of the analysis. See, for example, Kenneth Oye, ed., *Cooperation Under Anarchy* (1986). But note how Conybeare's article in that volume indicates how the type of unit might be relevant for such calculations. John Conybeare, "Trade Wars: A Comparative Study of Anglo-Hanse, Franco-Italian, and Hawley-Smoot Conflicts," in Oye, *Cooperation Under Anarchy*, pp. 147–172.

10. Dynamic density is thus "the quantity, velocity and diversity of transactions." Ruggie, "Continuity and Transformation," p. 142f.

11. For interesting discussions on the connection between political authority and spatial order, see, for example, Robert Dodgshon, *The European Past* (1987).

12. For good discussions of the differences between the feudal era and the contemporary state system, see, in addition to Ruggie's "Continuity and Transformation," Kratochwil, "Of Systems, Boundaries, and Territoriality"; and Holzgrefe, "The Origins of Modern International Relations Theory."

13. The attempts to create a state monopoly on the use of force arguably started as early as the mid-thirteenth century when Louis IX tried to limit the bearing of arms by the nobility. State monopoly over the means of violence, however, was not yet fully complete even in the nineteenth century. On the latter issue, see Janice Thomson, "Sovereignty in Historical Pespective: The Evolution of State Control over Extraterritorial Violence," in Caporaso, *The Elusive State*, pp. 227–254; and Janice Thomson, "State Practices, International Norms, and the Decline of Mercenarism," *International Studies Quarterly* 34 (March 1990), pp. 23–48.

14. The royal domain was seen as the personal property of the king. See Herbert Rowen, *The King's State* (1980).

15. This conclusion is similar to Wendt's argument that neorealism sees the system ontologically as separate units. Wendt, "The Agent-Structure Problem."

16. Consider, for example, how one might apply the contemporary vocabulary of international relations theorizing to the feudal era. Should one describe the system as tripolar consisting of Christian Europe, the Muslim world, and Mongol Eurasia? Would it be bipolar in terms of the contest of empire and papacy? Or was it multipolar? I would argue that the term *hyperpolar* seems more apt, in that a multitude of actors could wield

effective force. Even more problematic would be to define the international system. In short, what the modern state system has done is to make unambiguous what the system is and who the actors are.

17. Anthony Giddens describes structuration theory as having two main objectives. "First, to acknowledge the essential importance of a concept of action in the social sciences. . . . Second, to formulate such an account without relapsing into a subjectivist view, and without failing to grasp the structural components of the social institutions which outlive us." Anthony Giddens, *A Contemporary Critique of Historical Materialism* (1981), pp. 15. For adaptations in political science, see John Ruggie, "International Structure and International Transformation: Space, Time, and Method," in Czempiel and Rosenau, *Global Changes and Theoretical Challenges*, pp. 21–36; Wendt, "The Agent-Structure Problem"; David Dessler, "What's at Stake in the Agent-Structure Debate?" *International Organization* 43 (Summer 1989), pp. 441–473.

18. James Caporaso, "Microeconomics and International Political Economy: The Neoclassical Approach to Institutions," in Czempiel and Rosenau, *Global Changes and Theoretical Challenges*, p. 135.

19. Ashley, "The Poverty of Neorealism," p. 259.

20. For an example of a rich historical argument that the English state is a cultural construct, see Philip Corrigan and Derek Sayer, *The Great Arch* (1991).

21. Biersteker suggests that poststructuralism added to the epistemological debate surrounding international relations theory, but it has added little in the way of substantive social theory. Thomas Biersteker, "Critical Reflections on Post-Positivism in International Relations," *International Studies Quarterly* 33 (September 1989), pp. 263–267. For a suggestion on how to reconcile various approaches through more detailed historical analysis of nonstate logics of order, see Richard Mansbach and Yale Ferguson, "Between Celebration and Despair," *International Studies Quarterly* 35 (December 1991), pp. 363–386.

22. Dessler, "What's at Stake in the Agent-Structure Debate?" p. 447.

23. In this sense, I view Wendt's focus on symbolic interactionism as more problematic than his first critique of neorealism contained in "The Agent-Structure Problem." His later work takes the symbolic interactionist view. "Anarchy is What States Make of It: The Social Construction of Power Politics," *International Organization* 46 (Spring 1992), pp. 391–426.

24. In short, I see this work as a response to the earlier critique which required neorealism to specify how the system emerged, thus recognizing the historical specificity of the state system. That is how I read Ruggie and Wendt's earlier critiques. Ruggie, "Continuity and Transformation"; Wendt, "The Agent-Structure Problem." Redefining the nature of the system in an inductivist sense creates several problems. An inductive understanding based on a taxonomy of interactions becomes far less parsimonious. For example, Richard Rosecrance identifies nine systems in *Action and Reaction in World Politics* (1963). As Waltz notes, particularly in his critique of Rosecrance, an inductive "bottom up" generalization of actor behavior redefines the system in terms of agent behavior rather than in a priori structural dictates which constrain such behavior. See Waltz, *Theory of International Politics*, pp. 50, 64.

25. Waltz, *Theory of International Politics*, p. 89; and "Reflections on Theory of International Politics," p. 339.

26. See Michael Piore and Charles Sabel, *The Second Industrial Divide* (1984), for the argument that Fordist production systems are being pushed out by craftlike production systems.

27. Instead it is similar to Waltz's notion of Darwinian imperatives for socialization. See Waltz, *Theory of International Politics*, pp. 73–77.

28. Similarly, one could argue that the change from personalistic to more bureaucratic corporations was a structural change. See, for example, Alfred Chandler, *Strategy and Structure* (1962).

29. Giddens, *The Nation-State and Violence*, p. 255f.

30. An exception might be the entrance of new members to cartel-like arrangements.

31. This is well described by Marc Bloch, *Feudal Society* (1961).

32. See Thomson, "Sovereignty in Historical Perspective." For a fine description of the ambiguities of acceptable practice, see Robert Ritchie, *Captain Kidd and the War Against the Pirates* (1986).

33. Kratochwil comments of sovereignty that "it denotes internal hierarchy as well as external equality." By denying some types equal status, they were delegitimized as units in the system. Kratochwil, "Of Systems, Boundaries, and Territoriality," p. 35.

34. I will argue that city-leagues were incompatible with sovereign, territorial states because leagues, such as the Hansa, had no clear territorial boundaries. In their desire to extend their political control over their economic sphere of interaction, they would inevitably encroach on territorial units. Second, because of the absence of sovereign hierarchy, they lacked a clear focal point through which to coordinate their behavior. City-states were more compatible in that they did have specific territorial limits to their claims of authority. Hence, external sovereignty and juridical equivalence came easier to that logic of organization.

35. Robert H. Jackson, "Quasi-States, Dual Regimes, and Neoclassical Theory: International Jurisprudence and the Third World," *International Organization* 41 (Autumn 1987), pp. 519–549. He argues that the African states clearly lack the traditional empirical trappings of statehood but that they are juridically empowered. Also see, Giddens, *The Nation-State and Violence*, p. 272.

36. Kratochwil, "Of Systems, Boundaries, and Territoriality," p. 36.

37. For the difference between traditional universal empires and sovereign, territorial states, see particularly Roberto Unger, *Plasticity into Power* (1987); John Hall, *Powers and Liberties* (1985); Immanuel Wallerstein, *The Modern World System, vol. 1* (1974), p. 15; and Giddens, *The Nation-State and Violence*, p. 79f. Rundolph notes that it was only because of the failure of the Holy Roman Empire that Europe diverged from the world norm. Susanne Rundolph, "Presidential Address: State Formation in Asia— Prolegomenon to a Comparative Study," *Journal of Asian Studies* 46 (November 1987), p. 736.

38. Hedley Bull, *The Anarchical Society* (1977). Bull recognizes the existence of sovereign states but sees them as placed in a societal order (p. 24). Keens-Soper, also a Grotian, notes that this society was uniquely European: "The implications of political fragmentation did not call in question the continued spiritual and legal unity of Christendom." Maurice Keens-Soper, "The Practice of a States-System," *Studies in History and Politics*, vol. 2 (1981–82), p. 17. The Ottomans could play no part in this system. In Keens-Soper's interpretation, the Peace of Westphalia reinforced this notion of states self-consciously being part of an association of states united by a shared culture.

39. Bernard Lewis, *The Muslim Discovery of Europe* (1982), pp. 60–61.

40. On the universalist claims of Rome, see Hinsley, "The Concept of Sovereignty and the Relations Between States," p. 276. Similarly, the German emperor claimed to rule as *dominus mundi*, "lord of the world." Hinsley, *Sovereignty*, p. 60; Gerald Straus,

"Germany: Idea of Empire," in Joseph Strayer, ed., *Dictionary of the Middle Ages*, vol. 5 (1985), p. 495.

41. Ruggie rightly stresses the conceptual parallel between the exclusivity of property rights and sovereign territoriality. Ruggie, "Continuity and Transformation," p. 143.

42. To use the normal concept "international" relations, rather than translocal, indicates how the state transformed politics and how we perceive such interactions. See Ruggie, "Continuity and Transformation," p. 142.

43. Garett Mattingly, *Renaissance Diplomacy* (1988); Gordon Craig and Alexander George, *Force and Statecraft* (1983), p. 11.

44. Those who analyze the feudal-state transformation recognize that balancing and self-regarding behavior occur. The point is that neorealism implicitly assumes that it is evident who the actors are (states) and that it is clear when the condition of anarchy holds. That is, neorealism is premised on the separability of hierarchical and anarchical realms. It is that very separability that the emergence of the state system institutionalizes. I disagree here with Markus Fischer, "Feudal Europe, 800–1300: Communal Discourse and Conflictual Practices," *International Organization* 46 (Spring 1992), pp. 427–466. Ruggie similarly critiques Fischer's position as a misstatement of his position and the theoretical problem posed by the feudal-state transformation. John Ruggie, "Territoriality and Beyond: Problematizing Modernity in International Relations," *International Organization* 47 (Winter 1993), pp. 139–174, particularly note 57.

45. Stephen Jay Gould's view of evolution is a useful metaphor for an alternative understanding of institutional evolution. Gould likens biological evolution to water running down a slope. The water divides itself in different branches, the directions of which cannot be predicted. It is, however, possible to explain after the fact why a particular branch dried up, why it proved to be a dead end. In short, at critical junctures a multiplicity of alternatives emerge. Only over time do many of these turn out to be evolutionary dead ends. Gould, *The Panda's Thumb*, p. 140.

46. As said, of these three, Weber's views are the least unilinear.

47. I label this competitive efficiency, but one can read it as relative ability. I do not imply that there is a particular form of organization that is a priori optimally efficient. Efficiency is not to be understood absolutely but relatively; that is, a particular form of organization is more or less efficient vis-à-vis its rivals. It might be more efficient in reducing transaction costs, preventing freeriding, raising revenue, etc. Comparative efficiency thus stands for the comparative superiority of one form of organization over the other, in terms of effectiveness and efficiency.

48. Chapter 2 discusses this in greater detail.

49. Wallerstein, *The Modern World System, vol. 1*, p. 7.

50. Immanuel Wallerstein, *The Politics of the World Economy* (1984), p. 33.

51. Charles Tilly reaches a similar conclusion in *The Formation of National States in Western Europe* (1975), p. 601f. See also Bertrand Badie and Pierre Birnbaum, *The Sociology of the State* (1983), for a critique of functionalist and Marxist accounts of state emergence.

52. Aristide Zolberg argues that the development of states preceded the world economy, "Origins of the Modern World Economy," *World Politics* 33 (January 1981), pp. 253–281. See Baechler, Hall, and Mann, *Europe and the Rise of Capitalism*, for the argument that the development of states actually aided the development of capitalism. See also Hall, *Powers and Liberties*, and Gilpin, who argues that "the emergence of a world market economy was dependent on the pluralistic structure of the European (and,

subsequently, the global) political system." Gilpin, *War and Change*, p. 133. He rightly notes how earlier international markets were displaced by imperial economies.

53. Wendt, "The Agent-Structure Problem," p. 348.

54. Perry Anderson, *Passages from Antiquity to Feudalism* (1974), p. 198.

55. Perry Anderson, *Lineages of the Absolutist State* (1974), p. 18.

56. Durkheim, *The Rules of Sociological Method*, p. 138.

57. Badie and Birnbaum note that Durkheim "is less aware than Marx of the extreme diversity of modern processes of political centralization, and he is much more attached than Marx to a narrowly evolutionary view of state formation. He supposes that all states always develop according to the same laws." Badie and Birnbaum, *The Sociology of the State*, p. 12. Ruggie's earlier reliance on Durkheim's work to account for change does not satisfactorily explain sovereignty from my point of view because it cannot account for the variety in institutional types. Ruggie, "Continuity and Transformation," p. 142.

58. Consequently, one problem with a Weberian approach is that it does not easily lend itself to parsimonious theorizing. This evinces itself, for example, in the work of Reinhard Bendix. Bendix carefully retraces political developments in a variety of countries to examine why they resulted in monarchical or democratic rule. Reinhard Bendix, *Kings or People* (1978). Rueschemeyer says of Bendix's work: "Ad hoc explanations abound in Bendix's narrative." He believes that Bendix is skeptical of any systems theory. Dietrich Rueschemeyer, "Theoretical Generalization and Historical Particularity in the Comparative Sociology of Reinhard Bendix," in Skocpol, *Vision and Method in Historical Sociology*, pp. 151, 159.

59. This would, for example, be Habermas's interpretation of Weber. Jürgen Habermas, *The Theory of Communicative Action* (1984).

60. I believe that such accounts are prevalent in explanations of contemporary European developments. We are often told that a larger European community is "inevitable" because of increased competition. That actors who lose in this process might prevent further integration is not considered.

61. See, for example, Richard Bean, "War and the Birth of the Nation State," *Journal of Economic History* 33 (1973), pp. 203–221. See also David Friedman, "A Theory of the Size and Shape of Nations," *Journal of Political Economy* 85 (1977), pp. 59–77; and Leonard Dudley, "Structural Change in Interdependent Bureaucracies: Was Rome's Failure Economic or Military?" *Explorations in Economic History* 27 (April 1990), pp. 232–248.

62. For the usefulness of biological metaphors to explain social evolution see, for example, Krasner, "Approaches to the State." Runciman goes one step further by suggesting that biological evolution does not serve as a mere metaphor but that it and social evolution are analogues. W. G. Runciman, *A Treatise on Social Theory*, vol. 2 (1989), pp. 45–47, 449. I discuss my position at greater length in Chapter 2.

63. Many of the points raised here resemble Caporaso's discussion of weaknesses in rational choice theory. The close correspondence between flaws in rational choice theory and unilinear evolutionary views is not surprising. Both views run the risk of affirming the consequent. Caporaso argues that some of these weaknesses may be resolved through a clearer specification of alternatives, actual choices of individuals, and subsequent selective dynamics among these choices. All these points are very similar to my concerns regarding unilinear views, and my response in this book to those concerns is very similar to Caporaso's proposed research program. Caporaso, "Microeconomics and International Political Economy," pp. 135–160.

64. Eugene Rice, *The Foundations of Early Modern Europe, 1460–1559* (1970), p. 15.

65. As I already noted, this institutional phenomenon, a system of discrete but interacting units, is viewed as decisive in the rise of capitalism. See Baechler, Hall, and Mann, *Europe and the Rise of Capitalism*.

66. Caporaso uses the term *low level equilibrium trap*. Caporaso, "Microeconomics and International Political Economy," p. 150. Similarly, Elster notes how selection need not proceed to any optimal position. He speaks of *low maximum traps* wherein a higher optimum could only be reached after a brief decline. Consequently, new innovations that move toward the higher optimal result, but are initially inferior, will not be selected. The end result is that the higher optimum does not develop. Jon Elster, *Nuts and Bolts* (1989), pp. 72–73.

67. Like Gilpin, I will thus argue that unit change needs to be explained by the preferences of actors. Gilpin, *War and Change*, p. 42.

68. For a discussion of the advantages of rational choice applications, see Margaret Levi, *Of Rule and Revenue* (1988), particularly the conclusion and appendix. My analysis takes a methodological individualist approach but seeks to redress some problems with a strict rational choice approach.

CHAPTER 2

1. Tilly, *Coercion, Capital, and European States*, p. 11.

2. The economic transformation in the Late Middle Ages played such a role.

3. Fernand Braudel, *On History* (1980), pp. 3, 4, 27. For discussions of Braudel's work, see John Armstrong, "Braudel's Mediterranean," *World Politics* 29 (July 1977), pp. 626–636; Stuart Clark, "The Annales Historians," in Quentin Skinner, ed., *The Return of Grand Theory in the Human Sciences* (1985), pp. 177–198.

4. It has, for example, influenced Sahlins's work. He describes how individuals, whilst embedded in structures of signification, have some room to redefine the operational repertoire of that structure. Marshall Sahlins, *Islands of History* (1985), p. 125.

5. On this issue, see, for example, James Rosenau, "Global Changes and Theoretical Challenges: Toward a Postinternational Politics for the 1990s," in Czempiel and Rosenau, *Global Changes and Theoretical Challenges*, p. 15f.

6. The distinction is from Gilpin, *War and Change*, p. 40. Peter Katzenstein also uses this typology, albeit with a slight twist. He separates systems change from actor change, whereas the two are the same for Gilpin. Peter Katzenstein, "International Relations Theory and the Analysis of Change," in Czempiel and Rosenau, *Global Changes and Theoretical Challenges*, p. 294.

7. There are considerable debates on the periodization of such hegemonic shifts, particularly in long-cycle theory. For a good overview and discussion of different views, see Joshua Goldstein, *Long Cycles* (1988).

8. Since biologists see it as a model, I sometimes use that term. However, I pragmatically use it as a metaphor which helps us think through social evolution.

9. I say "ironically" because the idea of evolution as progressive and increasingly complex, which has influenced social science and everyday imagery, comes from misreading Darwinian selection.

10. The relevance of Gould's views of change for social science was particularly suggested by Krasner, "Approaches to the State."

11. Stephen Jay Gould, *Wonderful Life* (1989), p. 32.

12. Gould's theory can thus account for the problem of "missing links" which perplexed orthodox Darwinians. Such links simply never existed.

13. I do not deny that complexity can have advantages. Hominids with larger brain stems were more likely to survive than hominid types with smaller ones. Given a certain environment, complexity does have its rewards. But should the environment change in a dramatic manner, there is no reason to suppose that the most complex form will survive.

14. Gould, *The Panda's Thumb*, p. 79.

15. Krasner makes a compelling case for the relevance of this view for politics in "Approaches to the State"; and Krasner, "Sovereignty: An Institutional Perspective," in Caporaso, *The Elusive State*, pp. 69–96. For a variety of discussions on the punctuated equilibrium model, see Albert Somit and Steven Peterson, eds., *The Dynamics of Evolution* (1992). For the argument that biological evolution is not merely a metaphor for social evolution, see Runciman, *A Treatise on Social Theory*, vol. 2, p. 45f.

16. On this issue, see particularly Krasner, "Sovereignty."

17. One cannot identify a punctuation event a priori. However, one can suggest what types of changes might upset existing political coalitions or dramatically affect the probability that institutions will change. A punctuation is thus an event that alters domestic balances of power and lowers the costs of altering existing institutional arrangements. One can recognize the punctuation event on our level of historical analysis, unit change, by identifying which causal factor led to institutional innovation. I see no reason, however, why the logic of the punctuated equilibrium metaphor could not be extended to the levels of interaction change or hegemonic shifts.

18. This is, therefore, another example of how unilinear theories fail.

19. Otto Hintze, *The Historical Essays of Otto Hintze*, Felix Gilbert, ed. (1975).

20. Barrington Moore, *Social Origins of Dictatorship and Democracy* (1966).

21. Theda Skocpol, *States and Social Revolutions* (1979); Peter Gourevitch, "International Trade, Domestic Coalitions, and Liberty: Comparative Responses to the Crisis of 1873–1896," *Journal of Interdisciplinary History* 8 (Autumn 1977), pp. 281–313; Peter Gourevitch "Breaking with Orthodoxy: The Politics of Economic Policy Responses to the Depression of the 1930s," *International Organization* 38 (Winter 1984), pp. 95–129; and Peter Gourevitch, *Politics in Hard Times* (1986).

22. Part 2 of this book centers on that question.

23. A factor endowment model would not determine the outcome of social coalitions. First of all, the paucity of exact data makes the model difficult to apply to the medieval period. Even more troubling is the fact that whereas factor endowments might provide for a first guess of societal cleavages and incentives, they do not give a clear prediction of outcomes. For example, North and Thomas try to explain the decline of feudalism by the increase in the land/labor ratio. Because of the plague, shortage of labor led serfs to bargain their way out of their indentured conditions. Yet earlier in their work, North and Thomas attribute the decline of feudalism to a period of population growth. Douglass North and Robert Thomas, *The Rise of the Western World* (1973). See Alexander Field's critique of their model on this point, "The Problem with Neoclassical Institutional Economics: A Critique with Special Reference to the North-Thomas Model of Pre–1500 Europe," *Explorations in Economic History* 18 (April 1981), pp. 174–198. For use of the factor endowment model in a different context, see Ronald Rogowski, *Commerce and Coalitions* (1989).

24. A belief system is a conceptual framework through which individuals aggregate and evaluate social events. I take these as generalized insights into understanding and legitimating the social order beyond perceptions, which I see as more narrow. I will argue, and I will clarify this further in Chapter 4, that different social groups often have

different belief systems because of the elective affinity of interests and beliefs. For example, burghers had a different conception and different valuation of manual labor than the warrior aristocracy; the burghers valued Roman law for its established trial procedure and property rights, and they stressed merit rather than genealogy. For a similar understanding of belief systems in a different area of research, see Robert Legvold, "Soviet Learning in the 1980s," in George Breslauer and Philip Tetlock, eds., *Learning in U.S. and Soviet Foreign Policy* (1991), pp. 684–732.

25. Elster notes how evolution might get stuck in local maximum traps. Elster, *Nuts and Bolts*, p. 72. For a discussion of equilibrium traps and a suggestive critique of the new economics of organization, see Caporaso, "Microeconomics and International Political Economy."

26. Robert Keohane, *After Hegemony* (1984), p. 81. For other brief and insightful critiques of this problem, see Brian Barry, *Sociologists, Economists, and Democracy* (1978), p. 169; Beth Yarborough and Robert Yarborough, "International Institutions and the New Economics of Organization," *International Organization* 44 (Spring 1990), pp. 252–255; and Kathleen Thelen and Sven Steinmo, "Historical Institutionalism in Comparative Politics," in Sven Steinmo, Kathleen Thelen, and Frank Longstreth, eds., *Structuring Politics* (1992), pp. 7–10.

27. Caporaso, "Microeconomics and International Political Economy," p. 148. See also Gilpin's remarks on the limitations of new economic history. Gilpin, *War and Change*, p. 74.

28. Wilsford argues a similar point. David Wilsford, "The Conjuncture of Ideas and Interests," *Comparative Political Studies* 18 (October 1985), pp. 357–372.

29. For a discussion of Weber's understanding of elective affinity see, H. H. Gerth and C. Wright Mills, eds., *From Max Weber* (1946), pp. 62–63.

30. I have chosen France rather than England as the exemplar of state formation because the English case is actually atypical. England was unified early and by exceptional circumstances. "France, which had many provinces with widely differing institutions, was far more typical of the European political situation." Strayer, *On the Medieval Origins of the Modern State*, p. 49. For a different argument that France is a better case, see Robert Bates, "Lessons from History, or the Perfidy of English Exceptionalism and the Significance of Historical France," *World Politics* 40 (July 1988), pp. 499–516. Says Bates: "[T]he English case supports invalid inferences. Rather, it is the French case from which the lessons of history should be drawn" (p. 500). Likewise Corrigan and Sayer suggest that the English experience diverges from that of the continent. Corrigan and Sayer, *The Great Arch*.

31. I agree with Stephen Krasner's argument that Westphalia was neither the beginning of the sovereign state nor the end of all the old remnants. By my own account the beginning of sovereign, territorial statehood can be found at the end of the thirteenth century, but is not completed even after Westphalia. However, the Peace of Westphalia does serve as a useful indicator of this transition because it was understood by seventeenth-century writers themselves as something of a watershed. For Krasner's position, see Stephen Krasner, "Westphalia," (1991). Samuel Pufendorf, writing in about 1682 on the rights of the princes vis-à-vis the emperor, did perceive Westphalia as a juncture: "[T]ill in the Westphalian Peace their Rights and Authority have been expresly and particularly confirm'd and establish'd." In Herbert Rowen, ed., *From Absolutism to Revolution, 1648–1848* (1963), p. 75.

32. Note that an account of evolutionary selection bolsters the methodological individualist argument by clarifying the set of choices available at a particular point in time.

For related arguments, see Caporaso, "Microeconomics and International Political Economy"; Yarborough and Yarborough, "International Institutions and the New Economics of Organization"; and Keohane, *After Hegemony*. My work thus differs in two ways from standard rational choice accounts. First, I focus on the variety of institutional possibilities and then analyze why some were selected out over time. Second, I pay explicit attention to the importance of shared belief systems to clarify preferences and to link choices to outcomes.

33. Note that I do not contend that war is unimportant—far from it. Instead I argue that relative success in war itself needs to be explained. I explain success largely by institutional makeup.

34. This is somewhat similar to Axelrod's discussion of how particular types of units, even when in a minority, can become the dominant set. Robert Axelrod, "The Emergence of Cooperation among Egoists," *American Political Science Review* 75 (June 1981), pp. 306–318; Robert Axelrod, *The Evolution of Cooperation* (1984).

35. For a discussion of institutional mimicry, see Paul DiMaggio and Walter Powell, "The Iron Cage Revisited: Institutional Isomorphism and Collective Rationality in Organizational Fields," *American Sociological Review* 48 (April 1983), pp. 147–160.

36. One of my misgivings with Tilly's earlier explanations of state emergence was exactly that he did not account for the variety of forms in Europe; see *The Formation of National States in Western Europe*. Tilly's earlier work also did not distinguish the generative from the selective process. Both these problems are redressed in his challenging recent work *Coercion, Capital, and European States*.

37. In earlier arguments (1975 and 1985) Tilly stated that "war made states." This suggested a uniform response to a changing military environment. Tilly himself admits this.

38. Tilly, *Coercion, Capital, and European States*, p. 30.

39. Ibid., p. 30.

40. Tilly defines a national state as "states governing multiple contiguous regions and their cities by means of centralized, differentiated, and autonomous structures." He adds that "most states have been non-national: empires, city-states, or something else. The term national-state, regrettably, does not necessarily mean nation-state, a state whose people share a strong linguistic, religious, and symbolic identity." Tilly, *Coercion, Capital, and European States*, pp. 2–3.

41. Tilly is confusing on this issue. He concedes that if kings started to provide protection at Strayer's earlier date, then his argument is wrong. Indeed, there is evidence that kings already tried to regulate violence in the thirteenth and beginning of the fourteenth centuries. See, for example, Aline Vallee, "État et Securité Publique au XIVe Siècle. Une Nouvelle Lecture des Archives Royales Francaises," *Histoire, Economie et Societe*, vol. 1 (1987), pp. 3–15. Nevertheless, I do not see how this fact alone would be a decisive refutation of Tilly. The importance of coercive power remains emphasized. More important is the question of how this power was obtained in the first place, since the Capetian Dynasty started with very weak kings. In other words, Tilly is gracious in acknowledging possible counterarguments, but he misses the kernel of the counterargument that is presented by Strayer. That is, if state making preceded the military revolution, the centralization that occurred must have been based on factors other than military protection.

42. North and Thomas, *The Rise of the Western World*; and Douglass North, *Structure and Change in Economic History* (1981). Tilly, however, also includes property

rights as a central element, but he sees them as only tangentially related to either of the two paths. Tilly, *Coercion, Capital, and European States*, p. 100.

43. Tilly implies that the tsar possessed more power than rival aristocrats. The tsar had only to gradually overcome the competition. But if that is the case, there is little to explain—it is a simple matter of a strong monarch expanding his rule at the expense of the weaker. A more powerful version of Tilly's argument would be that the tsar had to strike a bargain with other actors, who were willing to ally with the tsar in exchange for particular benefits. An example of such a bargain would be the type of deal between the elector of Brandenburg-Prussia and the Junkers. Hans Rosenberg, "The Rise of the Junkers in Brandenburg-Prussia, 1410–1653," *American Historical Review* 49, part 1 (October 1943), pp. 1–22; and 49, part 2 (January 1944), pp. 228–242.

44. Tilly, *Coercion, Capital, and European States*, p. 36.

45. Empires concentrated coercive force but did not accumulate very much, whereas city-states and urban federations accumulated considerable force but in a highly fragmented fashion. Tilly, *Coercion, Capital, and European States*, p. 21.

46. Ibid., p. 160.

47. Of course, size does matter at some point. But for those who wish to explain Venetian decline by France's preponderant size, one does well to remember that the Dutch Republic, with roughly the same population as Venice (1.5 million) and only one tenth that of France, was on its way to becoming a near hegemonic power in that same period.

48. On this issue my views are similar to those of North and Weingast, who clarify how the institutional arrangements in England allowed it to raise more revenue than France. If we could classify seventeenth-century England as less coercive than absolutist France, particularly after the English Revolution, then the war-fighting ability of the English was enhanced, not diminished, by its greater reliance on bargaining with capital owners. Douglass North and Barry Weingast, "Constitutions and Commitment: The Evolution of Institutions Governing Public Choice in 17th Century England," *Journal of Economic History* 49 (December 1989), pp. 803–832.

49. Tilly, *Coercion, Capital, and European States*, p. 2.

50. Perhaps this is the reason why Spain under the Habsburgs is classified as an empire (an inefficient form of organization) and later as a national state (an efficient form). Empires are coercive intensive, capital poor, and have weak towns. Still there is something troubling about classifying Imperial Spain, with its Latin American gold and silver resources, as capital poor.

CHAPTER 3

1. Otto Gierke, *Political Theories of the Middle Age* (1987), p. 11. First published 1900.

2. Walter Schlesinger, "Lord and Follower in Germanic Institutional History," in Frederic Cheyette, ed., *Lordship and Community in Medieval Europe* (1975), p. 90.

3. Ruggie, "Territoriality and Beyond," p. 149. See also Kratochwil, "Of Systems, Boundaries, and Territoriality."

4. I refer to Eugen Weber's telling account of how even as late as the nineteenth century, France still contained many different language groups and much regional specificity. Eugen Weber, *Peasants into Frenchmen* (1976). Also see the discussion of Pizzorno, in which he distinguishes the state from kinship and religious organization.

Alessandro Pizzorno, "Politics Unbound," in Charles Maier, ed., *Changing Boundaries of the Political* (1987), pp. 27–62.

5. Dodgshon, *The European Past*.

6. Bernard Lewis, describing the Muslim logic of organization, captures the logic of such rule well. "The real difference was religion. Those who professed Islam were called Muslims and were part of God's community, no matter in which country or under what sovereign they lived. Those who rejected Islam were infidels." Lewis, *The Muslim Discovery of Europe*, p. 171.

7. As Kratochwil notes, sovereignty implied juridical equality among states. Kratochwil, "Of Systems, Boundaries, and Territoriality," p. 35.

8. Lucy Mair, *Primitive Government* (1962), p. 106. Authority is thus highly context dependent. It is exercised depending on the set of relationships in which that individual is embedded, for example, the specific of obligations one has to a feudal overlord or the conflicting obligations to the church. In short, one operates simultaneously in a variety of fields of authority. Which field happens to be relevant is case specific.

9. Charles Tilly notes five different possible forms of organization: feudalism, the church, the Holy Roman Empire, states, and federations of cities. Strayer suggests that the first three were no longer viable by 1300 and suggests that the issue was then already settled. Tilly, *The Formation of National States in Western Europe*, p. 26. But note that little attention is given to city-leagues and city-states. However, they had yet to reach their peak by 1300.

10. For a fine overview of these different points of view see Frederic Cheyette, ed., *Lordship and Community in Medieval Europe* (1975); also see Joseph Strayer, *Feudalism* (1965), p. 11; and Harold Berman, *Law and Revolution* (1983), p. 299.

11. There are many definitions of feudalism. Some emphasize the notion of reciprocal service, others emphasize the decentralization of authority, still others focus on the localization of production. One could argue that this variety of conceptualization proves that feudalism is not a generalizable concept. From my perspective, however, feudalism forms a valuable ideal type which aids in structuring that empirical environment. For a broad understanding of feudalism, see Bloch, *Feudal Society*; Archibald Lewis, *Knights and Samurai* (1974); and Michael Saltman, "Feudal Relationships and the Law," *Comparative Studies in Society and History* 29 (July 1987), pp. 514–532.

12. Strayer, *Feudalism*, p. 13.

13. See Bloch and Duby for descriptions of the impact of these invasions on the European economy and political infrastructure. Bloch, *Feudal Society*, chapters 1–3; Georges Duby, *The Early Growth of the European Economy* (1974), chapter 5.

14. Max Weber views the private character of military force as a critical feature of feudalism. See Gerth and Mills, *From Max Weber*, p. 47.

15. Thus one general precondition of feudalism in Europe and elsewhere seems to be chronic warfare. Owen Lattimore, "Feudalism in History," *Past and Present* 12 (November 1957), p. 50.

16. See White's emphasis on the development of the stirrup. Lynn White, *Medieval Religion and Technology* (1978), p. 78. See also White's "The Technology of Medieval Knighthood," in Stanley Chodorow, ed., *The Other Side of Western Civilization* (1973), p. 67. Others suggest that the success of particular technologies is directly related to efficiencies of scale. See, for example, Dudley, "Structural Change in Interdependent Bureaucracies."

17. By some estimates it required an estate of approximately 400 acres to maintain

one knight. Horst Fuhrmann, *Germany in the High Middle Ages, c. 1050–1200* (1986), p. 177.

18. Carl Stephenson, *Mediaeval Institutions* (1954), pp. 218–219. He argues that because this relationship is "thoroughly warlike," it is more Germanic rather than like the Roman patronage system, to which feudalism is sometimes traced. For the Germanic and Roman influences, also see Gianfranco Poggi, *The Development of the Modern State* (1978), p. 19f.

19. Both also value the practice of gift giving. This was not simply a matter of largesse and generosity; it also signaled appreciation and reward to those who served in battle. William Marshal, the right hand of several English kings, was thus highly praised by his contemporaries for his generosity and his disdain for material benefits.

20. Duby sees it as originating after 1000. Georges Duby, *The Three Orders* (1978).

21. Although the principle of vassalage was already in existence by the beginning of the seventh century, fragmentation of political authority only came into existence in the tenth. For a description of the contracts of these armed retainers, see Strayer, *Feudalism*, p. 82, document no. 4. Strayer argues that fragmentation was complete by the year 1000; see Strayer, *Feudalism*, p. 38.

22. One can easily see this as a classical principal-agent problem. As long as agents in the field were dependent on rewards from the center, they had little incentive to act independently. When remuneration became in-kind, in the form of land grants, and inheritable, incentives of course worked exactly in the opposite direction. Much of Carolingian royal administration and the later administration of the French Capetian kings were in a way all attempts to minimize these dangers. Indeed, the latter used roughly similar methods of administration to do so. For an excellent article that can be read in this vein, see James Fesler, "French Field Administration: The Beginnings," *Comparative Studies in Society and History* 5 (1962), pp. 76–111.

23. Many of Charlemagne's vassi dominici were related to him. By some accounts they were "a small body of selected families, half of them related to or allied by marriage with the Carolingian dynasty." Geoffrey Barraclough, *The Origins of Modern Germany* (1984), p. 14.

24. Consequently the later expansion of the economy following the latter part of the eleventh century is critical because it allowed kings to counteract such principal-agent problems.

25. To Polanyi, feudalism's important traits are a multiplicity of units, economy of kind, and the emergence of personal ties. Karl Polanyi, "Primitive Feudalism and the Feudalism of Decay," in George Dalton, ed., *Economic Development and Social Change* (1971), p. 146.

26. Bloch, *Feudal Society*, chapters 11, 12.

27. But this did not have to be the case; at no time in feudal history was every vassal also necessarily a landowner. Strayer, *Feudalism*, p. 22.

28. This has implications for the type of institutions that develop in the later Middle Ages. I have suggested that feudalism evolved around the particularities of Frankish kingship and reciprocal Germanic allegiance. Consequently, outside the Frankish home territory and outside the Germanic influence, we need not expect feudalism to be developed as such. And indeed Poggi notes how the ideal type of feudalism is absent in Italy. Poggi, *The Development of the Modern State*. In the argument yet to come, I suggest that this will influence the makeup of the political institutions that developed after the feudal era.

29. Lattimore, "Feudalism in History," p. 49.

30. Strayer, *On the Medieval Origins of the Modern State*, p. 83.

31. A declaration of multiple homage from the Glossarium of Du Cange. Cited in Strayer, *Feudalism*, p. 146, document no. 39.

32. This was a deviation from the traditional feudal formula. After giving homage to several lords, one still owed the knights service, as was specified for the fief held from the lords. If two overlords went to war, the lesser lord owed both of them the number of knights specified. However, the lesser lord himself should follow into war the over-lord to whom he owed primary allegiance. Hence, we might question Marshal's motives in counseling John against invading France to retrieve Normandy (1205), an act that would have jeopardized Marshal's holdings in Normandy should he have decided to fight Augustus. William Marshal refused to serve John because this would violate the homage he had done to Augustus. W. L. Warren, *King John* (1961), pp. 113–115.

33. For another example of multiple homage, see the granting of a fee by the Count of Troyes to Jocelyn d' Avalon, who already had obligations to the duke of Burgundy, the Count of Auxerre, and Gerard d' Arcy (1200). Brian Tierney, *The Middle Ages: Sources of Medieval History*, vol. 1 (1973), p. 108.

34. Augustus ended the practice of indebtedness to those bishops. His reign marks the beginning of the ligesse principle which set fealty to the king above all others. Fuhrmann, *Germany in the High Middle Ages*, p. 29.

35. Lattimore quoting Coulborn and Strayer, in Lattimore, "Feudalism in History," p. 47.

36. Saltman, "Feudal Relationships and the Law," p. 518.

37. Fuhrmann, *Germany in the High Middle Ages*, p. 20, notes the switch in the twelfth century with the Hohenstaufen from an identification based on ancestry to that of location. For an argument against the "tribalist" point of view, see Barraclough, *The Origins of Modern Germany*, p. 18.

38. Hallam notes that in the early Capetian reign the royal domain lacked clear boundaries—"and rights of justice, tolls and taxes appear on a map as a network, more concentrated in some areas than others, rather than as a unit of land." Elizabeth Hallam, *Capetian France, 987–1328* (1980), p. 82.

39. Bourdieu rightly observes that feudalism is not based on simply trust (fides) but on the confidence that one has in the inherent quality of the person. Pierre Bourdieu, *Outline of a Theory of Practice* (1977), p. 193.

40. Duby, *The Three Orders*, p. 28 Consequently, the common oaths that villagers and townspeople took when forming communes in the eleventh and twelfth centuries were an act of defiance.

41. Otto de Battaglia, "The Nobility in the European Middle Ages," *Comparative Studies in Society and History* 5 (1962), p. 60.

42. "A tout instant, chartes et sources narratives attribuent aux nobiles un esprit et des attitudes de classe et même de caste" (In every case characters and narrative sources attribute a class and even a caste spirit to the nobles). Leopold Genicot, "La Noblesse au Moyen Age Dans L'Ancienné 'Francie'; Continuité, Rupture ou Évolution?" *Comparative Studies in Society and History* 5 (1962), p. 53.

43. Marc Bloch notes that throughout the early feudal period ties of kinship remained strong. As evidence he cites the ubiquitousness of the feoda, similar to the contemporary vendetta, wherein kin members carried out private justice to avenge members of their tribe or kin. Bloch, *Feudal Society*, p. 125.

44. de Battaglia, "The Nobility in the European Middle Ages," p. 62. Poggi thus

describes the system as a network of interpersonal ties. Poggi, *The Development of the Modern State*, p. 25.

45. Genicot, "La Noblesse au Moyen Age Dans L'Ancienne 'Francie'," p. 54. See also Berman, *Law and Revolution*, chapter 9.

46. One of the earliest documents of vassalage notes how such a person when killed justified a higher wergild than one who was not a vassal. Strayer, *Feudalism*, p. 82.

47. This was true even after feudal law became more systematized. Berman, *Law and Revolution*, p. 314.

48. The underdeveloped nature of timekeeping is indicated by the fact that the infliction of physical pain, such as a blow to the head, was apparently one of the mnemonic methods used. Bloch, *Feudal Society*, pp. 113, 114.

49. Strayer, *On the Medieval Origins of the Modern State*, p. 40.

50. Saltman, "Feudal Relationships and the Law," p. 521. Likewise, Sahlins suggests that practical reason, conceptualizations which tailor to particular material interests, are only a part of the larger culture. Marshall Sahlins, *Culture and Practical Reason* (1976).

51. Berman, *Law and Revolution*, p. 321.

52. As a consequence there are three different interpretations of the extension of royal authority in France at the beginning of the Capetian reign. Is royal power constricted solely to the royal domain? Does it extend to the lands of the vassals who have paid homage and provide service? Or does it even include the lands of those who in feudal theory, but not in practice, are the king's inferiors? Usually the first criterion is used.

53. One of the clearest examples of such authority, even in the later Middle Ages, is Burgundy. It covered a widely disparate geographical basis of unconnected territories. It was based on the personal linkages of military aristocracy. Not surprisingly it is here that we find the last stand of feudalism, complete with the golden fleece and chivalric valor which served as means to enhance the aristocrats' castelike status. See Mann, who notes the translocal nature of Burgundy. Michael Mann, *The Sources of Social Power* (1986), pp. 438–440.

54. Strayer, *On the Medieval Origins of the Modern State*, p. 22.

55. Mann, *The Sources of Social Power*, p. 306.

56. The Roman Empire, like many other traditional empires, was a capstone government. Whereas elites were united horizontally, through common language and culture, the majority of society consisted of a plurality of groups, with their own identities and few links with others. These segmented groups were allowed to maintain their own religions and cultures, provided they did not interfere with Roman political rule. The empire stretched wide but not deep. The concept of a capstone government is discussed by Ernest Gellner, *Nations and Nationalism* (1983), chapter 2. For applications in historical sociology, see particularly Hall, *Powers and Liberties*.

57. Confucianism, by contrast, could readily become an immanent religion, overlaying and justifying the existing distribution of political power. It provided a set of rules, but more importantly it provided justification of civilian domination of the Han Empire. Bendix, *Kings or People*, p. 53f.

58. For an introductory exposition, see, for example, Norman Zacour, *An Introduction to Medieval Institutions* (1969), p. 156. The dioceses were grouped into the administrative unit of the province, which was headed by the metropolitan, the archbishop. For a slightly different classification, see Bendix, *Kings or People*, p. 27. Both acknowledge, though, the clear imperial legacy.

59. For the church's control of knowledge, see Luce Giard, "La Procès d'Emancipation de l'Anglais à la Renaissance," (1989); and Pizzorno, "Politics Unbound," p. 35. Pizzorno notes the translocal nature of Latin and the church's ability to keep written records, which allowed it to monopolize political discourse. Perhaps most important, the church claimed a monopoly on knowledge of ultimate ends.

60. The origins of the Frankish Empire are discussed in greater detail in the following section.

61. Brian Tierney, *The Crisis of Church and State, 1050–1300* (1964), p. 23.

62. Maurice Keen, *The Pelican History of Medieval Europe* (1968), p. 67.

63. Bloch, *Feudal Society*, p. 390f.; and Keen, *History of Medieval Europe*, p. 68.

64. Richard Southern, *Western Society and the Church in the Middle Ages* (1970), p. 94f.

65. Gierke, *Political Theories of the Middle Age*, p. 10.

66. Randall Collins, *Weberian Sociological Theory* (1986), chapter 3.

67. The following account draws from Vivian Green, "Taxation, Church," in Strayer, *Dictionary of the Middle Ages*, vol. 12, pp. 605–611. See also Alfred Haverkamp, *Medieval Germany 1056–1273* (1988), p. 53.

68. The manuscript demonstrated how the first Christian king, Constantine, who moved the capital of the Roman Empire to Constantinople, had donated the lands between Rome and Ravenna to the Bishop of Rome. Southern, *Western Society and the Church*, p. 92; Tierney, *The Crisis of Church and State*, p. 21.

69. Haverkamp, *Medieval Germany*, p. 53.

70. For a discussion of the tithe, see James Brundage, "Tithe," in Strayer, *Dictionary of the Middle Ages*, vol. 12, pp. 62–65; Georges Duby, *Rural Economy and Country Life in the Medieval West* (1968), pp. 56, 213; and James Scott, "Resistance Without Protest and Without Organization: Peasant Opposition to the Islamic Zakat and the Christian Tithe," *Comparative Studies in Society and History* 29 (July 1987), pp. 417–452. Approximately a quarter of the tithe went to the bishop, the second quarter to the parish clergy, the third to the maintenance of the church, and the last quarter was reserved for poor relief. Brundage, "Tithe," p. 63.

71. One of the cornerstones of the Benedictine rule was that absolute obedience was due the abbot. This is believed to be one of the main influences on the later developments of the hierocratic church. See Southern, *Western Society and the Church*, p. 218.

72. Aside from the routinized sources of revenue, the pope, the regular clergy, and secular clergy could all derive benefits from gifts and deeds. Goody notes how virtually every medieval will in England contained some clause benefiting the church. The church also had an established set of fees for clerical services, such as payments for baptism, marriage, and burial. Jack Goody, *The Development of the Family and Marriage in Europe* (1983), p. 105.

73. The Clunaic movement started with the abbey of Cluny, hence its name, and soon expanded to about one thousand monasteries. Its organization and integration served as a model for the movement to create a truly hierocratic church administered by the papacy. Particularly important was its explicit rejection of external authority, save that of the pope. Haverkamp, *Medieval Germany*, pp. 53–55; Tierney, *The Crisis of Church and State*, p. 26; and Berman, *Law and Revolution*, p. 89.

74. "The clergy became the first translocal, transtribal, transfeudal, transnational class in Europe to achieve political and legal unity. It became so by demonstrating that it was able to stand up against, and defeat, the one preexisting universal authority, the emperor." Berman, *Law and Revolution*, p. 108.

75. For the urban character of early Christianity, see Mann, *The Sources of Social Power*, p. 322 "Christianity was almost exclusively urban." It is ironic that later theological doctrine of the eleventh and twelfth centuries criticized the activities of the townspeople.

76. Zacour, *Medieval Institutions*, p. 179.

77. A decree of the council at Orleans in the sixth century. Quoted in Southern, *Western Society and the Church*, p. 152.

78. Goody, *Family and Marriage*, p. 109, note 3.

79. The College of Cardinals was first institutionalized in 1059 by Nicholas II. Southern, *Western Society and the Church*, p. 155; Zacour, *Medieval Institutions*, p. 192.

80. Fuhrmann, *Germany in the High Middle Ages*, p. 43.

81. Ibid.

82. Southern, *Western Society and the Church*, p. 176. Pope Nicholas I (856–867) asserted papal authority not only over bishops and priests but also over the emperor. Berman, *Law and Revolution*, p. 93.

83. Such clerical vassals would also provide for armed men to serve the lord when necessary. Monasteries and bishops often had armed retainers in service. The clergy provided three quarters of Otto II's army in his Italian campaign. Barraclough, *The Origins of Modern Germany*, p. 36.

84. Josef Fleckenstein, *Early Medieval Germany* (1978), pp. 122–128.

85. Goody, *Family and Marriage*, p. 105, points out how the large clerical holdings of property started as early as the sixth century. By the end of the seventh century, the church owned one-third of the arable land in France.

86. The tithe, the tax of one-tenth of gross revenue, became a transferable commodity. That is, one could sell it or transfer it, even if one was not a member of the clergy. This is further evidence of the intermingling of sacerdotal and secular capacity of the clergy. See Duby, *Rural Economy*, p. 239, note 17.

87. Tierney, *The Crisis of Church and State*, p. 14.

88. The claim that the pope was superior in secular matters as well would emerge at a later date, particularly in the pope's struggles with sovereign, territorial rulers.

89. Tierney, *The Middle Ages*, pp. 121–122, presents all twenty-seven theses. For discussions thereof, see Berman, *Law and Revolution*, p. 96f; and Barraclough, *The Origins of Modern Germany*, p. 113.

90. Tierney, *The Crisis of Church and State*, pp. 59–60; Tierney, *The Middle Ages*, p. 124.

91. Tierney, *The Crisis of Church and State*, p. 54.

92. For the argument that the Investiture Conflict was a revolution of world historical importance, see Berman, *Law and Revolution*, p. 87; Bloch, *Feudal Society*, p. 107; and Southern, *Western Society and the Church*, p. 34. Brown sees its importance in the separation of the sacred and the profane, which previously were intertwined. Peter Brown, "Society and the Supernatural: A Medieval Change," *Daedalus* 104 (Spring 1975), p. 134.

93. The Greek church had broken away in the Schism of 1054 which revolved around the exact nature of the trinity. The deal did not materialize at the time and was only concluded shortly before the fall of Constantinople, in 1453, when both the universalist claims of empire and papacy had effectively come to naught. Southern, *Western Society and the Church*, pp. 74–78. Recall also in this context that the Crusade of 1204 had been diverted to Constantinople, which was taken by the Crusaders two centuries before the Muslims.

94. On this issue, see particularly Berman, *Law and Revolution*, chapter 5; Tierney, *The Crisis of Church and State*, p. 116f.; and Harold Hazeltine, "Roman and Canon Law in the Middle Ages," in J. R. Tanner, ed., *The Cambridge Medieval History*, vol. 5 (1957), pp. 697–764.

95. Southern, *Western Society and the Church*, p. 109. Only ten papal letters survive for each year of pope Silvester II's reign (999–1003). The average number of letters per year was thirty-five until about 1130. After that it gradually increased. By the time of John XXII (1316–1324) there were an average of 3,646 letters per year.

96. Zacour, *Medieval Institutions*, p. 195.

97. Roberto Unger, *Plasticity into Power* (1987), p. 113. A similar point is made by Wallerstein in his discussion of how world economies were transformed into empires. Wallerstein, *The Modern World System*, vol. 1, pp. 15–16. Likewise Gilpin notes how expanding premodern markets were often turned into imperial economies. Gilpin, *War and Change*, p. 133. See also Kratochwil, "Systems, Boundaries, and Territoriality," pp. 35–36.

98. See the discussion of such rule in Susan Rudolph, "Presidential Address."

99. Giddens, *The Nation-State and Violence*, p. 81.

100. Fuhrmann, *Germany in the High Middle Ages*, p. 20.

101. Berman, *Law and Revolution*, p. 89.

102. For discussions of the idea of empire, see Straus, "Germany: Idea of Empire"; Bloch, *Feudal Society*, p. 390; and Barraclough, *The Origins of Modern Germany*, pp. 47, 62. The last, however, states that the emperor never asserted himself over the king of France. But note that there was an ideology arguing that kings were subject to the emperor, and Richard the Lionheart, when captured on his way back from the Crusades, was forced to recognize the emperor as his overlord. Fuhrmann, *Germany in the High Middle Ages*, pp. 156, 184.

103. Rudolph notes how universal empires were the traditional pattern elsewhere. "Had the Holy Roman Empire become the dominant polity in the twelfth century, Europe would have approximated the world 'norm' more closely." Rudolph, "Presidential Address," p. 736.

104. A full account of this is rendered in Chapter 6.

105. For overviews of this period, see Jacques Le Goff, *Medieval Civilization* (1988), chapters 1, 2; Duby, *The Early Growth of the European Economy*, chapters 4, 5.

106. Pope Gregory III's message to Charles Martel implored him for immediate aid. "You, oh son, will receive favor from the same prince of apostles here and in the future life in the presence of God, according as you render speedy aid to his church." Tierney, *The Middle Ages*, p. 82.

107. See Tierney, *The Crisis of Church and State*, pp. 22–23, for a variety of accounts. In Southern's view, "the idea of a western empire as a means of extending papal authority was a mistake from beginning to end . . . because in creating an emperor the pope created not a deputy, but a rival or even a master." Southern, *Western Society and the Church*, p. 99. However, one might equally argue that the emperor created the papacy. Berman, *Law and Revolution*, p. 91.

108. For overviews of this period, see Barraclough, *The Origins of Modern Germany*, chapters 2, 3; Bendix, *Kings or People*, pp. 129–145.

109. The emperors, however, were sensible enough to recognize the limits of their factual power. Although they claimed juridical supremacy over kings, they seldom asserted these claims against either the French or English monarchs. Their aims rather were to control the church and Italy. Moreover, their universalist rhetoric became more

strident as they faced an increasingly hierocratic church. Barraclough, *The Origins of Modern Germany*, pp. 68, 196.

110. France, by contrast, divided into roughly fifty-five distinct territorial units during the course of the tenth century. Barraclough, *The Origins of Modern Germany*, p. 17.

111. Fleckenstein, *Early Medieval Germany*, p. 109, discusses the return of these stem duchies. See also John Freed, "Germany: Stem Duchies," in Strayer, *Dictionary of the Middle Ages*, vol. 5, pp. 505–511. Barraclough disagrees with the classification, but note that he too acknowledges that authority in the east was always personal, not territorial, and that the territorial control of the counts was weak. Barraclough, *The Origins of Modern Germany*, p. 10.

112. Pizzorno thus labels the contest a struggle over absolute politics. The church claimed for itself the monopoly over knowledge, but even more important it claimed a monopoly over ultimate ends and loyalties. Pizzorno, "Politics Unbound." For the impossibility of compromise between these two theocratic authorities, also see Barraclough, *The Origins of Modern Germany*, p. 113.

113. The allies of the pope in the Investiture Conflict were the Normans, the Lombard communes, and the German aristocrats. Henry IV allied with German towns in the south and east, but this tended to alienate the bishops who opposed greater urban liberties. Barraclough, *The Origins of Modern Germany*, pp. 119–128. Henry V allied with the nobility against his own father, only to be defeated in battle, a prelude to the conflict between Frederick II and his son, which was similarly a conflict about pursuing an urban or a feudal alliance. Fuhrmann, *Germany in the High Middle Ages*, p. 86.

114. See the discussion of some of the implications in Berman, *Law and Revolution*, p. 98.

115. Around 1200 there were roughly four secular barons for every ecclesiastical one in England. In Germany, by contrast, there were six ecclesiastical barons for every secular lord. Fuhrmann, *Germany in the High Middle Ages*, p. 173.

116. Ibid., pp. 67–68.

117. This document, the Golden Bull, put a formal end to the German attempt to reunite the old empire, although in fact that policy had failed more than a century earlier. Barraclough, *The Origins of Modern Germany*, p. 316.

118. Le Goff, *Medieval Civilization*, p. 267. For his extravagant life style, see Keen, *History of Medieval Europe*, p. 165. For his messianic status see Norman Cohn, *The Pursuit of the Millennium* (1970), p. 111.

119. John Morrall, *Political Thought in Medieval Times* (1980), p. 28.

120. Leuschner, *Germany in the Late Middle Ages* (1980), p. 76.

121. Fuhrmann, *Germany in the High Middle Ages*, pp. 72, 147.

CHAPTER 4

1. Braudel, *The Perspective of the World*, p. 94.

2. Hinsley, *Sovereignty*, p. 1.

3. See his discussion in Bloch, *Feudal Society*, pp. 59–71. He speaks of an economic revolution which transformed the face of Europe. p. 69.

4. The literature on this issue is vast but unanimous in its conclusion that a dramatic economic transformation occurred. Duby marks it as "a major turning point in European economic history." Duby, *The Early Growth of the European Economy*, p. 269. See also Haverkamp, *Medieval Germany*, chapter 4; Carlo Cipolla, ed., *The Fontana Economic History of Europe: The Middle Ages*, vol. 1 (1972), pp. 11–24. See also Anderson, *Pas-*

sages from Antiquity to Feudalism, chapter 4. My account differs, however, from Anderson's in that he insists that the towns continued to be part of the feudal system.

5. Henri Pirenne, *Medieval Cities* ([1925], 1952), pp. 122, 132.

6. Indeed, much of his work focuses on the fortunes of great cities which managed to place themselves at the nexus of long-distance trade. Braudel, *The Perspective of the World*.

7. Jacques Le Goff argues that Pirenne is essentially correct. Towns formed the nodes of long-distance trade. Le Goff, *Medieval Civilization*, p. 78. Verhulst's critical evaluation of Pirenne's work basically ends up concluding that Pirenne was right for the period after 1000. Adriaan Verhulst, "The Origins of Towns in the Low Countries and the Pirenne Thesis," *Past and Present* 122 (1989), pp. 3–35. A variety of debates surrounding Pirenne's work are contained in Alfred Havighurst, *The Pirenne Thesis* (1976). See particularly the essay by Bryce Lyon. Note that most of the debates surround Pirenne's evaluation of the Merovingian and Carolingian periods. But even on that issue, Lyon notes how Pirenne's theory is convincing and credible. Havighurst (p. xi), concludes that Pirenne's main continued contribution lies in his economic history of the medieval city. Hohenberg and Lees take an approach similar to Pirenne's: "important cities sprang up on the basis of long-distance trade, and their economy from the beginning involved great specialization, distant markets, and large-scale financial complexity." Paul Hohenberg and Lynn Lees, *The Making of Urban Europe* (1985), p. 38. See also H. van Werveke, "The Rise of the Towns," in M. Postan, E. Rich, and E. Miller, eds., *The Cambridge Economic History of Europe*, vol. 3 (1963), pp. 3–41. Douglass North also stresses the importance of long-distance trade in *Institutions, Institutional Change and Economic Performance* (1990), p. 125.

8. Political geographers have substantiated this thesis by excavation and analysis of historical records. For a discussion of the urban structure, see Hohenberg and Lees, *The Making of Urban Europe*, pp. 23–37; Le Goff, *Medieval Civilization*, p. 73; and Pirenne, *Medieval Cities*, p. 142.

9. Fritz Rörig, *The Medieval Town* (1969), p. 35.

10. But even medieval Italy, the most urban region, added about two thousand settlements in the eleventh and twelfth centuries. Many of these could hardly be called towns, but clearly there was population growth and an increase in the number of villages. Marvin Becker, *Medieval Italy* (1981), p. 15.

11. This is hardly a startling or novel claim. For example, the political influence of contemporary French agriculture on French trade policy far outweighs the share of agricultural production within the overall French economy. Yet French farmers have been able to forestall trade liberalization on a much wider set of issues beyond agriculture.

12. Morrall, *Political Thought in Medieval Times*, p. 42. Likewise Poggi suggests that "the ascent of the towns marked the entrance of a new political force . . . such a force had to be taken into account in the shifting equilibrium between the territorial ruler and his feudatories, if only as a possible ally to be used by one against the other." Poggi, *The Development of the Modern State*, p. 37. See also Hohenberg and Lees, *The Making of Urban Europe*, pp. 40–41.

13. Poggi, *The Development of the Modern State*, p. 42.

14. Indeed, we know from medieval and postmedieval history that the areas where trade advanced the most, prior to the industrial revolution, were also the most urbanized. In the Late Middle Ages this was particularly true for Italy and the lowlands. Another way of thinking about this problem is by differentiating between central-place

towns and network towns. The first only performed a regional function. The latter were tied in to distant cities by means of commerce. See for this distinction Hohenberg and Lees, *The Making of Urban Europe*, pp. 4–6.

15. Jacques Bernard, "Trade and Finance in the Middle Ages, 900–1500," in Cipolla, *The Fontana Economic History of Europe*, vol. 1, p. 302.

16. There were basically two main trading areas, the Mediterranean basin and the North Sea-Baltic trade. Braudel, *The Perspective of the World*, p. 97f; Bernard, "Trade and Finance," p. 276. See also G. V. Scammel, *The World Encompassed: The First European Maritime Empires c. 800–1650* (1981). France fell outside these main maritime routes.

17. Bernard, "Trade and Finance," p. 299. There were some maritime ports that did attract trade, such as Bordeaux and La Rochelle. Not incidentally their political development and preferences differed from the rest of France. Fox speaks of two Frances, the maritime and the continental. Edward Fox, *History in Geographic Perspective* (1971). But for a critique of that view, see Braudel, *The Perspective of the World*, p. 243f.

18. Bernard, "Trade and Finance," pp. 308–310; Braudel gives a low estimate of 5 percent for the maritime bulk trade of the Hansa in *The Perspective of the World*, p. 103. Scammel notes it might have been higher. "In the Baltic, c. 1400 the average net profit was 15–25 percent." *The World Encompassed*, p. 77. I discuss the nature of trade in greater detail in the individual case studies. Miskimin reaffirms the differentiation between north and south: "in the northern trading region, the typical products were heavy, bulky goods of low value per unit. Certainly the greatest volume of trade occurred in these items." Harry Miskimin, *The Economy of Early Renaissance Europe, 1300–1460* (1975), p. 125.

19. The Champagne fairs did manage to attract some trade, but they were relatively short-lived and depended on the urbanized areas of the lowlands and Italy. See Le Goff, *Medieval Civilization*, p. 78; C. Verlinden, "Markets and Fairs," in Postan, Rich, and Miller, *The Cambridge Economic History of Europe*, vol. 3, pp. 119–153. Raymond de Roover suggests the fairs were finished by 1300, "The Organization of Trade," in Postan, Rich, and Miller, *The Cambridge Economic History of Europe*, vol. 3, p. 43.

20. Scammel, *The World Encompassed*, p. 48.

21. For the variety of sources documenting this range of profit margin, see chapter 7 on Italy which discusses Italian trade in greater detail. At this point I am simply arguing that trade in the south included, besides the basic bulk goods required to feed the populace of the cities, many expensive items of low volume but very high added value such as silk and spices. The term *spices* included many products, but particularly profitable were the "minute spices," wares sold in "small quantities at high prices." See the discussion in Miskimin, *The Economy of Early Renaissance Europe*, pp. 123–129, and the list of spices in Robert Lopez and Irving Raymond, *Medieval Trade in the Mediterranean World* (1967), p. 108f. De Roover likewise describes Italian trade as high-value, low-volume trade. The galley was not suited for bulk trade. De Roover, "The Organization of Trade," p. 100.

22. The term is Roberto Unger's. He contrasts it to autarkic empire and the state. Unger, *Plasticity into Power*, pp. 115–123. He argues that the state was less exploitive than the overlord-merchant and autarkic imperial forms of organization.

23. Scammel, *The World Encompassed*, p. 161.

24. One might speculate whether this created high barriers to entry for potential newcomers. Thus the highly advanced Venetian galley, with approximately two hun-

dred to three hundred men aboard, proved to be an ideal mix of merchant and warship. Lane speaks in this regard of a protection rent which accrued to the Venetians. See Frederic Lane, *Venice: A Maritime Republic* (1973). McNeill likewise discusses the exceptional ability of the Venetians to marry trade and military exploits. William McNeill, *The Pursuit of Power* (1982). The Hanseatic cog ship, by contrast, was relatively cheap to operate with small crews. See the discussion of these ships in Archibald Lewis and Timothy Runyan, *European Naval and Maritime History, 300–1500* (1985), chapters 4 and 6. They also reinforce the argument that trade in the north was largely bulk trade. "Though we have already noted that by the late tenth century some bulk cargoes already had begun to be transported by sea in northern Europe, such trade increased immensely in the twelfth and thirteenth centuries" (pp. 134–135).

25. Indeed, the rivalry between Genoa and Venice for control over the Black Sea provides an example. In 1204 Venice managed to divert the Crusaders to Constantinople and take that city, thus creating a Venetian monopoly to the Black Sea and the caravan connections to Asia. About sixty years later the ousted Byzantine emperor retook the city with Genoese help and thereupon received the monopoly for Black Sea trade. Documents demonstrate that internal monopolies were forbidden, whereas external monopolies were encouraged. See Lopez and Raymond, *Medieval Trade*, pp. 126–130. De Roover notes that the Italian cities were rivals, whereas the cities of the Baltic and North Sea banded together. De Roover, "The Organization of Trade," p. 105.

26. One cannot a priori predict what the outcome of particular recombinations will be. The nature of social evolution is indeterminate. One can, however, explain the observed outcomes of such recombinations once they have occurred. For a methodological exposition of this view, see Runciman, *A Treatise on Social Theory*. Runciman takes a more indeterminate view than I do. Since I trace the relative powers of social actors and their preferences, we can make reasoned inferences as to which type of institutions might develop.

27. Although social and political actors pursue their own specific goals, the eventual outcome need not be one intended by any actor. That is, the outcome of social realignments might, in the long run, result in unintended consequences. For example, the alliance between towns and French kings initially operated without established representation and oversight over royal revenue. Ad hoc negotiations benefited both town and king. In the long run however, the unintended consequence—at least for the towns—was an absolute monarchy. The king turned against the towns once his position was secure. The argument that king and towns were later sometimes at odds is thus not a rebuttal of my position. See, for example, the later opposition to royal absolutism in David Parker, "The Social Foundation of French Absolutism 1610–1630," *Past and Present* 53 (November 1971), pp. 67–89.

28. Because of the dual impact of external change and relative position of social actors, and the absence of hard data for this period, a factor endowment explanation such as Rogowski's is difficult to apply here, although I agree with his general approach. For example, prior to the plague, the population grew, but so did available land through the development of new agricultural areas. Was there then a high land/labor ratio or not? If there was, both France and Germany should have shown a high ratio. But the similarity does not explain the variation of political outcomes. For that reason I argue that the relative strength of social and political groups is more relevant for this set of cases than the distribution of productive factors. See Ronald Rogowski, *Commerce and Coalitions* (1989).

29. I do not deny that trade itself can be explained by other causal factors, such as weather, population shifts, and declining incursions from raiders. The latter variables in turn can be explained by yet other causal factors—ad infinitum. Nevertheless, it is legitimate to treat trade as an independent variable because it created a broad environmental shift which affected all actors in Europe, and over which no one actor had ultimate control. Admittedly, at a later stage the political changes set in motion by the economic transformation started to feed back on the level of trade. As I will argue, the emergence of a competitive state system was beneficial to the growth of trade.

30. Michael Walzer, "On the Role of Symbolism in Political Thought," *Political Science Quarterly* 82 (June 1967), p. 194. Walzer further suggests that political discourse is embedded in a larger unified vocabulary wherein it resonates with other realms of experience. For example, the idea of a "Body Politic" resonates with scientific and biological images. I argue that the transformation of the Late Middle Ages introduced a new unified vocabulary with new symbols and mental frames of reality. As Walzer points out, "in any complex civilization there exists what might be called symbols-in-reserve, or symbols alternative to the dominant ones, to which men freed for one or another reason from the dominant one can turn" (p. 197). I submit that the burghers were the ones who searched for and used alternative symbols, and they allied with political elites able to accommodate such new ideas.

31. "That is, the rule of the state not only extends throughout its territory, which gives it body, in which it is 'reified' (verdinglicht); it is also objectified (versachlicht)." Schlesinger, "Lord and Follower in Germanic Institutional History," in Cheyette, *Lordship and Community*, p. 88.

32. John of Salisbury already noted the distinction by the twelfth century. "He is, and acts as, a personal publica. And in that capacity he is expected to consider all issues with regard to the well-being of the res publica, and not with regard to his privata voluntas." Ernst Kantorowicz, *The King's Two Bodies* (1957), p. 95. For the view that the royal domain was seen as private possession by the early kings, see Rowen, *The King's State*.

33. Holzgrefe, "The Origins of Modern International Relations Theory"; Kratochwil, "Of Systems, Boundaries, and Territoriality"; Ruggie, "Continuity and Transformation."

34. For example, both the Chinese Empire and Japanese shogunate did not recognize the equivalent status of others.

35. These developments did not, of course, occur instantaneously. Here I can only suggest the enabling conditions that permitted for a later and fuller development of a theory of sovereignty. Nevertheless, as I will demonstrate in Chapter 5, the basis for the concept of sovereign authority had been laid by the end of the thirteenth century.

36. Indeed, the two areas that saw the first reemergence of ideas of sovereignty, Italy and Germany, ended up being the most fragmented.

37. See Max Weber, "The Social Psychology of the World Religions," in Gerth and Mills, *From Max Weber*. Their introduction gives a good description of the process of selection of ideas, which corresponds with my view on the matter. "But in time, ideas are discredited in the face of history, unless they point in the direction of conduct that various interests promote" (p. 63).

38. For a discussion of the ability of political entrepreneurs to manipulate cultural symbols, see David Laitin, *Hegemony and Culture* (1986).

39. Weber himself explicitly acknowledged this mutual dependence of ideas and interests; see Gerth and Mills, *From Max Weber*, p. 280: "Not ideas, but material and ideal interests, directly govern men's conduct. Yet very frequently the 'world images' that

have been created by 'ideas' have, like switchmen, determined the tracks along which action has been pushed by the dynamic of interest."

40. This does not claim to be a determinative account of why new ideas emerged in the late medieval era. The purpose is rather to explore which sets of ideas emerged and why certain social groups and political entrepreneurs had an affinity with some of these.

41. Bloch was the first to pioneer the concept of the medieval mentality as a structure determining individual actions. Many historians since then, such as Duby, Le Goff, and Braudel, similarly suggest that there was a comprehensive set of ideas which informed medieval human behavior. They sometimes call it *culture, civilization, collective mentality,* or *shared consciousness* (conscience collective). They seek to describe the way individuals perceived and made sense of their environment. It is different from the instrumental adoption of ideology for political expediency. I use the term *belief system,* since my focus is less on an overencompassing concept of culture and more on the systematized way people aggregate and explain political phenomena. This set of aggregations and explanations is moreover infused with personal and normative values. A belief system is thus a relatively enduring and related set of insights into reality. My understanding of what a belief system is shares a strong affinity with Robert Legvold's, although he uses it in a completely different realm. Legvold, "Soviet Learning in the 1980s."

42. Political geographers in particular have explored the correspondence of social order to the spatial extension of material activity in society. See, for example, Dodgshon, *The European Past.*

43. Le Goff, *Time, Work, and Culture* (1980), p. xiii, note 9.

44. There was a general feeling of pessimism, decay. Civilization had moved from east to west to its final stage. *Mundus senescit,* "the world is growing old." For others the prophecy of Daniel indicated that the end was near because of the decline of the Roman Empire. Scripture foretold that there would be but four empires—the Roman being the last. Others saw in famine, pestilence, and war signs of the horrors indicative of imminent final judgment.

45. Bloch notes how documents were seldom dated. Chroniclers often did not know the date. Bloch, *Feudal Society,* pp. 71–75.

46. The day was marked in blocks of our contemporary hours. The common measurement consisted of Matins (midnight); Lauds (3 A.M.); Prime (6 A.M.); Terce (9 A.M.); Sext (noon); Nones (3 P.M.); Vesper (6 P.M.); and Compline (9 P.M.). Le Goff, *Medieval Civilization,* p. 177.

47. Markers of differentiation could be manipulated depending on the instrumental purposes of those invoking scripture and clerical authority to argue their cause. Duby, *The Three Orders,* p. 63.

48. Ibid., p. 109.

49. Le Goff, *Time, Work, and Culture,* p. 58. De Roover notes that "merchants in any case, had no assigned place in the pattern of feudal society, and their activities, under the influence of Church doctrine, were regarded with distrust as something tainted with the stigma of usury or wickedness." De Roover, "The Organization of Trade," p. 46.

50. Le Goff, *Time, Work, and Culture,* pp. 60, 120.

51. Pizzorno discusses the particular nature of ecclesiastical knowledge. It was first of all a knowledge of ultimate ends. Furthermore, the use of Latin transcended the local-boundedness of vernaculars. Since it was knowledge of the general rather than the particular, it was considered superior to temporal knowledge. It bound society together "beyond the momentary and beyond the local." Pizzorno, "Politics Unbound," p. 36.

52. See the discussion in Hazeltine, "Roman and Canon Law in the Middle Ages." The personal nature of law made for great variation. A ninth-century bishop noted that "it often happened that five men were present or sitting together, and not one of them had the same law as another." Quoted in Morrall, *Political Thought in Medieval Times*, p. 17.

53. Bloch, *Feudal Society*, p. 116. "Teutonic custom, formulated later into feudal law, saw nothing inconsistent in the belief that the same piece of land could be owned by two or more persons. . . . Such divided ownership was quite foreign to the more severely logical Roman law." Morrall, *Political Thought in Medieval Times*, p. 15.

54. Brown argues that trial by ordeal functioned as ritualistic method of acquiring consensus. By the display of the ordeal, norms were made present to all. Brown, "Society and the Supernatural." For documents detailing the procedure of ordeals and a critical Arab view of Crusader justice, see Brian Tierney, *The Middle Ages*, pp. 60–61, 141–142.

55. Edouard Perroy, "Social Mobility Among the French Noblesse in the Later Middle Ages," *Past and Present* 21 (April 1962), p. 29.

56. de Battaglia, "The Nobility in the European Middle Ages," p. 60. See also the discussion of aristocratic society in Bendix, *Kings or People*, pp. 228–232.

57. Jean Dunbabin, *France in the Making, 843–1180* (1985), p. 247.

58. Karl Leyser, "The German Aristocracy from the Ninth to the Twelfth Century," *Past and Present* 41 (December 1968), p. 27. Leyser also notes how the Saxons claimed to have descended from Alexander the Great's army (p. 29).

59. Goody provides for a fascinating account of how the church favored a two-pronged strategy. First it stressed the importance of the elementary family rather than the wider kin group, and it advocated for primogeniture within that family. Second, it advocated written law rather than custom (bookland over folkland) because a written record provided better security against the claims of the descendant's kin. Goody, *Family and Marriage*, pp. 111, 118, 123. My thanks to John Hall for stressing this point with me. See also Hall, *Powers and Liberties*, pp. 130–132.

60. Some authors thus speak of the discovery of the individual. Although the church had condemned individualism as exaggerated pride, by breaking up traditional kinship ties it helped bring that very individualism about. Le Goff, *Medieval Civilization*, p. 279; Fuhrmann, *Germany in the High Middle Ages*, p. 30. Pizzorno suggests that subsequent territorial definition of individual identity facilitated market exchange. Pizzorno, "Politics Unbound," p. 48.

61. For a discussion of the Peace of God, see Bloch, *Feudal Society*, p. 412. For an example of the enforcement of the Peace of God by the duke of Normandy (in 1135), see Strayer, *Feudalism*, pp. 120–121, reading 25.

62. Strayer, *Feudalism*, p. 45. In Germany the feudal system was formally constituted through the Heerschild. In this rigid hierarchy there were five layers of lords and inferiors. Fuhrmann, *Germany in the High Middle Ages*, p. 171.

63. In the Eastern Roman Empire, Byzantium, the potential conflict between the two legal systems never arose because the basileus, the Byzantine emperor, came to have sacerdotal status. See Bendix, *Kings or People*, pp. 94–95; Le Goff, *Medieval Civilization*, p. 268. Southern, however, believes that the omnipotence of the Greek emperor has been exaggerated. Thus he explains the failure of the political package deal that the pope proposed: a unified Christian church with the pope as the sacerdotal authority, and the Byzantine emperor rather than the German to unite all Christendom in temporal mat-

ters. The pope misunderstood the political nature of the Greek church, and hence the deal failed. Southern, *Western Society and the Church*, pp. 74–78.

64. See Hazeltine, "Roman and Canon Law." How secular rulers specifically used Roman law will be discussed in the following chapters.

65. Kantorowicz, *The King's Two Bodies*, p. 87f.

66. In Weber's analysis of the protestant ethic, predestination creates anxiety in the believer. Because redemption is foreordained, all activity appears meaningless. It is up to the Calvinist to discover meaning in the world and meaning in the activity in which one is engaged. Max Weber, *The Protestant Ethic and the Spirit of Capitalism* (1958). The denial of legitimacy to monetary pursuits set similar forces in motion during the late medieval period. Duby mentions the rise of a capitalist mentality in twelfth-century Italy, well before Weber's discussion of the affinity between Protestantism and capitalism. Duby, *The Early Growth of the European Economy*, p. 261. Likewise Pirenne notes the existence of a capitalistic spirit well before the Renaissance. Pirenne, *Medieval Cities*, p. 118.

67. Hirschman argues that sixteenth- and seventeenth-century theorists saw a difference between the moderation of passions when engaged in commerce, as opposed to the absolute commitments of religion. Albert Hirschman, *The Passions and the Interests* (1977). The point is different than my own, but it suggests likewise the different beliefs entailed in either practice.

68. For the argument that the shift to territorial rule depended on an epistemic shift in perception, as evinced in the single point perspective in art, see John Ruggie, "Territoriality and Beyond." Likewise Le Goff sees this as an important indicator of changing views. Le Goff, *Time, Work, and Culture*, p. 37.

69. Le Goff, *Time, Work, and Culture*, p. 30

70. It is true that the church gradually developed a perspective that justified mercantile activity, and other previously illicit trades, by focusing on the intentions of actors. If actors had the intent to further the common good, then the activity was acceptable. This new view, however, demonstrated that there was a departure from the old medieval mentality. Indeed Le Goff suggests that the development of intentionality as a criterion was an important deviation from previous adherence to medieval symbolism, a point that I cannot further explore in this context.

71. The vassal kneels before his lord and places his hands between those of his lord. The position he takes is the same as that of prayer in the modern church. The vassal swears before God and guarantees his liegeship with his life before God. For the ritual of vassalage, see Bloch, *Feudal Society*, p. 146.

72. Becker, *Medieval Italy*, p. 25. Coleman suggests that other factors such as political centralization and Roman Law also might have had a lot to do with this shift to abstract ties. Janet Coleman, "The Civic Culture of Contracts and Credit: A Review Article," *Comparative Studies in Society and History* 28 (October 1986), pp. 778–784.

73. For that argument, see Duby, *The Early Growth of the European Economy*, pp. 48–57.

74. Becker, *Medieval Italy*, p. 15.

75. Bloch, *Feudal Society*, p. 118. For the urban preference for written law, also see Dunbabin, *France in the Making*, p. 253.

76. Edward Miller, "Government Economic Policies and Public Finance 1000–1500," in Cipolla, *Fontana Economic History*, p. 358.

77. Consequently, burghers would have had an affinity to rulers who changed legal procedures. For example, Hallam notes how Louis IX forbade trial by combat in a set of

ordinances (1257–1261). She adds that "this measure was greatly disliked by the nobility." Hallam, *Capetian France*, p. 244.

78. This development of Roman law coincides with the development of canonical law and the reemergence of scholasticism, as well as the beginnings of scientific procedure. Canon law particularly drew from the Decretum of Gratian (1140), which sought to interpret and update canonical law by substantive issues. This development of canonical law thereby provided the means to counteract encroachments on ecclesiastical property and reassert the supremacy of papal administration. Tierney, *The Crisis of Church and State*, p. 116f. In short, the strongest development of different bodies of law occurred when the conflict between church and secular authorities sharpened.

79. See also Pirenne's view on the distinctness of the noble and ecclesiastical points of view. Pirenne, *Medieval Cities*, p. 123.

CHAPTER 5

1. Quentin Skinner, *The Foundations of Modern Political Thought*, vol. 2 (1978), p. 351. The first precondition for the modern concept of the state is to see politics as a distinct branch of moral philosophy. Skinner basically retraces the possibility of a true "political" philosophy as opposed to its subservience to theological points of view.

2. Following the definition of Chapter 4, feudalism means political fragmentation, the exercise of public power through private actors, and the securing of military power by private contract. See Strayer, *Feudalism*, p. 13. I highlight this definition again because it clarifies whether the French political system after the Capetians can still be called feudal, as Hilton suggests. See R. H. Hilton, *English and French Towns in Feudal Society* (1992). I argue that it cannot.

3. The number of duchies and counties in France around the year 1000 is from Barraclough, *The Origins of Modern Germany*, p. 17. I have no figures on the number of castles in France, but by way of illustration, Heer suggests that there were about 10,000 castles in Germany. Friedrich Heer, *The Medieval World* (1961), p. 32. Whatever the equivalent number for France might have been, the disintegration of political authority was certainly high with military security basically revolving around a multiplicity of castle-holders.

4. Dunbabin, *France in the Making*, p. 4. The king was thus described as king of the Normans, Bretons, Aquitanians, Goths, and others, symbolizing the lack of a name for or identification with a particular territorial entity. See also Robert Fawtier, *The Capetian Kings of France* (1960), p. 60.

5. Joseph Strayer, *The Reign of Philip the Fair* (1980), p. 388.

6. James Fesler, "French Field Administration: The Beginnings," *Comparative Studies in Society and History* 5 (1962), p. 77. He also notes that by the end of the thirteenth century, the royal domain had expanded fortyfold.

7. Dunbabin, *France in the Making*, p. 27.

8. Sidney Painter, *The Rise of Feudal Monarchies* (1951), p. 10.

9. Strayer, *On the Medieval Origins of the Modern State*, p. 57. I would argue that Strayer overstates his point by generalizing the argument to Europe. Alternatives, such as the Hanseatic League and the Italian city-states, were viable and were yet to reach their zeniths. Strayer apparently discounts such forms. See Charles Tilly's comments on his discussion with Strayer, in Tilly, *The Formation of National States in Europe*, pp. 26–27. Strayer is right, however, in arguing that by then royalist centralization had largely succeeded.

10. Since 1066 the crown of England had been in hands of the duke of Normandy. Henry also ruled Anjou, Gascogny, and Acquitaine. Indeed, Henry II's holdings in 1152 consisted of virtually half of contemporary France.

11. Strayer, *The Reign of Philip the Fair*, pp. 388, 393.

12. Reynolds, *Kingdoms and Communities in Western Europe*. She explicitly disputes the idea that the king was merely primus inter pares, first among equals (p. 259). Paradoxically she notes on the very next page that Flanders and Normandy were also referred to as kingdoms. Yet nominally the Count of Flanders and the duke of Normandy were vassals of the French king. Indeed, the book refers to many other communities of identification than the kingdom.

13. Fawtier, *The Capetian Kings*, p. 108. He, too, seems to contradict himself. He notes on pp. 65–67 the prevalence of private wars against the king. On page 42 he suggests that Philip I (1060–1108) was little more than the lord of the Île-de-France. He adds on p. 199 that the kingdom need not have emerged.

14. Dunbabin, *France in the Making*, pp. 198, 205, 213; Hallam, *Capetian France*, pp, 37, 42, 52.

15. See his "War Making and State Making as Organized Crime" in Evans, Rueschemeyer, and Skocpol, *Bringing the State Back In*. As I already pointed out in Chapter 2, Tilly's earlier work did not pay attention to institutional variation. His later work, *Coercion, Capital, and European States*, does.

16. Bean, "War and the Birth of the Nation State"; Tilly, "War Making and State Making," p. 170; and Levi, *Of Rule and Revenue*.

17. Dunbabin, *France in the Making*, notes how in the eleventh century castles were increasingly constructed from stone rather than wood (p. 287). Rice, in *The Foundations of Early Modern Europe* (pp. 13–15), demonstrates how the fifteenth century saw a rise in the use of artillery and infantry warfare. Geoffrey Parker focuses on the absolute increase in the size of armies in the sixteenth and seventeenth centuries. See his "Warfare" in Peter Burke, ed., *New Cambridge Modern History*, vol. 13 (1979). Lawrence Stone suggests that sixteenth-century armies were much larger than medieval armies. See his comment in K. B. McFarlane et al., "War and Society 1300–1600," *Past and Present* 22 (July 1962), p. 13.

18. I have already discussed the merits of Tilly's nonlinear view of evolution in Chapter 2. Here I discuss the general theory that warfare is the determinative factor in the evolution of different types of units, and I use the French case as an empirical referent.

19. Dudley argues that the fiscal efficiency of small units is higher than that of large units because of lower transaction costs and fewer principal-agent problems. Since cavalry was more expensive, small units were more efficient in providing the resources for this type of warfare. Leonard Dudley, "Structural Change in Interdependent Bureaucracies."

20. From the fourteenth century onward, infantry gradually started to book successes against the mounted knight. See Le Goff's account of Courtrai (1302) in Le Goff, *Medieval Civilization*, pp. 282–284. See also Keegan's highly descriptive account of Agincourt in John Keegan, *The Face of Battle* (1976).

21. Walls were now constructed in the Trace Italienne, with cornered angles admitting less impact of artillery. Elaborate earthworks were built to protect the wall from direct gunfire. McNeill, *The Pursuit of Power*, pp. 90–93. See also Simon Pepper and Nicholas Adams, *Firearms and Fortifications* (1986).

22. For evidence in the rise of expenditure, see Bean, "War and the Birth of the Nation State"; Edward Ames and Richard Rapp, "The Birth and Death of Taxes: A

Hypothesis," *Journal of Economic History* 37 (1977), pp. 161–178; Parker, "Warfare"; Samuel Finer, "State and Nation Building in Europe: The Role of the Military," in Tilly, *The Formation of National States in Western Europe*; and Mann, *The Sources of Social Power*, chapter 13. I am not suggesting that all of these authors take a macrostructural view. What I argue against are interpretations of the historical evidence in a macrostructural manner that emphasize only efficiencies of scale.

23. Dudley, "Structural Change in Interdependent Bureaucracies." Even North, whose model basically explains the efficiency of particular organization in terms of the definition of property rights, sometimes resorts to efficiency-of-scale arguments. North, *Structure and Change in Economic History*, p. 64. See also Ruggie's discussion of North and Thomas in "Territoriality and Beyond," p. 156.

24. For a good discussion of the influence of economic, political, and ideological factors on the adaptation of technology across civilizations, see Hall, *Powers and Liberties*. He notes how Muslim, Brahman, and Chinese Imperial societies impeded technological evolution. For a discussion of how adaptation to technological change depends on major changes in the political and social organization, see Unger, *Plasticity into Power*.

25. In other words, the independent variable, the character of war, cannot explain variation on the dependent variable, the type of unit.

26. Douglass North and Barry Weingast make a somewhat similar argument in emphasizing property rights and credible commitments in their article. "Constitutions and Commitment." See also North and Thomas, *The Rise of the Western World*; and North, *Structure and Change in Economic History*.

27. Tilly's account in *Coercion, Capital, and European States* is of this type.

28. See my discussion in Chapters 1 and 2. Also see Thelen and Steinmo, "Historical Institutionalism in Comparative Politics," p. 8: "Rational choice institutionalists in effect 'bracket' the issue of preference formation theoretically . . . and generally they do so by deducing preferences of the actors from the structure of the situation itself."

29. An example is the opposition by the Mamluk light cavalry to the introduction of artillery. It was not due to a technical problem. The first evidence of the use of artillery by the Mamluks dates from 1366, shortly after it was introduced in Europe. White, *Medieval Religion and Technology*, p. 285. Carlo Cipolla notes that "as long as the social structure of the kingdom remained essentially feudal, the backbone of the army was necessarily represented by the knights and there was no possibility of giving a major role to other corps. Artillery was left to the black slaves who were the most despised human element in the kingdom." *Guns, Sails, and Empire* (1965), p. 92. See also Unger, *Plasticity into Power*, pp. 79, 163. Eugene Rice suggests that the adoption of this new technology depended on political actors, aspiring princes, who were willing to adopt it. *The Foundations of Early Modern Europe*, p. 15.

30. To some extent we can see this in the attempt to outlaw the adoption of the crossbow. Both nobles and ecclesiastics feared that this shift of technology would favor commoners.

31. Dunbabin suggests that stone castles favored centralization, whereas Petit-Dutaillis argues that stone castles enabled local defense and fragmentation. Dunbabin, *France in the Making*, p. 287; Charles Petit-Dutaillis, *The Feudal Monarchy in France and England* (1936), p. 17.

32. Strayer, *The Reign of Philip the Fair*, pp. 388–393.

33. I agree therefore with Strayer's statement that the formation of states cannot be explained by their ability to wage war. Strayer, *On the Medieval Origins of the Modern State*, p. 92. Ringrose notes that Bean's data do not bear out his conclusions on England.

David Ringrose, "Comment on Papers by Reed, de Vries, and Bean," *Journal of Economic History* 33 (1973), pp. 222–227. Indeed, Bean himself locates the main changes between 1400 and 1600. Strayer is right in arguing that by 1300 the basis of the French state already existed.

34. Estimating the size of medieval armies is a hazardous enterprise. Chroniclers often exaggerated the numbers, and later historians simply duplicated the fallacies. Thus the armies of Philip Augustus and of the German emperor, with his Flemish and English vassals, who fought each other at Bouvines (1215), were each reported to be between 40,000 and 100,000 strong. Delbrück suggests that it is far more likely that they were between 5,000 and 8,000. Hans Delbrück, *Medieval Warfare* (1982), p. 417. First published 1923.

35. Hallam, *Capetian France*, pp. 306–307.

36. Levi, *Of Rule and Revenue*, p. 106.

37. To uphold that argument, one would either have to say that the French king was actually quite strong from the outset or that his ideological position made him the preferred provider of protection. As I have already suggested, I reject both views.

38. As Michael Mann suggests, Flemish towns, the French state, and Italian communes alike strove to raise money for war. *The Sources of Social Power*, p. 428. Moreover, lords other than the king had their own means of raising revenue and their own administrations. The pipe rolls of the duke of Normandy and the Grote Brief (literally "long letter") of the Count of Flanders reveal fiscal machineries that were every bit as advanced and similar in function as the French king's. See Bryce Lyon and Adriaan Verhulst, *Medieval Finance* (1967).

39. Strayer sometimes suggests that he has no explanation of why this occurred. "It is difficult to decide what factors changed the behavior of possessing classes." Strayer, *On the Medieval Origins of the Modern State*, p. 91. At other points, however (pp. 93, 106), he does allude to the social mobility of the lower classes. His later work, *The Reign of Philip the Fair*, contains much information on how Philip's administration drew support from the lower nobility and commoners.

40. As Hilton suggests, the Flemish towns had more in common with northern Italy. Hilton, *English and French Towns*, p. 1. We may add that their political objectives, to maintain independence from central authority, also looked similar.

41. An exception were the periodic fairs, such as those in Champagne. However, these fairs basically depended on itinerant traders, that is, merchants accompanying their goods. Once this type of trade declined, the fairs declined as well. C. Verlinden, "Markets and Fairs." Even when long-distance trade developed in the sixteenth century in such cities as Lyons, Marseille, and La Rochelle, its impact was relatively small. Robin Briggs, *Early Modern France, 1560–1715* (1977), p. 55. In *English and French Towns*, p. 101, Hilton also notes the relatively underdeveloped mercantile element in French towns.

42. Fawtier, *The Capetian Kings*, p. 207. Although I would argue that a city-league, such as the ones the German towns developed, would be a possibility, Fawtier is right that the Italian option of individual city-states was not viable in France.

43. The efforts of the king to standardize weights and measures and centralize coinage are discussed in Chapter 8. There I compare the success of sovereign, hierarchical institutions to that of nonsovereign organizations.

44. James Given has similarly suggested that medieval state building needs to clarify which social groups benefited and which suffered. *State and Society in Medieval Europe*, p. 258.

45. Duby, *The Early Growth of the European Economy*, p. 252. Immanuel Waller-stein argues that the importance of the towns depended not on their magnitude but on their bargaining position. *The Modern World System, vol. 1*, p. 20, note 14. Hallam suggests that the towns were more important than the countryside. *Capetian France*, p. 139.

46. Pirenne submits that money, rather than in-kind transfers, allowed the change from royal suzerainty, feudal overlordship, to sovereignty. *Medieval Cities*, pp. 213, 226. Likewise Hallam emphasizes the importance of these new sources of revenue. *Capetian France*, p. 112.

47. In the words of P. S. Lewis, "a rich king with a taste for power can buy troops to browbeat the unbribable and can bribe the unbeatable." *Essays in Later Medieval French History* (1985), p. 7.

48. Of course I do not deny that there is a coercive element to paying tax as well. Individuals and towns prefer to shirk without the political power of towns to support them were no doubt exploited against their will. The point I am making is that coercion alone is relatively inefficient. As Scott demonstrates in his discussion of the tithe, indi-viduals can easily subvert taxation processes, that are considered unfair or too high. James Scott, "Resistance Without Protest." Similarly, Margaret Levi argues that taxation implies at least quasi-compliance. *Of Rule and Revenue*, p. 52f.

49. Carolyn Webber and Aaron Wildavsky, *A History of Taxation and Expenditure in the Western World* (1986), p. 198. David Parker notes that the taille had become the most important revenue source, by far outstripping aides and domainal revenue, which were previously important sources of money. *The Making of French Absolutism* (1983), pp. 10–15.

50. Initially the king relied on many methods of revenue raising. From those who owed military service he could receive payments in substitution for military service, the scutage. The king could ask aides to pay for special occasions such as the wedding of a son or daughter. He could also impose taxes on movable goods, such as the gabelle, the salt tax. Some money was raised by charging exports. Then there were a host of special sources of revenue raising such as confiscating property of Jews and Templars. Default-ing on loans and manipulation of currency were other common means of generating revenue. Webber and Wildavsky, *A History of Taxation*, p. 181f. See also John Baldwin, *The Government of Philip Augustus* (1986), p. 44f.

51. See the discussions of Given, *State and Society*, p. 23; and Hallam, *Capetian France*, p. 12.

52. Duby, *The Early Growth of the European Economy*, p. 228. He further notes that it was considered the most burdensome by reason of its arbitrary character. See also Duby, *Rural Economy*, pp. 225–228, 247. Likewise John Baldwin sees it as an "arbitrary payment." *The Government of Philip Augustus*, pp. 45, 49. Myers shares this assessment. Henry Myers, *Medieval Kingship* (1982), p. 312.

53. Stephenson, *Mediaeval Institutions*, p. 41.

54. Duby, *The Early Growth of the European Economy*, p. 200. In my account, the end of feudalism therefore comes before the black death. This solves one of the prob-lems noted by Field, who argues that the decline of feudalism in the North-Thomas model precedes the factor endowment explanation that they use to explain the decline of serfdom after the plague. For the discussion of that problem, see Field, "The Problem with Neoclassical Institutional Economics."

55. Stephenson, *Mediaeval Institutions*, p. 117.

56. For example, Scott has argued that peasants resisted the church tithe. It was

228   NOTES TO CHAPTER 5

technically meant to guarantee the availability of local religious service, but in fact five-sixths went to the higher ranks of the clergy. Strategies to evade such taxation were numerous. Scott, "Resistance Without Protest," p. 443f. For descriptions of the tithe, see Duby, *Rural Economy*, pp. 56, 213, 239.

57. Hence the well-known adage of the medieval town, *Stadtluft macht frei nach Jahr und Tag* "City air makes free after a year and a day." For a variety of examples of this practice across western Europe, see John Mundy and Peter Riesenberg, *The Medieval Town* (1958), documents 23–26, pp. 137–142.

58. For the provisions in the Charter of Lorris, see Tierney, *The Middle Ages*, p. 161. See therein also the liberties granted to English and Italian towns, p. 162f. For similar discussions and examples of demands in these charters, see Duby, *Early Growth of the European Economy*, p. 207; Hilton, *English and French Towns*, pp. 36, 38, and particularly 128; Hallam, *Capetian France*, p. 140; Painter, *Medieval Society*, pp. 72–73; and Dunbabin, *France in the Making*, p. 269.

59. Duby suggests this happened toward the latter part of the twelfth century. *Early Growth of the European Economy*, p. 228. See also Miskimin, *The Economy of Early Renaissance Europe*, p. 7.

60. Strayer, *The Reign of Philip the Fair*, p. 106. On occasion communes would purchase this from the prévôts, the royal tax officials; see William Jordan, *Louis IX and the Challenge of the Crusade* (1979), p. 161. See also Duby, *Rural Economy*, pp. 243–248.

61. Given, *State and Society*, p. 196.

62. Myers, *Medieval Kingship*, p. 198. This is probably the reason why John Henneman distinguishes an intermediate stage between seigneurial taille and royal taille as the phase of the municipal taille. "Taille, Tallage," in Strayer, *Dictionary of the Middle Ages*, vol. 12, p. 576.

63. This decentralized and ad hoc bargaining was a tedious process. It involved haggling and reneging. The taxfarmers, the prévôts, were relatively uncontrolled, despite efforts by their supervising baillis, and hence apt to reroute considerable revenue to their own pockets. Still, compliance was relatively high during the late Capetian era according to Strayer. *The Reign of Philip the Fair*, p. 208.

64. For a good discussion of the contrasting strategies of French and English Crown, see Given, *State and Society*.

65. See Jan Rogozinski, "The Counsellors of the Seneschal of Beaucaire and Nimes, 1250–1350," *Speculum* 44 (July 1969), pp. 421–439; Strayer, *The Reign of Philip the Fair*, pp. 43–44.

66. This continued well into the fifteenth and sixteenth centuries despite the emergence of French absolutism. The negotiations did not follow any formalized rules (*se placent dans un dialogue qui n'admet aucune règle posée d'avance*, "took place in a dialogue that did not acknowledge any previously established rule"). Bernard Chevalier, "L'État et les Bonnes Villes en France au Temps de leur Accord Parfait," in Bulst and Genet, *La Ville, La Bourgeoisie et La Genèse de L'État Moderne* (1988), p. 74. Fryde notes how in one instance Rouen obtained one-third of its tax back. "The Financial Policies of the Royal Governments and Popular Resistance to Them in France and England c. 1270–1420," in E. B. Fryde, *Studies in Medieval Trade and Finance* (1983), p. 854.

67. P. S. Lewis, "The Failure of the French Medieval Estates," *Past and Present* 23 (1962), p. 14. In *Capetian France*, p. 303, Hallam likewise notes the relative unimportance of assemblies.

68. There is some debate on this issue. According to some accounts, the alliance started to fall apart during the fourteenth century when higher taxes were imposed on the towns, and it certainly was not very strong by the seventeenth century. However, it would be wrong to argue, based on an understanding of the seventeenth century, that there never was an understanding between towns and monarchy, as David Parker seems to suggest in "The Social Foundation of French Absolutism." Chevalier argues, by contrast, that the alliance of towns and kings, begun in the Late Middle Ages, lasted at least until 1550. What upset the balance were the wars of religion. Chevalier, "L'État et les Bonnes Villes."

69. Fawtier, *The Capetian Kings*, p. 77.

70. Eleanor Lodge, "The Communal Movement, Especially in France," in Tanner, *The Cambridge Medieval History*, vol. 5 (1957), p. 629.

71. As the townsmen of Marseille put it, they would prefer ideally to hold from God and no one else. Mundy and Riesenberg, *The Medieval Town*, p. 49.

72. Lodge, "The Communal Movement," p. 638; Strayer, *The Reign of Philip the Fair*, p. 356; and Tierney, *The Middle Ages*, p. 158. Hallam also notes a general dislike of ecclesiastical lordship. *Capetian France*, p. 141.

73. Painter, *The Rise of Feudal Monarchies*, pp. 15–16; Duby, *Rural Economy*, pp. 76–77; and Poggi, *The Development of the Modern State*, p. 42.

74. Many historians support this description of towns as antifeudal. See Heer, *The Medieval World*, p. 75; Fawtier, *The Capetian Kings*, pp. 206–207; Duby, *The Early Growth of the European Economy*, pp. 244–245. Given the discussion of the content of urban charters and their demands for liberties, I cannot interpret the towns' objectives any other way. Nevertheless, Hilton, taking a neo-Marxist position, wants to embed towns within the feudal order. He does so by focusing on feudalism as a social formation and argues that it did not alter despite the emergence of towns. Hilton, *English and French Towns*. I discuss this position in more detail in my conclusion to this chapter.

75. Rörig, *The Medieval Town*, p. 28.

76. Dunbabin, *France in the Making*, p. 274. On pg. 275 she adds: "No lords appreciated the possibilities inherent in the movement so clearly as Louis VI and Louis VII." Given argues that the king offered Toulouse a better deal than the Count of Toulouse. *State and Society*, p. 58. That town, however, wanting more, went back and forth in its loyalties between king and count. Petit-Dutaillis suggests that the king granted more liberties to the towns than rival lords granted to them and that hence burghers outside the domain would demand royal justice. *The Feudal Monarchy*, pp. 153, 197, 309.

77. Hallam, *Capetian France*, pp. 136, 186; Fawtier, *The Capetian Kings*, p. 207.

78. Baldwin, *The Government of Philip Augustus*, pp. 61–64.

79. Baldwin, *The Government of Philip Augustus*, p. 59f. See also Rörig, *The Medieval Town*, p. 58.

80. Hallam, *Capetian France*, pp. 141, 142.

81. Lyon and Verhulst, *Medieval Finance*, p. 94.

82. Baldwin, *The Government of Philip Augustus*, pp. 152–175. Additional extraordinary revenue might come from the church in times of Crusades.

83. See Strayer, *The Reign of Philip the Fair*, p. 394. Fryde notes that particularly the debasements of the fourteenth century mobilized determined opposition. At those times kings would have to return to hard currency. "The Financial Policies," p. 835.

84. Strayer, *The Reign of Philip the Fair*, pp. xii, 79, 394; Fawtier, *The Capetian Kings*, p. 194.

85. Philippe Contamine, *War in the Middle Ages* (1984), p. 79.

86. It was particularly difficult to levy knight service from areas outside the royal domain. For example, the knight service that Philip Augustus could extract in 1215 when confronted with the forces of the German emperor, English king, Count of Flanders, and their allies at Bouvines was relatively small. His army of 1,300 knights was "a surprisingly small number summoned from Philip's entire feudal resources at the most critical moment of his reign." Baldwin, *The Government of Philip Augustus*, p. 286.

87. Contamine, *War in the Middle Ages*, p. 83.

88. There were two types of pounds—the livre tournois (l.t.) outside the Île-de-France area and the livre parisis (l.p.) within the Parisian area. Strayer, *The Reign of Philip the Fair*, p. xvii; and Baldwin, *The Government of Philip Augustus*, p. xv. There were twelve deniers (pence) to a sous (shilling), and twenty sous to a livre. The livre tournois was worth about 20 percent less than the livre parisis. Given provides an example of the king's strategy in the south. *State and Society*, p. 169.

89. Strayer, *The Reign of Philip the Fair*, p. 349.

90. James Collins, *The Fiscal Limits of Absolutism* (1988), p. 27. See also Fryde, "The Financial Policies," pp. 837, 858.

91. See P. S. Lewis, "The Failure of the the French Medieval Estates," p. 12.

92. See the argument of Randall Collins, *Weberian Sociological Theory* (1986).

93. The general assessment is that there was an alliance between the church and king. Painter, *The Rise of Feudal Monarchies*, p. 13; Dunbabin, *France in the Making*, pp. 121–122, 167. But even though there were seventy-seven bishoprics, the general weakness of the early Capetians meant they only controlled perhaps as few as fourteen. Fawtier, *The Capetian Kings*, p. 73; Baldwin, *The Government of Philip Augustus*, p. 48; Hallam, *Capetian France*, p. 86.

94. Tierney, *The Crisis of Church and State*, p. 173.

95. Louis IX thus obtained about 900,000 l.t. for his first crusade. Jordan, *Louis IX*, p. 82. Significantly, the towns contributed a large amount, about 274,000 l.t., as well (p. 98).

96. Baldwin, *The Government of Philip Augustus*, p. 178; Dunbabin, *France in the Making*, p. 43.

97. Myers, *Medieval Kingship*, p. 316. The king's lawyers had already in 1289 used legal codes against an archbishop to argue for the supremacy of royal jurisdiction. Strayer, *The Reign of Philip the Fair*, p. 243. According to Hallam, "lay jurisdiction was constantly encroaching on ecclesiastical jurisdiction." Hallam, *Capetian France*, p. 310.

98. For an account of this campaign, see Strayer, *The Reign of Philip the Fair*, p. 319.

99. See Le Goff, *Medieval Civilization*, p. 282.

100. Tierney, *The Crisis of Church and State*, p. 182. It is interesting to speculate why the French king succeeded where the German emperor failed. One reason is that the king's position vis-à-vis ecclesiastical lords was stronger than the German emperor's at the time of the Investiture Struggle (1075 and on). The German emperor had used a greater number of ecclesiastical than secular lords. Fuhrmann, *Germany in the High Middle Ages*, p. 173. Moreover, the king only moved against the pope after he had built a solid domestic alliance with the towns from which the lords received side payments.

101. The next seven popes were subsequently Frenchmen. Of the 134 cardinals appointed by these popes, 112, maybe 113, were French. Half of papal revenue in 1328 came from ecclesiastical intake in the French kingdom. Francis Oakley, *The Western Church in the Later Middle Ages* (1979), pp. 38–55; Heer, *The Medieval World*, p. 338.

102. Petit-Dutaillis, *The Feudal Monarchy*, p. 206.

103. Ibid., p. 235.

104. In essence the king was confronted with a classical principal-agent problem. Given the inability to supervise agents on a frequent basis, how could he make sure that agents were pursuing policies that met his objectives?

105. This distinction of four stages of administration is from Fesler, "French Field Administration."

106. As general agents they performed military, administrative, fiscal, and judiciary functions. Their offices quickly became hereditary, and the pagi established themselves as counts. This corresponded with the Merovingian practice of land grants to those who rendered military service to the chieftain. Stephenson, *Mediaeval Institutions*, p. 211.

107. Dunbabin, *France in the Making*, p. 6f.

108. These appeared for the first time around 1050. Hallam, *Capetian France*, p. 83.

109. A moment's reflection suggests the logic of this type of administration. The king had no established core of personnel to raise such revenue, nor could he hire them in view of his lack of money. Economic conditions, being what they were, did not allow for easy means of revenue increases through tolls or indirect taxes. In other words, the transaction and enforcement costs of levying taxes were high. What the king did possess was a modest royal domain. Since he had no means at his disposal to raise revenue, adjudicate disputes, and make his presence felt, he offered others a part of the proceeds of the revenue they could raise. Thus he acquired personnel at little cost to himself. For a description of this system, see Fawtier, *The Capetian Kings*, p. 175; Lyon and Verhulst, *Medieval Finance*, p. 92.

110. I use the terms *bailli* and *bailiff* interchangeably. Fawtier dates their emergence at around 1180. *The Capetian Kings*, p. 177. See also Baldwin, *The Government of Philip Augustus*, p. 126.

111. This third aspect, the prefectoral model of administration, reveals the efficiency of royal policy. Since the king lacked the means to control his agents on a day-to-day basis and to continually instruct his agents, he, as the principal, wished to duplicate the policy of the principal in the agent. The model for this form of administration was in many ways the Catholic church in which the bishop duplicated the pope. Furthermore, since the center of control was undifferentiated—it still formed an amorphous Curia Regis—the agents in the field could not be specialized either.

112. Hallam, *Capetian France*, p. 239. There is considerable research on the origins of the men who served the king. Strayer argues that the careers of about a one thousand men who served Philip the Fair can be traced in some detail. He suggests that the use of nonnobles was stronger in the south than the north. Strayer, *The Reign of Philip the Fair*, p. 37. The input and participation of the bourgeois are well documented. See Fawtier, *The Capetian Kings*, p. 184. Jordan adds: "The majority of baillis . . . came from knightly and bourgeois backgrounds." Jordan, *Louis IX*, p. 48. Hallam speaks of "nouveaux riches officials" in *Capetian France*, pp. 159, 160, 296; Strayer, *Feudalism*, p. 65 and documents 45 and 46 on pp. 159–162.

113. Dunbabin, *France in the Making*, p. 284; Mundy and Riesenberg, *The Medieval Town*, pp. 90, 91.

114. Strayer, On the *Medieval Origins of the Modern State*, p. 51; Given, *State and Society*, p. 173; Jordan, *Louis IX*, p. 160.

115. Some bailiffs would serve thirty or forty years and as many as five successive kings. Strayer, *The Reign of Philip the Fair*, p. 416.

116. For comparison, a skilled worker might earn one to one and a half sous (shilling) a day. If he worked 300 days, he would earn about 300 shilling, or 15 livres (pounds). See Strayer, *The Reign of Philip the Fair*, p. 56. He argues that even lower officials did

reasonably well. Walter Prevenier has suggested to me that this estimate of the number of working days is too high and that 200 to 240 was more common because of the large number of holy days. If so, this reinforces my point that the agents of the king were well remunerated.

117. Petit-Dutaillis argues that the pay was not very high, but one must keep in mind that he focuses primarily on the period leading up to the end of Augustus's reign with less emphasis on the later half of the thirteenth century. Petit-Dutaillis, *The Feudal Monarchy*, p. 296. Fawtier notes that salaries were low(!) but then argues they were between 292 and 739 livres. *The Capetian Kings*, p. 182. Baldwin and Fesler suggest that the pay was indeed high. See Fesler, "French Field Administration," p. 94; Baldwin, *The Government of Philip Augustus*, p. 109.

118. Jan Rogozinski, "The Counsellors." Jordan likewise notes that the prévôts established strong local ties. *Louis IX*, pp. 161–162.

119. See particularly Fesler, "French Field Administration," for this discussion.

120. Strayer, *The Reign of Philip the Fair*, p. 89.

121. Fawtier, *The Capetian Kings*, p. 185.

122. Hallam, *Capetian France*, p. 160.

123. Rörig, *The Medieval Town*, p. 60.

124. Duby stresses the importance of this. *The Early Growth of the European Economy*, p. 253.

125. See, for example, Ruggie, "Territoriality and Beyond." Many others have raised similar points of view. Useful starting points for a variety of discussions are Nicholas Onuf, "Sovereignty: Outline of a Conceptual History," *Alternatives* 16 (1991), pp. 425–466; Robert Walker and Saul Mendlovitz, *Contending Sovereignties: Rethinking Political Community* (1990).

126. To reiterate, I take a Weberian position on this issue. I take ideas as exogenous. Their routinization, however, depends on both material conditions and their empowerment by social actors and political entrepreneurs.

127. Hinsley, *Sovereignty*, pp. 41, 159.

128. "Quod principi placuit, legis habet vigorem" (What pleases the prince, has the power of law). P. Gerbenzon and N. E. Algra, *Voortgangh des Rechtes*, (1975), p. 106. About a century earlier, Henry IV had first entertained the idea of using Roman law to support his position against the pope. He did not, however, use it as a systematic means to enhance imperial control as did Frederick Barbarossa. Particularly the Diet of Roncaglia (1156) is important in this regard. See Fuhrmann, *Germany in the High Middle Ages*, pp. 72, 147, 148.

129. "Rex Franciae in regno suo princeps est, nam in temporalibus superiorem non recognoscit" (The King of France is prince in his own Kingdom, for in temporal affairs he recognizes no superior). Gerbenzon and Algra, *Voortgangh des Rechtes*, p. 106. See also Keen, *History of Medieval Europe*, p. 204.

130. Stanley Benn and Richard Peters, *Social Principles and the Democratic State* (1959), p. 255.

131. Kantorowicz, *The King's Two Bodies*, pp. 131, 132.

132. Fuhrmann argues that this alliance between the French king and papacy formed in the twelfth century. Fuhrmann, *Germany in the High Middle Ages*, p. 103. Pope Innocent III recognized in 1202 that the king of France had no superior in temporal affairs, but the king like the emperor was subject to the universal church. Hinsley, *Sovereignty*, p. 80; Fawtier, *The Capetian Kings*, p. 86.

133. Hallam, *Capetian France*, pp. 262–269, 308–309. To the notion of sovereignty

that the legists put forward, Marsilius of Padua added in his Defensor Pacis (1324–1326) that the state was a creation of reason. Heer, *The Medieval World*, p. 344.

134. Fawtier, *The Capetian Kings*, p. 95.

135. Mundy and Riesenberg, *The Medieval Town*, p. 87.

136. Marvin Becker discusses the importance of the growth of trust and confidence in abstract exchange in order for a market economy to take hold. *Medieval Italy*.

137. See the discussion by V. G. Kiernan, "Private Property in History," in Jack Goody, Joan Thirsk, and E. P. Thompson, eds., *Family and Inheritance* (1976), pp. 374, 376, and note the importance of Roman law on p. 378.

138. The royal court thus advanced a theory of delegated powers, in which the highest authority lay with the royal court. Strayer, *Feudalism*, pp. 47, 131.

139. See Baldwin, *The Government of Philip Augustus*, pp. 229, 318f.; Strayer, *The Reign of Philip the Fair*, p. 230.

140. Mundy and Riesenberg, *The Medieval Town*, p. 61.

141. For an example of the towns' resistance to privileged juridical procedures for knights, see Dunbabin, *France in the Making*, pp. 270, 280.

142. Hallam, *Capetian France*, p. 244.

143. Petit-Dutaillis, *The Feudal Monarchy*, pp. 288, 310.

144. Fawtier, *The Capetian Kings*, p. 39.

145. For the standardization and codification of customs, see Dunbabin, *France in the Making*, p. 277; Hallam, *Capetian France*, pp. 265–266.

146. In short, the king's actions changed the political order in favor of the merchants. "One thing is certain, the political action of the sovereign that dismantled the ecclesiastical organization, the redistribution of land, the secularization of the administration that began in the preceding century, changed the balance, broke the routine, accelerated the rise of the merchants and the servants of the Crown, partially renewed a superior class, and contributed to the decline of the ideal life associated with the old warrior aristocracy" (my translation). Giard describes in particular how the advance of vernacular language coincided with the empowerment of new actors. Previously, Latin had been the language of knowledge, power, and belief. Luce Giard, "La Procès d'Émancipation de l'Anglais à la Renaissance," pp. 2, 13. An example of the nonfeudal character of the crown was that legal training became more important for service. For example, Nogaret, one of Philip the Fair's closest advisors, had been a faculty member of law at the University of Montpellier, which was well known for its study of Roman law. Strayer, *The Reign of Philip the Fair*, p. 52. For the influence of Montpellier, also see Hallam, *Capetian France*, p. 57; Heer, *The Medieval World*, p. 343.

147. Strayer, *The Reign of Philip the Fair*, p. xii.

148. From a new institutionalist perspective, one might add that a shared ideology made it easier to overcome freerider problems and lower the costs of forming alliances.

149. Strayer, *The Reign of Philip the Fair*, p. 314.

150. Dunbabin, *France in the Making*, p. 49.

151. A nice enumeration of reasons for this alliance is also given by Myers, *Medieval Kingship*, pp. 197–199.

152. Gradually kings became more involved in trade because of its economic benefits. Rather than letting the merchants rely on self-help to settle grievances, the king himself would seek redress from his royal counterpart and thus create more certitude in the merchants' business practices. See Frederic Cheyette, "The Sovereign and the Pirates, 1332" *Speculum* 45 (January 1970), pp. 40–68.

153. Hallam, *Capetian France*, p. 154. "The medieval universities were predominantly urban institutions." Edith Ennen, *The Medieval Town* (1979), p. 203.

154. Indeed, the expansion of that system became one of France's continual fiscal woes in the centuries to come. That story is well known. See, among others, Collins, *The Fiscal Limits of Absolutism*; Parker, *The Making of French Absolutism*; Briggs, *Early Modern France*; Hilton Root, *Peasants and King in Burgundy: Agrarian Foundations of French Absolutism* (1987).

155. Thus in the Hundred Years War the king could claim with considerable plausibility that only he, not any other lords, should be the one to sign treaties with the English. Aline Vallée, "État et Securité Publique au XIVe Siècle."

156. See Hilton, *English and French Towns*, pp. 11, 25.; A. B. Hibbert, "The Origins of the Medieval Town Patriciate," *Past and Present* 3 (February 1953), p. 17; Anderson, *Lineages of the Absolutist State*, p. 18.

157. Hilton thus denies an alliance between king and towns (p. 15) and argues that the divisions within the towns reflect the agricultural division of lord and tenant (pp. 16–17). He places towns within the feudal system (pp. 78, 88, 132, 150). Yet he also notes the towns' desires for freedom from lordly exactions (pp. 36–38), the rivalry on jurisdiction (p. 53), that English towns were ruled by merchants capitalists, and that the French bourgeois became royal officials (p. 104). Hilton, *English and French Towns*. Similarly, Anderson notes that the "Absolutist State increasingly centralized political power" (p. 40) but argues that "the nobility could deposit power with the monarchy, and permit the enrichment of the bourgeoisie: the masses were still at its mercy" (p. 41). From my point of view, if the previously independent lords surrendered political power to the king, this should be understood as a decline of feudalism. To argue otherwise is inconsistent with Anderson's own definition of feudalism as "parcellized sovereignty" on p. 18 of his book. For a similar critique of Anderson, see Mary Fulbrook and Theda Skocpol, "Destined Pathways: The Historical Sociology of Perry Anderson," in Skocpol, *Vision and Method in Historical Sociology*, p. 186.

158. Hallam, *Capetian France*, pp. 290, 305; Given, *State and Society*, p. 16; Jordan, *Louis IX*, p. 15; Fawtier, *The Capetian Kings*, p. 210.

159. Although the Hundred Years War threatened the centralized power, it nevertheless did not see the rise of independent lordships. At best we may call this bastard feudalism. See Jean-Philippe Genet, "Conclusion," in Bulst and Genet, *La Ville, La Bourgeoisie et La Genèse de L'État Moderne*, p. 347. Strayer disagrees with that term, because although some groups tried to capture parts of central government, they did not establish quasi-independent fiefs. Strayer, *On the Medieval Origins of the Modern State*, p. 62.

160. Wim Blockmans, "Princes Conquérants et Bourgeois Calculateurs," in Bulst and Genet, "*La Ville, La Bourgeoisie et La Genèse de L'État Moderne*," pp. 178–180; Chevalier, "L'État et les Bonnes Villes," pp. 72–83; Parker, *The Making of French Absolutism*, pp. 103–105.

CHAPTER 6

1. Scammel, *The World Encompassed*, p. 24.

2. After Otto I (936–973), the king who was crowned emperor in 962 in Rome, virtually every German king was also emperor. In most cases, we can use the two terms interchangeably without suggesting that usage of one or the other has specific political meaning. However, the German king was basically approved by, and later elected by,

the German nobility. The imperial title was granted by the pope. The two elective procedures therefore did not have to, and later did not, converge on the same candidate. Where such an issue arises, this will be made clear in the text.

3. The phrase *Roman Empire* was introduced by the German kings who sought to gain control over the kingdoms of Burgundy, Italy, and Germany. It was introduced in the later part of the tenth century when the German kings sought to make Rome the capital of the empire. Frederick I (1152–1190) added the adjective *Holy* to denote the special status of the empire.

4. The confusing set of political organizations plagued Germany for many centuries. Harris aptly describes the anachronism of the empire in the seventeenth century. "It consisted of well over 300 separate States; there were over 200 ruling princes, some ruling more than one State; there were 51 Free Towns, and in addition nearly 1,500 Free Knights, a special mediaeval curiosity, each ruling a tiny State with an average of 300 subjects." R. W. Harris, *Absolutism and Enlightenment, 1660–1789* (1966), p. 187.

5. See Hajo Holborn, *A History of Modern Germany: The Reformation* (1959), p. 37.

6. Du Boulay, like Barraclough, affirms the Pirenne thesis (see Chapter 4 of this book) and stresses the importance of long-distance trade. F. R. Du Boulay, *Germany in the Later Middle Ages* (1983), p. 116; Barraclough, *The Origins of Modern Germany*, p. 4; Rörig, *The Medieval Town*, p. 20. Holborn notes the importance of migration and expansion in the formation of new towns. Holborn, *A History of Modern Germany*, p. 10.

7. I discuss these profit margins in greater detail in the section on the Hansa in this chapter.

8. Consequently, when imperial authority regained a measure of effectiveness under the Hapsburgs, the Hanseatic towns sought imperial protection. Leo Lensen and Willy Heitling, *De Geschiedenis van de Hanze* (1990), p. 37.

9. In practice, election usually meant affirmation. Only after the Investiture Conflict did this become a serious impediment to monarchy, because election was then tied to the criterion of suitability.

10. Rörig, *The Medieval Town*, p. 23.

11. Rhiman Rotz, "German Towns," in Strayer, *Dictionary of the Middle Ages*, vol. 5, p. 459.

12. Leuschner, *Germany in the Late Middle Ages*, p. 85; Rörig, *The Medieval Town*, p. 24.

13. Since the differences between townsfolk on the one hand, and feudal lords and church on the other, were basically similar to cleavages in France, I have not discussed them in detail. The point is that because the German case lacked a political actor who was willing to capitalize on these differences, these cleavages did not evolve into the basis for a political coalition.

14. For a discussion of this sequence of events, see Fuhrmann, *Germany in the High Middle Ages*, pp. 86–90.

15. Ibid., p. 147.

16. See the description in David Abulafia, *Frederick II: A Medieval Emperor* (1988), p. 73. According to some German historians, such as A. Hauck, that date already marks the end of German imperial pretensions. Fuhrmann, *Germany in the High Middle Ages*, p. 161.

17. Fuhrmann, *Germany in the High Middle Ages*, p. 166.

18. Consequently their rivalry was also fought out in Italy where the two parties were called the Ghibelline (after Waiblingen, a Hohenstaufen castle) and the Guelph (Welf).

19. Barraclough, *The Origins of Modern Germany*, p. 154.

20. Haverkamp, *Medieval Germany*, p. 244.

21. Barraclough, *The Origins of Modern Germany*, p. 236. Barraclough argues (p. 234) that "the Statutum . . . was directed first and foremost against the rising towns." Leuschner also evaluates it as an explicit strategy in favor of the secular and ecclesiastical princes and against the cities. *Germany in the Late Middle Ages*, p. 57. See also the text of the Statutum in Tierney, *The Middle Ages*, p. 248. Although Abulafia agrees that these agreements gave the princes extensive rights of intervention in towns, he is somewhat less critical than Barraclough and Holborn of the imperial strategy and suggests it conformed with an overall imperial position of nonintervention in de facto independent units. Abulafia, *Frederick II*, p. 231f.

22. Holborn, *A History of Modern Germany*, p. 23.

23. Leuschner, *Germany in the Late Middle Ages*, p. 55f; Abulafia, *Frederick II*, pp. 230–241; Barraclough, *The Origins of Modern Germany*, p. 237.

24. The royal domain was only three-fourths the size of the margravate of Brandenburg. Barraclough, *The Origins of Modern Germany*, p. 246.

25. Leuschner, *Germany in the Late Middle Ages*, pp. 80–81.

26. Leuschner, *Germany in the Late Middle Ages*, pp. 155–161; Barraclough, *The Origins of Modern Germany*, pp. 316–321.

27. Barraclough, *The Origins of Modern Germany*, p. 320.

28. This was not the full-fledged sovereignty of the French state. The external relations of these lords were still in the hands of the emperor. At the Peace of Westphalia (1648) these principalities would also gain external standing, despite the fact that the empire continued to exist until 1806. Gradually, from the decline of the Hohenstaufen until Westphalia, the princes would increasingly start to behave like their regular sovereign counterparts.

29. Holborn, *A History of Modern Germany*, p. 28.

30. Holborn, *A History of Modern Germany*, p. 23–24. Rotz makes a similar assessment: "Unlike the English or French monarchs or the Dukes of Burgundy in the Low Countries, the German King never used towns as a foundation for his authority." Rotz, "German Towns," p. 459.

31. Fleckenstein, *Early Medieval Germany*, p. 189.

32. Fuhrmann, *Germany in the High Middle Ages*, p. 148. This estimate basically conforms with the estimates of Louis VII's revenue that we saw in Chapter 5.

33. Abulafia, *Frederick II*, p. 14. The estimate is probably too high, but no doubt there were considerable gains to be had from Sicily.

34. As I have already pointed out, the German king relied more on ecclesiastical lords than did the English or French kings. Fuhrmann, *Germany in the High Middle Ages*, p. 173. The reason for that might have been the strength of the stem duchies. That is, the king initially tried to use the clergy as a counterweight to the German high aristocracy. See Holborn for that argument. *A History of Modern Germany*, p. 19.

35. Keen, *History of Medieval Europe*, p. 165; Leuschner, *Germany in the Late Middle Ages*, p. 53; Straus, "Germany," p. 495. For the eschatological status of the emperors, see also Abulafia, *Frederick II*, p. 77; and Fuhrmann, *Germany in the High Middle Ages*, p. 135.

36. It continues to be a matter of debate whether the emperors only professed universalist ideas or also tried to follow through on them. Holborn thus suggests that the German emperors only claimed preeminence over kings, not actual dominion. *A History of Modern Germany*, p. 20. Abulafia, however, argues that the emperor did act on ideological claims of competence to judge kings. For example, the emperor forced Richard

of England to do homage to him as his vassal and interfered with the Kingdom of Cyprus, claiming that it, as all kingdoms, fell under his jurisdiction. Abulafia, *Frederick II*, pp. 69, 232.

37. Barraclough, *The Origins of Modern Germany*, pp. 254–262; Rotz, "German Towns," p. 459.

38. Barraclough, *The Origins of Modern Germany*, p. 221.

39. Alexander Boswell, "The Teutonic Order," in J. R. Tanner, ed., *The Cambridge Medieval History*, vol. 7 (1958), pp. 248–269.

40. Rörig, *The Medieval Town*, p. 25; de Battaglia, "The Nobility," p. 66. It is virtually impossible to say where this movement first started. It is clear, however, that communes were aware of similar movements throughout Europe and that they consciously copied each other's substantive demands.

41. Rotz, "German Towns," p. 459.

42. Fuhrmann, *Germany in the High Middle Ages*, p. 80. See also Rörig for the general disagreeableness of clerical overlordship. *The Medieval Town*, p. 22.

43. The imperial towns, sixty to eighty in number, owed no allegiance to any lord and were placed directly under the emperor. Lübeck obtained the status of imperial city early on. Imperial cities (Reichsstädte), such as Lübeck and Nürnberg, were usually large and only owed the emperor a certain amount of tax. As far as policy was concerned, imperial towns were basically indistinguishable from free towns. Free towns, such as Mainz, Cologne, and Strasbourg, were nominally subject to bishops but had gained independence. Territorial towns (Landstädte), by contrast, were controlled by secular or ecclesiastical lordships. These were usually the least independent. Leuschner, *Germany in the Late Middle Ages*, p. 85; Ennen, *The Medieval Town*, p. 178; Du Boulay, *Germany in the Later Middle Ages*, p. 126.

44. Hans-Joachim Behr, "Die Landgebietspolitik Nordwestdeutscher Hansestädte," *Hansische Geschichtsblätter* 94 (1976), p. 18.

45. Gerald Straus, "Germany: 1254–1493," in Strayer, *Dictionary of the Middle Ages*, vol. 5, pp. 485–491; Leuschner, *Germany in the Late Middle Ages*, p. 63f.

46. Barraclough, *The Origins of Modern Germany*, pp. 342–352.

47. Edward Miller, "Government Economic Policies and Public Finance 1000–1500," in Cipolla, *The Fontana Economic History*, vol. 1, p. 347.

48. Steven Rowan, "Germany: Principalities," in Strayer, *Dictionary of the Middle Ages*, vol. 5, p. 503.

49. Ennen, *The Medieval Town*, p. 98.

50. Rörig, *The Medieval Town*, p. 32. He relates the early formation of town councils to the business groups which had helped found the towns. Fuhrmann talks of consortia of merchants. *Germany in the High Middle Ages*, p. 151.

51. Rörig, *The Medieval Town*, p. 35.

52. For a discussion of the functions of guilds and the Hanse, see Ennen, *The Medieval Town*, pp. 98–99; Lensen and Heitling, *De Geschiedenis van de Hanze*, pp. 31–32.

53. Philippe Dollinger, *The German Hansa* (1970), p. 24. This is still the seminal historical work on the Hansa.

54. The Saxon, Westphalian, and Wendish leagues were all formed during the twelfth century, partially for reasons of military security. Bruce Gelsinger, "Hanseatic League," in Strayer, *Dictionary of the Middle Ages*, vol. 6, p. 93.

55. See the efforts to perform such economic functions described in Rowan, "Germany: Principalities," p. 503; Straus, "Germany: 1254–1493," p. 490. For the Hansa's attempt to regulate measures and weights, see Otto Held, "Hansische Einheitsbestre-

bungen im Mass- und Gewichtswesen bis zum Jahre 1500," *Hansische Geschichtsblätter* 45 (1918), pp. 127–167; Rotz, "German Towns," p. 464.

56. Fuhrmann, *Germany in the High Middle Ages*, p. 165.

57. In 1254 the Rhenisch League formed to take over a semblance of central government after Frederick II's policies had failed. There were also: the Westphalian League (1246), the lower Saxon League (1246), the Wendish League (1280), the Hansa League (1294 or 1356), the League of Thüringen (1304), the ten cities of the Elzas (1354), the Swabian League (1376), the new Rhenisch League (1381), and the Saxon League (1382). Lensen and Heitling, *De Geschiedenis van de Hanze*, p. 28; Ennen, *The Medieval Town*, p. 179; Dollinger, *The German Hansa*, p. 47.

58. Barraclough, *The Origins of Modern Germany*, p. 238. See also Du Boulay for the argument that city-leagues were often antifeudal. They attempted to ameliorate the effects of political fragmentation. *Germany in the Later Middle Ages*, p. 125.

59. Matthias Puhle, "Der Sächsische Städtebund und die Hanse im späten Mittelalter," *Hansische Geschichtsblätter* 104 (1986), pp. 21–34.

60. The Hansa also had provisions to maintain the ruling patriciate against the patriciate's internal opponents. Indeed, patrician rule was a prerequisite for membership. When Brunswick's government was overthrown in 1374, the town was excluded from the Hansa for five years. Ennen, *The Medieval Town*, p. 177. Such provisions were not superfluous given the large number of urban uprisings. The German historian Maschke estimates that there might have been as many as 210 throughout Germany between 1300 and 1550. Cited in Du Boulay, *Germany in the Later Middle Ages*, p. 146.

61. Rotz, "German Towns," p. 464f.

62. See Ennen, *The Medieval Town*, p. 179. Consequently the emperor allied with the princes against the Swabian-Rhenisch League in 1388. Leuschner, *Germany in the Late Middle Ages*, p. 141.

63. The adage "Unity at Home. Peace Abroad" is inscribed above the Holstein gate of Lübeck. See Johannes Schildhauer, *The Hansa* (1988), p. 86. In a way it symbolizes both the objectives and the problems of the Hansa. Because the league was a confederation of towns, collective action problems were one of the main concerns for Hanseatic internal unity. At the same time, the Hansa sought to protect its members from deprivations abroad and to provide a larger degree of certainty in their long-distance commerce.

64. The etymology of the word is difficult to trace. Early on it denoted a group or fellowship for which the medieval Latin *hansa* or old German *hanse* are both used. It might also derive from *hos* which is an armed contingent. A. Weiner, "The Hansa," in Tanner, *The Cambridge Medieval History*, vol. 7, p. 216. See also Ruth Schmidt-Wiegand, "Hanse und Gilde. Genossenschaftliche Organisationsformen im Bereich der Hanse und ihre Bezeichnungen," *Hansische Geschichtsblätter* 100 (1982), p. 22; Ennen, *The Medieval Town*, p. 129; Lensen and Heitling, *De Geschiedenis van de Hanze*, p. 12. When I discuss the *Hansa*, I mean the Hanseatic League. With *hansa*, I refer generically to any group of merchants.

65. Scammel notes how the Hansa in the fifteenth century had profit margins of about 15 to 25 percent. Italian profit margins ranged between 20 and 150 percent. Portuguese trade with the East Indies, by contrast, could yield extraordinary profits of up to 2000 percent. Scammel, *The World Encompassed*, p. 77. See also Chapter 7 of this book for a discussion of the nature of Italian trade. Braudel suggests lower profit margins for the Hansa, i.e., between 5 and 15 percent. Braudel, *The Perspective of the World*, p. 103. The difference between Italian and northern commerce also shows up in ship design. The Hansa ships were "designed for carrying bulk cargoes of only moderate value." J. H.

Parry, *The Discovery of the Sea* (1981), p. 19. For a similar assessment, see Lewis and Runyan, *European Naval and Maritime History*, pp. 130–136. The cog and later the hulk were bulk carriers. For an enumeration of the most important products, see Dollinger, *The German Hansa*, p. 214f.

66. I have relied heavily in this section on the extensive discussion by Walter Stark, "Untersuchungen zum Profit beim Hansischen Handelskapital in der ersten Hälfte des 15. Jahrhunderts," in *Abhandlungen zur Handels und Sozialgeschichte* (1985).

67. In general, German business knowledge and training lagged behind that of the Italians. There was little double-entry accounting. Training was largely by experience and socialization. Only by the seventeenth century did such education improve. Pierre Jeannin, "Das Handbuch in der Berufsausbildung des Hansischen Kaufmanns," *Hansische Geschichtsblätter* 103 (1985), pp. 101–120; Scammel, *The World Encompassed*, p. 76; Dollinger, *The German Hansa*, p. 165.

68. Stark suggests that Töhner might have had an extraordinary profit of 48.7 percent. Stark, or perhaps Töhner himself, does not specify whether this is calculated from twelve or eleven marks to the great pound. Stark, "Untersuchungen zum Profit," p. 136. If it is calculated by twelve instead of eleven, then the profits according to my calculation would be about 27 percent. Once again this demonstrates the information costs involved in commerce of this period. It also explains why the Hansa made considerable effort to come to an agreement with the Count of Flanders not to change the coinage. Lensen and Heitling, *De Geschiedenis van de Hanze*, p. 15. This became a general demand. The Treaty of Stralsund, which was drafted after the Hansa's victory over Denmark in 1370, included provisions on the stability of currency. Weiner, "The Hansa," p. 222.

69. Lensen and Heitling, *De Geschiedenis van de Hanze*, p. 35. This consequently meant that the consumer also faced considerable information costs.

70. Both words are used synonymously in early texts. Schmidt-Wiegand, "Hanse und Gilde," pp. 20, 30, 35.

71. Dollinger, *The German Hansa*, pp. 164–165.

72. Ibid., pp. 40, 41, 56–58.

73. It thus restricted the Dutch and English from sailing in the Baltic. Lewis and Runyan, *European Naval and Maritime History*, p. 152.

74. Scammel, *The World Encompassed*, p. 44.

75. Consequently, German historiography used it in the 1930s to justify claims to a greater Germany. Lensen and Heitling, *De Geschiedenis van de Hanze*, chapter 15.

76. For a discussion of Lübeck's founding and its subsequent efforts to found daughter cities, see Scammel, *The World Encompassed*, p. 41.

77. For a fuller discussion of these orders, see Boswell, "The Teutonic Order," p. 250f.; Barraclough, *The Origins of Modern Germany*, p. 270; Leuschner, *Germany in the Late Middle Ages*, p. 130; E. Lönnroth, "The Baltic Countries," in Postan, Rich, and Miller, eds., *Economic Organization and Policies in the Middle Ages*, vol. 3 (Cambridge, 1963), pp. 364, 375f.

78. Gelsinger, "Hanseatic League," p. 92; Du Boulay, *Germany in the Later Middle Ages*, p. 124.

79. Recall that French communes also sought to be placed as high as possible in the feudal hierarchy since this diminished the number of overlords to be served.

80. Dollinger, *The German Hansa*, p. 40.

81. Rörig, *The Medieval Town*, p. 39.

82. One might argue that it is not therefore possible to give a history of the German town. The variation of towns is well documented and not contested here. However, the

very formation of city-leagues such as the Saxon League, the Swabian-Rhenisch League, and the Hanseatic League, as well as many other regional organizations, suggests that the towns recognized similar interests. This chapter clarifies these shared interests and explains why the towns resorted to the particular formation of leagues to serve their interests rather than another type of organization.

83. Lönnroth, "The Baltic Countries," p. 391. See also Gelsinger, "Hanseatic League," p. 92. The Teutonic Order itself was, true to the crosscutting jurisdictions of feudalism, subject to the emperor and the pope. In practice it proved to be virtually an independent body. Boswell, "The Teutonic Order," p. 261.

84. The Kontor was a combination of diplomatic representative, judicial body, office, living quarters, and storage facility.

85. The Hansa thus acquired a form of extraterritoriality. The same holds true for the private property of Hanseatic merchants in some non-Hansa towns. These properties (*fed*) were administered by the bailiff of the local town, but Lübeck law exceeded all other law. In other words, Hanseatic merchants were tried by the law of one of the dominant Hansa towns rather than by local law. C. Verlinden, "Markets and Fairs," pp. 148–149.

86. Dollinger, *The German Hansa*, p. 91; Wernicke (p. 34) also notes that a simple majority decision could bind even those who were not present. Hence, the towns had an added incentive to be present. Horst Wernicke, "Die Städtehanse 1280–1418," in *Abhandlungen zur Handels und Sozialgeschichte* Bd. 22 (1983), pp. 1–204. Lensen and Heitling confirm the simple majority vote. *De Geschiedenis van de Hanze*, p. 31.

87. Dollinger, *The German Hansa*, p. 334.

88. Ibid., p. 92.

89. Gelsinger, "Hanseatic League," p. 90. Leuschner suggests a membership of seventy active members with about ninety peripheral members. Leuschner, *Germany in the Late Middle Ages*, p. 145. Scammel and Heer give roughly similar estimates. Scammel, *The World Encompassed*, p. 53; Heer, *The Medieval World*, p. 90. For estimates of around two hundred, see Lensen and Heitling, *De Geschiedenis van de Hanze*, p. 17; Du Boulay, *Germany in the Later Middle Ages*, p. 133.

90. Leuschner mentions the Wendish, Saxon, Prussian, Rhenisch, Westphalian, and Brandenburg groups. *Germany in the Late Middle Ages*, p. 145. Wernicke mentions the Wendish towns, the Prussian, the Livonian, the Westphalian, the Dutch towns on the Southern Sea, and the Saxon group. "Die Städtehanse," p. 31. See also Weiner, "The Hansa," p. 220. Some of this variation depends on the period chosen by the historian. After 1500 many of the towns in Russia had fallen under territorial control.

91. Dollinger, *The German Hansa*, p. 51. Ennen gives a similar ordering in *The Medieval Town*, p. 173.

92. Lensen and Heitling, *De Geschiedenis van de Hanze*, pp. 22–23.

93. Dollinger, *The German Hansa*, pp. 98, 99.

94. Wernicke, "Die Städtehanse," p. 63. For example, the eighteen board members of Bruges were divided into three *Drietel* ("thirds") of six. Each third represented the towns of its regional group.

95. Wernicke, "Die Städtehanse," p. 56. Smaller Hansa settlements (Niederlassungen) were supervised by mother towns (Funktionalstädte). Antwerp, for example, was supervised by Dortmund.

96. This is a general phenomenon. Where merchants face a variety of local obstacles to trade and lack some reliable enforcement mechanism, they must rely on self-help mechanisms. To guarantee that agents in the field are not cheating and to have access to

help overseas, individuals rely on group associations and social mechanisms to overcome short-run, self-interested behavior. The most common method is to conduct trade through members of the family. Consequently, ethnic communities with strong kinship affiliations are prevalent in long-distance trade in general. See, for example, Philip Curtin, *Cross-Cultural Trade in World History* (1984). De Roover notes the general principal-agent problem in commerce. From necessity, agents have a large amount of freedom. De Roover, "The Organization of Trade," p. 87.

97. Lensen and Heitling, *De Geschiedenis van de Hanze*, p. 41.

98. The logic of overcoming collective action problems by establishing some semblance of hierarchy and reducing the number of actors involved is, of course, also well known in today's business practices. See, for example, the account of Charles Lipson on how the major banks subdivide responsibilities to control a larger number of subordinate banks in the restructuring of Latin American debt. Charles Lipson, "Bankers' Dilemmas: Private Cooperation in Rescheduling Sovereign Debts," in Kenneth Oye, ed., *Cooperation Under Anarchy* (1986), pp. 200–225.

99. Weiner, "The Hansa," p. 229.

100. Rörig, *The Medieval Town*, chapter 2.

101. This is Wernicke's main contention. He draws particular attention to the existence of enforcement rules by majority decisions in the Hansetag. Wernicke, "Die Städtehanse," p. 12f. Georg Fink suggests that the Hansa was not really a confederation because it did not have a founding document and did not wage war using all its members. He argues that wars were only conducted by a given number of members within the Hansa. Fink, however, acknowledges that the Hansa performed the tasks noted by Dollinger and Wernicke. Georg Fink, "Die Rechtliche Stellung der Deutschen Hanse in der Zeit ihres Niedergangs," *Hansische Geschichtsblätter* 61 (1936), pp. 122–137.

102. Lensen and Heitling, *De Geschiedenis van de Hanze*, pp. 31–32.

103. Wernicke, "Die Städtehanse," p. 114.

104. Dollinger, *The German Hansa*, p. 211.

105. Dollinger, *The German Hansa*, p. 332; Lensen and Heitling, *De Geschiedenis van de Hanze*, p. 37.

106. For brief discussions of the Hansa and some of these conflicts, see de Roover, "The Organization of Trade," p. 185; Ennen, *The Medieval Town*, p. 174; Holborn, *A History of Modern Germany*, p. 74.

107. For example, records show that Deventer was assessed and paid 1,000 pounds in 1368 and 1369 prior to the war with Denmark. In 1394 towns were assessed for a certain number of troops and armed contingents, again against Denmark. Lübeck was to contribute 6 cogs with 100 men each, including 20 archers. Stralsund was assessed 4 ships, Greifsfeld 2, and Stettin 2, and the Prussian towns were to contribute 10 ships with 100 men each. Lensen and Heitling, *De Geschiedenis van de Hanze*, pp. 140–143. See also the discussion of the Tohopesate, the league assessment of armed troops, in Wilhelm Bode, "Hansische Bundesbestrebungen in der ersten Hälfte des 15. Jahrhunderts," *Hansische Geschichtsblätter* 25 (1919), pp. 173–246 and 26 (1920/21), pp. 174–193. Wernicke notes that there were special decisions and agreements by the Hanse Tag to raise troops and revenue for war. Wernicke, "Die Städtehanse," pp. 75, 114, 158.

108. For discussions of the nature and effects of such boycotts or blockades, see Lönnroth, "The Baltic Countries," p. 393; Dollinger, *The German Hansa*, pp. 48, 72; and Lensen and Heitling, *De Geschiedenis van de Hanze*, p. 164.

109. Even as late as the Peace of Westphalia (1648), the Hansa sought, and gained, limited representation as a league. This recognition as an international actor was highly

contested. Soon thereafter the league was not recognized as such, and even the recognition at Westphalia was only on certain issues. It is interesting to note, and this is important in terms of status as an international actor, that the imperial cities were recognized without objection. Hans-Bernd Spies, "Lübeck, die Hanse und der Westfälische Frieden," *Hansische Geschichtsblätter* 100 (1982), pp. 110–124.

110. Rörig, *The Medieval Town*, p. 36; Dollinger, *The German Hansa*, p. 361; Lensen and Heitling, *De Geschiedenis van de Hanze*, p. 32.

111. Rörig, *The Medieval Town*, p. 168; Behr, "Die Landgebietspolitik," p. 19.

112. For a discussion of the law merchant, see W. A. Bewes, *The Romance of the Law Merchant* (1923); Lensen and Heitling, *De Geschiedenis van de Hanze*, p. 13. For the spread of "families" of law codes, see Fuhrmann, *Germany in the High Middle Ages*, p. 80; Ennen, *The Medieval Town*, pp. 109–110; Heer, *The Medieval World*, p. 94. Weiner suggests that Lübeck law was adopted by nineteen towns by 1300. Urban submits that eventually one hundred cities governed themselves by Lübeck law. Weiner, "The Hansa, " p. 218; William Urban, "Lübeck," in Strayer, *Dictionary of the Middle Ages*, vol. 7, p. 680.

113. "Damit schufen die hansischen Städtemitglieder ein relativ geschlossenes Rechtssystem" (With that the Hansa city members created a relatively closed legal system). Wernicke, "Die Städtehanse," p. 124.

114. Wernicke makes that point. "Die Städtehanse," p. 12f.

115. For this description of Postan's position, see Rotz, "German Towns," p. 460.

116. Rörig, *The Medieval Town*, p. 27.

117. Giddens, *The Nation-State and Violence*, p. 80.

CHAPTER 7

1. From the chronicles of Otto of Freising, *The Deeds of Frederick Barbarossa* (1953). The bishop, the uncle of the emperor, narrated the first years of Frederick Barbarossa's reign (1152–1156). After Otto of Freising's death, the narrative was brought up to 1160 by Rahewin. Freising here laments the strength of the Italian towns and their unwillingness to submit to the emperor.

2. Lauro Martines, *Power and Imagination* (1979), p. 9.

3. Anderson, *Lineages of the Absolutist State*, p. 46.

4. Rotz, "German Towns," p. 464.

5. Daniel Waley, *The Italian City-Republics* (1969), p. 84.

6. For the Genoese estimate, see Scammel, *The World Encompassed*, p. 161. The Venetians had about 20,000 men available for war by the early fifteenth century. In 1450 they could muster approximately 40,000 land and 20,000 naval forces. Denys Hay and John Law, *Italy in the Age of the Renaissance, 1380–1530* (1989), p. 89; William McNeill, *Venice: The Hinge of Europe, 1081–1797* (1974), p. 70.

7. Scammel, *The World Encompassed*, p. 86.

8. Scammel, *The World Encompassed*, pp. 86, 90, 101. For a similar description of Italian trade, see de Roover, "The Organization of Trade," p. 100. De Roover also notes that the galleys used for such transport were not suited for bulk trade because of their high freight costs and inability to take large loads. Because of the low-volume, high-value nature of trade, the number of ships engaged in such commerce was relatively small. "In good years, Venice sent out several fleets: twelve galleys . . . to Syria and Alexandria, four to Constantinople, four or five to Flanders and England, and two or three to Barbary." De Roover, p. 101.

9. Braudel, *The Perspective of the World*, p. 103.

10. Schumann suggests a profit margin of 20 to 100 percent. Reinhold Schumann, *Italy in the Last Fifteen Hundred Years* (1986), p. 107. Scammel notes a profit margin of about 40 percent but suggests that Genoese privateering, which was not that different from their regular trading practices, yielded profit margins of 50 to 100 percent. Scammel, *The World Encompassed*, pp. 101, 200. Waley believes profits of up to 150 percent were possible. Waley, *The Italian City-Republics*, p. 47. For the average investor, who was not a direct partner in a venture, profits were also high. Braudel argues that these would be around 40 percent. Braudel, *The Perspective of the World*, p. 121. De Roover suggests that short trips would yield profits of about 25 percent and that longer trips, such as from Genoa to Constantinople would yield about 42.5 percent. De Roover, "The Organization of Trade," p. 56. McNeill also finds profit margins of about 40 percent. *Venice*, p. 61. Kedar, analyzing the recession of the fourteenth century, suggests that profit margins were a good deal lower for that period. But even in the later part of the fourteenth century it was possible to make reasonable profits of between 33 and 36 percent per year, as the commoner Nicolo Picacio did. Benjamin Kedar, *Merchants in Crisis* (1976), pp. 64–65.

11. Scammel, *The World Encompassed*, p. 128. See also McNeill, *Venice*, for a discussion of their maritime technology.

12. Scammel, *The World Encompassed*, p. 159.

13. It was rather appropriately called the Synod of the Corpse. Schumann, *Italy in the Last Fifteen Hundred Years*, p. 33.

14. According to some historians, this occurred along feudal lines, which system had been introduced by the Carolingians. Schumann, *Italy in the Last Fifteen Hundred Years*, p. 31. Others, such as Tabacco, see this as less feudal, because the counts and dukes were basically freeholders rather than holders of fiefs, subject to the emperor. However, even Tabacco admits that the second in line held as vassals, similar to the feudal system. Giovanni Tabacco, *The Struggle for Power in Medieval Italy* (1989), p. 159.

15. Schumann, *Italy in the Last Fifteen Hundred Years*, p. 76.

16. As I have previously discussed, Pirenne's argument concerning the nature of long-distance commerce and the growth of towns has largely been substantiated, particularly regarding northwestern Europe. However, his claim that the Carolingian Empire rose because the Muslims had basically closed off Mediterranean commerce has been severely contested. For an overview of this debate, see Havighurst, *The Pirenne Thesis*.

17. Martines, *Power and Imagination*, p. 18. However, by some accounts these communes first appeared around 1015. See Ennen, *The Medieval Town*, p. 119.

18. Schumann sees the commune as an association directed against secular and ecclesiastical lords and royal control. Schumann, *Italy in the Last Fifteen Hundred Years*, pp. 81, 88. Martines has the same view in *Power and Imagination*, pp. 18–21. Tabacco emphasizes the anti-ecclesiastical nature of the commune and sees it as "an urban collectivity which was potentially able to provide itself with an autonomous political order, in the shadow of and in opposition to the power of the prelate." Tabacco, *The Struggle for Power*, p. 185. For a similar evaluation, see Barraclough, *The Origins of Modern Germany*, p. 149.

19. Martines, *Power and Imagination*, pp. 14, 175.

20. Waley, *The Italian City-Republics*, pp. 57, 58.

21. Tabacco, *The Struggle for Power*, p. 219; Schumann, *Italy in the Last Fifteen Hundred Years*, p. 62; Waley, *The Italian City-Republics*, p. 111.

22. Martines, *Power and Imagination*, p. 16.

23. Tabacco denies, in fact, that the election of the communal government, the rule by consuls, was styled after the Romans, despite the similarity in titles. But for opposing views, see Ennen, *The Medieval Town*, p. 119; Abulafia, *Frederick II*, p. 67.

24. The Lombards had gradually been assimilated under Roman culture and adopted written law. This presence of written law was further aided by the proximity of Byzantine rule, which maintained a foothold in Italy until 1059, and the Papal State, both of which maintained written law. Schumann, *Italy in the Last Fifteen Hundred Years*, pp. 76, 77. Brown notes that the theory of classical republicanism was important because it provided a model of political order without the church. Alison Brown, "Florence, Renaissance and Early Modern State: Reappraisals," *Journal of Modern History* 56 (June 1984), p. 299.

25. The focus on northern Italy, rather than on Italy as a whole, has several reasons. First, virtually all the large towns, except three, were located in the north. The independent city-states thus arose in the north. Second, the southern towns were dominated by foreign powers, first the Byzantines, then the Normans, Hohenstaufen, French, and Aragonese. They never developed the autonomy of the northern city-states. For the Norman policy toward towns, see Abulafia, *Frederick II*, p. 16. Ennen discusses the lesser development of southern Italy. Ennen, *The Medieval Town*, p. 147.

26. Martines, *Power and Imagination*, p. 14.

27. Tabacco, *The Struggle for Power*, p. 148.

28. Waley, *The Italian City-Republics*, p. 24.

29. Diane Owen-Hughes, "Urban Growth and Family Structure in Medieval Italy," *Past and Present* 66 (February 1975), p. 5; Martines, *Power and Imagination*, p. 11.

30. Hibbert contrasted the towns of northwestern Europe to those of Italy in order to criticize Henri Pirenne's old (1925) thesis that new mercantile towns were dramatically different from the old towns dominated by the nobles. Hibbert, "The Origins of the Medieval Town Patriciate," pp. 15–27. Arguably, however, Pirenne in fact limits his conclusions to northwestern Europe. Hence, both Pirenne and Hibbert reaffirm the distinct nature of the Italian towns.

31. See Rörig, *The Medieval Town*; Straus, "Germany: 1254–1493," in Strayer, *Dictionary of the Middle Ages*, vol. 5, p. 490f.

32. Genoa obliged its landed aristocracy to live in the city for a certain number of days per year. Likewise, Florence required the feudal aristocracy to live in town. Ennen, *The Medieval Town*, pp. 118, 143.

33. Heer, *The Medieval World*, p. 75.

34. Schumann, *Italy in the Last Fifteen Hundred Years*, p. 53.

35. Le Goff, *Time, Work, and Culture*, p. 69; Anderson, *Passages from Antiquity to Feudalism*, p. 165.

36. Although feudalism also contained Roman elements, the strong influence of Germanic custom was a critical element in the feudal character of German and French relations. Both Stephenson and Poggi see Roman authority as distinct from feudal principles of rule. Poggi, *The Development of the Modern State*, pp. 19, 26; Stephenson, *Mediaeval Institutions*, p. 210.

37. Waley, for example, notes the persistence of a military ethos which denigrated the commoner. Waley, *The Italian City-Republics*, p. 48.

38. McNeill views this combination as a critical element in explaining the success of the Italian maritime cities. McNeill, *Venice*, particularly chapter 2.

39. For the Genoese, piracy, trade, and war were all intertwined. See, for example, Scammel, *The World Encompassed*, pp. 157–159.

40. That the inhabitants of the towns were quite aware of these differences is well discussed by Martines, *Power and Imagination*, p. 46.

41. Schumann, *Italy in the Last Fifteen Hundred Years*, p. 116.

42. For example, the Alberghi, the clans in Genoa, thus claimed that their genealogy was traceable to that of old Roman patricians. Scammel, *The World Encompassed*, p. 210. Such clans consisted of kin, clients, and neighbors who were willing to take the same last name and aid each other. Hay and Law, *Italy in the Age of the Renaissance*, p. 246.

43. John Mundy, "Medieval Urban Liberty," manuscript (1993), p. 7.

44. Martines, *Power and Imagination*, p. 30.

45. Owen-Hughes, "Urban Growth and Family Structure," pp. 3, 20, 23.

46. This also served to demarcate nobles from commoners, since the latter did not have this extended family concept.

47. Martines, *Power and Imagination*, p. 35.

48. Waley, *The Italian City-Republics*, p. 175f.; Owen-Hughes, "Urban Growth and Family Structure," p. 6; Martines, *Power and Imagination*, p. 36.

49. Confusingly, *popolo* might sometimes also refer to nobles. In that context, it was used as an honorary title, because these were "good" nobles who were on the side of the popolo (commoners). Waley, *The Italian City-Republics*, p. 167. For another enumeration of these different groups, see also Heer, *The Medieval World*, pp. 78–79.

50. Martines, *Power and Imagination*, p. 77.

51. Waley, *The Italian City-Republics*, pp. 197–199.

52. These geographic divisions still exist today. They are, for example, symbolized by the palio horse race in Siena in which each of the contrade sends its champion. Dundes and Falassi note that these contrade almost formed city-states within the city, with their own government, flag, armed companies, and constitution. Alan Dundes and Alessandro Falassi, *La Terra in Piaza* (1975), p. 13.

53. "In many towns the inhabitants of the different rioni gathered in the main square to throw stones at each other, a violent sport in which there were many casualties; at Siena the bactallia in campo Fori between the three regions (terzi) is witnessed by documents as early as 1238. Stone throwing of this sort was an organized sport in a number of towns, as were various other forms of fighting and wrestling." Waley, *The Italian City-Republics*, p. 199.

54. Schumann, *Italy in the Last Fifteen Hundred Years*, p. 35.

55. Ibid., p. 48.

56. Tabacco, *The Struggle for Power*, p. 240.

57. To appease the pope, who feared German control of northern and southern Italy, the emperor argued that the kingdom of Sicily (the regnum) was not part of the empire (the imperium). Thus the king of Sicily need not be in the hands of the German emperor. This was of course but a legalistic ploy since factual control remained in the hands of the Hohenstaufen.

58. By some estimates Sicilian revenues equaled half those of France. Tabacco, *The Struggle for Power*, p. 249. The revenues from Palermo alone purportedly rivaled those of the entire English kingdom. Abulafia, *Frederick II*, p. 14. (Abulafia is unclear on whether that was an accurate estimate.)

59. The Guelphs named themselves after the Welfs, the Saxon opponents of the king in Italy. *Ghibelline* refers to the Hohenstaufen castle Waiblingen. At one point, Tuscany thus tended to favor the emperor, whereas the Lombard towns tended to favor the pope. Barraclough, *The Origins of Modern Germany*, p. 150. For reasons why factions within the towns might favor the Hohenstaufen, see Abulafia, *Frederick II*, p. 72.

60. Waley, *The Italian City-Republics*, p. 201.

61. He claimed that he was the legitimate overlord of Sicily since he had granted this area to the Normans for their ousting of the Muslims.

62. For a discussion of this episode, see Schumann, *Italy in the Last Fifteen Hundred Years*, p. 111; Tabacco, *The Struggle for Power*, p. 247.

63. Schumann, *Italy in the Last Fifteen Hundred Years*, p. 113f: Tabacco, *The Struggle for Power*, p. 252f.

64. Nevertheless, as late as 1313 Henry VII would still claim universal domination. Tabacco, *The Struggle for Power*, p. 269.

65. Waley, *The Italian City-Republics*, p. 210. These terms continued to be used even after the decline of the Hohenstaufen and the decline of the French fortunes in Sicily.

66. Thus Castruccio Castracani converted the podesta in Lucca, a temporary position, into a permanent despotism by allying with Ghibelline forces in the city. Louis Green, "Lucca under Castruccio Castracani," *I Tatti Studies* 1 (1985), pp. 137–159.

67. Waley, *The Italian City-Republics*, p. 206; Tabacco, *The Struggle for Power*, p. 261.

68. Moreover, because of their fierce struggles, the church and empire succeeded in demythologizing their own claims to rule. Tabacco, *The Struggle for Power*, p. 221.

69. See Tabacco, *The Struggle for Power*, p. 215, for this argument. This conforms with my earlier general assessment of the tension between feudal organization and urban life.

70. For the abstractness of protocapitalist relations, see Becker, *Medieval Italy*. For a good discussion of Becker's work, see Janet Coleman, "The Civic Culture of Contracts and Credit." Coleman disagrees with Becker that public trust in the communal government was based on the availability of credit. Instead, she focuses on the political and social reasons why such an abstract set of social relations could develop. That is, for her, credit and abstract contract are a consequence of, rather than an anterior condition to, different political relations. Coleman's position is closer to my own.

71. Schumann, *Italy in the Last Fifteen Hundred Years*, p. 85.

72. Waley, *The Italian City-Republics*, p. 176.

73. Hay and Law, *Italy in the Age of the Renaissance*, p. 4.

74. In accordance with the Germans' Norman predecessors, German imperial policy favored feudal obligations rather than seeking an urban alliance. "This was, clearly and unequivocally, a resumption of the preceding Norman experiment." Tabacco, *The Struggle for Power*, p. 245.

75. This might have been an additional reason why the German emperors tried to pursue a feudal strategy in Germany rather than seek an urban alliance.

76. For a discussion of this development, see Martines, *Power and Imagination*, p. 42; Schumann, *Italy in the Last Fifteen Hundred Years*, p. 120; Heer, *The Medieval World*, pp. 81–82. For an example of the functions and installation of the podesta, see the excerpt of John Viterbo's book on government (1228) in Mundy and Riesenberg, *The Medieval Town*, p. 121f, document 14.

77. Waley, *The Italian City-Republics*, p. 66. Because of the levels of violence, the size of the police force was always considerable. Bowsky suggests that Siena between 1280 and 1350 had a police to citizens ratio of between 1:73 and 1:145. The contemporary ratio for New York City is about 1:285. William Bowsky, "Keeping the Urban Peace," in Stanley Chodorow, ed., *The Other Side of Western Civilization*, vol. 1 (1973), pp. 176–187.

78. One cannot attribute the ascent of the signoria to internal strife alone. In many instances communes turned to seigneurial government even when internal strife was minimal. Martines, *Power and Imagination*, p. 71.

79. Schumann, *Italy in the Last Fifteen Hundred Years*, p. 111. Waley notes how these lords allied with the emperor or the Angevins; *The Italian City-Republics*, p. 231.

80. This example relies on Green, "Lucca under Castruccio Castracani."

81. Martines, *Power and Imagination*, p. 101.

82. For a discussion of the Venetian government, see Schumann, *Italy in the Last Fifteen Hundred Years*, p. 122; Hay and Law, *Italy in the Age of the Renaissance*, p. 34; McNeill, *Venice*, p. 34. Martines suggests that this amounted to thirty to forty family clans. Martines, *Power and Imagination*, pp. 131, 154f.

83. Hay and Law, *Italy in the Age of the Renaissance*, pp. 252, 259; Brown, "Florence," p. 288f.

84. Becker argues that oligarchy was the typical form of government in Florence from 1282 to 1382. Marvin Becker, "Some Aspects of Oligarchical, Dictatorial and Popular Signorie in Florence 1282–1382," *Comparative Studies in Society and History* 2 (July 1960), pp. 421–439.

85. Hans Baron agrees with Becker but suggests that this development continued past 1382. He notes as evidence, for example, the famous castato, the property tax of 1427, which went against the interests of the oligarchs, who opposed direct taxes. Hans Baron, "The Social Background of Political Liberty in the Early Italian Renaissance," *Comparative Studies in Society and History* 2 (July 1960), p. 446. He also notes how social mobility and the strength of an industrial middle class, based on wool manufacturing, kept the oligarchy at bay (p. 448).

86. Martines, *Power and Imagination*, p. 148.

87. See the discussion by Martines, *Power and Imagination*, p. 139.

88. Residency requirements for citizenship status could be as high as thirty years, as it was in Pisa. Waley, *The Italian City-Republics*, p. 106.

89. Peter Riesenberg, "Civism and Roman Law in Fourteenth-Century Italian Society," in Herlihy et al., eds., *Economy, Society and Government in Medieval Italy* (1969), p. 241. This differed quite markedly from the Hansa towns which openly copied laws and business practices from fellow Hansa members. It viewed non-Hansa individuals as distinct and forbade its members intermarriage, thus creating more social cohesion between the Hansa towns.

90. Glenn Olson, "Italian Merchants and the Performance of Papal Banking Functions in the Early Thirteenth Century," in Herlihy et al., *Economy, Society and Government in Medieval Italy*, pp. 43–63.

91. Scammel, *The World Encompassed*, p. 148.

92. Schumann, *Italy in the Last Fifteen Hundred Years*, p. 116f.

93. Braudel, *The Perspective of the World*, pp. 119, 120. For more extensive listings of Venetian revenues, see Lane, *Venice: A Maritime Republic*, p. 426; Michael Knapton, "City Wealth and State Wealth in Northeast Italy, 14th–17th Centuries," in Bulst and Genet, *La Ville, La Bourgeoisie et La Genèse de L'État Moderne*, p. 203; McNeill, *Venice*, p. 262, note 68. For revenues of other Italian towns in the 1470s, see Denys Hay, *Europe in the Fourteenth and Fifteenth Centuries* (1989), p. 180. For a discussion of the types of taxes, see Waley, *The Italian City-Republics*, pp. 78–81; McNeill, *Venice*, p. 71; Hay and Law, *Italy in the Age of the Renaissance*, p. 101; and Gene Brucker, *Renaissance Florence* (1969), p. 58.

94. Parry, *The Discovery of the Sea*, p. 70. Taxes in Genoa in 1293 yielded by some estimates three and a half times those of France; see Anderson, *Passages from Antiquity to Feudalism*, p. 193.

95. For a brief discussion of the rivalry between Genoa and Venice, see Janet Abu-Lughod, *Before European Hegemony* (1989), pp. 110, 121; Scammel, *The World Encompassed*, p. 96. For a chronicler's account of the brutal Pisan war in 1284, see the description of the Franciscan Salimbene in Mundy and Riesenberg, *The Medieval Town*, p. 107, document 6.

96. Hay and Law, *Italy in the Age of the Renaissance*, p. 113.

97. Brown, "Florence," pp. 298–299; Hay and Law, *Italy in the Age of the Renaissance*, p. 255.

98. McNeill, *Venice*, p. 123.

99. Martines, *Power and Imagination*, pp. 222, 228.

100. There were good reasons to try to keep with the old galley ships. First, the Mediterranean did not always provide sufficient wind. Furthermore, the Venetian Arsenal had perfected its design and was able to manufacture the ships along assembly-line techniques. Galleys were also difficult to combine with sailing ships. Hence, the Venetian navy would have had to be completely overhauled. Thus, although the Venetians experimented with alternative models, the galley remained the ship of preference. McNeill, *Venice*, p. 130.

101. Martines, *Power and Imagination*, p. 172. Although not as spectacular as the profits in long-distance commerce, profits on landed wealth could yield between 15 and 20 percent. Hay and Law, *Italy in the Age of the Renaissance*, p. 53.

102. This war was partially propelled by Florentine concerns over a secure grain supply. Florentine worry with their food supply was of long standing. In the thirteenth century, for example, they actually aided bishopric control over their contado provided the bishop remained subject to the town council and provided the city with grain. George Dameron, "Episcopal Lordship in the Diocese of Florence and the Origins of the Commune of San Casciano Val di Pesa, 1230–1247," *Journal of Medieval History* 12 (June 1986), pp. 135–154.

103. Heer, *The Medieval World*, p. 77.

104. Leuschner, *Germany in the Late Middle Ages*, p. 106; Hay and Law, *Italy in the Age of the Renaissance*, p. 275.

105. Paul Coles, "The Crisis of Renaissance Society: Genoa 1488–1507," *Past and Present* 11 (April 1957), p. 21.

106. I borrow the term from Charles Tilly, *Coercion, Capital, and European States*, p. 21.

107. Peter Burke, "City-States," in John Hall, ed., *States in History* (1986), pp. 142, 151. He goes on to provide a rather tautological definition of the city-state by essentially describing the character traits of the Italian city-state, but he provides no answer as to their differences with sovereign states.

108. That would also be empirically inaccurate. The Venetian republic was qua population no smaller than the Dutch Republic of the sixteenth century or Portugal. In territorial terms, it was also a good deal larger than the Dutch provinces, and yet Portugal and the Dutch Republic were to become world powers. In short, *small* is often used as a posterior assessment.

109. Giorgio Chittolini, "Cities, 'City-States,' and Regional States in North-Central Italy," *Theory and Society* 18 (September 1989), p. 699.

110. Tilly makes the general point that strong centralized states emerged where

towns were weakest. Charles Tilly, "Cities and States in Europe, 1000–1800," *Theory and Society* 18 (September 1989), pp. 563–584. I discuss the implications of the status of subject cities in greater detail in Chapter 8.

111. The reasons why this might be the case are potentially very interesting. I, however, do not deal with this topic in this book. I am not explaining why kings exist, or what special position they have. I merely wish to analyze how they operate vis-à-vis other political actors.

112. Braudel, *The Perspective of the World*, p. 89.

113. Note that I am not merely suggesting that the towns dominated the rural areas politically. One might, for example, counter that Paris also dominated the provinces. The population of the French provinces, however, were still full French subjects. The position of subjects in Italian territories almost resembled semicolonial status.

CHAPTER 8

1. Giddens, *The Nation-State and Violence*, p. 281.

2. My research strategy is endogenous. I explain the relative success of different institutions in a similar environment. That is, the advent of a monetarized economy with considerable trade eroded the old feudal order and gave rise to a variety of institutions. The changed economic context created roughly similar environmental opportunities for which some institutional responses were more suited than others. The alternative is ecological analysis which explains success of similar institutions in different types of environments. For the difference between these two strategies, see Robert Putnam et. al., "Explaining Institutional Success: The Case of Italian Regional Government," *American Political Science Review* 77 (March 1983), p. 55.

3. For the discussion of sovereignty as a constitutive element of the state system, see, for example, Onuf, "Sovereignty"; Robert Walker and Saul Mendlovitz, *Contending Sovereignties: Rethinking Political Community* (1990). Although my analysis focuses on the European alternatives to the state, the argument clearly has implications for the spread of this system of rule in general. That is, there were specific advantages to units that were internally hierarchical and limited in their territorial jurisdiction.

4. See, for example, Herbert Heaton, *Economic History of Europe* (1948), p. 259.

5. The popular account, however, that the circumnavigation of Africa by the Portuguese and Spanish pushed the Italians out of the spice trade is not uncontested. The Italians soon restored their trading position through the Mideast. See McNeill, *Venice*, p. 127; Martines, *Power and Imagination*, p. 171.

6. We have already seen this in the spread of the idea and organization of the independent commune. Similarly, early fiscal administration in Normandy and, through the Norman conquest, also in England paralleled developments in Capetian France.

7. For example, Gilpin, *War and Change*; Goldstein, *Long Cycles*.

8. Gilpin, *War and Change*, p. 42.

9. By competitive superiority I mean that the sovereign, territorial state survived and became the dominant form of organization in the international system, rather than its alternatives. Such superiority is not to be understood in a functionalist, teleological sense.

10. Gilpin, *War and Change*, p. 41.

11. Bean, "War and the Birth of the Nation State"; Dudley, "Structural Change in Interdependent Bureaucracies."

12. The *Adler*, for example, measured 3,000 tons and carried sixty-eight guns, perhaps the largest gun platform of its time. Dollinger, *The German Hansa*, p. 338.

13. White, *Medieval Religion and Technology*, p. 149f. This particular account is interesting in that it demonstrates how patent law was instrumental in bringing intellectual talent to England and in fostering inventions.

14. For a textbook account, see, for example, Lewis Spitz, *The Renaissance and Reformation Movements* (1971), chapter 9. Even very informed and sophisticated accounts sometimes suggest that efficiency of scale is critical. See, for example, Hay and Law, *Italy in the Age of the Renaissance*, p. 260; Tilly, *Coercion, Capital, and European States*, p. 65. Tilly, however, simultaneously notes the theoretical problem posed by the continued existence of small states.

15. See Ringrose, "Comment on Papers by Reed, de Vries, and Bean," p. 222f.

16. Mackenney argues that Venice was still a considerable military force by the late sixteenth century. In the 1570s it had about 33,000 troops which compared quite favorably with some sovereign states. The English army in Ireland, for example, numbered about 18,000 troops. Richard Mackenney, *The City-State* (1989).

17. Of course, I do not deny that the international arena is a predatorial one. Indeed, that is one core premise in explaining my view of institutional, unit selection. But the historical and empirical oddities suggest that an explanation of selection needs to account for some puzzling phenomena such as the success of relatively small entities.

18. Mark Greengrass, among others, notes the problem in his recent work. See Mark Greengrass, *Conquest and Coalescence* (1991), p. 4.

19. On this issue my focus lies close to that of North and Weingast, "Constitutions and Commitment." At some point size does matter. David does not always beat Goliath. However, I suggest that the efficiency of institutions has often been neglected whereas efficiency-of-scale arguments have been overemphasized.

20. For some of these explanations, see McNeill, *The Pursuit of Power*; Brian Downing, *The Military Revolution and Political Change* (1992); Geoffrey Parker, *The Military Revolution* (1988).

21. Myers, *Medieval Kingship*, p. 318.

22. Ronald Zupko, "Weights and Measures, Western European," in Strayer, *Dictionary of the Middle Ages*, vol. 12 (1989), p. 582. For a discussion of the variation in Mediterranean weights and measures, see Lopez and Irving, *Medieval Trade*, p. 11f.

23. For a fascinating account, see Witold Kula, *Measures and Men* (1986). Representational measurement lent itself to regional specificity. Even attempts at standardization were particularistic. For example, the standard ell in Bremen was allegedly defined as the distance between the knees of the statue of Roland in front of the town hall.

24. Kula, *Measures and Men*, pp. 5, 162, 163.

25. Held, "Hansische Einheitsbestrebungen."

26. Lensen and Heitling, *De Geschiedenis van de Hanze*, p. 24.

27. Held, "Hansische Einheitsbestrebungen," p. 166. "Bei den übrigen Massen ist eine Einheitlickeit nicht erzielt werden. . . . Nicht anders verhielt es sich mit den Längenmassen. . . . Was das Gewicht anbetrifft, so fehlte es auch da an einer Einheit" (With the other measures no unity was achieved. . . . It was no different with measures of length. As far as weight is concerned, there was no standardization either).

28. Lensen and Heitling, *De Geschiedenis van de Hanze*, p. 36.

29. The classic work on freeriding in the absence of a dominant actor is Mancur Olson, *The Logic of Collective Action* (1965).

30. Baldwin, *The Government of Philip Augustus*, p. 348.

31. See Hallam, *The Capetian Kings*, p. 284; Heaton, *Economic History of Europe*, pp. 289, 294.

32. Kula, *Measures and Men*, p. 168.

33. Ibid., p. 169.

34. Ibid., p. 220.

35. Ibid., pp. 172, 183.

36. Briggs, *Early Modern France*, p. 149. For a discussion of the efforts of the English Crown at standardization, see Ronald Zupko, *British Weights and Measures* (1977). See particularly chapter 3.

37. I am fully aware that this was a lengthy process. Economic standardization in France took many centuries to complete. The point is that such standardization can only come about when there is hierarchical authority with a claim to final jurisdiction. There needs to be an actor who can overcome freeriding. Thus Germany only standardized after 1870. See Zupko, "Weights and Measures."

38. See the tabulation in Kula, *Measures and Men*, p. 224.

39. "One can only imagine the difficulties of poor Thomas Betson, when into his counting-house there wandered in turn the Andrew guilder of Scotland, the Arnoldus gulden of Gueldres (very much debased), the Carolus groat of Charles of Burgundy, new crowns and old crowns of France, the David and Falewe of the Bishopric of Utrecht, the Hettinus groat of the Counts of Westphalia, the Lewe or French Louis D'Or, the Limburg groat, the Milan groat, the Nimuegen groat, the Phelippus or Phillipe d'Or of Brabant, the Plaques of Utrecht, the Postulates of various bishops, the English Ryall . . . the Scots Rider or the Rider of Burgundy . . . the Florin Rhenau of the Bishopric of Cologne and the Setillers. He had to know the value in English money of them all, as it was fixed by the time being by the Fellowship, and most of them were debased past all reason." Eileen Power, *Medieval People* (1963), p. 148.

40. There are two issues in this context with which we might be concerned: the diversity of coinage and the issue of debasement. My primary interest in this context is the variety of mints and coinage, which raised transaction and information costs. Debasement compounded the problem, because not only would merchants have had to figure out what the prevalent exchange rates were, but they would also have needed to have some idea of whether the currency to which they were exchanging had been debased or not, or was about to be debased. The complexity bedevils even modern economic historians. See Lopez and Raymond, *Medieval Trade*, p. 11.

41. Wilhelm Jesse, "Die Münzpolitik der Hansestädte," *Hansische Geschichtsblätter* 53 (1928), p. 79.

42. Dollinger, *The German Hansa*, p. 205f.

43. Peter Spufford, "Coinage and Currency," *The Cambridge Economic History of Europe*, vol. 2 (1987), p. 813. See also Leuschner's comments: "The more the German Empire split up into principalities, the more the princes were privileged to issue coins, the more important became the recurrent attempts—which it must be added, always failed—to maintain a uniform currency." Leuschner, *Germany in the Late Middle Ages*, p. 19.

44. See Holborn for that conclusion. The estimate of the number of local authorities is also his. Holborn, *A History of Modern Germany*, pp. 38–39, 68.

45. There were some attempts to simplify currency in the Wendish currency union, to which also some non-Hansa towns were part, but "they were only very partially adhered to." Dollinger, *The German Hansa*, p. 208.

46. Only for a brief period in medieval history, during the English kingdom of Wessex (970) through the Danish and Norman periods, until the reign of Henry II (1180), was English coin symbolic. That is, the value of the coin was not equivalent to the real

value of the coin in metal (silver, gold, or an alloy). Spufford, "Coinage and Currency," pp. 808, 809. The relative stability of English currency might account for the prevalence of sterling throughout the North Sea and Baltic, before the English made significant inroads there. Lewis and Runyan, *European Naval and Maritime History*, p. 142. Overall, merchants were aware that debasement was detrimental to their business. The charter of Speyer (not in the Hansa) had a clause that stated that "the coinage was not to be altered except with the common consent of the citizens." Ennen, *The Medieval Town*, p. 134. The Hansa towns, therefore, did not tend to debase their currency as a source of revenue. Dollinger, *The German Hansa*, p. 207. However, the minting of coinage in some Hansa towns, such as Westphalia, was still under the control of the bishops and hence less amenable to Hanseatic interests.

47. Particularly from Philip Augustus onward, kings tried to extend royal coinage through the entire realm. Berman, *Law and Revolution*, p. 467; Spufford, "Coinage and Currency," p. 809. For the large number of mints in France prior to centralization, see Duby, *The Early Growth of the European Economy*, p. 249; Spufford, "Coinage and Currency," pp. 802, 806.

48. Jordan, *Louis IX*, p. 208.

49. Myers, *Medieval Kingship*, p. 319.

50. Heaton, *Economic History of Europe*, p. 175. He also notes that "the German cities strove to conform to a common standard, but the general picture was one of great diversity."

51. Spufford, "Coinage and Currency," p. 812.

52. Spufford, "Coinage and Currency," p. 853. But this apparently occurred less than sometimes thought. Hicks argues that the currencies were actually relatively stable over the centuries. John Hicks, *A Theory of Economic History* (1969), pp. 88, 89. This was particularly true for the great currencies rather than the local ones.

53. Thus Philip the Fair could only use that policy instrument sporadically. Strayer, *The Reign of Philip the Fair*, pp. 394–395. Nobles and clergy, who increasingly relied on fixed rents, as well as bankers and ordinary merchants, became consistent enemies of such policies. See Fryde, "The Financial Policies," p. 834.

54. Cipolla notes how English coinage debased the least; French debased a good deal more, but less than that of the Italian city-states. This is partially due to nonpolitical factors such as the scarcity of precious metals. He argues that England debased the least because minting was centralized and the baronage would therefore not benefit from debasement, whereas the French system was less centralized, and hence they could debase their own coinage. Paradoxically, he notes that the Italian merchants benefited from debasement by requiring their credits to be paid in gold. My argument would suggest that the more fragmented sovereignties might have had reasons to debase more, perhaps because short-run strategies predominated in such systems. Carlo Cipolla, "Currency Depreciation in Medieval Europe," *The Economic History Review* 15 (1963), pp. 413–422.

55. Governments manipulated their currency, but "this situation generally discouraged outright debasement, since governments were aware of the dangerous implications this would have for their international position." Briggs, *Early Modern France*, p. 44. Note that this was an advantage of a competitive state system over imperial alternatives as in the Mideast and the Orient. See also Hall, *Powers and Liberties*, p. 137. Hicks also notes the possibility of capital flight. Hicks, *A Theory of Economic History*, p. 90.

56. Although kings of course had fiscal reasons to manipulate currency to their advantage, their authority was not unlimited. The townsfolk did resist, as in, for example, the

kingdom of Aragon. There "it was the merchants who put a stop to royal coin-debasing." Myers, *Medieval Kingship*, p. 227. Petit-Dutaillis notes how the Capetian kings consulted with the towns on currency issues. Petit-Dutaillis, *The Feudal Monarchy*, p. 238. In exchange for stability in currency, the towns made explicit agreements with high lords and kings to pay certain taxes. See, for example, the agreement with Philip Augustus in the early thirteenth century. Thomas Bisson, *Conservation of Coinage* (1979), p. 44.

57. Some standardization occurred within Germany and the Baltic when towns adopted the laws of their mother cities. But even so, this led to more than a dozen legal systems. Forty-three towns adopted Lübeck law, forty-nine Frankfurt law, four Hamburg law, and two Bremen law. Berman, *Law and Revolution*, p. 376.

58. It only drafted a formal constitution after the Hansetag of 1557.

59. For these claims of the king as arbitrator, see Jordan, *Louis IX*, pp. 202–203. Indeed, the whole idea of sovereignty, as it was gradually established by the scholars of Roman law and by the actual practice of kingship, was that the king was the final judge.

60. Hallam, *Capetian France*, p. 244.

61. "Contracts are to be honored." Berman, *Law and Revolution*, pp. 476, 477. "Other laws extended the royal coinage to the entire realm, enforced more rigorous control over the towns, and, in general, increased the efficiency of royal government."

62. We must be cautious, however, in identifying this with a modern state. The king did manage to codify local codes, and exercise high justice, but on many lesser issues the 80,000 seigneurial courts still had considerable local influence. Parker, *The Making of French Absolutism*, p. 22. Consolidation was under way, but it was a slow and gradual process.

63. Webber and Wildavsky, *A History of Taxation*, p. 198. See also Miller, "Government Economic Policies," p. 346. For a longer time perspective on French royal finance, see Collins, *The Fiscal Limits of Absolutism*, who suggests that the tax system from the Late Middle Ages went unchanged for many centuries.

64. This does not always have to be a problem for a city-league provided it can overcome collective action problems. For example, Athens was so predominant in the Delian League that it could enforce compliance with general levies on all its members. Donald Kagan, *The Outbreak of the Peloponnesian War* (1969), p. 98f. However, one might question whether this is more rightly called the Athenian Empire rather that a true league.

65. Guenee notes that the Rhineland states of the fifteenth century derived 60 percent of state revenue from tolls. Simultaneously, Louis XI (1461–1483) obtained most of his revenue by direct tax. Bernard Guenee, *States and Rulers* (1985), p. 109. From this we might conclude that the king had less reason to rely on the incidental tolls.

66. See Conybeare's account in *Trade Wars* (1987).

67. Matthias Puhle, "Der Sächsische Städtebund und die Hanse im Späten Mittelalter," p. 29.

68. Lensen and Heitling, *De Geschiedenis van de Hanze*, p. 155.

69. T. H. Lloyd, *England and the German Hanse 1157–1611* (1991), p. 175. The Zuiderzee and Prussian towns were unwilling to support the Wend towns in their war with Denmark in 1426. Dollinger, *The German Hansa*, p. 296. In the War of the Roses in England, the Hanseatics differed on which claimant to support. Weiner, "The Hansa," p. 238.

70. Heaton, *Economic History of Europe*, p. 259; Lloyd, *England and the German Hanse*, pp. 361–362.

71. Ralph Davis, *English Overseas Trade 1500–1700* (1973), p. 29; Dollinger, *The German Hansa*, p. 359.

72. Davis, *English Overseas Trade*, p. 43. In other words, Hanseatic decline started well before the Thirty Years War.

73. Lübeck and the other Wend towns were no doubt the most important elements in the league. Wernicke, "Die Städtehanse," p. 28. Nevertheless, Lübeck was almost excluded from the league in 1440 for acting against the league's best interest.

74. Dietrich Schäfer, "Zur Frage nach der Einführung des Sundzolls," *Hansische Geschichtsblätter* 5 (1875), pp. 33–43.

75. Davis, *English Overseas Trade*, p. 11.

76. Miller, "Government Economic Policies," p. 356.

77. Already in the thirteenth century, royal interventionism proved beneficial to newly incorporated areas. In Languedoc, for example, trade expanded following the ousting of local coin and the implementation of early mercantilist policies of the Capetians. Given, *State and Society*, pp. 145–146.

78. Heaton, *Economic History of Europe*, p. 289; Braudel, *The Perspective of the World*, p. 315.

79. John Nef, *Industry and Government in France and England 1540–1640* (1957), chapter 3.

80. Bernard notes how in the fourteenth century there were forty tolls on the Garonne and more than seventy on the Loire, which added more than 20 percent to the price. On the Seine, such tolls added up to 50 percent. Bernard, "Trade and Finance in the Middle Ages," p. 313. Colbert tried to reduce the number of tolls by dividing the country into three zones. In the north, in the Cinq Grandes Fermes, there were to be no tolls at all. The two other areas of France were regarded as "reputed foreign" and "effectively foreign," and movement between these zones thus still required customs. Heaton, *Economic History of Europe*, p. 298. Even though Braudel suggests that the importance of these tolls is overstated, since they did not raise the price on many commodities by a high margin, he does note that even as late as the nineteenth century there were still many tolls that were time consuming. Braudel, *The Perspective of the World*, p. 290.

81. The English king had started with mercantilist type policies at an even earlier date. Edward II tried to prevent imports of foreign cloth in the early fourteenth century. By 1331 Edward III was trying to attract Flemish weavers. In 1381 the English Crown passed its first navigation acts, thus precluding foreigners from transporting English goods. (Hence the importance of gaining privileges such as those of the Hansa which provided exceptions to such regulations.) Shepard Clough, *The Economic Development of Western Civilization* (1959), p. 115.

82. Parker, *The Making of French Absolutism*, p. 17. Likewise Poggi argues that towns favored the commercial extension of the sovereign state. Poggi, *The Development of the Modern State*, pp. 63, 64, 78. Central government also had an interest in protecting taxpayers from aristocratic and ecclesiastical exploitation. Briggs, *Early Modern France*, p. 50. Rörig likewise notes that the towns tended to favor the king because they preferred a large unified area of trade. Rörig, *The Medieval Town*, p. 182.

83. The Hundred Years War was a major factor in this development. The later stages of this war, in the middle of the fifteenth century, saw the formation of standing Companies d'Ordonnances of approximately 12,000 men. C. W. Previté-Orton, ed., *The Shorter Cambridge Medieval History*, vol. 2 (1971), p. 983. But note that this development only reinforced the monarchy. By then the position of the king as the logical defender of the realm had already been established.

84. For some evidence on this point, see Vallee, "État et Securité Publique," The king was particularly opposed to aristocrats' negotiations with the English.

85. The quote is from the French historian Olivier-Martin in Rowen, *The King's State*, p. 13.

86. When Charles VII was willing to cede Normandy to the English during the Hundred Years War, the bishop of Laon objected because the king was "the administrator, tutor, curator, and procurator" of the kingdom. Rowen, *The King's State*, p. 23.

87. Kantorowicz, *The King's Two Bodies*, p. 126. The law became synonymous with the king. "Lex est rex."

88. Ibid., pp. 95–96.

89. Ibid., p. 340.

90. Dollinger, *The German Hansa*, p. xvii.

91. Lewis and Runyan, *European Naval and Maritime History*, p. 152.

92. Holborn notes that the Hansa did not close its ranks against territorial lords in Holland, England, and Russia. Holborn, *A History of Modern Germany*, pp. 81–82. Rörig notes that the Hansa ultimately lost to England because it lacked a central power. Rörig, *The Medieval Town*, p. 70. Dollinger argues that "the main cause of the Hanseatic failure . . . was their lack of unity." Dollinger, *The German Hansa*, p. 195. Lloyd emphasizes the divergent interests of regional versus Hanseatic diets. Lloyd, *England and the German Hanse*, p. 366. Puhle notes how the Saxon towns were gradually subjected to territorial rulers during the 1480s and 1490s without much aid from the Hansa. Puhle, "Der Sächsische Städtebund," p. 30. Likewise the towns in Livonia gradually came under Swedish and Russian territorial influence. Dollinger, *The German Hansa* p. 338.

93. Scammel, *The World Encompassed*, pp. 44, 64; Dollinger, *The German Hansa*, p. 344; Holborn, *A History of Modern Germany*, pp. 82, 85.

94. Hicks, *A Theory of Economic History*, p. 60.

95. Dollinger, *The German Hansa*, p. 367.

96. In effect, Giddens raises the same issue. Transnational communication and exchange require the state's administration of domestic conditions (such as the maintenance of property rights) and reciprocal agreements between states. For a discussion of this point, see Justin Rosenberg, "A Non-Realist Theory of Sovereignty? Giddens' 'The Nation-State and Violence,'" *Millenium* 19 (1990), p. 254.

97. Lloyd, *England and the German Hanse*, p. 294.

98. Ibid., p. 304.

99. Fink, "Die Rechtliche Stellung der Deutschen Hanse," p. 134. Although the Hansa had actually handed over a list in reaction to the demands of the Privy Council in 1560, the English objected to the inclusion of certain towns, and the Hansa did not accept the final agreement. Lloyd, *England and the German Hanse*, p. 319. The demand for such a list, by the way, preceded this period by more than a century. On the English demands for such a list, also see Weiner, "The Hansa," p. 226.

100. Dollinger, *The German Hansa*, p. 85f.

101. The Hansa thus refused to provide a list because such a list "might be used as a basis for collective claims for compensation and demands for indemnities." The Hansa refused to accept that principle. Dollinger, *The German Hansa*, pp. 86, 106–107. For another argument that the Hansa deliberately obfuscated membership to avoid responsibility, see Volker Henn, "Die Hanse: Interessengemeinschaft oder Städtebund?" *Hansische Geschichtsblätter* 102 (1984), p. 120.

102. Lloyd, *England and the German Hanse*, p. 370.

103. "Finally, it was difficult to enforce any agreements that were reached, primarily

because of domestic disunity on both sides. . . . The English claimed it was difficult to control piracy and the Hanse found it nearly impossible to get any trade agreement with England adhered to by all Hanse cities." Conybeare, *Trade Wars*, p. 115. (During the time focused on by Conybeare, English disunity was due to the War of the Roses.) See also Zupko who notes that the Hansa used the internal dissent to obtain better privileges. Zupko, *British Weights and Measures*, p. 72.

104. Lloyd, *England and the German Hanse*, pp. 204, 311.

105. Lensen and Heitling, *De Geschiedenis van de Hanze*, p. 148.

106. Bernard, "Trade and Finance," p. 314.

107. For an example, see Mundy and Riesenberg, *The Medieval Town*, p. 42.

108. For an illuminating example, see Cheyette, "The Sovereign and the Pirates."

109. This was not unique to the French Crown. Sawyer says this of the English king: "One of the prerogatives claimed by the English kings in the thirteenth and fourteenth centuries was the right to regulate merchants and commerce. They freed particular groups of merchants from various obligations, they licensed markets, granted charters of privilege to boroughs and to guilds of merchants and craftsmen, they levied customs and controlled the coinage. One obvious motive was to increase revenue." P. H. Sawyer and I. N. Wood, eds., *Early Medieval Kingship* (1977).

110. See Thomson, "Sovereignty in Historical Perspective," and her discussion of the control of nonstate coercive force in "State Practices, International Norms, and the Decline of Mercenaries."

111. For the gradual shift of state policy regarding piracy, see Ritchie, *Captain Kidd and the War against the Pirates*.

112. In game theoretic terms, the interaction between the Hansa and sovereign states, such as England, proved to be noniterative. Arguably the Hansa preferred a situation of deadlock. It sought to maintain its monopoly over northern trade no matter what the other actor did. For a discussion of this logic, see Oye, *Cooperation Under Anarchy*, particularly chapter 1.

113. Nicholas Abercrombie, "Knowledge, Order and Human Autonomy," in James Hunter and Stephen Ainlay, eds., *Making Sense of Modern Times* (1986), p. 18.

114. This is Giddens's argument. "But imperial expansion tends to incorporate all significant economic needs within the domain of the empire itself, relations with groups on the perimeter tend to be unstable. . . . Imperial systems . . . do not adjoin other domains of equivalent power, as nation-states may do today." Giddens, *The Nation-State and Violence*, pp. 80–81. For a brief discussion of empire and economy, see also Wallerstein, *The Modern World System*, vol. 1, pp. 15, 16.

115. See the excellent discussion in Kratochwil, "Of Systems, Boundaries, and Territoriality."

116. Werner Link, "Reflections on Paradigmatic Complementarity in the Study of International Relations," in Czempiel and Rosenau, *Global Changes and Theoretical Challenges*, p. 101.

117. The properties of Hanseatic merchants thus acquired "a kind of extraterritoriality." They were administered by the bailiff of the local town, but Lübeck law exceeded all other, i.e., local law. Verlinden, "Markets and Fairs," pp. 148–149. In England the Hansa had acquired charters that granted them immunity from parliamentary statutes. Lloyd, *England and the German Hanse*, p. 375.

118. Holborn, *A History of Modern Germany*, p. 82.

119. Lloyd, *England and the German Hansa*, p. 181.

120. Lensen and Heitling, *De Geschiedenis van de Hanze*, p. 155.

121. Spies, "Lübeck, die Hanse und der Westfälische Frieden."

122. Ibid., p. 114. My translation.

123. The Peace of Westphalia in itself was only one point in a long process in which nonsovereign forms of organization were weeded out.

124. "The territorial rulers of Germany were the chief winners of the peace negotiations of Osnabrück and Münster. Their power over their own subjects, their ius territoriale, or droit de souveraineté, as the French draft called it, was recognized without reservations." Holborn also notes that "at the end of the Age of Reformation the states emerged as sovereign agencies in foreign affairs. At the same time their internal sovereignty had grown immensely." Holborn, *A History of Modern Germany*, pp. 371, 373.

125. There is some debate on the importance of Westphalia. Krasner argues that Westphalia was less important than often suggested and that developments toward a state system predated the Peace. Nor did the conference end medieval elements such as the free knights and the Holy Roman Empire. Krasner, "Westphalia." Although I agree that the Peace did not mark the beginning of a state system—indeed, my entire account dates the origin of the state several centuries earlier—the Peace was perceived as significant by contemporaries such as Pufendorf (see note 129). For contemporary arguments about the importance of Westphalia, see Kalevi Holsti, *Peace and War: Armed Conflicts and International Order 1648–1989* (1991), chapter 2; Adam Watson, *The Evolution of International Society* (1992), chapter 17. (There is also some confusion about terminology. Tilly, for example, speaks of the *Treaty* of Westphalia on page 165 of *Coercion, Capital, and European States*, but Krasner and most others use the term *Peace* since two conferences were involved.)

126. DiMaggio and Powell, "The Iron Cage Revisited." They place less emphasis on competition than I do. This is probably due to the fact that they are largely concerned with organizations within a domestic setting. Such an environment differs from the anarchical environment of international politics.

127. This is somewhat similar to what DiMaggio and Powell call *coercive isomorphism*. Such isomorphism results from "pressures exerted on organizations by other organizations upon which they are dependent and by cultural expectations in the society within which such organizations function." DiMaggio and Powell, "The Iron Cage Revisited," p. 150.

128. As in sovereign states that formed earlier, the use of Roman law was important, as was the recruitment from the burgher classes. Holborn, *A History of Modern Germany*, pp. 35, 57; Barraclough, *The Origins of Modern Germany*, pp. 279, 342, 349.

129. Consequently, Pufendorf observed in 1682: "But besides this, the Estates of Germany some of which have great and potent countries in their possession, have a considerable share of the Sovereignty over their subjects; and tho' they are Vassals of the Emperour and Empire, nevertheless they ought not to be consider'd as Subjects . . . for they are actually possess'd of the supreme Jurisdiction in the Criminal Affairs; they have power to make Laws and to regulate Church Affairs . . . to dispose of the Revenues rising out of their Own Territories; to make Alliances, as well among themselves as with Foreign States . . . they may build and maintain Fortresses and Armies of their own, Coin Money and the like." In Rowen, *From Absolutism to Revolution*, p. 75. See also Barraclough, *The Origins of Modern Germany*, p. 382.

130. In the discussion to come of the Italian city-states, I give a rough comparison of the growth of their respective revenues.

131. There is only sporadic evidence of individual assessments. The common treasury was only established by 1612, when the Hansa was just a shell of its former self.

132. The Reformation also contributed to centralization of authority in the many German principalities. The Reformation put control over ecclesiastical institutions squarely under the prince. Barraclough, *The Origins of Modern Germany*, p. 374. "The whole weight of the organized churches, including their influence over education and morality, was thrown into the scales on the side of government: they were content to preach the duty of obedience to divinely-appointed authority."

133. The emperor chose not to support the Hansa's claims against England. Lloyd, *England and the German Hanse*, p. 331. Religious differences between the Catholic emperor and the largely Protestant towns might have made cooperation more difficult.

134. Lensen and Heitling, *De Geschiedenis van de Hanze*, p. 37. For other descriptions of the Hansa's attempts to reinvigorate its organizational strength, see Dollinger, *The German Hansa*, p. 332f.

135. Weiner, "The Hansa," p. 247.

136. Leuschner, *Germany in the Late Middle Ages*, p. 139. Similarly, Barraclough argues that the German towns benefited from territorial princes through the reduction of localism. Barraclough, *The Origins of Modern Germany*, p. 351. This was not always a voluntary process; some towns were forced into making the choice. Brandenburg, for example, forced all its cities to leave the Hanseatic League. Holborn, *A History of Modern Germany*, p. 32.

137. Lensen and Heitling, *De Geschiedenis van de Hanze*, p. 39.

138. At the last Hanseatic Diet only three cities (Hamburg, Bremen, and Lübeck) were present.

139. Thus we find the oddity that at the signing of the Declaration of Paris—a treaty sponsored by France and England against piracy—many German cities and ministates signed on a par with the Netherlands, Sweden, and Portugal. Hamburg, Bremen, Lübeck, landlocked Frankfurt, Hanover, and many other German cities and territories each individually signed the treaty in 1856. See Thomson, "Sovereignty in Historical Perspective."

140. See Peter Burke on the difficulty of giving a general definition of city-states. In effect, he ends up simply describing the Italian city-states. Burke, "City-States."

141. For example, see the description of Francesco Pegolotti in Brucker, *Renaissance Florence*, p. 70.

142. Braudel, *The Perspective of the World*, p. 89.

143. Chittolini, "Cities, 'City-States,' and Regional States in North-Central Italy," p. 699. See also Wim Blockmans, "Voracious States and Obstructing Cities: An Aspect of State Formation in Preindustrial Europe," *Theory and Society* 18 (September 1989), pp. 733–756. Extension over other important towns was easier if local rule was left intact. See Hay and Law, *Italy in the Age of the Renaissance*, pp. 113–114.

144. Brian Pullan, ed., *Crisis and Change in the Venetian Economy in the Sixteenth and Seventeenth Centuries* (1968), p. 15. For a similar assessment, see Knapton, "City Wealth," p. 191. Mackenney sees in this a more federalist form of organization rather than subjection. Mackenney, *The City-State*, p. 49. In any case, it was not integrated as a coherent whole.

145. Eric Cochrane, *Florence in the Forgotten Centuries, 1527–1800* (1973), p. 9.

146. Runciman notes how in general the extension of citizenship is an important element of fostering allegiance with the dominant center. Runciman, *A Treatise on Social Theory*, p. 438.

147. Cochrane, *Florence in the Forgotten Centuries*, p. 66.

148. Hay and Law, *Italy in the Age of the Renaissance*, pp. 59, 105.

149. See Richard Rapp, *Industry and Economic Decline in Seventeenth Century Venice* (1976), p. 141.

150. There has been relatively little research on the period of economic decline. See, for example, Pullan's comments in the introduction to Pullan, *Crisis and Change*. Hay and Law note further that the history of the subject cities has been neglected. Hay and Law, *Italy in the Age of the Renaissance*, p. 113.

151. Hay and Law, *Italy in the Age of the Renaissance*, pp. 79–80.

152. Spufford, "Coinage and Currency," p. 814.

153. For this suggestion, see Braudel, *The Perspective of the World*, p. 289, although he does not delve deeply into this matter. See also Cochrane, *Florence in the Forgotten Centuries*, p. 66.

154. Knapton, "City Wealth," p. 189. Hocquet suggests that Venice was a mosaic of different communities. Venice "did not dream of issuing an ordinance that might have applied to the entire city-state." Jean-Claude Hocquet, "Venise, les Villes et les Campagnes de la Terreferme, XVe–XVIe Siècles," in Bulst and Genet, *La Ville, La Bourgeoisie*, p. 210.

155. Hay and Law, *Italy in the Age of the Renaissance*, p. 117; Cochrane, *Florence in the Forgotten Centuries*, p. 47; Eric Cochrane, *Italy 1530–1630* (1988), p. 9.

156. Cochrane, *Italy 1530–1630*, p. 47.

157. Hay and Law, *Italy in the Age of the Renaissance*, p. 261. Anderson is right in his assessment that in contrast to territorial monarchs, Italian leadership was often perceived as illegitimate. Anderson, *Lineages of the Absolutist State*, p. 163.

158. Hay and Law, *Italy in the Age of the Renaissance*, p. 118.

159. Benedict, for example, argues that French commerce and the wealth of the cities increased between 1560 and 1700, while this consolidation of a national economy was proceeding. Philip Benedict, *Cities and Social Change in Early Modern France* (1992), p. 31.

160. Hay and Law, *Italy in the Age of the Renaissance*, p. 157; Craig and George, *Force and Statecraft*, p. 11. And for a full discussion, see Mattingly, *Renaissance Diplomacy*.

161. Rice, *The Foundations of Early Modern Europe*, p. 115.

162. Braudel sometimes seems to suggest that city-states were simply too small. Braudel, *The Perspective of the World*, p. 61. At other times he dispels the notion that size is critical: "immediate visible differences—those of size and area—are less important than they appear." Instead what matters is that "cities and territories both attached themselves in identical fashion to an international political economy." Braudel, *The Perspective of the World*, p. 295. He goes on to argue that city-states might even have an advantage in that they focus on high added value commodities rather than agriculture. See pp. 296, 325. This comes far closer to my own view that success is determined by how well institutional forms cue in to the particular economic environment.

163. Cochrane, *Florence in the Forgotten Centuries*, pp. 51–59.

164. Ibid., p. 66.

165. Thus Woolf speaks of "obstacles to trade . . . and the survival of innumerable transit duties." There was a continued existence of "protectionist duties and internal barriers to trade" and "innumerable checks to internal trade." Stuart Woolf, *A History of Italy 1700–1860* (1979), pp. 52, 59, 60.

166. Cochrane, *Italy*, p. 48.

167. Lane, *Venice: A Maritime Republic*, p. 430; James Davis, *The Decline of the Venetian Nobility as a Ruling Class* (1962), pp. 109, 118–124.

168. Davis, *The Decline of the Venetian Nobility*, p. 104. Cochrane notes that the constitutional bodies of the city-states had to be nobles or citizens of the dominant city. There was thus little room for entry by influentials from the subject towns. Cochrane, *Italy*, p. 45.

169. Lane, *Venice: A Maritime Republic*, pp. 427, 431.

170. Rapp, *Industry and Economic Decline*, p. 160. Knapton notes several other areas in which Venice was reluctant to develop the mainland economy. Knapton, "City-Wealth," p. 194.

171. Woolf, *A History of Italy*, p. 63.

172. This is Romano's explanation. Ruggiero Romano, "Italy in the Crisis of the Seventeenth Century," in Peter Earle, ed., *Essays in European Economic History 1500–1800* (1984), p. 195.

173. Hay and Law, *Italy in the Age of the Renaissance*, p. 65.

174. Woolf, *A History of Italy*, p. 14. Feudal forms of tenure likewise survived as obstacles to the possession of full property rights (p. 51).

175. Woolf, *A History of Italy*, pp. 84–85. The task of such enlightened rulers was to remove obstacles to the economy and the code of law.

176. A rough indicator is revenue. By the end of the 1400s, Venetian revenue was roughly equal to that of France: approximately 1 million ducats. Counting the Terra Ferma, Venetian revenue was 60 percent higher. But then the French intake started to rise dramatically. During the reign of Charles VII (middle of the fifteenth century) revenue was between 1.8 and 2.25 million livres. By Francis I (1515–1547) that had gone up to 8 million. In 1549, it was 8.3 million and in the 1580s about 30 million. For these estimates see Collins, *The Fiscal Limits of Absolutism*, pp. 48, 51, 55. Parker estimates these revenues more conservatively and suggests that revenues in the 1620s were about 16 million, 33 million in 1635, and 38 million by 1640. Parker, *The Making of French Absolutism*, p. 140. For another set of estimates, roughly between those of Collins and Parker, see Richard Bonney, *The European Dynastic States 1494–1660* (1991), pp. 352–353. See also Briggs, *Early Modern France*, p. 213f. By contrast, Venetian revenue had only doubled by 1570 (2 million ducats), reached 2.45 million in 1602, and 3.4 million by 1621. Lane, *Venice: A Maritime Republic*, p. 426. Similar figures are provided by Rapp, *Industry and Economic Decline*, p. 141f. In real terms Venetian revenue was probably declining, whereas French revenue in real terms was increasing. Knapton, "City Wealth," p. 204. (Precise calculations are very difficult because inflation and the real intake of revenue are hard to estimate.)

177. Even so, we must be cautious when looking back into history. The size of the French army was not particularly great until the defeat of the Swedish at the battle of Nordlingen in 1634. Only then was there a significant rise in the number of troops. Downing, *The Military Revolution*, p. 121f.

178. The Dutch Republic would appear at first glance to violate this thesis, because of the considerable autonomy of its provinces. It should have had similar problems of defection and freeriding as the Hanseatic League and the Italian city-states. I would argue, however, that in practice the fragmentation of the republic was severely curtailed by the predominance of Amsterdam which by some accounts provided two-thirds of the Dutch budget. Mackenney, *The City-State*, p. 31. For a more conservative estimate, see R. J. Holton, *Cities, Capitalism and Civilization* (1986), p. 108. It would be interesting to examine, although I do not do it here, whether the failure of the Dutch to meet the challenge of the English was to some extent due to the lack of consolidation of the republic. Holton follows the historian Swart in suggesting that this was indeed the case. See also Boxer: "The result of this political deadlock was that nothing effective was done

to improve the condition of either the army or the navy." C. R. Boxer, *The Dutch Seaborne Empire 1600–1800* (1965), pp. 119–120.

179. Whereas some scholars have looked at relative efficiency and effectiveness between territorial states, I extend that argument to nonstate forms. My argument thus complements analyses that compare the relative merits of states such as that in North and Thomas, *The Rise of the Western World*, and North and Weingast, "Constitutions and Commitment." I do not claim that absolutist sovereign states were the best states available. Indeed, as North and Weingast show, more democratic forms might have had considerable advantages. I have, however, argued that sovereignty, with a hierarchical actor who can prevent freeriding and defection and who has a vested stake in overcoming localism, had advantages over institutional forms that failed to meet those criteria. Such advantages were internal as well as external.

180. Of course I recognize the implications of anarchy. Sovereigns might defect from agreements. The point is that the negotiators of the Hansa could not commit their members even if they wanted to, because a means of internal control over defectors was absent. Seen from the perspective of a two-level game, the Hanseatic negotiators could not credibly claim control over the domestic side of the bargain. Whatever might be agreed in international fora need not have had any bearing on the commitment of the Hanseatic members. Imagine, if you will, a contemporary analogue wherein international negotiators had little ability to commit their societies to the terms of a treaty. For some reflections on the nature of two-level games, see Robert Putnam, "Diplomacy and Domestic Politics: The Logic of Two-Level Games," *International Organization* 42 (Summer 1988), pp. 427–460.

181. Similarly, the postcolonial era empowered many societies as states. Jackson, "Quasi-states, Dual Regimes, and Neoclassical Theory." He argues that the African states clearly lacked the European traits of statehood but that they were juridically empowered as such. See also Giddens, *The Nation-State and Violence*, p. 272.

182. From a game theoretic perspective, these allow for long-run iterative benefits. See Axelrod, "The Emergence of Cooperation"; and his *The Evolution of Cooperation*.

183. See Nettl, "The State as a Conceptual Variable."

184. This view of the development of the state system concurs with Giddens's argument concerning agent-structure interaction. Giddens, *The Nation-State and Violence*. See also Dessler, "What's at Stake in the Agent-Structure Debate?"; Wendt, "The Agent-Structure Problem." Their arguments have largely been epistemological in nature with a call for more empirical work on the origins of the state. I believe this explanation is quite compatible with their intent.

CHAPTER 9

1. Rosenau, "Global Changes and Theoretical Challenges," p. 2.

2. For the argument that three roughly coequal regions are developing, see John Zysman, "Technology and Power in a Multi-Polar Global Economy," Berkeley Roundtable on International Economy (1990).

3. Strange and Russett both believe that American decline is vastly overstated. Susan Strange, "The Persistent Myth of Lost Hegemony," *International Organization* 41 (Autumn, 1987), pp. 551–574. Bruce Russett, "The Mysterious Case of Vanishing Hegemony: Or Is Mark Twain Really Dead?" *International Organization* 39 (Spring 1985), pp. 207–231. For a discussion of the hegemonic stability literature, see, for example, Keohane, *After Hegemony*.

4. One of the first to question the relevance of the state given the development of

nuclear weapons was John Herz, *The Nation-State and the Crisis of World Politics*, chapter 3. Lipshutz and Conca, for example, discuss the relation between the global ecology and the state. Ronnie Lipshutz and Ken Conca, eds., *The State and Social Power in Global Environmental Politics* (1993). Some of these epic changes are also highlighted by John Ruggie, "Unraveling Trade: Global Institutional Change and the Pacific Economy," Fulbright Symposium paper (1991).

5. For a popular and readily accessibly account, see Jeffry Frieden, *Banking on the World* (1989), p. 238.

6. For a discussion of the explosive growth of Eurocurrencies, see Bryant, *International Financial Intermediation*, See particularly his figures in chapter 3.

7. The Reformation postdates the advent of these institutional types and thus does not explain the lack of state formation in, for example, Germany.

8. "Evolution to professionals, is adaptation to changing environments, not progress." Gould, *Wonderful Life*, p. 32.

9. Note that biological science is unable to predict the direction of evolution. At best, evolutionary theorists can provide explanations of why particular paths turned out to be dead ends. Their discipline is a retrodictive one. Even in the midst of such change, one need not recognize it or dare predict it.

10. The idea that Gould's view of punctuated equilibrium might serve as a metaphor for understanding institutional change is from Krasner, "Approaches to the State." See also Krasner, "Sovereignty," p. 80. Katzenstein refers to this view of history as "a sequence of big bangs." Katzenstein, "International Relations Theory," p. 296.

11. For an intuitive argument that the nation is becoming increasingly irrelevant, see Robert Reich, *The Work of Nations* (1991). Although Porter argues that nations continue to be important in the international economy, the nation-state is not the relevant unit of analysis. One understands the international economy not as states competing under anarchy but as firms competing in international markets. The unit of analysis is the industry with the state as one actor affecting the proximate environment of that industry. Michael Porter, *The Competitive Advantage of Nations* (1990), p. 33. Ruggie also discusses the changes in the international economic environment in "Territoriality and Beyond."

12. See, for example, Peter Cowhey, "The International Telecommunications Regime: The Political Roots of Regimes for High Technology," *International Organization* 44 (Spring 1990), pp. 169–200.

13. As I implied earlier, it would be wrong to suggest that the decline of the state might occur as the result of a linear process of increased communication and exchange. Broad environmental changes are a necessary but not sufficient cause. Such changes are mediated by political entrepreneurs and social groups.

14. Vaubel, for example, makes that type of argument. Roland Vaubel, "A Public Choice Approach to International Organization," *Public Choice* 51 (1986), pp. 39–57.

15. Social actors might make international contracts transaction-specific for both parties, so that both parties have an incentive to adhere to the agreement without the necessity of enforcement by national governments. For a discussion of transaction specificity and its implications for cooperation, see Yarborough and Yarborough, "International Institutions"; and their "Cooperation in the Liberalization of International Trade: After Hegemony, What?" *International Organization* 41 (Winter 1987), pp. 1–26.

16. David Held, *Political Theory and the Modern State* (1989), pp. 214–242. Even the idea that the state has diminished in scope, which Held takes as evident, can be contested. Kahler suggests that the economic policies of the European states have not been

dramatically altered by changes in their environment. Miles Kahler, "The Survival of the State in European International Relations," in Charles Maier, ed., *Changing Boundaries of the Political* (1987), pp. 287–319.

17. Sbragia makes that argument in "Thinking About the Future: The Uses of Comparison," in Alberta Sbragia, ed., *Europolitics* (1992), pp. 257–291.

18. Although the changes in economic environment are preconditions for such changes, they cannot explain why certain arrangements for the internal market were chosen over alternatives that also would have represented Pareto improvements for EC members. Geoffrey Garrett, "International Cooperation and Institutional Choice: The European Community's Internal Market," *International Organization* 46 (Spring 1992), pp. 533–560. For another critique of neofunctionalism which stresses the importance of intergovernment bargains, see Andrew Moravcsik, "Negotiating the Single European Act: National Interests and Conventional Statecraft in the European Community," *International Organization* 45 (Winter 1991), pp. 19–56. See also Linda Cornett and James Caporaso, "'And Still It Moves.' State Interests and Social Forces in the European Community," in Rosenau and Czempiel, *Governance Without Government*, pp. 219–249.

19. Wayne Sandholtz and John Zysman, "1992: Recasting the European Bargain," *World Politics* 42 (October 1989), p. 128.

20. Goodman notes that integration has proceeded far more on competition and trade policy than on monetary and tax issues. John Goodman, "Do All Roads Lead to Brussels? Economic Policymaking in the European Community," in Norman Ornstein and Mark Perlman, eds., *Political Power and Social Change* (1991). Even for supposedly strong states, trade policy rests to considerable extent in Brussels. Helen Milner, "Resisting the Protectionist Temptation: Industry and the Making of Trade Policy in France and the United States During the 1970s," *International Organization* 41 (Autumn 1987), p. 654.

21. See, for example, recent comments in *The Economist*: "Nevertheless, some American officials admit to feeling frustrated with Europe's Byzantine way of organizing foreign policy. It is not always clear whether they should deal with officials from the commission, the council or an individual country. . . . Political co-operation is a particularly slow animal to deal with, since it cannot take a position until 12 foreign ministries have reached a consensus." *The Economist* 316 (July 7, 1990), p. 11 (European Community Survey).

22. That is, the role of the sovereign state as an ordering device of both domestic as well as international relations is not that easy to replace. This would conform with Krasner's argument that the state system will not be easily dislodged. Krasner, "Sovereignty." Even Frieden, who highlights the globalization of finance, notes how national governments continue to be critical players in international financial markets, particularly in periods of crisis. "Nevertheless, the Euromarkets are not stateless." Frieden, *Banking on the World*, p. 116.

23. A relatively new body of literature concerning the relation of state and identity is the field of gender studies. Unfortunately my work is incognizant on the implications of such study for the future of the territorial state.

24. To what extent growing economic interdependence and modernization are causes for a search for alternative identities is a matter of great debate and a complex question which I do not address here. Some of the literature on nationalism certainly suggests that economic transformation does provoke changes in people's loyalties, identities, and interests. Hobsbawn, for example, sees the recent surge of ethnic and linguistic agitation as a defensive move against modernity. E. J. Hobsbawn, *Nations and Na-*

tionalism Since 1780 (1990), p. 164. Benedict Anderson notes how modernity and particularly the advance of vernacular print-language can affect national consciousness. *Imagined Communities* (1991). For a set of essays dealing with the tension between increasing global interdependence and individual affinities, see Zdravko Mlinar, ed., *Globalization and Territorial Identities* (1992).

25. For that argument, see James Piscatori, *Islam in a World of Nation-States* (1986). Gregory Gause notes the continued existence of the state system in the Mideast despite the historical challenges to it under the principle of Pan-Arabism. Gregory Gause, "Sovereignty, Statecraft and Stability in the Middle East," *Journal of International Affairs* 45 (Winter 1992), pp. 441–469.

26. For a discussion of African states and their empowerment see Jackson, "Quasi-States"; Jeffrey Herbst, "The Creation and Maintenance of National Boundaries in Africa," *International Organization* 43 (Autumn 1989), pp. 673–692.

27. Krasner, "Sovereignty."

28. International organizations empower actors as juridical equals in international affairs. Giddens, *The Nation-State and Violence*, chapter 10.

29. See Ruggie's argument in "Territoriality and Beyond."

30. To paraphrase Wendt's claim, I argue that "states make anarchy." See Wendt, "Anarchy is What States Make of It." It is exactly because of the historical development of territorially circumscribed and exclusive jurisdictions that we today take anarchy as a self-evident concept. Wendt suggests that identities play a critical role in understanding how states behave under anarchy. My focus is a different one in that I argue that what anarchy means is partially determined by the nature of the units.

Abercrombie, Nicholas. "Knowledge, Order and Human Autonomy." In James Hunter and Stephen Ainlay, eds., *Making Sense of Modern Times*. London: Routledge & Kegan Paul, 1986.

Abulafia, David. *Frederick II: A Medieval Emperor*. New York: Oxford University Press, 1988.

Abu-Lughod, Janet L. *Before European Hegemony*. New York: Oxford University Press, 1989.

Allison, Graham. *Essence of Decision*. Boston: Little, Brown & Co., 1971.

Ames, Edward, and Richard Rapp. "The Birth and Death of Taxes: A Hypothesis." *Journal of Economic History* 37 (1977), 161–178.

Anderson, Benedict. *Imagined Communities*. New York: Verso, 1991.

Anderson, Perry. *Passages from Antiquity to Feudalism*. London: Verso, 1974.

———. *Lineages of the Absolutist State*. London: Verso, 1974.

Armstrong, John. "Braudel's Mediterranean." *World Politics* 29, 4 (July 1977), 626–636.

Ashley, Richard. "The Poverty of Neorealism." In Robert Keohane, ed., *Neorealism and Its Critics*. New York: Columbia University Press, 1986.

Axelrod, Robert. "The Emergence of Cooperation among Egoists." *American Political Science Review* 75, 2 (June 1981), 306–318.

———. *The Evolution of Cooperation*. New York: Basic Books, 1984.

Badie, Bertrand, and Pierre Birnbaum. *The Sociology of the State*. Translated by Arthur Goldhammer. Chicago: University of Chicago Press, 1983.

Baechler, Jean, John Hall, and Michael Mann, eds. *Europe and the Rise of Capitalism*. London: Basil Blackwell, 1988.

Baldwin, John. *The Government of Philip Augustus*. Berkeley: University of California Press, 1986.

Baron, Hans. "The Social Background of Political Liberty in the Early Italian Renaissance." *Comparative Studies in Society and History* 2, 4 (1960), 440–451.

Barraclough, Geoffrey. *The Origins of Modern Germany*. New York: W. W. Norton, 1984.

Barry, Brian. *Sociologists, Economists and Democracy*. Chicago: University of Chicago Press, 1978.

Bartlett, Christopher, and Sumantra Ghoshal. *Managing Across Borders*. Cambridge: Harvard University Press, 1989.

Bates, Robert. "Lessons from History, or the Perfidy of English Exceptionalism and the Significance of Historical France." *World Politics* 40, 4 (1988), 499–516.

de Battaglia, Otto. "The Nobility in the European Middle Ages." *Comparative Studies in Society and History* 5, 1 (1962), 60–75.

Bean, Richard. "War and the Birth of the Nation State." *Journal of Economic History* 33 (1973), 203–221.

Becker, Marvin. "Some Aspects of Oligarchical, Dictatorial and Popular Signorie in Florence, 1282–1382." *Comparative Studies in Society and History* II, 4 (1960), 421–439.

———. "Changing Patterns of Violence and Justice in Fourteenth- and Fifteenth-Century Florence." *Comparative Studies in Society and History* 18, 3 (1976), 281–296.

Becker, Marvin. *Medieval Italy*. Bloomington: Indiana University Press, 1981.

Behr, Hans-Joachim. "Die Landgebietspolitik Nordwestdeutscher Hansestädte." *Hansische Geschichtsblätter* 94 (1976), 17–37.

Beik, William. *Absolutism and Society in Seventeenth-Century France*. Cambridge: Cambridge University Press, 1985.

Bendix, Reinhard. *Kings or People: Power and the Mandate to Rule*. Berkeley: University of California Press, 1978.

Benedict, Philip. *Cities and Social Change in Early Modern France*. New York: Routledge, 1992.

Benn, Stanley. "Sovereignty," In Paul Edwards, ed., *The Encyclopedia of Philosophy*, vol. 7/8. New York: MacMillan, 1967, 501–505.

Benn, Stanley, and Richard Peters. *Social Principles and the Democratic State*. London: George Allen and Unwin, 1959.

Berman, Harold. *Law and Revolution: The Formation of the Western Legal Tradition*. Cambridge: Harvard University Press, 1983.

Bernard, Jacques. "Trade and Finance in the Middle Ages, 900–1500." In Carlo Cipolla, ed., *The Fontana Economic History of Europe: The Middle Ages*, vol. 1. Glasgow: Collins/Fontana, 1972.

Bernstein, Richard. *The Restructuring of Social and Political Theory*. New York: Harcourt Brace Jovanovich, 1976.

———, ed. *Habermas and Modernity*. Cambridge: MIT Press, 1985.

———, ed. *Philosophical Profiles*. Philadelphia: University of Pennsylvania Press, 1986.

Bewes, W. A. *The Romance of the Law Merchant*. London: Sweet & Maxwell, 1923.

Biddick, Kathleen. "People and Things: Power in Early English Development." *Comparative Studies in Society and History* 32, 1 (January 1990), 3–23.

Biersteker, Thomas. "Critical Reflections on Post-Positivism in International Relations." *International Studies Quarterly* 33, 3 (September 1989), 263–267.

Bisson, Thomas. *Conservation of Coinage*. Oxford: Clarendon Press, 1979.

Bloch, Marc. *Feudal Society*, 2 vols. Chicago: University of Chicago Press, 1961.

Blockmans, Wim. "Princes Conquérants et Bourgeois Calculateurs." In Neithard Bulst and Jean-Philippe Genet, eds., *La Ville, La Bourgeoisie et La Genèse de L'État Moderne* Paris: CNRS, 1988.

———. "Voracious States and Obstructing Cities: An Aspect of State Formation in Preindustrial Europe." *Theory and Society* 18, 5 (September 1989), 733–756.

Bode, Wilhelm. "Hansische Bundesbestrebungen in der ersten Hälfte des 15. Jahrhunderts." *Hansische Geschichtsblätter* 25 (1919), 173–246; 26 (1920/21), 174–193.

Bonney, Richard. *The European Dynastic States, 1494–1660*. New York: Oxford University Press, 1991.

Boswell, Alexander. "The Teutonic Order." In J. R. Tanner, ed., *The Cambridge Medieval History*, vol. 7. Cambridge: Cambridge University Press, 1958.

Bourdieu, Pierre. *Outline of a Theory of Practice*. Cambridge: Cambridge University Press, 1977.

Bouwsma, William. "Swanson's Reformation." *Comparative Studies in Society and History* 10, 4 (July 1968), 486–491.

Bowsky, William. "Keeping the Urban Peace." In Stanley Chodorow, ed., *The Other Side of Western Civilization*, vol. 1. New York: Harcourt Brace Jovanovich, 1973.

Boxer, C. R. *The Dutch Seaborne Empire, 1600–1800*. London: Penguin, 1965.

Braudel, Fernand. *On History*. Translated by Sarah Matthews. Chicago: University of Chicago Press, 1980.

———. *The Perspective of the World*. Translated by Sian Reynolds. New York: Harper and Row, 1984.

Briggs, Robin. *Early Modern France, 1560–1715*. Oxford: Oxford University Press, 1977.

Brinton, Crane, John Christopher, and Robert Wolff. *A History of Civilization*, vol. 1. Englewood Cliffs, N.J.: Prentice-Hall, 1955.

Brown, Alison. "Florence, Renaissance and Early Modern State: Reappraisals." *Journal of Modern History* 56, 2 (June 1984), 285–300.

Brown, Peter. "Society and the Supernatural: A Medieval Change." *Daedalus* 104, 2 (Spring 1975), 133–151.

Brucker, Gene. *Renaissance Florence*. Berkeley: University of California Press, 1969.

Brundage, James. "Tithe." In Joseph Strayer, ed., *Dictionary of the Middle Ages*, vol. 12. New York: Charles Scribner's Sons, 1989.

———. "Usury." In Joseph Strayer, ed., *Dictionary of the Middle Ages*, vol. 12. New York: Charles Scribner's Sons, 1989.

Bryant, Ralph. *International Financial Intermediation*. Washington: The Brookings Institution, 1987.

Bull, Hedley. *The Anarchical Society*. New York: Columbia University Press, 1977.

Bulst, Neithard, and Jean-Philippe Genet, eds., *La Ville, La Bourgeoisie et La Genèse de L'État Moderne*. Paris: CNRS, 1988.

Burke, Peter. "City-States." In John Hall, ed., *States in History*. New York: Basil Blackwell, 1986.

———. "Republics of Merchants in Early Modern Europe." In Jean Baechler, John Hall, and Michael Mann, eds., *Europe and the Rise of Capitalism*. London: Basil Blackwell, 1988.

Caporaso, James, ed. *The Elusive State*. Newbury Park, Calif.: Sage, 1989.

———. "Microeconomics and International Political Economy: The Neoclassical Approach to Institutions." In Ernst-Otto Czempiel and James Rosenau, eds., *Global Changes and Theoretical Challenges*. Lexington, Mass.: D. C. Heath, 1989.

Chandler, Alfred. *Strategy and Structure*. Cambridge: MIT Press, 1962.

Chevalier, Bernard. "L'État et les Bonnes Villes en France au Temps de leur Accord Parfait." In Neithard Bulst and Jean-Philippe Genet, eds., *La Ville, La Bourgeoisie et La Genèse de L'État Moderne*. Paris: CNRS, 1988.

Cheyette, Frederic. "The Sovereign and the Pirates, 1332." *Speculum* 45, 1 (1970), 40–68.

———, ed. *Lordship and Community in Medieval Europe*. New York: Robert E. Krieger, 1975.

Chittolini, Giorgio. "Cities, 'City-States' and Regional States in North-Central Italy." *Theory and Society* 18, 5 (September 1989), 689–706.

Cipolla, Carlo. "Currency Depreciation in Medieval Europe." *The Economic History Review*. 15, 2 (1963), 413–422.

———. *Guns, Sails, and Empires*. Manhattan, Kansas: Sunflower University Press, 1965.

———, ed. *The Fontana Economic History of Europe: The Middle Ages*, vol. 1. Glasgow: Collins/Fontana, 1972.

———. *Before the Industrial Revolution*. New York: W. W. Norton, 1980.

Clark, Stuart. "The Annales Historians." In Quentin Skinner, ed. *The Return of Grand Theory in the Human Sciences*. New York: Cambridge University Press, 1985.

Clough, Shepard. *The Economic Development of Western Civilization*. New York: McGraw Hill, 1959.

Cochrane, Eric. *Florence in the Forgotten Centuries, 1527–1800*. Chicago: University of Chicago Press, 1973.

———. *Italy, 1530–1630*. Julius Kirshner, ed. London: Longman, 1988.

Cohn, Norman. *The Pursuit of the Millenium*. New York: Oxford University Press, 1970.

Coleman, Janet. "The Civic Culture of Contracts and Credit: A Review Article." *Comparative Studies in Society and History* 28, 4 (October 1986), 778–784.

Coles, Paul. "The Crisis of Renaissance Society: Genoa, 1488–1507." *Past and Present* 11 (April 1957), 17–47.

Collins, James. *The Fiscal Limits of Absolutism*. Berkeley: University of California Press, 1988.

Collins, Randall. *Weberian Sociological Theory*. Cambridge: Cambridge University Press, 1986.

Contamine, Philippe. *War in the Middle Ages*. Translated by Michael Jones. New York: Basil Blackwell, 1984.

Conybeare, John. "Trade Wars: A Comparative Study of Anglo-Hanse, Franco-Italian, and Hawley-Smoot Conflicts." In Kenneth Oye, ed., *Cooperation Under Anarchy*. Princeton, N.J.: Princeton University Press, 1986.

———. *Trade Wars*. New York: Columbia University Press, 1987.

Cornett, Linda, and James Caporaso. "'And Still It Moves.' State Interests and Social Forces in the European Community." In James Rosenau and Ernst-Otto Czempiel, eds., *Governance Without Government: Order and Change in World Politics*. New York: Cambridge University Press, 1992.

Corrigan, Philip, and Derek Sayer. *The Great Arch*. Cambridge: Basil Blackwell, 1991.

Cowhey, Peter. "The International Telecommunications Regime: The Political Roots of Regimes for High Technology." *International Organization* 44, 4 (Spring 1990), 169–200.

Craig, Gordon, and Alexander George. *Force and Statecraft*. New York: Oxford University Press, 1983.

Crone, Patricia. *Pre-Industrial Societies*. Oxford: Basil Blackwell, 1989.

Curtin, Philip. *Cross-Cultural Trade in World History*. New York: Cambridge University Press, 1984.

Czempiel, Ernst-Otto, and James Rosenau, eds. *Global Changes and Theoretical Challenges*. Lexington, Mass.: D. C. Heath, 1989.

Dameron, George. "Episcopal Lordship in the Diocese of Florence and the Origins of the Commune of San Cascaiano Val di Pesa, 1230–1247." *Journal of Medieval History* 12, 2 (June 1986), 135–154.

Davis, James. *The Decline of the Venetian Nobility as a Ruling Class*. Baltimore: Johns Hopkins Press, 1962.

Davis, Ralph. *English Overseas Trade, 1500–1700*. London: MacMillan, 1973.

Delbrück, Hans. *Medieval Warfare*. Translated by Walter Renfroe. Lincoln, Neb.: University of Nebraska Press, 1982. First published 1923.

Dessler, David. "What's at Stake in the Agent-Structure Debate?" *International Organization* 43, 3 (Summer 1989), 441–473.

Deutsch, Karl. *Political Community and the North Atlantic Area*. New York: Greenwood Press, 1956.

DiMaggio, Paul, and Walter Powell. "The Iron Cage Revisited: Institutional Isomorphism and Collective Rationality in Organizational Fields." *American Sociological Review* 48 (April 1983), 147–160.

Dodgshon, Robert. *The European Past: Social Evolution and Spatial Order*. New York: MacMillan, 1987.

Dollinger, Philippe. *The German Hansa*. Translated by D. Ault and S. Steinberg. Stanford, Calif.: Stanford University Press, 1970.

Doran, Charles, and Wes Parsons. "War and the Cycle of Relative Power." *American Political Science Review* 74, 4 (December 1980), 947–965.

Downing, Brian. *The Military Revolution and Political Change*. Princeton, N.J.: Princeton University Press, 1992.

Doyle, Michael. *Empires*. Ithaca, N.Y.: Cornell University Press, 1986.

Du Boulay, F. R. *Germany in the Later Middle Ages*. London: Athlone Press, 1983.

Duby, Georges. *Rural Economy and Country Life in the Medieval West*. Columbia, S.C.: University of South Carolina Press, 1968.

———. *The Early Growth of the European Economy*. Ithaca, N.Y.: Cornell University Press, 1974.

———. *The Three Orders*. Chicago: University of Chicago Press, 1978.

Dudley, Leonard. "Structural Change in Interdependent Bureaucracies: Was Rome's Failure Economic or Military?" *Explorations in Economic History* 27 (April 1990), 232–248.

Dunbabin, Jean. *France in the Making, 843–1180*. Oxford: Oxford University Press, 1985.

Dundes, Alan, and Alessandro Falassi. *La Terra in Piazza*. Berkeley: University of California Press, 1975.

Durkheim, Emile. *The Division of Labor in Society*. New York: Free Press, 1933.

———. *The Rules of Sociological Method*. Steven Lukes, ed. New York: Free Press, 1982.

Earle, Peter, ed. *Essays in European Economic History 1500–1800*. Oxford: Clarendon Press, 1984.

Elster, Jon. *Nuts and Bolts*. Cambridge: Cambridge University Press, 1984.

Ennen, Edith. *The Medieval Town*. Translated by Natalie Fryde. Amsterdam: North-Holland Publishing, 1979.

Evans, Peter, Dietrich Rueschemeyer, and Theda Skocpol, eds. *Bringing the State Back In*. Cambridge: Cambridge University Press, 1985.

Fawtier, Robert. *The Capetian Kings of France*. New York: St. Martin's Press, 1960.

Fesler, James. "French Field Administration: The Beginnings." *Comparative Studies in Society and History* 5 (1962), 76–111.

Field, Alexander. "The Problem with Neoclassical Institutional Economics: A Critique with Special Reference to the North-Thomas Model of Pre-1500 Europe." *Explorations in Economic History* 18 (April 1981), 174–198.

Finer, Samuel. "State and Nation Building in Europe: The Role of the Military." In Charles Tilly, ed., *The Formation of National States in Western Europe*. Princeton, N.J.: Princeton University Press, 1975.

Fink, Georg. "Die Rechtliche Stellung der Deutschen Hanse in der Zeit ihres Niedergangs." *Hansische Geschichtsblätter* 61 (1936), 122–137.

Fischer, Markus. "Feudal Europe, 800–1300: Communal Discourse and Conflictual Practices." *International Organization* 46, 2 (Spring 1992), 427–466.

Fleckenstein, Josef. *Early Medieval Germany*. Translated by Bernard Smith. Amsterdam: North-Holland Publishing Company, 1978.

Fox, Edward. *History in Geographic Perspective*. New York: W. W. Norton, 1971.

Francois, Martha. "Reformation and Society: An Analysis of Guy Swanson's Religion and Regime." *Comparative Studies in Society and History* 14, 3 (June 1972), 289–305.

Freed, John. "Germany: 843–1137." In Joseph Strayer, ed., *Dictionary of the Middle Ages*, vol. 5. New York: Charles Scribner's Sons, 1985, 473–478.

————. "Germany: 1138–1254." In Joseph Strayer, ed., *Dictionary of the Middle Ages*, vol. 5. New York: Charles Scribner's Sons, 1985, 478–485.

————. "Germany: Stem Duchies." In Joseph Strayer, ed., *Dictionary of the Middle Ages*, vol. 5. New York: Charles Scribner's Sons, 1985, 505–511.

————. "Translation of Empire." In Joseph Strayer, ed., *Dictionary of the Middle Ages*, vol. 12. New York: Charles Scribner's Sons, 1989, 143.

Freising, Otto of. *The Deeds of Frederick Barbarossa*. Translated by Charles Mierow. New York: W. W. Norton, 1953.

Frieden, Jeffry. *Banking on the World*. Oxford: Basil Blackwell, 1989.

Friedman, David. "A Theory of the Size and Shape of Nations." *Journal of Political Economy* 85 (1977), 59–77.

Friedrichs, Christopher. "Capitalism, Mobility and Class Formation in the Early Modern German City." *Past and Present* 69 (November 1975), 24–49.

Fryde, E. B. "The Financial Policies of the Royal Governments and Popular Resistance to Them in France and England c. 1270–1420." In E. B. Fryde, *Studies in Medieval Trade and Finance*. London: Hambledon Press, 1983.

Fuhrmann, Horst. *Germany in the High Middle Ages c. 1050–1200*. Cambridge: Cambridge University Press, 1986.

Fulbrook, Mary, and Theda Skocpol. "Destined Pathways: The Historical Sociology of Perry Anderson." In Theda Skocpol, ed., *Vision and Method in Historical Sociology*. Cambridge: Cambridge University Press, 1984.

Garrett, Geoffrey. "International Cooperation and Institutional Choice: The European Community's Internal Market." *International Organization* 46, 2 (Spring 1992), 533–560.

Gause, Gregory. "Sovereignty, Statecraft and Stability in the Middle East." *Journal of International Affairs* 45, 2 (Winter 1992), 441–469.

Geertz, Clifford. *The Interpretation of Cultures*. New York: Basic Books, 1973.

Gellner, Ernest. *Nations and Nationalism*. Ithaca, N.Y.: Cornell University Press, 1983.

Gelsinger, Bruce. "Hanseatic League." In Joseph Strayer, ed., *Dictionary of the Middle Ages*, vol. 6. New York: Charles Scribner's Sons, 1985, 90–97.

Genicot, Leopold. "La Noblesse au Moyen Age Dans L'Ancienne 'Francie': Continuité, Rupture ou Évolution?" *Comparative Studies in Society and History* 5, 1 (1962), 52–59.

Gerbenzon, P., and N. Algra. *Voortgangh des Rechtes*. Groningen: Tjeenk Willink, 1975.

Gerth, H. H., and C. Wright Mills, eds. *From Max Weber*. New York: Oxford University Press, 1946.

Giard, Luce. "La Procès d'Emancipation de l'Anglais à la Renaissance." Paris: CNRS, LP 21 (manuscript), 1989.

Giddens, Anthony. *A Contemporary Critique of Historical Materialism*. Berkeley: University of California Press, 1981.

————. *The Nation-State and Violence*. Berkeley: University of California Press, 1987.

Gierke, Otto. *Political Theories of the Middle Age*. Translated by F. Maitland. Cambridge: Cambridge University Press, 1987. First published 1900.

Gilpin, Robert. *War and Change in World Politics*. Cambridge: Cambridge University Press, 1981.

_____. "The Richness of the Tradition of Political Realism." In Robert Keohane, ed., *Neorealism and Its Critics*. New York: Columbia University Press, 1986.

Given, James. *State and Society in Medieval Europe*. Ithaca, N.Y.: Cornell University Press, 1990.

Goldstein, Joshua. *Long Cycles*. New Haven, Conn.: Yale University Press, 1988.

Goodman, John. "Do All Roads Lead to Brussels? Economic Policymaking in the European Community." In Norman Ornstein and Mark Perlman, eds., *Political Power and Social Change*. Washington: AEI Press, 1991.

Goody, Jack. *The Development of the Family and Marriage in Europe*. Cambridge: Cambridge University Press, 1983.

Gould, Stephen Jay. *The Panda's Thumb*. New York: W. W. Norton, 1980.

_____. *Wonderful Life*. New York: W. W. Norton, 1989.

Gourevitch, Peter. "International Trade, Domestic Coalitions and Liberty: Comparative Responses to the Crisis of 1873–1896." *Journal of Interdisciplinary History* 8, 2 (Autumn 1977), 281–313.

_____. "The Second Image Reversed. The International Sources of Domestic Politics." *International Organization* 32, 4 (Autumn 1978), 881–911.

_____. "Breaking with Orthodoxy: The Politics of Economic Policy Responses to the Depression of the 1930s." *International Organization* 38, 1 (Winter 1984), 95–129.

_____. *Politics in Hard Times*. Ithaca, N.Y.: Cornell University Press, 1986.

Green, Louis. "Lucca under Castruccio Castracani." *I Tatti Studies* 1 (1985), 137–159.

Green, Vivian. "Taxation, Church." In Joseph Strayer, ed., *Dictionary of the Middle Ages*, vol. 12. New York: Charles Scribner's Sons, 1989.

Greengrass, Mark. *Conquest and Coalescence*. London: Edward Arnold, 1991.

Gross, Leo. "The Peace of Westphalia, 1648–1948." In Richard Falk and Wolfram Hanrieder, eds., *International Law and Organization*. Philadelphia: J. B. Lippincott, 1968.

Guenee, Bernard. *States and Rulers*. Oxford: Basil Blackwell, 1985.

Haas, Ernst. "Technocracy, Pluralism, and the New Europe." In Joseph Nye, ed., *International Regionalism*. Boston: Little, Brown and Co., 1968.

Habermas, Jürgen. *Toward a Rational Society*. Boston: Beacon Press, 1970.

_____. *The Theory of Communicative Action*, vol. 1. Boston: Beacon Press, 1984.

Hagen, William. "How Mighty the Junkers? Peasant Rents and Seigneurial Profits in Sixteenth-Century Brandenburg." *Past and Present* 108 (August 1985), 80–116.

_____. "Capitalism and Countryside in Early Modern Europe: Interpretations, Models, Debates." *Agricultural History* 62, 1 (1988), 13–47.

Hall, John. *Powers and Liberties*. Berkeley: University of California Press, 1985.

_____, ed. *States in History*. New York: Basil Blackwell, 1986.

Hallam, Elizabeth. *Capetian France, 987–1328*. New York: Longman, 1980.

Harris, R. W. *Absolutism and Enlightenment, 1660–1789*. New York: Harper and Row, 1966.

Haskins, George. *The Growth of English Representative Government*. New York: Perpetua, 1960.

Haverkamp, Alfred. *Medieval Germany, 1056–1273*. New York: Oxford University Press, 1988.

Havighurst, Alfred. *The Pirenne Thesis*. Lexington, Mass.: D. C. Heath, 1976.

Hay, Denys. *Europe in the Fourteenth and Fifteenth Centuries*. London: Longman, 1989.

Hay, Denys, and John Law. *Italy in the Age of the Renaissance, 1380–1530*. London: Longman, 1989.

Hazeltine, Harold. "Roman and Canon Law in the Middle Ages," In J. R. Tanner, ed., *The Cambridge Medieval History*, vol. 5. Cambridge: Cambridge University Press, 1957.

Heaton, Herbert. *Economic History of Europe*. New York: Harper and Row, 1948.

Heer, Friedrich. *The Medieval World*. Translated by Janet Sondheimer. New York: New American Library, 1961.

Held, David. *Political Theory and the Modern State*. Stanford, Calif.: Stanford University Press, 1989.

Held, Otto. "Hansische Einheitsbestrebungen im Mass und Gewichtswesen bis zum Jahre 1500." *Hansische Geschichtsblätter* 45 (1918), 127–167.

Henn, Volker. "Die Hanse: Interessengemeinschaft oder Städtebund?" *Hansische Geschichtsblätter* 102 (1984), 119–126.

Henneman, John. *Royal Taxation in Fourteenth Century France*. Princeton, N.J.: Princeton University Press, 1971.

————. *The Medieval French Monarchy*. Hinsdale, Illinois: Dryden Press, 1973.

————. "Taille, Taillage." In Joseph Strayer, ed., *Dictionary of the Middle Ages*, vol. 11. New York: Charles Scribner's Sons, 1988.

Herbst, Jeffrey. "The Creation and Maintenance of National Boundaries in Africa." *International Organization* 43, 4 (Autumn 1989), 673–692.

Herz, John. *The Nation-State and the Crisis of World Politics*. New York: David McKay, 1976.

Hibbert, A. B. "The Origins of the Medieval Town Patriciate." *Past and Present* 3 (February 1953), 15–27.

Hicks, John. *A Theory of Economic History*. Oxford: Oxford University Press, 1969.

Hilton, R. H. *English and French Towns in Feudal Society*. Cambridge: Cambridge University Press, 1992.

Hinsley, F. H. "The Concept of Sovereignty and the Relations Between States." In W. J. Stankiewicz, ed., *In Defense of Sovereignty*. New York: Oxford University Press, 1969.

————. *Sovereignty*. Cambridge: Cambridge University Press, 1986.

Hintze, Otto. *The Historical Essays of Otto Hintze*. Felix Gilbert, ed. New York: Oxford University Press, 1975.

Hirschman, Albert. *Exit, Voice, and Loyalty*. Cambridge: Harvard University Press, 1970.

————. *The Passions and the Interests*. Princeton, N.J.: Princeton University Press, 1977.

Hobsbawn, E. J. *Nations and Nationalism Since 1780*. New York: Cambridge University Press, 1990.

Hocquet, Jean Claude. "Venise, les Villes et les Campagnes de la Terreferme, XVe–XVIe Siècles." In Neithard Bulst and Jean-Philippe Genet, eds., *La Ville, La Bourgeoisie et La Genèse de L'État Moderne*. Paris: CNRS, 1988.

Hohenberg, Paul, and Lynn Lees. *The Making of Urban Europe*. Cambridge: Harvard University Press, 1985.

Holborn, Hajo. *A History of Modern Germany: The Reformation*. Princeton, N.J.: Princeton University Press, 1959.

Holsti, Kalevi. *Peace and War: Armed Conflicts and International Order, 1648–1989*. New York: Cambridge University Press, 1991.

Holton, R. J. *Cities, Capitalism and Civilization*. London: Allen and Unwin, 1986.

Holzgrefe, J. L. "The Origins of Modern International Relations Theory." *Review of International Studies* 15 (1989), 11–26.

Iggers, Georg. *New Directions in European Historiography*. Middletown, Conn.: Wesleyan University Press, 1984.

Jackson, Robert. "Quasi-States, Dual Regimes, and Neoclassical Theory: International Jurisprudence and the Third World." *International Organization* 41, 4 (Autumn 1987), 519–549.

Jeannin, Pierre. "Das Handbuch in der Berufsausbildung des Hansischen Kaufmanns." *Hansische Geschichtsblätter* 103 (1985), 101–120.

Jesse, Wilhelm. "Die Münzpolitik der Hansestädte." *Hansische Geschichtsblätter* 53 (1928), 78–96.

Johnston, R. J. *Geography and the State*. London: MacMillan, 1982.

Jones, E. *The European Miracle*. Cambridge: Cambridge University Press, 1987.

Jordan, William. *Louis IX and the Challenge of the Crusade*. Princeton, N.J.: Princeton University Press, 1979.

Kagan, Donald. *The Outbreak of the Peloponnesian War*. Ithaca, N.Y.: Cornell University Press, 1969.

Kahler, Miles. "The Survival of the State in European International Relations." In Charles Maier, ed., *Changing Boundaries of the Political*. Cambridge: Cambridge University Press, 1987.

Kantorowicz, Ernst. *The King's Two Bodies*. Princeton, N.J.: Princeton University Press, 1957.

Katzenstein, Peter. "International Relations Theory and the Analysis of Change." In Ernst-Otto Czempiel and James Rosenau, eds., *Global Changes and Theoretical Challenges*. Lexington, Mass.: D. C. Heath, 1989.

Kedar, Benjamin. *Merchants in Crisis*. New Haven, Conn.: Yale University Press, 1976.

Keegan, John. *The Face of Battle*. New York: Dorset, 1976.

Keen, Maurice. *The Pelican History of Medieval Europe*. Harmondsworth: Penguin, 1968.

Keens-Soper, Maurice. "The Practice of a States-System." *Studies in History and Politics*, 2, 2 (1981–82), 15–36.

Kennedy, Paul. *The Rise and Decline of Great Powers*. New York: Random House, 1987.

Keohane, Robert. *After Hegemony*. Princeton, N.J.: Princeton University Press, 1984.

———, ed. *Neorealism and Its Critics*. New York: Columbia University Press, 1986.

Keohane, Robert, and Joseph Nye. *Power and Interdependence: World Politics in Transition*. Boston: Little, Brown and Co., 1977.

———. "Power and Interdependence Revisited." *International Organization* 41, 4 (Autumn 1987), 725–753.

Kiernan, V. G. "Foreign Mercenaries and Absolute Monarchy." *Past and Present* 11 (April 1957), 66–86.

———. "State and Nation in Western Europe." *Past and Present* 31 (July 1965), 20–38.

———. "Private Property in History." In Jack Goody, Joan Thirsk, and E. P. Thompson, eds., *Family and Inheritance*. Cambridge: Cambridge University Press, 1976.

Kinder, Hermann, and Werner Hilgemann. *The Anchor Atlas of World History*, vol. 1. Translated by Ernest Menze. New York: Anchor Press, 1974.

Knapton, Michael. "City Wealth and State Wealth in Northeast Italy, 14–17th centuries." In Neithard Bulst and Jean-Philippe Genet, eds., *La Ville, La Bourgeoisie et La Genèse de L'État Moderne*. Paris: CNRS, 1988.

Krasner, Stephen. "Approaches to the State: Alternative Conceptions and Historical Dynamics." *Comparative Politics* 16, 2 (January 1984), 223–246.

———. "Sovereignty: An Institutional Perspective." In James Caporaso, ed., *The Elusive State*. Newbury Park, Calif.: Sage, 1989.

———."Westphalia." Unpublished manuscript. Stanford University, 1991.

Kratochwil, Friedrich. "Of Systems, Boundaries, and Territoriality: An Inquiry into the Formation of the State System." *World Politics* 39, 1 (October 1986), 27–52.

Kula, Witold. *Measures and Men*. Princeton, N.J.: Princeton University Press, 1986.

Laitin, David. *Hegemony and Culture*. Chicago: University of Chicago Press, 1986.

Lake, David. "The Expansion of Sovereignty: Imperialism, Decolonization, and the Constitutive Principle of International Relations." Paper delivered to the American Political Science Association, Chicago, August 1987.

———. "The State and the Production of International Security: A Microeconomic Theory of Grand Strategy." Discussion paper no. 1. Los Angeles: Center for International Studies, University of Southern California, 1990.

Lane, Frederic. *Venice: A Maritime Republic*. Baltimore: Johns Hopkins University Press, 1973.

Lattimore, Owen. "Feudalism in History." *Past and Present* 12 (November 1957), 47–57.

Leff, Gordon. "Heresy and the Decline of the Medieval Church." *Past and Present* 20 (November 1961), 36–51.

Le Goff, Jacques. *Time, Work, and Culture in the Middle Ages*. Chicago: University of Chicago Press, 1980.

———. *Medieval Civilization*. New York: Basil Blackwell, 1988.

Legvold, Robert. "Soviet Learning in the 1980s." In George Breslauer and Philip Tetlock, eds. *Learning in U.S. and Soviet Foreign Policy*. Boulder, Col.: Westview Press, 1991.

Lensen, Leo, and Willy Heitling. *De Geschiedenis van de Hanze*. Deventer: Arko, 1990.

Leps, Curt. "Das Zunftwesen der Stadt Rostock bis um die Mitte des 15. Jahrhunderts." *Hansische Geschichtsblätter* 58 (1933), 122–156.

Leuschner, Joachim. *Germany in the Late Middle Ages*. Translated by Sabine MacCormack. Amsterdam: North Holland Publishing Company, 1980.

Levi, Margaret. *Of Rule and Revenue*. Berkeley: University of California Press, 1988.

Lewis, Archibald. *Knights and Samurai*. London: Temple Smith, 1974.

Lewis, Archibald, and Timothy Runyan. *European Naval and Maritime History, 300–1500*. Bloomington: Indiana University Press, 1985.

Lewis, Bernard. *The Muslim Discovery of Europe*. New York: W. W. Norton, 1982.

Lewis, P. S. "The Failure of the French Medieval Estates." *Past and Present* 23 (November 1962), 3–24.

———. *Essays in Later Medieval French History*. London. Hambledon Press, 1985.

Leyser, Karl. "The German Aristocracy from the Ninth to the Twelfth Century." *Past and Present* 41 (December 1968), 25–53.

Link, Werner. "Reflections on Paradigmatic Complementarity in the Study of International Relations." In Ernst-Otto Czempiel and James Rosenau, eds., *Global Changes and Theoretical Challenges*. Lexington, Mass.: D. C. Heath, 1989.

Lipshutz, Ronnie, and Ken Conca, eds. *The State and Social Power in Global Environmental Politics*. New York: Columbia University Press, 1993.

Lipson, Charles. "Bankers' Dilemmas: Private Cooperation in Rescheduling Sovereign Debts." In Kenneth Oye, ed., *Cooperation Under Anarchy*. Princeton, N.J.: Princeton University Press, 1986.

Lloyd, T. H. *England and the German Hanse, 1157–1611*. New York: Cambridge University Press, 1991.

Lodge, Eleanor. "The Communal Movement, Especially in France." In J. R. Tanner, ed., *The Cambridge Medieval History*, vol. 5. Cambridge: Cambridge University Press, 1957.

Lönnroth, E. "The Baltic Countries." In M. Postan, E. Rich, and E. Miller, eds., *Economic Organization and Policies in the Middle Ages*. Cambridge: Cambridge University Press, 1963.

Lopez, Robert, and Irving Raymond. *Medieval Trade in the Mediterranean World*. New York: W. W. Norton, 1967.

Lyon, Bryce, and Adriaan Verhulst. *Medieval Finance*. Providence, R.I.: Brown University Press, 1967.

Mackenney, Richard. *The City-State*. London: MacMillan, 1989.

Maier, Charles, ed. *Changing Boundaries of the Political*. Cambridge: Cambridge University Press, 1987.

Mair, Lucy. *Primitive Government*. Harmondsworth: Penguin, 1962.

Mann, Michael. *The Sources of Social Power*. Cambridge: Cambridge University Press, 1986.

Mansbach, Richard, and Yale Ferguson. "Between Celebration and Despair." *International Studies Quarterly* 35, 4 (December 1991), 363–386.

Markovits, Andrei, and Warren Oliver. "The Political Sociology of Integration and Social Development: A Comparative Analysis of Emile Durkheim and Karl Deutsch." In Richard Merritt and Bruce Russett, eds., *From National Development to Global Community*. London: George Allen and Unwin, 1981.

Martines, Lauro. *Power and Imagination*. New York: Vintage, 1979.

———. "Italy, Rise of Towns In." In Joseph Strayer, ed., *Dictionary of the Middle Ages*, vol, 7. New York: Charles Scribner's Sons, 1986, 12–18.

Mattingly, Garrett. *Renaissance Diplomacy*. New York: Dover, 1988.

McFarlane, K. B., et al., "War and Society 1300–1600." *Past and Present* 22 (July 1962), 3–35.

McNeill, William. *Venice: The Hinge of Europe, 1081–1797*. Chicago: University of Chicago Press, 1974.

———. *The Pursuit of Power*. Chicago: University of Chicago Press, 1982.

Milgrom, Paul, Douglass North, and Barry Weingast. "The Role of Institutions in the Revival of Trade: The Law Merchant, Private Judges, and the Champagne Fairs." *Economics and Politics* 2 (1990), 1–23.

Miller, Edward. "Government Economic Policies and Public Finance, 1000–1500." In Carlo Cipolla, ed., *The Fontana Economic History of Europe: The Middle Ages*, vol. 1. Glasgow: Collins/Fontana, 1972.

Milner, Helen. "Resisting the Protectionist Temptation: Industry and the Making of Trade Policy in France and the United States during the 1970s." *International Organization* 41, 4 (Autumn 1987), 639–666.

Miskimin, Harry. *The Economy of Early Renaissance Europe, 1300–1460*. New York: Cambridge University Press, 1975.

Mlinar, Zdravko, ed. *Globalization and Territorial Identities*. Aldershot: Avebury, 1992.

Modelski, George. "The Long Cycle of Global Politics and the Nation-State." *Comparative Studies in Society and History* 20 (April 1978), 214–235.

———. "Is World Politics Evolutionary Learning?" *International Organization* 44, 1 (Winter 1990), 1–24.

Moore, Barrington. *Social Origins of Dictatorship and Democracy*. Boston: Beacon Press, 1966.

Moravcsik, Andrew. "Negotiating the Single European Act: National Interests and Conventional Statecraft in the European Community." *International Organization* 45, 1 (Winter 1991), 19–56.

Morrall, John. *Political Thought in Medieval Times*. Toronto: University of Toronto Press, 1980.

Mundy, John. "Medieval Urban Liberty." Unpublished manuscript. New York, 1993.

Mundy, John, and Peter Riesenberg. *The Medieval Town*. New York: Van Nostrand Publishing, 1958.

Myers, Henry. *Medieval Kingship*. Chicago: Nelson-Hall, 1982.

Nef, John. *Industry and Government in France and England, 1540–1640*. Ithaca, N.Y.: Great Seal Books, 1957.

Nettl, J. P. "The State as a Conceptual Variable." *World Politics* 20, 4 (1968), 559–592.

Nicholas, David. "Economic Reorientation and Social Change in Fourteenth Century Flanders." *Past and Present* 70 (February 1976), 3–29.

North, Douglass. "A Framework for Analyzing the State in Economic History." *Explorations in Economic History* 16 (1979), 249–259.

———. *Structure and Change in Economic History*. New York: W. W. Norton, 1981.

———. *Institutions, Institutional Change and Economic Performance*. Cambridge: Cambridge University Press, 1990.

North, Douglass, and Robert Thomas. *The Rise of the Western World*. Cambridge: Cambridge University Press, 1973.

North, Douglass, and Barry Weingast. "Constitutions and Commitment: The Evolution of Institutions Governing Public Choice in 17th Century England." *Journal of Economic History* 49 (December 1989), 803–832.

Oakley, Francis. *The Western Church in the Later Middle Ages*. Ithaca, N.Y.: Cornell University Press, 1979.

Olson, Glenn. "Italian Mechants and the Performance of Papal Banking Functions in the Early Thirteenth Century." In David Herlihy, Robert Lopez, and Vsevolod Slessarev, eds. *Economy, Society and Government in Medieval Italy*. Kent, Ohio: Kent State University Press, 1969.

Olson, Mancur. *The Logic of Collective Action*. Cambridge: Harvard University Press, 1965.

———. *The Rise and Decline of Nations*. New Haven, Conn.: Yale University Press, 1982.

Onuf, Nicholas. "Sovereignty: Outline of a Conceptual History." *Alternatives* 16 (1991), 425–446.

Owen-Hughes, Diane. "Urban Growth and Family Structure in Medieval Italy." *Past and Present* 66 (February 1975) 3–28.

Oye, Kenneth, ed. *Cooperation Under Anarchy*. Princeton, N.J.: Princeton University Press, 1986.

Painter, Sidney. *Mediaeval Society*. Ithaca, N.Y.: Cornell University Press, 1951.

———. *The Rise of the Feudal Monarchies*. Ithaca, N.Y.: Cornell University Press, 1951.

Parker, David. "The Social Foundation of French Absolutism, 1610–1630." *Past and Present* 53 (1971), 67–89.

———. *The Making of French Absolutism*. New York: St. Martin's Press, 1983.

Parker, Geoffrey. "Warfare." In Peter Burke, ed., *New Cambridge Modern History*, vol. 13. Cambridge: Cambridge University Press, 1979.

———. *The Military Revolution*. New York: Cambridge University Press, 1988.

Parry, J. H. *The Discovery of the Sea*. Berkeley: University of California Press, 1981.

Pepper, Simon, and Nicholas Adams. *Firearms and Fortifications*. Chicago: University of Chicago Press, 1986.

Perroy, Edouard. "Social Mobility Among the French Noblesse in the Later Middle Ages." *Past and Present* 21 (April 1962), 25–38.

Petit-Dutaillis, Charles. *The Feudal Monarchy in France and England*. London: Kagan, Paul, Trench & Trubner, 1936.

Piore, Michael, and Charles Sabel. *The Second Industrial Divide*. New York: Basic Books, 1984.

Pirenne, Henri. *Medieval Cities*. Princeton, N.J.: Princeton University Press, 1952. First published 1925.

———. *Economic and Social History of Medieval Europe*. New York: Harcourt Brace Jovanovich, 1956.

Piscatori, James. *Islam in a World of Nation-States*. New York: Cambridge University Press, 1986.

Pitz, Ernst. "Steigende und Fallende Tendenzen in Politik und Wirtschaftsleben der Hanse im 16. Jahrhundert." *Hansische Geschichtsblätter* 102 (1984), 39–77.

Pizzorno, Alessandro. "Politics Unbound." In Charles Maier, ed., *Changing Boundaries of the Political*. Cambridge: Cambridge University Press, 1987.

Poggi, Gianfranco. *The Development of the Modern State*. Stanford, Calif.: Stanford University Press, 1978.

Polanyi, Karl. "Primitive Feudalism and the Feudalism of Decay." In George Dalton, ed., *Economic Development and Social Change*. New York: Natural History Press, 1971.

Porter, Michael. *The Competitive Advantage of Nations*. New York: Free Press, 1990.

Post, Gaines. "Patriapotestas, Regia Potestas and Rex Imperator." In David Herlihy, Robert Lopez, and Vsevolod Slessarev, eds., *Economy, Society, and Government in Medieval Italy*. Kent, Ohio: Kent State University Press, 1969.

Power, Eileen. *Medieval People*. New York: Barnes and Noble, 1963. First published in 1924.

Previté-Orton, C. W., ed. *The Shorter Cambridge Medieval History*, 2 vols. Cambridge: Cambridge University Press, 1971.

Puhle, Matthias. "Der Sächsische Städtebund und die Hanse im Späten Mittelalter." *Hansische Geschichtsblätter* 104 (1986), 21–34.

Pullan, Brian, ed. *Crisis and Change in the Venetian Economy in the Sixteenth and Seventeenth Centuries*. London: Methuen and Co., 1968.

Putnam, Robert, et al. "Explaining Institutional Success: The Case of Italian Regional Government." *American Political Science Review* 77, 1 (March 1983), 55–74.

———. "Diplomacy and Domestic Politics: The Logic of Two-Level Games." *International Organization* 42, 3 (Summer 1988), 427–460.

Rapp, Richard. *Industry and Economic Decline in Seventeenth Century Venice*. Cambridge: Harvard University Press, 1976.

Rasler, Karen, and William Thompson. "War Making and State Making: Governmental Expenditures, Tax Revenues, and Global War." *American Political Science Review* 79, 2 (June 1985), 491–507.

Reich, Robert. *The Work of Nations*. New York: Alfred Knopf, 1991.

Reynolds, Susan. *Kingdoms and Communities in Western Europe, 900–1300*. Oxford: Clarendon Press, 1984.

Rice, Eugene. *The Foundations of Early Modern Europe, 1460–1559*. New York: W. W. Norton, 1970.

Riesenberg, Peter. "Civism and Roman Law in Fourteenth-Century Italian Society." In David Herlihy, Robert Lopez, and Vsevolod Slessarev, eds., *Economy, Society, and Government in Medieval Italy*. Kent, Ohio: Kent State University Press, 1969.

Ringrose, David. "Comment on Papers by Reed, de Vries, and Bean." *Journal of Economic History* 33 (1973), 222–227.

Ritchie, Robert. *Captain Kidd and the War Against the Pirates*. Cambridge: Harvard University Press, 1986.

Rogowski, Ronald. *Commerce and Coalitions*. Princeton, N.J.: Princeton University Press, 1989.

Rogozinski, Jan. "The Counsellors of the Seneschal of Beaucaire and Nimes, 1250–1350." *Speculum* 44, 3 (July 1969), 421–439.

Romano, Ruggiero. "Italy in the Crisis of the Seventeenth Century." In Peter Earle, ed., *Essays in European Economic History, 1500–1800*. Oxford: Clarendon Press, 1984.

Root, Hilton. *Peasants and King in Burgundy: Agrarian Foundations of French Absolutism*. Berkeley: University of California Press, 1987.

de Roover, Raymond. "The Organization of Trade." In M. Postan, E. Rich, and E. Miller, eds., *The Cambridge Economic History of Europe*, vol. 3. Cambridge: Cambridge University Press, 1963.

Rörig, Fritz. *The Medieval Town*. Berkeley: University of California Press, 1969.

Rosecrance, Richard. *Action and Reaction in World Politics*. Boston: Little, Brown, 1963.

———. "International Theory Revisited." *International Organization* 35, 4 (Autumn 1981), 691–713.

———. *The Rise of the Trading State: Commerce and Conquest in the Modern World*. New York: Basic Books, 1986.

———. "Long Cycle Theory and International Relations." *International Organization* 41, 2 (Spring 1987), 283–302.

Rosenau, James. "Global Changes and Theoretical Challenges: Toward a Postinternational Politics for the 1990s." In Ernst-Otto Czempiel and James Rosenau, eds., *Global Changes and Theoretical Challenges*. Lexington, Mass.: D. C. Heath, 1989.

Rosenau, James, and Ernst-Otto Czempiel, eds., *Governance Without Government: Order and Change in World Politics*. New York: Cambridge University Press, 1992.

Rosenberg, Hans. "The Rise of the Junkers in Brandenburg-Prussia, 1410–1653." *American Historical Review* 49, part 1, (October 1943), 1–22; 49, part 2 (January 1944), 228–242.

Rosenberg, Justin. "A Non-Realist Theory of Sovereignty? Giddens' 'The Nation-State and Violence.'" *Millenium* 19, 9 (1990), 249–259.

Rotz, Rhiman. "German Towns." In Joseph Strayer, ed., *Dictionary of the Middle Ages*, vol. 5. New York: Charles Scribner's Sons, 1985, 457–471.

Rowan, Steven. "Germany: Electors." In Joseph Strayer, ed., *Dictionary of the Middle Ages*, vol. 5. New York: Charles Scribner's Sons, 1985, 491–493.

———. "Germany: Principalities." In Joseph Strayer, ed., *Dictionary of the Middle Ages*, vol. 5. New York: Charles Scribner's Sons, 1985, 498–504.

Rowen, Herbert, ed. *From Absolutism to Revolution, 1648–1848*. New York: MacMillan, 1963.

———. *The King's State*. New Brunswick, N.J.: Rutgers University Press, 1980.

Rudolph, Susanne. "Presidential Address: State Formation in Asia—Prolegomenon to a Comparative Study." *Journal of Asian Studies* 46, 4 (November 1987), 731–746.

Rueschemeyer, Dietrich. "Theoretical Generalization and Historical Particularity in the Comparative Sociology of Reinhard Bendix." In Theda Skocpol, ed., *Vision and Method in Historical Sociology*. Cambridge: Cambridge University Press, 1984.

Ruggie, John. "Continuity and Transformation in the World Polity." In Robert Keohane, ed., *Neorealism and Its Critics*. New York: Columbia University Press, 1986.

———. "International Structure and International Transformation: Space, Time, and Method." In Ernst-Otto Czempiel and James Rosenau, eds., *Global Changes and Theoretical Challenges*. Lexington, Mass.: D. C. Heath, 1989.

———. "Unraveling Trade: Global Institutional Change and the Pacific Economy." Paper prepared for the Fulbright Symposium on Managing International Economic Relations in the Pacific of the 1990s. Canberra, December 1991.

———. "Territoriality and Beyond: Problematizing Modernity in International Relations." *International Organization* 47, 1 (Winter 1993), 139–174.

———. *Planetary Politics: Ecology and the Organization of Global Political Space*. Forthcoming.

Runciman, W. G. "Origins of States: The Case of Archaic Greece." *Comparative Studies in Society and History* 24 (July 1982), 351–377.

———. *A Treatise on Social Theory*, vol. 2. Cambridge: Cambridge University Press, 1989.

Russell, J. C. "Population in Europe, 500–1500." In Carlo Cipolla, ed., *The Fontana Economic History of Europe: The Middle Ages*, vol. 1. Glasgow: Collins/Fontana, 1972.

Russett, Bruce. "The Mysterious Case of Vanishing Hegemony: Or Is Mark Twain Really Dead?" *International Organization* 39, 2 (Spring 1985), 207–231.

Sahlins, Marshall. *Culture and Practical Reason*. Chicago: University of Chicago Press, 1976.

———. *Islands of History*. Chicago: University of Chicago Press, 1985.

Saltman, Michael. "Feudal Relationships and the Law: A Comparative Inquiry." *Comparative Studies in Society and History* 29, 3 (July 1987), 514–532.

Sandholtz, Wayne, and John Zysman. "1992: Recasting the European Bargain." *World Politics* 42, 1 (1989), 95–128.

Sauveplanne, J. G. "Codified and Judge Made Law." Report of the Dutch Royal Academy of Sciences. New Series 45/4. Amsterdam: North Holland Publishing Company, 1982, 95–120.

Sawyer, P. H., and I. Wood, eds. *Early Medieval Kingship*. Leeds: University of Leeds, 1977.

Sbragia, Alberta. "Thinking About the Future: The Uses of Comparison." In Alberta Sbragia, ed., *Europolitics*. Washington: Brookings Institution, 1992.

Scammel, G. V. *The World Encompassed: The First European Maritime Empires c. 800–1650*. Berkeley: University of California Press, 1981.

Schäfer, Dietrich. "Zur Frage nach der Einführung des Sundzolls." *Hansische Geschichtsblätter* 5 (1875), 33–43.

Schelling, Thomas. *The Strategy of Conflict*. Cambridge: Harvard University Press, 1980.

Schildhauer, Johannes. *The Hansa*. Translated by Katherine Vanovitch. New York: Dorset Press, 1988.

Schlesinger, Walter. "Lord and Follower in Germanic Institutional History." In Frederic Cheyette, ed., *Lordship and Community in Medieval Europe*. New York: Robert Krieger, 1975.

Schluchter, Wolfgang. *The Rise of Western Rationalism: Max Weber's Developmental History*. Translated by Guenther Roth. Berkeley: University of California Press, 1981.

Schmidt-Wiegand, Ruth. "Hanse und Gilde. Genossenschaftliche Organisationsformen im Bereich der Hanse und ihre Bezeichnungen." *Hansische Geschichtsblätter* 100 (1982), 21–40.

Schumann, Reinhold. *Italy in the Last Fifteen Hundred Years*. Lanham, Md.: University Press of America, 1986.

Scott, James. "Resistance Without Protest and Without Organization: Peasant Opposition to the Islamic Zakat and the Christian Tithe." *Comparative Studies in Society and History* 29, 3 (July 1987), 417–452.

Scott, Martin. *Medieval Europe*. New York: Dorset Press, 1964.

Skinner, Quentin. *The Foundations of Modern Political Thought*, 2 vols. Cambridge: Cambridge University Press, 1978.

————, ed. *The Return of Grand Theory in the Human Sciences*. Cambridge: Cambridge University Press, 1985.

Skocpol, Theda. *States and Social Revolutions*. Cambridge: Cambridge University Press, 1979.

————, ed. *Vision and Method in Historical Sociology*. Cambridge: Cambridge University Press, 1984.

Solo, Robert. "The Formation and Transformation of States." In W. Ladd-Hollist and F. Lamond Tullis, eds. *International Political Economy*. Boulder, Colo.: Westview Press, 1985.

Somit, Albert, and Steven Peterson, eds. *The Dynamics of Evolution*. Ithaca, N.Y.: Cornell University Press, 1992.

Southern, Richard. *Western Society and the Church in the Middle Ages*. London: Penguin, 1970.

Spies, Hans-Bernd. "Lübeck, die Hanse und der Westfälische Frieden." *Hansische Geschichtsblätter* 100 (1982), 110–124.

Spitz, Lewis. *The Renaissance and Reformation Movements*, vol. 1. St. Louis, Mo.: Concordia, 1971.

Spufford, Peter. "Coinage and Currency." In M. Postan, E. Rich, and E. Miller, eds., *The Cambridge Economic History of Europe*, vol. 2. Cambridge: Cambridge University Press, 1987.

Stankiewicz, W. J. *In Defense of Sovereignty*. New York: Oxford University Press, 1969.

Stark, Walter. "Untersuchungen zum Profit beim Hansischen Handelskapital in der ersten Hälfte des 15. Jahrhunderts": *Abhandlungen zur Handels und Sozialgeschichte*, Bd. 24. Weimar: Hermann Böhlaus Nachfolger, 1985, 1–147.

Stephenson, Carl. *Mediaeval Institutions*. Ithaca, N.Y.: Cornell University Press, 1954.

Strange, Susan. "The Persistent Myth of Lost Hegemony." *International Organization* 41, 4 (Autumn 1987), 551–574.

Straus, Gerald. "Germany: 1254–1493." In Joseph Strayer, ed., *Dictionary of the Middle Ages*, vol. 5. New York: Charles Scribner's Sons, 1985, 485–491.

————. "Germany: Idea of Empire." In Joseph Strayer, ed., *Dictionary of the Middle Ages*, vol. 5. New York: Charles Scribner's Sons, 1985, 493–497.

Strayer, Joseph. *Feudalism*. New York: Van Nostrand Reinhold, 1965.

————. *On the Medieval Origins of the Modern State*. Princeton, N.J.: Princeton University Press, 1970.

————. *The Reign of Philip the Fair*. Princeton, N.J.: Princeton University Press, 1980.

———. *Dictionary of the Middle Ages*, 13 vols. New York: Charles Scribner's Sons, 1985–1989.

"Survey of the European Community." *The Economist* 316 (July 7, 1990).

Tabacco, Giovanni. *The Struggle for Power in Medieval Italy*. Cambridge: Cambridge University Press, 1989.

Thelen, Kathleen, and Sven Steinmo. "Historical Institutionalism in Comparative Politics." In Sven Steinmo, Kathleen Thelen, and Frank Longstreth, eds., *Structuring Politics*. New York: Cambridge University Press, 1992.

Thompson, William. "Long Waves, Technological Innovation, and Relative Decline." *International Organization* 44, 2 (Spring 1990), 201–234.

Thomson, Janice. "Sovereignty in Historical Perspective: The Evolution of State Control over Extraterritorial Violence." In James Caporaso, ed., *The Elusive State*. Newbury Park, Calif.: Sage, 1989.

———. "State Practices, International Norms, and the Decline of Mercenarism." *International Studies Quarterly* 34, 1 (March 1990), 23–48.

Tierney, Brian. *The Crisis of Church and State, 1050–1300*. Englewood Cliffs, N.J.: Prentice Hall, 1964.

———. *The Middle Ages: Sources of Medieval History*, vol. 1. New York: Alfred Knopf, 1973.

Tilly, Charles, ed. *The Formation of National States in Western Europe*. Princeton, N.J.: Princeton University Press, 1975.

———. "War Making and State Making as Organized Crime." In Peter Evans, Dietrich Rueschemeyer, and Theda Skocpol, eds., *Bringing the State Back In*. Cambridge: Cambridge University Press, 1985.

———. "Cities and States in Europe, 1000–1800." *Theory and Society* 18, 5 (September 1989), 563–584.

———. *Coercion, Capital, and European States, AD 990–1990*. Cambridge: Basil Blackwell, 1990.

Tracy, James, ed. *The Rise of Merchant Empires*. New York: Cambridge University Press, 1990.

Unger, Roberto. *Plasticity into Power*. New York: Cambridge University Press, 1987.

Urban, William. "Lübeck." In Joseph Strayer, ed., *Dictionary of the Middle Ages*, vol. 7. New York: Charles Scribner's Sons, 1986.

Vallee, Aline. "État et Securité Publique au XIVe Siècle: Une Nouvelle Lecture des Archives Royales Francaises." *Histoire, Economie et Societe*, vol. 1 (1987), 3–15.

Van Houtte, J. "The Rise and Decline of the Market of Bruges." *Economic History Review* 19, 1 (1966), 29–47.

Vaubel, Roland. "A Public Choice Approach to International Organization." *Public Choice* 51 (1986), 39–57.

Verhulst, Adriaan. "The Origins of Towns in the Low Countries and the Pirenne Thesis." *Past and Present* 122 (1989), 3–35.

Verlinden, C. "Markets and Fairs." In M. Postan, E. Rich, and E. Miller, eds., *The Cambridge Economic History of Europe*, vol. 3. Cambridge: Cambridge University Press, 1963.

Waley, Daniel. *The Italian City-Republics*. New York: McGraw-Hill, 1969.

Walker, Robert, and Saul Mendlovitz, eds., *Contending Sovereignties: Rethinking Political Community*. Boulder, Colo.: Lynne Rienner, 1990.

Wallerstein, Immanuel. *The Modern World System*, vol. 1. Orlando, Fla.: Academic Press, 1974.

Wallerstein, Immanuel. *The Politics of the World Economy*. Cambridge: Cambridge University Press, 1984.

Waltz, Kenneth. *Theory of International Politics*. New York: Random House, 1979.

———. "Reflections on Theory of International Politics: A Response to My Critics." In Robert Keohane, ed., *Neorealism and Its Critics*. New York: Columbia University Press, 1986.

Walzer, Michael. "On the Role of Symbolism in Political Thought." *Political Science Quarterly* 82, 2 (June 1967), 191–204.

Warren, W. L. *King John*. Berkeley: University of California Press, 1961.

Watson, Adam. *The Evolution of International Society*. London: Routledge, 1992.

Webber, Carolyn, and Aaron Wildavsky. *A History of Taxation and Expenditure in the Western World*. New York: Simon and Schuster, 1986.

Weber, Eugen. *Peasants into Frenchmen: The Modernization of Rural France, 1870–1914*. Stanford, Calif.: Stanford University Press, 1976.

Weber, Max. *The City*. Translated by Don Martindale and Gertrud Neuwirth. New York: Free Press, 1958.

———. *The Protestant Ethic and the Spirit of Capitalism*. Translated by Talcott Parsons. New York: Charles Scribner's Sons, 1958.

Weiner, A. "The Hansa." In J. R. Tanner, ed., *The Cambridge Medieval History*, vol. 7. Cambridge: Cambridge University Press, 1958, 216–247.

Wendt, Alexander. "The Agent-Structure Problem in International Relations Theory." *International Organization* 41, 3 (Summer 1987), 335–370.

———. "Anarchy is What States Make of It: The Social Construction of Power Politics." *International Organization* 46, 2 (Spring 1992), 391–426.

Wernicke, Horst. "Die Städtehanse 1280–1418," in *Abhandlungen zur Handels und Sozialgeschichte* Bd. 22. Weimar: Hermann Böhlaus Nachfolger, 1983, 1–204.

van Werveke, H. "The Rise of the Towns." In M. Postan, E. Rich, and E. Miller, eds., *The Cambridge Economic History of Europe*, vol. 3. Cambridge: Cambridge University Press, 1963.

White, Lynn. *Medieval Religion and Technology*. Berkeley: University of California Press, 1978.

———. "The Technology of Medieval Knighthood." In Stanley Chodorow, ed., *The Other Side of Western Civilization*. New York: Harcourt Brace Jovanovich, 1973.

Wight, Martin. *Systems of States*. N.J.: Humanities Press, 1977.

Wilsford, David. "The *Conjoncture* of Ideas and Interests." *Comparative Political Studies* 18, 3 (October 1985), 357–372.

Wolf, Eric. *Europe and the People Without History*. Berkeley: University of California Press, 1982.

Wolf, John. *The Emergence of the Great Powers*. Westport, Conn.: Greenwood Press, 1951.

Wolfe, Martin. *The Fiscal System of Renaissance France*. New Haven, Conn.: Yale University Press, 1972.

Woolf, Stuart. *A History of Italy, 1700–1860*. London: Methuen and Co., 1979.

Wright, Quincy. *A Study of War*, vol. 2. Chicago: University of Chicago Press, 1942.

Wuthnow, Robert. "Processes of Early State Development: A Review Article." *Comparative Studies in Society and History* 28, 1 (1986), 107–113.

Yarborough, Beth, and Robert Yarborough. "Cooperation in the Liberalization of International Trade: After Hegemony, What?" *International Organization* 41, 1 (1987), 1–26.

————. "International Institutions and the New Economics of Organization." *International Organization* 44, 2 (Spring 1990), 235–259.

Zacour, Norman. *An Introduction to Medieval Institutions*. Toronto: MacMillan, 1969.

Zolberg, Aristide. "Strategic Interactions and the Formation of Modern States: France and England." *International Social Science Journal* 32 (1980), 687–716.

————. "Origins of the Modern World System: A Missing Link." *World Politics* 33, 2 (January 1981), 253–281.

Zupko, Ronald. *British Weights and Measures*. Madison, Wis.: University of Wisconsin, 1977.

————. "Weights and Measures, Western European." In Joseph Strayer, ed., *Dictionary of the Middle Ages*, vol. 12. New York: Charles Scribner's Sons, 1989, 582–596.

Zysman, John. "Technology and Power in a Multi-Polar Global Economy." Berkeley Roundtable on International Economy, Berkeley, Calif., Manuscript. September 1990.